Also by Sandra Mackey

The Reckoning: Iraq and the Legacy of Saddam Hussein
Lebanon: Death of a Nation
Passion and Politics: The Turbulent World of the Arabs
The Iranians: Persia, Islam, and the Soul of a Nation

The
Saudis

Inside the
Desert Kingdom

Sandra Mackey

W. W. Norton & Company
New York London

The quotation from Adonis' *The Blood of Adonis* from *Transformations of the* 1 *Lover* (Byblos Press, 1982) reprinted by permission of International Poetry Forum. The quotations from Fouad Adjami's *The Arab Predicament: Arab Political Thought and Practice since 1967* (Cambridge University Press, 1982) reprinted with permission of Cambridge University Press. The quotations from Wilfred Thesiger's *Arabian Sands* © Wilfred Thesiger, 1959, reprinted by permission of Curtis Brown Group Ltd/ Pitt Rivers Museum, University of Oxford. The map from *Atlas of Saudi Arabia's Oil: Proven Resources, Producing Fields and Neutral Zone* by Hussein Hamza Bindagi (Oxford University Press, 1978) reproduced by permission of Oxford University Press.

The text of this book is composed in Times New Roman with the display set in Skjald.
Manufacturing by The Haddon Craftsmen, Inc.

Library of Congress Cataloging-in-Publication Data

Mackey, Sandra, 1937–
The Saudis : inside the desert kingdom / Sandra Mackey.
p. cm.
Originally published: Boston : Houghton Mifflin, 1987. With new introd.
Includes bibliographical references and index.
ISBN 0-393-32417-6 pbk.
1. Saudi Arabia. I. Title.

DS204.M23 2002
965—dc21   200275388

W. W. Norton & Company, Inc.
500 Fifth Avenue, New York, N.Y. 10110
www.wwnorton.com

W. W. Norton & Company Ltd.
Castle House, 75/76 Wells Street, London W1T 3QT

2 3 4 5 6 7 8 9 0

p.127 Daughter of° until son is born
p.152 having only daughters is like being
childless

To Dan

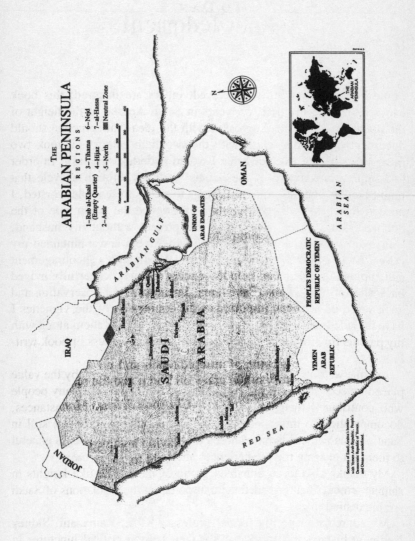

THE
ARABIAN PENINSULA
R E G I O N S

1–Rub al-Khali   6–Nejd
  (Empty Quarter)   7–al-Hassa
2–Assir   ▨ Neutral Zone
3–Thama
4–Hijaz
5–North

Miles 0   100   200   300   400

N

ARABIAN GULF

IRAQ

JORDAN

SAUDI ARABIA

UNION OF ARAB EMIRATES

OMAN

PEOPLE'S DEMOCRATIC REPUBLIC OF YEMEN

YEMEN ARAB REPUBLIC

RED SEA

ARABIAN SEA

THE ARABIAN PENINSULA

Sections of Saudi Arabia's borders with Yemen Arab Republic, People's Democratic Republic of Yemen, and Oman are undefined.

Acknowledgments

Some books are carefully conceived, others are inspired; this book evolved. During my first two years in Saudi Arabia, at the height of the oil boom, I became engrossed with the idea that someone should document the Saudis' clash with the twentieth century. It took two more years before I decided that I would undertake the task. In order to complete the record of the Saudis' fortunes through a cycle that might be described as going from rags to riches to sensible worsted, I needed to return to the kingdom to experience the down side of the boom. I could never have begun this project without my husband, Dan, who provided my entree into Saudi Arabia and maintained my cover. And I could never have completed it without his encouragement and support. I also must thank my son, Colin, who cheerfully moved back and forth to Saudi Arabia and whose powers of observation and keen sense of humor added immeasurably to some of the vignettes I have included in the book. Most of all, I thank both of them along with my parents for simply living through the arduous process of book writing.

Anyone writing on Saudi Arabia is greatly handicapped by the value placed on secrecy by the whole society. For this reason, many people who contributed their knowledge, insights, and, in some instances, documentation to this book must remain nameless. Some are still in Saudi Arabia and others have chosen to remain anonymous. I am grateful to them for sharing their experiences and expertise with me.

My thanks also to an unnamed group of men who, like knights in shining armor, often provided the transportation the regulations of Saudi Arabia denied me.

My appreciation to my former professor R. K. Ramazani, Sidney Nettleton Fisher, and Joe Sabah for their help at critical junctures in the manuscript.

Special thanks go to Helen Rees, who over many months never gave up faith in my idea, and to Pamela Painter, whose special talents helped

viii ACKNOWLEDGMENTS

mold a mountain of material into shape. And to my editor, Robie Macauley, whose gentle direction, great wisdom, and mellow humor helped so much along the way.

Finally, I have a whole group of friends whose help, support, and encouragement meant so much. Many thanks to Bob Burghardt, who was at the last stand; Reynolds and Sally Couch, who took care of so many things for me while I was in Saudi Arabia; Julie Brawner, for all those thick envelopes she carried out of Saudi Arabia; Betty Jones, for acting as my agent; Rosemary Kittrell and Bettye Sue Wright, for their editing skills; Lynne and A. J. Land, for the use of their mountain retreat; Clay and Barbara Moore, for contributing so much to my emotional stability; and Joy Garrett, for her never-failing interest and enthusiasm.

Contents

Contents

Author's Note

The transliteration of Arabic to English is problematic at best. There is no standard system recognized for either academic or general audiences. Consequently, Moslem is also spelled Muslim. Mohammed can be spelled Muhammed, Muhamed, or Muhamid. The names of the kings Faisal, Khalid, and Fahd appear in any one of several forms, and I have seen sixteen different spellings for the city of Jeddah. No method of transliteration is without its critics. I have chosen to use the simplified forms of Arabic commonly used in the newspapers in the United States. The diacritical marks, glottal stops, consonant sounds unique to Arabic, and marks for long vowels have been omitted. For words that are not easily recognized in English, I have used what might be termed the "consensus spelling" of the Saudis themselves. Quotations from other writers are retained in the original. The spellings of tribe and town names, as well as the names of geographic areas, are taken from the 1978 edition of the *Atlas of Saudi Arabia* published by the Oxford University Press.

After much thought, I have made two significant deviations from Arabic in the interest of clarity for nonspecialist readers. The prefix "al" means "the"; "al-Sauds," therefore, translates as "the Sauds." In references to the royal family, the reader will notice that I have used the redundant "the al-Sauds" as a concession to the natural flow of English. In the second deviation, I have pluralized a number of Arabic words by simply adding "s." In Arabic, the plural of a word changes form. *Yom* ("day"), for instance, becomes *ayam* ("days"), which is confusing to English readers.

Conversion from Saudi *riyals* to U.S. dollars is complicated by fluctuating exchange rates and varying levels of inflation. My concern is to convey a sense of the amounts of money cited, not figures deduced in terms of constant *riyal* to dollar amounts. Conversions have been made on the formula of SR 3.4 = $1.00, the most representative rate of exchange throughout the oil boom. The names of all persons in this book with the exception of public figures and my family have been changed. The name of the ship *Portia* is a pseudonym.

Introduction

In Saudi Arabia, it was late in the afternoon of September 11, 2001. The punishing heat of the desert summer had moderated but not waned. Inside the air-conditioned comfort of one of Riyadh's glitzy shopping malls, veiled Saudi women enveloped in black cloaks and men draped in triangular headcloths browsed the marble corridors during that period of commerce that falls between the prayer calls of afternoon and sunset. None of the shoppers knew that 6524 miles to the west, American Airlines Flight 11 had just slammed into the north tower of Manhattan's World Trade Center. But minutes later, Saudis, joined by their foreign employees, crowded in front of the windows of stores selling state-of-the-art, large-screen television sets to watch the inferno created by roughly eleven thousand gallons of burning jet fuel. Eighteen minutes later, they saw United Airlines Flight 175 plow into the second of the twin towers. As the stunned Saudis, wrapped in the protective cocoon of their oil wealth for almost three decades, watched the buildings burn, they regarded themselves as bystanders in the most spectacular act of terrorism the world had ever seen. It was an illusion.

Within days, fifteen of the nineteen hijackers of four U.S. airliners had been identified as Saudis. Islamic militants, most of them had obtained their visas for the United States in Riyadh and Jeddah. It also became known that some of the recruiting, financing, and planning for the attack on America had occurred on Saudi soil. The ruling House of Saud staggered. While the United States was the victim, the assault on the World Trade Center also amounted to a strike at the House of Saud from the very core of its political base. Suddenly the images of the collapsing towers translated into the image of a collapsing regime.

Since the consolidation of Saudi Arabia in the early 1920s, the House of Saud had invested its legitimacy in the promotion of Islam and the defense of the faith's two holiest sites, Mecca and Medina, which lie in western Saudi Arabia. Yet twice, in 1929 and 1979, religious dissidents had rebelled against what they saw as a broken social contract between the House of Saud and the large number of extremely conservative Moslems within the population. Now Saudi Arabia's rulers seemed threatened again, this time by a dissident element in the Saudi population that deeply resents the House of Saud's apparent rejection of traditional society and its alliance with the United States. Reacting according to its cherished axiom that no news is good news, the House of Saud barricaded itself behind its well-fortified wall of censorship. What little information was released regarding the attacks on New York and Washington was pruned and sanitized before being packaged as brief spots for state-run television. Meanwhile, officials of the government either refused to comment on allegations of Saudi involvement, played ignorant, or issued denials. Yet behind the scenes, the highest levels of authority sent down word that forbid Saudi journalists from digging for information that linked the hijackers to Saudi Arabia. To the consternation of the United States, Saudi Arabia's rulers continued to dribble morsels of insignificant facts. When the mounting evidence could no longer be denied, the House of Saud was forced to publicly acknowledge the Saudi origins of at least some of the hijackers. They were described as "misfits of society." Picking up the theme, Prince Naif, the longtime head of the Ministry of Interior, said, "We will not forget that those who now are in their caves and burrows, they are the ones who do harm to the kingdom and Muslims are being held accountable for them although Islam is innocent."[*]

The Saudi who had expropriated Islam from the House of Saud and hurled it at the regime was Osama bin Laden. He was the scion of one of the wealthiest families in Saudi Arabia that had gained its riches by being cozy with the al-Sauds since the earliest days of the kingdom. In 1992, the zealous bin Laden broke with his family when he called on the Saudis to topple the thirty-thousand-member royal family on charges of corruption and Westernization. From exile in Sudan and later Afghanistan, he operated al-Qaeda, an organization he founded that fed on the ideology and militancy of politicized Islam. Under bin Laden's leadership, al-Qaeda focused hatred on the al-Sauds and the United States, the symbol of a despised secular West. Although recruits for al-Qaeda came from many Islamic societies, a number were from Saudi Arabia, particularly the southwestern region of the Assir, one of the poorest areas of the kingdom. In November 1995, al-Qaeda struck at the heart of the al-Sauds' kingdom and the presence of the United States by detonating a bomb in Riyadh that killed five Americans. In June 1996, a second bomb exploded at an air base in Al Khobar, killing nineteen American airmen and wounding hundreds, including Saudi civilians. Outside the kingdom, al-Qaeda

---

[*]Quoted in Elaine Sciolino and Neil MacFuarquhar, "Naming of Hijackers as Saudis May Further Erode Ties to U.S.," *New York Times*, October 25, 2001, p. B4.

targeted symbols of the United States. In 1998, two American embassies
served as the targets of terrorism. In 2000, it was the American destroyer
Cole, anchored in the port of Aden in southern Yemen, that took the wrath
of Islamic militancy.

While most Saudis shied away from the violent aspects of al-Qaeda's
jihad, the grievances bin Laden articulated resonated powerfully through
many segments of Saudi society. Before September 11, this was the internal challenge to the House of Saud. After September 11, the external
challenge came from a chorus of voices raised within the borders of the
al-Sauds' principal ally—the United States. Editorials in all the major
American newspapers including the *New York Times*, the *Wall Street Journal*, the *Chicago Tribune*, and the *Los Angeles Times* called into question
the Saudi commitment to the war on terrorism. As a result, the vital, long-
standing alliance between Saudi Arabia and the United States, which has
always been fraught with misunderstanding, insecurity, and ignorance,
became strained as never before.

Under the assault, the House of Saud remained largely silent, yet
increasingly bitter about what it regarded as American failure to recognize
the depth of its service to the United States. Ever since the explosion
of oil prices in 1973, the House of Saud has adjusted its oil production up and down in order to hold prices at or below $30 per barrel.*
It has done so at the expense of domestic opposition to what most
Saudis see as the wholesaling of national resources. Furthermore,
Saudis almost universally condemn American foreign policy that
defends the Israeli occupation of the Palestinian territory and that for
eleven years after the Gulf War kept the weight of broad economic
sanctions pressed on the Iraqi people. These issues only added to the
challenge of internal politics that has always required the House of
Saud to placate a population that adheres to the most fundamental of
Islamic sects—Wahhabism.

Even though the Saudis have long frustrated American policy makers
with their ambivalence on military matters, regional diplomacy, and intelligence gathering, Washington struggled to paper over its differences with
Riyadh concerning the newborn war on terrorism. No matter how vexed
the United States was, no American government could escape the reality
that the world runs on oil and the Saudis are the linchpin of the oil production that feeds the global economy. Saudi Arabia holds an estimated
204.5 trillion cubic feet of natural gas and 259 billion barrels of proven oil

---

*Saudi oil policy has served two goals—shielding the economy of the House of Saud's American protector
and preventing nonpetroleum energy sources from becoming an economically attractive alternative to oil.

reserves, more than one-fourth of the world's total.* In quantity and quality, it is oil that cannot be replaced in world markets no matter how much
consumers might wish. Thus, Saudi Arabia is the indispensable nation in
the equation of U.S. strategic interests. Yet, at the same time, it is perhaps
the least understood of all U.S. allies.

The forces threatening the political stability of Saudi Arabia took form
during the oil boom of the 1970s, which grabbed the Saudis out of their
medieval past and catapulted them into the late twentieth century dominated by the West. Over the six-year period chronicled in this book, I lived
in Saudi Arabia and watched what was, at times, an absurd comedy and, at
other times, a serious drama in which the Saudis reveled in their newfound
wealth and suffered the disruption of their insular, traditional society. During my time in the kingdom, I came to understand the Saudis as a people
who live in a materially rich yet psychologically tormented society. In the
fifteen years since *The Saudis: Inside the Desert Kingdom* first went into
print, little has changed in the basic dynamics of the country. Since September 11, 2001, I have watched the familiar patterns of leadership, the
uneasy relationship between Saudi Arabia and the United States, and the
tensions between Saudi modernizers and Saudi traditionalists unfold in
what seems like a time warp. What has changed in the last decade and a
half is the intensity and immediacy of the pressures within Saudi Arabia
that were released by the oil boom. Thus now, even more than when this
book was originally published, all Americans need to comprehend how a
people caught between great wealth and an endangered society think, feel,
and function in a fragile state that is crucial to American security.

---

*This does not include an additional 5 billion barrels of proven oil reserves in the Neutral Zone shared by
Saudi Arabia and Kuwait.

What narrow yesterdays,
what stale and shriveled years . . .
Even storms come begging
when the sky matches the gray of the sand,
leaving us stalled between seasons

Adonis [Ali Ahmad Said]
The Blood of Adonis

I

The Oil Boom

1974–1980

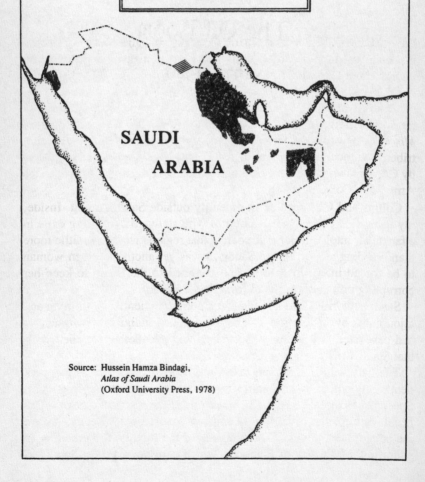

OIL

Proven reserves
Producing fields
Neutral zone
Offshore drilling not indicated

SAUDI

ARABIA

Source: Hussein Hamza Bindagi,
Atlas of Saudi Arabia
(Oxford University Press, 1978)

I

The Coming of a Foreigner

I AM Michael Collins. I am Justin Coe. I am Sandra Mackey. Behind my male pseudonyms of Collins and Coe, I spent four years as an underground journalist in Saudi Arabia.

From 1978 to 1980 and again from 1982 to 1984, I wrote on poli tics, the royal family, the economy, conflicts in the society, military tensions, foreign policy, and everyday life for the *Christian Science Monitor*, newspaper syndicates, and business journals. I also contributed an academic article to the *Washington Quarterly*, published by Georgetown Center for Strategic Studies, and another article to the Army War College.

Collins and Coe became my identity outside Saudi Arabia. Inside, my friends perceived me as a dutiful wife stalwartly suffering exile in a fanatical, intolerant Islamic society that regards women as little more than breeding stock. To the Saudis, I was yet another foreign woman to be forced into a long dress and confined to the house to keep her corrupting influences isolated from Saudi society.

Saudi authorities had no idea that a political scientist by training and a journalist by inclination — and as an added indignity, a woman — had penetrated the carefully constructed and relentlessly patrolled walls that Saudi Arabia retains around itself.

The only way I gained entrance into Saudi Arabia was as a dependent of my physician husband, who was on the staff of the King Faisal Specialist Hospital in Riyadh. Since this is the hospital that provides health care for the royal family and top government officials, it gave me entrée into the palaces and homes of the mighty. I worked as an editor in the Ministry of Planning, which is responsible for Saudi Arabia's massive development plans. Papers containing the goals and spending priorities of every government ministry passed across my desk. Yet surprisingly my greatest advantage in reporting on Saudi Arabia was not my strategic position but rather the fact that I am a woman.

The Saudis regard women as such mindless creatures that I was able to ask questions without raising much suspicion. No man could have walked into the headquarters of the Palestine Liberation Organization and interviewed the PLO chief for Saudi Arabia and succeeded in convincing him that his interest was nothing more than idle curiosity, as I did. But above all, being a woman gave me access to the secluded world of Saudi women. I went into their houses and tents. I watched them shop in the sequestered women's *souqs*. I went to their weddings. I questioned and probed about their lives, their marriages, their children, their ambitions, and their lifestyles.

Through it all, I guarded my anonymity for one reason only: to stay out of jail. I constantly lived with the fear of being caught. My male pseudonyms not only gave me credibility in the Western press (still not totally liberated from the male mystique) but also afforded an added measure of protection. Publishing under a woman's name in the male-dominated Saudi society would have sent up a red flag to the Ministry of the Interior, leading agents of the secret police to ferret through their files for Western female suspects.

The need for my deception arose from the very core of the Saudi psyche — an obsession with how they appear to others. The government's strictures on foreign journalists serve to protect Saudi society's image of itself as much as to protect the political interests of the House of Saud. Saudi Arabia is a highly secretive, super-sensitive society that distrusts anyone beyond family or tribe. Since the oil boom, the Saudis have come to regard themselves as a family facing the outside world. In a culture where image is paramount to reality, the Saudis want both to bask in the glory of their wealth and progress and, at the same time, hide anything that threatens their self-esteem.

With general public support, then, the government bans all foreign news organizations from the country. The only press reports that come out of the kingdom are those written by journalists invited to visit Saudi Arabia under the auspices of the Ministry of Information. Anyone breaking the rules is severely punished. During my time in Saudi Arabia, the most infamous example of Saudi sensitivities involved a

British subject, Keith Carmichael, a freewheeling entrepreneur in the construction business who was arrested in October 1981 while trying to cross the border into Qatar to escape debts exceeding a million dollars. The claims against his indebtedness would have been resolved in about a year if Carmichael had not had the effrontery to embarrass Saudi Arabia in the Western press by writing a series of letters to the editor of the London *Observer,* protesting what he called his brutal treatment in primitive jails. The Saudi government held Carmichael in jail for three years, until 1984, when Margaret Thatcher purportedly tied the sale of British-made weapons to Saudi Arabia to Carmichael's release.

Only a few trusted Western friends in Saudi Arabia knew that I was a writer. They took my rough drafts to the desert to burn, carried copy out of the country when they went on vacation, and stored my notes when I had reason to believe that the secret police might be closing in. Yet writing the story was not the only problem. While in Saudi Arabia I was totally cut off from my publishers. All communication had to be handled by a friend in the United States who received the copy and sent it on. The only time I knew when an article had been published was when I received a coded letter saying, "Your picture of the new rare bird sighted in Saudi Arabia [in this case the arrival of the U.S. AWACS] has been hung by the gallery in Boston."

My motivation to continue my underground reporting was a desire to record the extraordinary conjunction of time and place. In 1973 Saudi Arabia quarterbacked the oil embargo against the world. Almost overnight this increasingly prosperous but largely ignored country on the Arabian peninsula catapulted into world prominence. As a result, a deeply traditional society now struggled to define itself while trying to cope with an influx of enormous wealth and the arrival of legions of foreigners. From the outset, the progress of the economic and social planners ran head on into a rigid Islamic society that had not changed for fourteen hundred years. This clash between the progressives and traditionalists was repeated as the xenophobic Saudis tried to control the forces unleashed by the presence of great numbers of expatriates, Westerners particularly.

To appreciate just what was happening, reflect on the fact that almost every Saudi man thirty years old or older in 1973 had, at one time, made his own shoes. Although the national income in the 1960s was far greater than ever before, the average Saudi had little in the way of material goods or human comforts. Few people who did not actually live in Saudi Arabia before the oil bonanza realize just how hard life actually was, even for the well-to-do in urban coastal areas such as Jeddah. As one member of a prominent Jeddah merchant family said, when criticized by a Westerner for tearing down the family's historic old tabby house to make way for a new stucco and marble one, "If all you remembered from that house was heat, foul smells, and disease, you would tear it down, too."

As late as 1945, at the end of World War II, King Abdul Aziz ibn Saud and his countrymen were living on charity. After two years of production, Saudi Arabia's infant oil industry had closed down for the duration of the war. The kingdom was forced to return to living on the receipts of pilgrims making the *hajj* to Mecca; but pilgrimages too had been all but shut down by the war. Nature added its vengeance as a severe drought parched the country for several years in the early 1940s.

Saudi Arabia survived on British and American aid supplemented by loans from the California Arabian Standard Oil Company. The generosity of governments and the oil company was not all selfless altruism but instead was motivated by the need to protect their individual and collective interests in Saudi Arabia's oil. When Abdul Aziz died in 1953, he was still living in his mud-walled palace in Riyadh.

During the 1950s, the royal family and the merchant families began to reap the rewards of their oil production. Revenues from oil, which went directly into the king's personal treasury, rose from $56.7 million in 1950 to $333.7 million by 1960. Members of the royal family undertook highly publicized shopping trips to the United States and Europe, but the money was in the hands of only a few. Most of the people still lived in their goat-hair tents or clustered around oases in small, poorly ventilated houses made of straw and mud. They had no electricity, no education, no medical care. But the common people seldom went hungry. In the tradition of Abdul Aziz, who traveled around his kingdom with the public treasury in a chest on the back of a camel, King Saud, his oldest son and successor, continued to dole out the national wealth. There was no system of distribution, only the personal gifts of the king or the coins Saud threw from his car whenever he went out among his people.

It was not long before the profligate spending habits of the royal family and the generosity of the king plunged the country into near bankruptcy. After all, Saudi Arabia was producing only 1.4 million barrels of oil a day and the oil companies were paying less than $2.00 a barrel. King Saud's abdication, forced by the royal family in 1964, ushered in the era of King Faisal, the mastermind of the oil embargo and guru of Saudi Arabia's development policies.

By 1970 the world's appetite for oil was bringing in $1.2 billion a year, which relieved some of Saudi Arabia's major economic problems. Basic services such as water and electricity were creeping into the cities. The port cities of Jeddah on the west and Dammam on the east began to see more consumer goods than ever before. The blessings of air conditioning spread and cars became common. But the new prosperity did not spread much beyond the urban areas. Even Riyadh remained out of the mainstream of prosperity that was overtaking the coasts, although King Faisal did build an impressive new palace of buff-colored stone with a green slate roof in a date grove on the edge of Riyadh, and his favorite sister moved into a tasteless square palace near the center of the city. A few trees sprang up and some concrete-block stores appeared, but basically the city slumbered.

By 1973 Saudi Arabia was producing 7.6 million barrels of oil a day and selling it for $3.60 a barrel. So much money was coming in that the government had no way to spend it all. Therefore it was not primarily economics but politics that motivated King Faisal to impose the oil embargo. Since 1967 the honor of the mystical entity known as the "Arab nation" had stood blemished by the Israeli victory over the Arabs in the Six Day War. Saudi Arabia felt the Arab loss for its own particular reasons. Emotionally, the loss of Jerusalem, the third of Islam's holiest sites, was a blow from which Faisal never recovered. Politically, the bitterness of the Palestinians continued to destabilize the Middle East and threaten the House of Saud.

When Egypt attacked Israel to avenge Arab honor for the Six Day War, Anwar Sadat already had Faisal's promise to unleash the Arabs' ultimate weapon, oil. Ten days after the October 6, 1973, war began, oil sales to nations supporting Israel were suspended. The embargo was on. It was not to end until March 19, 1974.

The oil embargo exposed a critical weakness in the West — a dependence on Arab oil. Greed took over from politics as OPEC moved to maximize its price advantage. By the end of 1974, oil prices had quadrupled to $11.65 per barrel and Saudi Arabia's revenues hit $22.5 billion and were climbing. The kingdom was swimming in money.

It was the quest for a share in the Saudis' money that brought hundreds of foreigners into the interior of Saudi Arabia, which was largely untouched by the outside world. Legitimate businessmen, con artists, and hucksters poured into Riyadh to solicit every Saudi who could read as a business partner. But Saudi Arabia was not prepared for the onslaught. In Riyadh the only hotel that could be called habitable was the Al Yamama, located on the narrow road that ran between the central town and the airport. Room reservations at the Al Yamama meant nothing. It was essentially first come, first served. Bribery helped, of course, but even if a room were obtained, it still meant sharing it with three other men. The lobby was like a pilgrims' rest, as exhausted businessmen from a dozen different countries sprawled on the sparse furniture or stretched out on the floor, their luggage spread out around them defining their space. There was constant turmoil as other desperate men pleaded for a room or searched for floor space. Groups of two, three, or four buzzed in corners, hallways, or the one restroom on the main floor, as eager businessmen plotted strategies to win contracts or to cut the price of the Saudi "agent" or middleman.

According to an American farm equipment salesman, there was only one place in all of Riyadh where Westerners would risk eating — a small, dingy restaurant over a shop near the old Riyadh supermarket, called the Green something (dirt and grime obliterated the last word). The menu was rice and lamb alternating with lamb and rice. Customers brought their own bottled water.

Logistics for the businessman were difficult if not impossible. In town, taxis were available for those with a careless regard for life. Rental cars were nonexistent. A businessman who was in the kingdom for only a few weeks often was forced to buy a car, if he could find one. Even with transportation, other obstacles remained. The road connecting Riyadh, the capital, with Dhahran, the home of the Arabian-American Oil Company (ARAMCO),* was impassable in anything less than a four-wheel-drive vehicle. So most people were forced to depend on Saudia, Saudi Arabia's national airline, for transportation between cities. The Arabian Express, the commuter service between Riyadh and Dhahran and Riyadh and Jeddah, was like the hotels, always overbooked. A man could wait a week or forever to get a seat. An alternative means of reaching Dhahran was to go to al-Kharj, about

---

*ARAMCO, the Arabian-American Oil Company, was formed in 1948 by Standard Oil of California, Texaco, Standard Oil of New Jersey, and Mobil to produce Saudi Arabia's oil.

40 kilometers south and east of Riyadh, and take the old, wheezing train that ARAMCO had built for Abdul Aziz in 1951. The 250-mile trip took eight hours if all went well.

By 1975 foreigners began to arrive to staff the schools and hospitals that were opening. Housing that approached a Western standard was all but nonexistent. Some of my friends who arrived during this period lived in a succession of abominable places. Most were housed in dark, dank apartments not far from the Baatha *souqs* overlooking an open sewage canal. The evaporative coolers (air conditioning had arrived only in the newest buildings) whirled day and night, throwing water-cooled air into the stuffy rooms. The men went to work while the women stayed trapped in their quarters, except when they went out in groups to buy fruit, a few vegetables, and perhaps a little meat to prepare on the hot plates in their rooms. Life was hard and few people were willing to endure it. Yet I was about to join them.

Saudi Arabia was desperate for skilled labor. A majority of the Saudis were illiterate, and those who were educated had been taught the traditional curriculum of classical Arabic and the Koran, but no technical skills. To build the large infrastructure projects needed for economic development and to deliver the services that the Saudis now demanded required that the country import a highly skilled work force, primarily from the West, where most of these needed skills were found. To woo these Westerners to come live in the adverse conditions existing at the beginning of the boom, the Saudis were willing to pay well and to provide lavish fringe benefits. Everything — housing, utilities, transportation, sheets to sleep on, and pans to cook in — was provided by the employer. Children could attend the finest boarding schools anywhere in the world and the Saudis paid. Vacation time was generous: for most, about sixty days a year. The opportunity for travel was unparalleled. Every employee got a round-trip ticket home once a year for himself and his dependents. So many people flew first class, courtesy of the Saudis, that most of the planes going in and out of Saudi Arabia were reconfigured to expand the size of the first-class section to about a third of the plane.

Even before the oil embargo, as a political scientist, I had developed a consuming interest in the Middle East. Watching events in Saudi Arabia that followed the embargo, I was pulled to the country as if by a magnet. I wanted to live there, to bury myself in events, to experience what was happening to this medieval society. But I could not go on my own. Females received visas only as dependents of foreign workers or for critical jobs such as nursing. Fortunately, my husband shared my enthusiasm and began to send out feelers for job possibilities in Saudi Arabia.

In the fall of 1977, the King Faisal Specialist Hospital (KFSH) in Riyadh asked Dan to come fill in for a dermatologist who was on vacation for a month. The hospital had been founded by the former king, Faisal, who was assassinated in 1975 just before the facility officially opened. The 250-bed hospital was conceived by the king as a royal clinic to keep members of his vast family from escaping to London, Geneva, or Los Angeles on the pretext of needing medical care. Perhaps smarting from the grumbling about the hospital's cost and grandeur, Faisal, just before he died, expanded its role from royal clinic to the medical referral center for Saudi Arabia. But because housing at the hospital was in such short supply, I was denied a visa. So we decided that while Dan was working in Saudi Arabia, I would make my own tour of Syria, Jordan, and Israel.

At the end of the month, I met Dan in Amman and we returned home. He had been fascinated by the professional challenges presented by the quantity and diversity of rare diseases he had seen in Riyadh, and I was, by now, inescapably addicted to life in the Middle East. When the King Faisal Hospital called a few weeks later to ask Dan to come as a staff physician on a two-year contract, we seized the opportunity.

The decision to go to Saudi Arabia in 1978 was not to be taken lightly, but perhaps it was less difficult for Dan and me than it might have been for many others. This would not be our first foreign living experience. In 1962, shortly after we were married, Dan was awarded a fellowship to study primitive medicine, and we spent four months in the interior of Borneo living with the Ibans, a tribe of former headhunters. I experienced outdoor privies, snakes, cockroaches, monkey meat entrees, giant lizards, mosquitoes, and a face-to-face encounter with a Komodo dragon while happily surviving life in the jungle.

In 1978 Saudi Arabia in its own way was as much a frontier as Borneo had been. Few had blazed the trail before us. There were essentially no books on Saudi Arabia, and few people outside the oil industry had ever even been there. The orientation provided by Hospital Corporation International, the American management company for KFSH, was meager. But one fact that was indelibly impressed on

me was the importance of respecting Saudi customs about the pro-
scribed dress for women. In public I was to wear a long dress with a
high neck and long sleeves, and I was to cover my hair. From the few
things I was able to learn about Saudi Arabia, I quickly realized that
the kingdom presented an unparalleled opportunity for a journalist.

While Dan shifted his patients in Atlanta to the care of other doctors,
I packed, put our business affairs in the hands of strangers, took our
nine-year-old son, Colin, out of school, closed up my house, told my
friends good-by, and left my parents with a family portrait in case we
never came back. Three months after making our decision to leave,
we boarded an airplane for Riyadh.

It was the first part of May 1978, the height of Saudi Arabia's oil
boom. The Saudia airlines jumbo jet from London was fully loaded
that night, as it had been for months before and as it would be for
months ahead. The airline was the conduit through which the outside
world was shuttled into and out of the secluded microcosm of Saudi
Arabia. Except for a smattering of Saudi nationals returning home from
holiday in London, the passengers were all foreigners. They represented a new kind of servant class, highly skilled and highly paid,
recruited literally to build a country.

Near midnight the 747 touched down on a runway laid out on a
barren and seemingly lifeless desert. Beyond the mounds of pale, sandy
soil lining the tarmac, there was nothing — no houses, no highways,
no parallel runways, no lofty structures — just the crusty dirt and one
low, rambling building defined as an airport only by the blinking light
atop its flat roof.

As the pilot touched the brakes, the Saudis in the oversize first-class
section began to gather near the exit door. The men, dressed in long
white shirtdresses known as *thobes** and white head coverings held in
place by a black double-corded ringlet, carried packages from Har-

---

*One of the distinguishing characteristics of Saudi society is the uniformity of dress among men.
Except for the coolest months of the winter, when he might don light wool or polyester, a Saudi
man wears the white *thobe*. His head gear is composed of a skull cap over which is placed a
gutra, a triangular folded cloth of either white or red-and-white check. It is held in place by an
agal, which the Bedouins traditionally used to tether their camels.

The *abaaya*, or black cloak, worn by women has large sleeves and hangs over the head. Unlike
the Iranian *chador*, it does not cover the face. Two styles of veils are seen on Saudi women.
Rural women commonly wear a veil that drops from a velvet band across the forehead and leaves
the wearer's eyes exposed. Urban women wear veils made of a heavy gauzelike fabric that
completely covers their faces and is anchored at the top of the head by the *abaaya*.

rods, the tailors of Savile Row, and the chic shops of Regent Street. Their women were formless figures engulfed in black cloaks and heavy veils. Clutched to their shrouded bodies were big, heavy cosmetics bags filled with the promises of the London perfumeries and cosmeticians.

As the plane rolled to a stop on the tarmac, I could see a miniature collection of the world's luxury cars of the period — Rolls Royces, Mercedes, Cadillacs — clustered below the wings of the aircraft, their drivers leaning against the expensive bodies. When the exit ramp locked into place, the cabin crew threw open the door and quickly moved to block the aisle while the world's new ultrarich deplaned. The men, their wives trailing behind, descended the steps and embraced the men meeting them, planting a kiss on each cheek and then the nose. Within moments, the cars were loaded and sped off into the night.

The rest of us tumbled out into the heavy heat. Spring was long past, and the summer was already upon us. We were herded toward a bus, not old but rattling and wheezing from lack of maintenance. I gathered up my requisite long skirt and struggled aboard the bus. The crowd behind me surged forward and the crowd in front staggered under the weight of sleeping children and heavy hand luggage.

We neophytes to Saudi Arabia were in a trance. Physical fatigue, anxiety, and the enormous emotional drain associated with total uprooting lay over me like a sodden blanket. The people crammed together in the wheezing, belching bus laboring toward the terminal spoke very little. Suddenly we jerked to a stop. I took my son's hand and followed my husband into the great unknown.

The scene inside the airport was chaos. Baggage handlers of a dozen different nationalities, speaking a dozen different languages, were tossing luggage off an antiquated conveyor belt into a makeshift holding pen. Passengers who missed their bags as they flew by yelled at the handlers while climbing over the barricades in a frantic effort to retrieve their suitcases. Others who had arrived days earlier wandered through the mountains of unclaimed baggage in an odyssey of despair, searching for their lost possessions.

The confusion was made even worse by the number of bags most of us had. We were coming to an underdeveloped country in the midst of frantic expansion, where everything was in short supply. Essentially we had brought along everything we needed for a whole year. My family, which had a history of going to Europe for two weeks with one carry-on bag apiece, had twelve large pieces of luggage, including a typewriter.

There were no porters and only six dilapidated luggage carts, so the fifty feet from the baggage claim area to customs presented a major logistics problem. We picked up as many bags as we could carry and pushed the rest along with our feet. The arrival "lounge" was so small that the lines before the three customs counters snaked in and out of each other. Even the ever-polite British, the originators and vigilant defenders of the queue, were pushing and shouting as they tried to get through the mob with their suitcases. Gathered along the walls in casual chatting groups was a sampling of Saudi men. With no apparent purpose in the general scheme of things, they fondled their plastic prayer beads and watched as their new servants struggled toward the gates of the kingdom. The plane had landed at midnight. It was approaching 2:00 A.M. when we presented ourselves for customs inspection.

Saudi Arabia probably has the most tyrannical customs organization in the world. The list of items forbidden in the country is long and vigorously enforced, a list whose restrictions are rooted in the Koran and the politics of the Arab world.

Saudi Arabia is the cradle of the Islamic religion. Mohammed, the seventh-century prophet whose revelations became the foundation of Islam, was a native of the scruffy, dry mountains of western Saudi Arabia, where the holy city of Mecca nestles. As possessors of two of the three holy sites of Islam, Mecca and Medina, the Saudis see themselves as having a certain birthright as defenders of the faith. Therefore, if other Moslems are pious, the Saudis must be even more pious. If other Moslems are faithful to the teachings of the Prophet, the Saudis must be even more faithful.

Coupled with their assumed birthright as the elect among Moslems, the Saudis are the Puritans of the Moslem world. They are followers of Wahhabism, a sect that is among the most fundamental, rigid, and intolerant in Islam. Wahhabism demands of its adherents exacting compliance with the dictates of Mohammed. At the same time, the Saudis harbor an almost pathological fear that temptation on the path of religious purity is beyond man's ability to resist. For centuries, Saudi Arabia's barren deserts protected its purity from invasion by outside sin. But with the oil boom, the country was suddenly being flooded with thousands of heretics from the Christian West who brought the sins of their decadence with them. The religious authorities and the House of Saud had made it an article of faith to stop temptation at the borders of the kingdom. Standing like a bulwark between Saudi society and eternal damnation was the Saudi customs agent, charged with the preservation of purity.

Customs was one of the few areas of government employment in which only Saudi nationals were permitted. Manning its borders with nothing but Saudis presented sparsely populated Saudi Arabia with an enormous manpower problem. To meet the personnel demands, young men were pulled out of villages, given a crash course in English, and sent to the front. Before the late 1970s, the average Saudi customs agent, in all likelihood, had never been exposed to anything outside the confines of his own village, did not possess much beyond the essentials of life, and was probably a devout adherent of the Wahhabi sect of Islam. At his post, he was mildly resentful of the infusion of foreigners coming into his world and was charged with the responsibility of protecting his country and his society from the ravages of sin. Little wonder that he was a tyrant.

The big three on the forbidden list were pork, alcohol, and pornography. Because the Moslems follow some of the same dietary restrictions as orthodox Jews, pork is regarded as unclean and banned from the country. Alcohol, in any form, is totally forbidden to a Moslem and is, therefore, banned from the kingdom. Lust in any disguise is forbidden by the Koran and so anything that compromises the modesty of women is banned.

When a customs agent went through an incomer's luggage, his eye would move beyond the obvious, such as a bottle of gin or *Penthouse* magazine. Everything entering the country was suspect. Mouthwash was often seized because it might contain alcohol. Fashion magazines with ads for lingerie were destroyed. I had a book of knitting patterns mutilated, apparently because the models were too scantily clad. Guide books to the museums of Europe were confiscated, for the Venus Di Milo, the paintings of Botticelli, and the *David* were all classified as pornography. Even the Mona Lisa's seductive smile on occasion fell victim to seizure.

Added to these was the restriction on anything that propagated another religion. Reading material about or symbols of other religions, including Bibles and crucifixes, were contraband. And those who had failed to heed the warnings about shipping in artificial Christmas trees or other Christmas decorations with their household goods paid the price. The trees were invariably seized. While one helpless family stood by, I watched while customs officials dropped its Christmas ornaments, one at a time, on the floor and crushed them under their sandals. A few bewildered little girls even saw their dolls torn apart because an inspector regarded them as idols.

Any printed matter that reflected unfavorably on the Saudis or Moslems in general was confiscated. The definition of unfavorable covered virtually everything about Saudi Arabia, the Arabs, the Middle East, or Islam that was not printed by Saudi Arabia's own Ministry of Information.

In addition, Saudi customs carried on the Arabs' political war against the state of Israel. Products made, or suspected of being made, in Israel were taken. Coca-Cola and a range of other common products whose companies did business in Israel were banished from Saudi Arabia. Books by Jewish authors were confiscated. During one period, Saudi customs decided James Michener was Jewish and seized all of his books carried in by arriving passengers.

In almost every case, the decision about what would be permitted in the country and what would be confiscated rested with the individual customs agent. There was little chance of appeal.

In fact, however, vigilance on the part of the Saudis was a necessity since almost every Westerner, at some time, engaged in petty smuggling. Yeast for homemade wine was brought in, disguised as aspirin or sewn in the hems of women's dresses. Book jackets were substituted to get banned books into the kingdom. And someone was always trying to smuggle in canned ham.

But this was something I would learn in the future. Now I was facing the customs officer. Poised over my bag, he raised his arms high above his head and swooped down, running his hands along each inner side of the suitcase until he had plunged to the very bottom. There he burrowed until his parted hands met, clasped them together, and raised them up again as if seeking air after a deep dive. Neatly folded clothes went everywhere as a second customs man rummaged through the heap. Shaving kits and cosmetics bags were dumped out, the contents thoroughly searched. Reading material was examined for author and content. I had with me the classic sociological study of the Arabs, *The Arab Mind,* by the well-known scholar Raphael Patai. It was grabbed out of my hand and thrown on the mound of books already seized.

Inspection completed, we were dismissed. Dan and I nervously stuffed our possessions into our bags while the Saudi who had done all of the damage yelled at us to move on. The scrutiny of my possessions had left me feeling violated. But even stronger was the feeling of humiliation that Saudi customs imposed on all the foreigners who passed through. We were herded like animals, treated with contempt, and finally shoved out the door to confront Saudi Arabia.

It was now 3:00 A.M. Staggering through the door of the arrivals section, we were overwhelmed by the mob scene beyond. The airport police were beating self-appointed porters with night sticks, vainly trying to keep a path cleared in front of the door. Beyond this narrow neutral zone, which continued to change in size and shape as the crowd surged and ebbed, was a mob of at least a hundred people holding signs reading "Holtzman," "Corps of Engineers," "BAC," "Bechtel," "Seimens," "Lockheed." This was the rendezvous point for the new arrival and his employer. The company representatives were there night after night to collect the ever-increasing numbers of Westerners coming into the country. One of the enduring mysteries of Riyadh was that all international flights, arriving or departing, operated sometime between midnight and 2:00 A.M.

There was no sign for the King Faisal Specialist Hospital bobbing in the crowd. We had no idea where to go or what to do. With nowhere to sit (the airport had no chairs), we gathered up the luggage once more and crawled over sleeping people scattered across the floor until we found a protected place to stand while Dan went in search of a telephone.

My immediate problem was somehow to keep control of our luggage. Scurrying through the crowd were tiny little men dressed in skirts and turbans. They were Yemenis, natives of the southern end of the Arabian Peninsula. Left without oil, the dwarfish Yemenis migrated north early in the boom to become the backbone of Saudi Arabia's manual labor force. They mixed cement during the day and carried bags at night. I found that it took everything short of brute force to keep them from seizing our bags and running off to load them into our nonexistent vehicle.

For anyone arriving in Saudi Arabia for the first time, being met by a resident was crucial. And because whole systems were not yet functioning in the kingdom, new arrivals were missed as often as they were met. The reasons varied. The telex with the arrival date and flight

number may never have made it through the inadequate and over-
loaded communications system. Or the flight had been overbooked and
the expected new arrival might not have been able to secure a seat for
five days. The car coming to pick up the passenger may have been hit
by one of the new Saudi drivers, and since there were no public telephones and absolutely no message service at the airport, a person delayed had no way of notifying anyone.

The newly arrived novice was unaware of the monumental problem
he faced in moving from point A to point B. Ground transportation
from the airport was all but nonexistent, for limousines and public
buses had yet to reach this Arabian frontier. The only public transportation available was the hundreds of yellow Toyota taxicabs whose
drivers were eager to take people anywhere for an outlandish price if
the destination could only be established.

Language was at the root of much of the newly arrived foreigner's
difficulties in functioning. Most Westerners did not have even a smattering of Arabic. And the Saudis had not yet been forced into learning
English in order to communicate with their new servant class. That left
the new arrival to cope as best he could.

If the stranded traveler had a telephone number to call, and access
to the airport director's personal phone, he was fortunate. Riyadh had
no telephone directories. But even if the caller actually reached someone, the person at the other end, in all likelihood, spoke no English
and would hang up. If the caller then, in desperation, tried the number
again, the telephone by this time probably was no longer working.

Pleas for assistance from Arabic-English speaking Saudia employees were fruitless, as they were overwhelmed by the mobs in front of
the ticket counters trying to get on departing flights.

So the next step was to gather up the bags and move outside to get
a taxi. In the rush toward modernization, it seemed, the government
had bought every Saudi a car and made him a taxi driver. Taxis were
everywhere, with every driver blowing his horn for customers. If the
stranded traveler could make himself heard over the noise, he could
tell the driver where he wanted to go. But since the driver probably
could speak no English, the well-prepared arrivee might have a card
printed with the name of his company, on one side in English, one side
in Arabic, on the off chance that the taxi driver could read. The problem remained that there could be no address on this card, since Riyadh
had few street names and no house numbers.

In the end the only way anyone could move around the city was to know exactly where he was going so he could direct the driver there street by street, corner by corner, in Arabic.

More than a few stranded Westerners were taken home for the night by other hospitable Westerners who might well have been in the same situation at one time.

Fortunately, Dan was able to use the director's precious telephone to get through to the hospital and talked to an English-speaking Egyptian, who dispatched a car to fetch us. The Yemenis were still swarming around our luggage as I sat on the floor, snapping and snarling at them. Colin, clutching his worn and much-loved Curious George doll, was sprawled across my lap, asleep.

At last the Sudanese driver from the hospital arrived. He spoke no English except "King Faisal." He held the horde of Yemenis at bay while three of them loaded the luggage. Apparently, the fifteen Saudi *riyals* (approximately $4.40) apiece to carry the bags fifty feet was considered an inadequate tip. The porters, in their distinctive skirts and rubber sandals, shook their fists and screamed as the driver bundled us into his car and sped away through the maze of yellow taxi cabs, drivers and potential passengers engaged in the Middle East's timeless ritual of bargaining.

Riyadh, in the middle of the night, embodied in miniature what was happening to the country as a whole. There were stretches of the road from the airport to the hospital that were so quiet they seemed to have been asleep for centuries. But interrupting the tranquility were the massive construction sites, where tons of steel rose out of the dust of millennia. The frantic race to build something where nothing existed before went on twenty-four hours a day. Bathed in the light of huge round floodlights, hard-hatted construction workers, with gauze masks over their faces to filter the rising dust, crawled through the superstructures. Foremen shouted orders; trucks plied in and out of the sites. And looming overhead like the new national bird of Saudi Arabia were the ubiquitous bright yellow construction cranes.

The effect was to make Riyadh look like a surrealistic painting. Small mud houses and scruffy stucco apartment houses slumbered in the foreground, while rising out of the placid background and dominating the scene were machines contorted out of shape by the harsh lights and operated by seemingly grotesque figures bent on their urgent activity. In those early morning hours, few of Riyadh's inhabitants were yet aware of how menacing the pace of development was to their traditional lifestyles.

By 4:00 A.M. we arrived at the gate to the King Faisal Specialist Hospital. The hospital complex was located at the edge of Riyadh on land donated by the royal family. Former King Faisal's palace, with its green tile roof rising through the palm trees, was just beyond the main gate. KFSH was the showplace of the capital. The buff stone building exceeded in design and quality anything else in the city. Sitting on the site of a former date grove now carefully landscaped, the institution had the feeling of a garden. Dominating the entrance was a spewing fountain highlighted with garish colored lights. Cool water cascaded down into a pool, breaking the stillness of the night. New trees, struggling to sink in their roots, were scattered about in the greatest luxury of all — grass! KFSH boasted the only public grass in all of Riyadh.

The employee housing compound across the street had been left much as the rest of Riyadh, bare and dusty. As we pulled to a stop at the gate, I began to see the outlines of the buildings where I would live. Numb by this time, I did not yet feel the full impact of the gap between the recruiting company's promises about life in Riyadh, presented in their color brochures and 35-mm slides, and the reality. All I wanted was a bed.

The guard on the gate was Lebanese. He had his job because he could speak some English. I soon learned that a great gulf existed between being able to speak *some* English and being able to speak English. The same was true of those of us who struggled to speak some Arabic and those of us who could actually operate in the language.

My husband slowly pronounced his name and then spelled it. The guard consulted his official-looking clipboard, perused the list, and said there was no Dr. Mackey listed. With great patience, Dan said that he must be on the list. The hospital had known for several months when he would be arriving.

Through the list again. No, the only doctor expected that night was a Dr. Sandstorm. Finally the guard was convinced that, regardless of the name on his list, there was no other doctor in sight. The stalemate ended and our car proceeded through the forbidding gate into a cluster of prefab townhouse apartments laid out like a little community. Not a soul stirred. The night shift workers had long since gone, and the morning shift was still drifting through its dreams.

The car stopped in front of 13E. We all grabbed for the bags and staggered in the door. There we faced what was to be our new home.

The front door opened into the dining area, which contained a Formica-topped table and four stainless steel chairs. The kitchen was just large enough for one person. On the counter was a survival package designed to get us through the first few days. It contained tea bags from India, instant coffee from the United States, cubed sugar from Singapore, a box of salt from China, a jar of jelly from Switzerland, a loaf of bread of local origin, and some powdered milk, origin unknown.

The living room was furnished with a foam rubber cube covered in bright purple fabric, which I later learned was the sofa, a plastic coffee table, and a collapsible wooden chair, sitting under an enormous paper lantern. Upstairs there were two tiny bedrooms and a bath. All of the walls of the 800-square-foot apartment were cheap imitation wood paneling.

By now it was 4:30 A.M. We stood amid our mountain of luggage in a daze. Colin was bleary-eyed and far beyond whining and complaining. I numbly wondered, Where is the three-bedroom apartment we were promised? Where is the bougainvillea lazily creeping over stucco walls? Where are the exotic bazaars and the mystery and intrigue of the East? I finally collapsed into bed just as the mournful sounds of the *muezzin* calling the faithful to morning prayers drifted over the compound and Saudi Arabia's newest arrivals. We were there; now it was up to the Saudis to decide if they wanted us, and the rest of the new servant class, to stay.

This is the question that the Saudis have never answered for themselves. As I rode through Riyadh that first night, the contrast I observed between the tranquility of the sleeping Saudis and the mad pace of the working foreigners characterized the great truth of the oil boom. The people and their leaders believed that they could buy the physical development that they wanted without disturbing the stability of their traditional society. It is an illusion they still fight to preserve.

2

The Magic Kingdom

IN SAUDI ARABIA, there is no early hour of daylight when the soft shades of pink creep over the landscape, gradually waking a sleeping world. Morning comes early and comes forcefully. Within minutes of rising, the sun falls on the landscape with full intensity, savagely pounding the flat roofs and baked earth.

As I opened my eyes that first morning in Saudi Arabia, I saw the morning light powering its way through the draped windows. Struggling to wake up, I became aware of a deathly quiet seeping into my consciousness. There were no birds chirping outside the window and almost no sound of human activity. Here at the edge of the city, we still had the luxury of the tranquil desert. But even in the residential neighborhoods in the heart of the city, the streets were almost deserted, as the combination of the climate and the culture kept the Saudis in their houses, protected from the cruelty of the sun and the prying eyes of strangers.

My first day in Riyadh was spent touring the city with others who had just arrived at the King Faisal Specialist Hospital. When the car sent to pick me up stopped in front of my apartment that afternoon, and I walked out of the air conditioning into the blazing sun, the thermometer mounted on the shaded wall outside registered a late-springtime temperature of 114 degrees. It would reach 120 degrees and more by June and would stay there until late September.

I fought to keep my long skirt from tangling between my legs as I climbed up into the four-wheel-drive Chevrolet Suburban and crawled into the back seat between two nurses. It was unbelievably hot. We bumped along on half-finished roads, dodging heavy Mercedes water trucks and deep construction pits. The sun hammered the car, and the air conditioner groaned and labored to keep the temperature just bearable. An intense glare, interrupted only by the optical illusion of waves washing across the road, rose up from the flat landscape. The heat that had sent everyone indoors created a stillness that was somehow lonely. As I looked at the overwhelming ugliness around me, a heavy feeling of depression overcame me. The landscape was an endless monotone of grayish tan. There were no trees, hardly a shrub. The newer buildings were flat-topped squares of dingy stucco that merged with the colorless ground. Mountains of rubble stood everywhere. In the mad rush of construction, bulldozers ceaselessly pushed dirt and debris from one building site to the next, increasing the size and content of the piles as the city spread outward.

The bulk of the government's development funds were being poured into Riyadh. Before the oil boom, Riyadh, ancestral home of the House of Saud and capital of the kingdom, produced nothing of economic value except dates. What little economic activity there was in Saudi Arabia before the Second World War was centered around the port of Jeddah, which received religious pilgrims from the Moslem world and a pitiful volume of goods from the West. In the 1950s and 1960s, the oil belt in the Eastern Province became prosperous with the development of the petroleum industry, shifting the kingdom's economy from the west coast to the east and still largely ignoring Riyadh. The oil boom of the seventies would provide the funds to make Riyadh, at last, the commercial and governmental center of the kingdom of the al-Sauds. But in 1978, the new star of Saudi Arabia was more like a desert outpost than an international city.

Much of Riyadh was still composed of cramped mud buildings, especially near the center of the city. The driver and guide on this tour was an American who had been in Saudi Arabia since 1976. In the manner of a cheerleader, he chatted on to his passengers about how much living conditions were improving and how much easier life had become as electricity, telephones, and supermarkets gradually established themselves. On each side of the street, I could see the brown porcelain of the newly installed electrical insulators clinging precariously from the walls of old mud constructions.

Emerging from a twisting side street, we drove into the central square of Riyadh, dominated by the nondescript flat architecture and humble minaret of the main mosque. Circling right, away from the mosque, we passed the entrance to the Dirrah *souqs* ("markets"). Bright brass coffee pots hung along the outside wall and mysterious scents filtered through the air, imparting the timeless quality of the Oriental bazaar. Knots of three or four faceless women, totally clad in black, moved together toward the main entrance. An occasional lone woman, escorted by a man or her adolescent son, entered through one of the beckoning doors. Other men stood in the shadows of their shops or sprawled on intricately woven carpets of deep red, drinking tea from petite glass cups.

The car turned right again and went into the vegetable markets, where trucks from a dozen countries supplying Saudi Arabia with food unloaded their cargoes. We drove back toward the mosque and around the clock tower, an incongruous structure that some member of the royal family must have commissioned after a trip to Switzerland. Then on to Baatha, another marketing district. The area's cardinal feature was a broad, open sewage canal, which six months before had accommodated everything from human feces to the bloated bodies of dead donkeys. But now it was being filled in and within the year would become a wide, asphalt thoroughfare.*

We drove along Intercontinental Road, Pepsi Road, Chicken Street, and Continuous Flyover Road, all names devised by Westerners to compensate for the absence of street names. As we came back around the water tower, Riyadh's most distinguishing landmark, our guide offered typical directions to places Westerners were likely to frequent. The silver shops in Baatha were just left of the live chicken *souq*. And to reach a good picnic spot we should drive nine kilometers from Riyadh's last paved road and turn left where a bumper of a wrecked Mercedes stuck up out of a pile of rocks, then proceed across the desert to the first thorny tree that might provide some shade.

On the way back to the hospital, we passed one construction site after another where foreign workers raced to complete buildings to house government or business and apartment houses to accommodate the influx of foreigners. At the same time, the Saudis clung to their homes and shops, wary of the Western world that had camped in their midst. It was a wariness that would turn to hostility as Saudi Arabia's

---

*In the interim, a spate of new T-shirts showed up among the Westerners. Out was the pristine white one with "Baatha Yacht Club" sedately printed in navy blue on the upper left front, and in was the yellow-orange one that screamed "Save the Baatha Canal."

mad dash into the twentieth century progressed. The oil boom and its aftermath is not only economic history, it is a history of the relationship between Saudi Arabia and the West. Recruited by the Saudis, the Westerners marched into Saudi Arabia armed with blueprints, construction equipment, organizational charts, and management skills. Originally welcomed as liberators, the Westerners in time came to be regarded as an army of occupation bent on destroying the Saudis' traditional values. Through the various controls they could exert over the Westerners, the Saudis staged a defense of their society, while the Westerners with subtle determination resisted the Saudis' attempts to crush their own lifestyle. The Saudis and their Western work force coexisted in a state of tension that was not the result of ill will on the part of either, but rather resulted from a combination of Saudi insecurities and Western insensitivities. The Saudis with their money and the Westerners with their skills each fought to shape Saudi Arabia in its own image. Neither has succeeded in winning the battle.

Saudi Arabia in the 1970s was both exciting and exhausting for Westerners. No one attuned to world events could deny that living in the kingdom at that particular time in history was a unique opportunity. If one had the stamina, the sense of building a country from scratch was highly romantic. But not everyone was able to cope. The long hours and tremendous pressures of working in the midst of chaos produced a sizable number of cases of battle fatigue. It was stressful to live with the dictates of Saudi culture and the Saudi psyche. It was wildly frustrating when everything — the air conditioning, the stove, the water pump, the telephone — broke down and no one could fix them for days or weeks. It was maddening to reach the airport with confirmed reservations on a flight for a much-needed vacation to learn no such flight existed or that the plane was delayed for three days. Many became bored in a country where there were no movies, theaters, clubs, golf courses, or sports events and only a handful of restaurants. While many Westerners happily chalked up one year after another, various studies done for Western companies sending large numbers of employees to Saudi Arabia estimated that as many as a third could not cope with the demands of their jobs, an alien culture, and the difficult living conditions. I saw a few leave within days. Others waited for their first leave, a vacation from which they never returned. Ian Dylan, a seasoned veteran of Saudi Arabia who had spent three years tracking the movement of nomads in the northern part of the kingdom, arrived at his new job at the Ministry of Industry and Electricity to learn that his predecessor was in a London psychiatric hospital. And Peter Wright, an American equipment company representative, arrived in al-Khobar to replace a man who precipitously fled the country to check into the Mayo Clinic with a whole spectrum of physical and emotional complaints. The most difficult aspect of living in Saudi Arabia was that life totally lacked any predictability. Every day was a surprise as the Saudis went through the throes of modernization. So much had happened so quickly that there were no systems in place. Procedures for paying phone bills and regulations governing the conduct of business changed from week to week, leaving everyone in a state of confusion. The Saudis themselves were so confused about where they were going, and if they even wanted to go, that much of life was characterized by abrupt starts and stops. The House of Saud, for its part, played an intricate game of pushing ahead with strong policies for economic and social development, while claiming to uphold age-old religious traditions that conflicted with modernization in order to placate the religious leaders. Government policy affecting all aspects of the lives of foreigners living and doing business in the country shifted daily, causing periodic waves of wonder and apprehension. Moreover, the lack of order and organization, concepts alien to Saudi culture, forced foreigners to pick their way through a minefield of conflicting messages and demands. One misstep that violated an obscure law or offended a Saudi's sense of honor could lead to immediate expulsion from the country. Yet the reward at the end of any trying day was to stand on a corner in Baatha, with a *shwarma** in one hand and in the other a tepid Pepsi bought from the galvanized tub of a street vendor, for the sole purpose of experiencing the tempo of the time. Harried Western businessmen carrying fine leather briefcases picked their way along the sidewalk through crowds of Egyptians in flowing *galabias*. Tall Sudanese with lineal designs burned in their faces strode along among Yemenis, their heads swathed in bright colored turbans. Saudis straight off the desert honked the horns of their new Toyota pickups and raced through the newly installed red lights. There were those among us who had found a niche in Saudi Arabia.

---

*A Middle Eastern sandwich made from thin layers of lamb sliced off a standing rack slowly turning on a rotisserie and served in flat Arabic bread with a mixture of parsley, tomatoes, lemon juice, and spices.

A colorful kaleidoscope of people was drawn to Riyadh during those first years of the boom. In addition to businessmen, physicians, para-medics, administrators, and consultants, I counted among my friends and acquaintances the son of the last Turkish governor of Palestine, the heir apparent to the nonexistent throne of Kurdistan, and a stocky Irishman with a missing front tooth who appeared regularly at diplo-matic functions in Jeddah, claiming to be chief of an obscure tribe in the Cameroons.

That first year in Saudi Arabia, I wrote almost as many stories about the Western experience in Saudi Arabia as I did about the Saudis. Although the Westerners were being paid phenomenal salaries, they lived with the same shortages with which the Saudis lived. Saudi Ar-abia's primitive transportation system was overwhelmed by the king-dom's insatiable appetite for steel, cement, machinery, electrical sup-plies, automobiles, and consumer goods. With enormous amounts of money chasing scarce supplies, market shelves stayed largely bare. But it was the essentials that were missing, not the luxuries. The Sau-dis' passionate love of perfume kept the shops stocked with hundreds of gallons of expensive French scents, but there were no fly swatters. There were Rolex watches but no Band-Aids. In the scramble to ac-commodate, Westerners found ingenious substitutions for all manner of things that they took for granted at home. With no Thermos bottles, the children went to school swinging plastic bottles of frozen water encased in a sock for insulation. A wide array of metal springs were pressed into service for curtain rods. Prayer rugs became pictures for the wall. Big empty fruit and vegetable cans scavenged from com-munal kitchens were turned into waste baskets. Bits of aluminum foil from air-conditioning insulation, boxes, string, and plastic bags were hoarded, for nothing was casually thrown away.

The shortage of consumer goods extended to food. There were only two "supermarkets" in Riyadh when I arrived, the Western-style Spinney's and, down the street, the small, dark, and odorous Riyadh supermarket. Both were miserable places to shop. The shelves at Spin-ney's were usually empty of the basics, while the cramped quarters of the Riyadh supermarket were stuffed with dented, long outdated tin cans of milk and tuna, molding cheese, and spoiled meat.

The supermarket was for staples like flour, sugar, and tea. Potato chips, cookies, ice cream, spaghetti sauce, and breakfast cereal were only memories of another time and place. There was an ample supply of vegetables and eggs, but meat was a major problem. The mutton, camel, and goat from the local butcher were slaughtered among flies and rats and hung in the open without refrigeration. There were frozen chunks of low-grade beef, scrawny Bulgarian chickens, and plastic tubes filled with a little ground beef and a lot of ground soybeans that the few cold-storage houses in Riyadh imported. The only place where quality meat was available was from a roving meat truck, the project of an enterprising American who imported frozen beef and sold it at exorbitant prices to Western expatriates. Unfortunately, the truck was closed down in 1980 for selling smoked turkey that tasted suspiciously like ham.

Although no one ever faced going hungry, Islam forbade us pork because it was deemed unclean and vanilla extract because it contains alcohol. Local law forbade ground nutmeg, which was believed by officials to be hallucinogenic. The Arab black list forbade us Coca-Cola. And port congestion frequently forbade us everyday items such as sugar, cocoa, or coffee. With the high transportation costs and the delays in the ports, prices were exorbitant. The Saudi government heavily subsidized the staples of the Saudi diet — lamb, rice, and flour — keeping their costs inordinately low. It was imported food, food to satisfy the tastes and desires of the Westerners, that was so expensive. In 1978 prices, a can of green beans cost $1.50, a box of laundry soap was priced at $7.00, and six small wedges of cheese sold for $2.80.

Even with all the other shortages, it was the shortage of housing more than anything else that caused Westerners the most anguish. Very little housing existed that approached a Western standard. And like everything else, incessant demand had pushed housing prices to soaring levels. Since foreigners are barred from owning property in Saudi Arabia, Saudi nationals who were in favorable positions to acquire land became wealthy by using interest-free government loans to build rental property, which they then leased to Westerners. In 1973 a modern three-bedroom house in Riyadh rented for about $8,800 a year. By the end of 1975, this same house would bring an annual rent of $26,460. And by 1978, the luxury villas (the Saudi term for a single-family house) could cost $147,058 a year, payable in advance. Westerners recouped their costs by simply upping the prices on their contracts. Thus, the petrodollars the West paid for its oil circulated through the Saudi economy and back to the West.

In my first two years in Saudi Arabia, I moved from the tiny prefab townhouse we first occupied to a house in a compound of ten villas in a Saudi neighborhood and, finally, to a metal prefab behind Medical City Village that was about the size and style of a double-wide trailer. Each place had its own personality. The kitchen in the townhouse was so small that unless the wastebasket sat in the hall the refrigerator door would not open. The villa was a great, graceless barn of approximately 4500 square feet, built of cement block and stucco, void of even one piece of interior wood, and with only enough furniture to fill the 800 square feet I had just left. As was customary in a Saudi-style house, the front door opened onto an enormous foyer that served as a prayer area, complete with two lavatories for washing before prayers.

The house stood in an upper-class Saudi neighborhood. Directly across the street from the compound was an empty lot strewn with debris. A minor prince in the royal family lived on one side, while on the other side was a group of Bedouins, the nomads of the Arabian Peninsula. They lived in packing cases, and their bright new taxicabs, which had been presented to them by the government, were parked outside. And like true nomads, they had brought their flocks to the city with them. When our children ran through the compound yelling "goat alert," it was the signal to grab mops, brooms, and broken boards and charge out to chase the large, long-haired Nejdi sheep out of the garbage cans.

Ten months later we moved to Rainbow Villas, a collection of metal prefabs that had all the ambience of Stalag 17. There were twenty-four such houses in all, with five washing machines to share among us. The air-conditioning unit was mounted on the unshaded flat roof of the house so that it caught the full heat of the sun. The temperature in the house never dropped below ninety degrees in the afternoon, and because none of the water pipes was laid below ground, heat rose out of the toilets all summer long. Moreover, the metal construction expanded so much during the day that the house groaned all night as it cooled off.

It was life on the frontier. Packs of wild dogs that might attack any animal or human that got in their way still roamed Riyadh in 1978. There were also rats, scorpions, snakes, an occasional wild donkey, and horde upon horde of aggressive flies that mercilessly attacked the eyes, nose, and mouth in their desperate search for moisture. And someone was always falling down an unmarked construction hole.

Although Westerners existed with the hardships and did without everything but the bare necessities, we had the best of what was available. Everything about our lives was governed by a set of conditions different from those governing the rest of the expatriate work force* and even the Saudis themselves. We had the best housing, the highest salaries, and access to whatever recreation was available, for the Saudi government was pragmatic about its labor needs. To attract and keep the Westerners whose particular skills they so desperately wanted, the Saudis had to make life as painless as possible for the Westerners while still protecting their own culture. Even with the high salaries, a Westerner deprived of recreation and crowded into intolerable housing was not going to stay. Everyone else, from the illiterate manual laborers from the Third World to the highly educated and urbane Lebanese, suffered more from the physical shortages and the Saudis' strict code of conduct than did the Westerners. Although the Saudis in the work force rejected the recreational amenities provided to the Westerners because of their religious beliefs, they chafed under the two-tier salary and housing system in which the Westerners dominated. But there were so few Saudis in the work force at the time that the political repercussions for the House of Saud were inconsequential to the goal of recruiting Westerners to develop the country. In essence, the House of Saud often allowed the Saudi nationals to lose out to the demands of the Westerners.

As a result of the different conditions imposed on the various segments of the population, Saudi Arabia was a composite of several separate worlds. The manual laborers from the Third World lived in construction barracks, worked long hours, and stayed largely confined to their quarters after hours. The Westerners' lives were divided between the strict culture of Saudi Arabia that existed outside the walls of their housing compounds and the best imitation of the Western world that they could create inside. Finally, the Saudis lived in a world being physically torn apart, their culture under attack by the presence of their Western work force while they themselves tenaciously clung to their past.

While the Saudis outwardly flattered and indemnified the Westerners for their services, they were deeply ambivalent toward the Western presence. While the riches and exhilaration of the oil boom eclipsed much of the Saudis' internal conflicts over the challenge to their tra-

---

*When large numbers of foreigners began to arrive, the Saudi government and press commonly referred to members of the kingdom's imported work force as "expatriates." To Saudis and Westerners alike, the term came to mean a foreign national working in Saudi Arabia.

ditional values, deep hostility toward the Westerners grew and was fed by the Saudis' own xenophobia. There is an arrogance among the Saudis, especially among the religiously conservative Wahhabis of central Saudi Arabia, that comes from a profound belief in their own superiority. This self-perception has little to do with the Saudis' immense wealth but rather extends back through the centuries when the vast majority of Saudis lived within the confines of family and tribe, experienced nothing of the outside world, and remained smug in their puritanical religion and their ability to survive the harshness of the desert.

With the oil boom, these clannish and withdrawn people were suddenly confronted with hordes of new arrivals, not just from neighboring tribes but from cultures outside the world of Islam. Many of the Saudis in the interior of the country had never seen a non-Moslem before the sweep of the economic strategists planted Westerners in every corner of the kingdom. With the Westerners in place, the Saudis' xenophobia took on a new dimension. Now added to an innate sense of spiritual and racial superiority was a defensiveness that arose from their embarrassed bewilderment when confronted by technology they did not understand. It was this technology that undercut the Saudis' undoubting perception of themselves. Haughty in their wealth and sense of self, the Saudis nonetheless suffered from the reality that they knew how to do very little except herd goats and barter in the marketplace.

It was not only the Westerners to whom the Saudis felt inferior. The educated Arabs whom Saudi Arabia imported from Egypt, Lebanon, and elsewhere were contemptuous of the Saudis. For centuries the Arabs outside the Arabian Peninsula had placed the Saudis near the bottom of the Middle East's pecking order, considering them culturally and intellectually inferior to the Arabs from Islam's traditional centers of learning. Yet it was the attitude of the Westerners that most challenged the Saudis' self-perception.

The Westerners' behavior toward the Saudis was no better than that of the other Arabs and in many respects caused more pain. Most Westerners felt an overwhelming air of superiority toward their Saudi employers. So intense was their feeling of preeminence that it could be characterized as barely concealed scorn, a scorn that regarded the most sophisticated Saudi as either "a primitive European or retarded American."* From this attitude, which was conveyed to the Saudis in

---

*Ghazi A. Algosaibi, *Arabian Essays* (London: Kegan Paul, 1982), p. 115.

hundreds of poorly hidden messages, deep resentments grew. While gladly lavishing money on the machines of the West, the Saudis saw the Westerners themselves as thieves who were stealing their money and threatening to steal their values.

The Saudis' defense against these conflicting feelings of superiority and inferiority toward the foreign work force was managed by allowing only as many foreigners into the country as was necessary to build what the Saudis wanted and keeping those who were admitted isolated from Saudi society.

The Saudis' most lethal weapon against the uncontrolled influx of foreigners was the entry visa. Regardless of foreigners' complaints about the illogical administration of the visa process, the entry visa performed a vital function for Saudi Arabia. It was the kingdom's only real defense against the swarms of both honest and corrupt foreigners hungering after a bite of Saudi Arabia's golden apple. But in the bureaucratic inefficiency of the visa process, the people the Saudis needed were kept out along with those who were not wanted.

The push for visas was like an avalanche. Businessmen chased lucrative contracts from the government or fledgling Saudi entrepreneurs. Massive public works projects cried for engineers and laborers. The airlines, the lifeline between the kingdom and its sources of supply, needed pilots and mechanics. The new schools clamored for teachers. The deluge of imports demanded stevedores to unload ships and truck drivers to deliver the cargoes. But everything depended on access to entry visas controlled by the Ministry of the Interior.

Without an entry visa, the gates of Saudi Arabia stayed shut to the foreigner. In fact, a foreigner could not even apply for a visa; that could be done only by a Saudi national who agreed to sponsor him. This agreement then bound foreigner and sponsor together as long as the expatriate was in the country.

Although a visa could be approved only in Saudi Arabia, it had to be issued by the Saudi embassy or consulate in the foreigner's country of origin. While a Saudi sitting on a $15 million construction project dependent on the specialized skills of an electrical engineer pushed to move the paper work through the visa office in Saudi Arabia, the engineer hounded his nearest Saudi consulate for confirmation that the telex of approval had been received from Saudi Arabia and, once received, was stamped in his passport. Each step in the process was arduous. I knew an Arab-American, fluent in Arabic, who spent four weeks persuading a resistant consulate employee in Houston to open his stamp pad to imprint the visa in his passport.

Even for those foreigners the government itself demanded on a priority basis, the wait could go on for several months. Departure dates for a hefty percentage of people needed desperately in Saudi Arabia were set back time after time while they waited for their visas to clear. Screaming telephone calls back and forth between the employee at home and his sponsor in Saudi Arabia sometimes got the bureaucratic ball rolling and sometimes not. Numbers of people fell through the cracks. Some who had already sold their houses and prepared to depart never left their own countries.

The Saudis incurred enormous costs in time and money in these tangles over visas. But expense was of no concern to Saudi Arabia during the 1970s; security and control over foreigners was. Therefore, the documentation process for foreigners only began with the entry visa.

Once in the country, a foreigner surrendered his passport to his Saudi sponsor and was subject to the laws of Saudi Arabia. A foreigner could be deported on administrative order of the Ministry of the Interior. If deported, he had no legal rights to protect his contract. Employment in the kingdom, even over a long period of time, gave an expatriate no claim to citizenship. Babies born in Saudi Arabia to expatriate parents were denied Saudi citizenship. All political parties, organizations of foreigners, and trade unions were prohibited. Public demonstrations, strikes, and political protests were forbidden. Criticism of the government and its policies was banned.*

To exit Saudi Arabia, a foreigner needed an exit visa, which also could be obtained for him only by his Saudi sponsor. To reside in the kingdom required a residency permit, to travel within the country required written approval of the Saudi sponsor, and to work required an *igama*, or work permit, that served as an identity card. All had to be obtained by the foreigner's Saudi sponsor. The Saudi government's rationale for these regulations was that they bound a foreign worker to his Saudi sponsor. In theory, by keeping a worker always tied to his sponsor, the government was able to control the expatriate's movements, thus easing its own concerns. This was of little comfort to the

* All rules governing entry and exit visas and work permits, as well as the restrictions on foreigners' rights, still stand.

expatriate. With his passport in his employer's hands and unable to seek an exit visa on his own, the foreigner was at the mercy of his Saudi employer.

Of all the regulations, it was the expatriate's inability to leave the country without an exit visa that was the most anxiety provoking. Every expatriate knew of foreigners becoming trapped in Saudi Arabia. Expatriates were held captive for suspected criminal offenses or by sponsors who refused to release them, or they simply became victimized by the system. A British engineer I once knew was forced to stay a month beyond his contract because his passport was stuck under the short leg of a desk in the visa office.

Western embassies could do little other than make inquiries to help their nationals escape the country. Embassies had as many problems dealing with the Saudi government as did their nationals, so what clout foreign governments had was conserved for affairs of state, not for intervening in exit visa controversies. Yet when an American was standing on a street corner in Riyadh shouting that the Saudis were grinding up Thai and Pakistani workers and selling them as hamburger meat in the Panda supermarket, the Saudis were only too happy to cooperate with his embassy to arrange for his speedy departure from the kingdom.

Underlying the stern rules of documentation, which were based on apprehensions about the uncontrolled mobility of labor, was a fear that if foreigners were not rigidly controlled, Saudi culture would fall victim to alien ways. The Saudis' anxiety about foreigners was not unique to the oil boom. The Wahhabis had always sensed a danger of corruption from contact with foreigners. This feeling was based on the notion that somehow Wahhabism is valid only as long as it is not challenged by other ideas and philosophies. Yet there was a second fear that contributed to the control of foreigners: the House of Saud's fear of a backlash against its development policies from the religious fundamentalists. Development in the form of housing, airports, roads, hospitals, and perhaps schools for boys were politically acceptable ways to spend the Saudis' oil revenues. It was the importation of the Western work force that threatened to upset the tenuous balance that the al-Sauds had struck between progress and tradition. Throughout the history of the House of Saud, Saudi Arabia, except for the coastal areas, had remained remarkably free of outside influences, especially those of the West. Responding to the Wahhabis' distrust of anyone outside the realm

34 THE SAUDIS

of Islam, the House of Saud had kept at bay the few Westerners in the kingdom before the oil boom. ARAMCO's Western work force, present since the late 1940s, had been contained in their own town of Dhahran. The idea was to allow Westerners to produce the Saudis' oil but to spare Saudi society disruption by the introduction of Western ideas. The same principle was applied to the new wave of Westerners in the 1970s. The House of Saud devised various ways, primarily in housing and schooling, to contain Western influence.

Saudi law required that employers provide foreign laborers with housing. Originally designed to relieve the pressure on housing demands by balancing the number of housing units with the number of foreigners admitted into the kingdom, the requirement quickly created a means to corral foreigners. With the exception of sales representatives of Western firms, freewheeling entrepreneurs, some consultants, and executives of companies with only one or two families assigned to a Saudi city, Westerners lived in housing compounds owned and operated by their employers. In Riyadh there was the Lockheed compound, the B-2 and C-3 compounds of the U.S. Army Corps of Engineers, the Bell Canada compound, and the BAC compound, all operating as towns unto themselves. Surrounded by walls with guards posted on the gates, the Westerners lived according to their own ways and the Saudis were kept out. As long as a Westerner stayed within the confines of those walls, he could watch Western movies at the recreation center, make a little homemade wine, and put his arm around his wife in public. She could play tennis in shorts or lie by the swimming pool in a bikini. At the recreation centers, unmarried men and women were allowed to play bingo together or swim together as long as they stayed hidden from the eyes of the Saudis.

The same principle applied to education of expatriate children. In education, religion marked the great dividing line between the Saudis and their foreign servants. Christian Arabs were as split from the Saudis as the Westerners. Before the oil boom, schooling for non-Moslem expatriate children outside of ARAMCO and the diplomatic community in Jeddah was almost nonexistent. With no government support, Genevra Abou Seoud, a Christian Lebanese educator living in Riyadh, had pieced together a curriculum with the help of a few women with teaching experience and had opened a school in a ramshackle old villa near Riyadh's Maalaz district in 1965. Using English as the language of instruction, the school served the non-Moslem population of Riyadh that was barred from the local schools. In 1977, overwhelmed by the numbers of children arriving in Saudi Arabia, the Ministry of Education gave official sanction to the principle of expatriate education by providing land outside of Riyadh for the construction of an international school. Similar schools were sanctioned elsewhere in the kingdom. Supported by tuition paid by parents or their employers, the Riyadh International Community School became a microcosm of nationalities working in Riyadh. Throughout the 1970s, however, Moslems of any nationality were forbidden to attend. Until the British and French founded their own schools, the Riyadh International Community School was the receptacle for every non-Moslem child in Riyadh. Americans, Canadians, Swedes, Lebanese, Koreans, Indians, Finns, Germans, all went to school together through the ninth grade. Afraid foreign teenagers would somehow corrupt Saudi youth, the government sent high-school-age students to boarding schools abroad.

Even though there has been a significant foreign presence in Saudi Arabia since 1973, few expatriates have ever cracked the wall that separates the Saudis from everyone except their own kin. Saudi Arabia never was nor is likely ever to be a melting pot. Its society, built on family and tribe, is incapable of assimilating outsiders even on a casual basis. The Saudis expected the Westerner to come with his skills, collect his extravagant salary, and go home when his job was finished. From the highest princes to the lowliest peasants, the Saudis constantly served up notice to the foreigner that he was there at the pleasure of his Saudi master.

No Westerner consciously saw himself as a missionary of Western culture. Yet by his very presence, he introduced new ideas and mores, many of which struck at the tenets of Wahhabism. Conforming to the society enough to stay employed, the Westerner nonetheless imposed a wide range of his own values on the bureaucracy, the educational system, and the new Western-educated middle class. It would not be until the oil boom died that the extent of Western infiltration and Saudi reaction against Westernization would become evident.

During my years in Saudi Arabia, the most vivid depiction I saw of the Saudi attitude toward Westerners occurred at the airport in Abha, a small city in the mountains of the southwest. A woman of perhaps fifty, heavyset, draped in veils, her skin patterned with henna dye, lumbered into the ladies room, where she angrily confronted a group of Western women waiting to use the toilets. With disgust, she pushed everyone aside as she went to the front of the line. Dispossessing the occupant from one of the stalls, she turned to the next woman waiting in line and handed her her black *abaaya* as if she were a parlor maid. When she emerged from the toilet, she took her *abaaya* again and draped it over her head. Turning toward us, she glared and waved her hand over the crowd as if she were shooing flies, as she said with contempt, *"Bas Saudi, bas Saudi"* — "Only Saudis!"

3

Managing the Boom

DAYS BEGAN EARLY in Saudi Arabia. By 7:30 A.M. the men were at work and the children long on their way to school. By 9:00 the daily household chores were done. By 10:30 the shopping bus had made its daily run and was back. It was then that the deathly reality of the whole day with nothing to do and nowhere to go confronted me. Though we faced the risks of personal injury and harassment, the major threat to Western women living in Saudi Arabia was complete and utter boredom. Locked in my apartment, confined behind the walls of the compound I was in a stupor as day followed day in unbroken repetition. I lasted nine days in this atmosphere before I went to work.

There was one mammoth obstacle to female employment — it was against the law. In conforming to the religious dictates of Wahhabism, Saudi law forbid women to be employed in any occupation other than teaching or nursing. But because there was such a desperate shortage of labor, a thriving pool of black market female labor quickly developed. Wages were high. Simple clerical work paid about $10 an hour (in 1978 dollars), with no taxes withheld. Yet the chief appeal of employment was not money but something to do. A job was an anchor of sanity.

Employers and their female employees played a constant cat-and-mouse game with the Ministry of Labor, which patroled business establishments, rooting out women. There were also raids by the *matawain*, the religious police, who conducted their own searches to confirm that the Ministry of Labor was doing its job in protecting the morals of Saudi Arabia. As a result, harried businessmen unwilling to risk arrest were forced to hire couriers to scuttle between the office and secretaries safely ensconced in their apartments, equipped with type-writers and filing cabinets. Others put women to work on the premises and risked the consequences. So desperate were women to keep their jobs, they were willing to work under bizarre conditions. I knew one woman who worked in an office but typed at a tiny table in a closet. Outside the closet door an assortment of mops and brooms stood wait-ing to be thrown in for a screen if the authorities were spotted ap-proaching the building. One business firm hired a Saudi to sit outside the door of its office to divert authorities while the women employees escaped through a back door. I had one friend who worked in an office building in downtown Riyadh where the door was rigged with a cord strung with bells. Employees of the office always shouted a password before they opened the door, jangling the bells. If the bells rang with-out warning, the woman dove out the window.

The raiding parties were not always fooled. A woman was caught from time to time. Nothing happened to her personally except that she was sent back to her compound. It was her employer and her husband who were responsible to the authorities. The employer was heavily fined and, for a woman caught more than once, her husband was sum-moned to court to explain his inability to control his wife. Owen Ford, a physicist at the King Faisal Specialist Hospital, was once threatened with deportation if his wife were caught working one more time.

My first job in Saudi Arabia was a legal one. The Saudi government had contracted with the U.S. Corps of Engineers to supervise many of the massive construction projects under way in the kingdom. The Corps was given a special dispensation to hire Western women in Corps of-fice compounds, operating under a sort of extra-territorial status. The Corps paid only about 25 percent more than stateside salaries, much less than anyone else, but they never had trouble hiring people because of the fringe benefits. Local employees had access to a commissary that stocked directly from the United States. It had delectable things such as Oreo cookies and Fritos, unknown elsewhere in Riyadh. Best of all, a Corps employee could buy pork chops and ham. Not the least of the fringe benefits of Corps employment was the highly secret "tea ration." The Saudi government quietly allowed foreign missions, un-der a loose interpretation of diplomatic immunity, to bring in alcohol. Once a month, the Corps' female employees boarded the bus that took us to work carrying small suitcases, canvas tote bags, various heavy plastic sacks, or anything that was not transparent, to transport home the five bottles of liquor we were allowed each month. Under the U.S. government's understanding with Saudi authorities, the label on every empty bottle had to be soaked off and the bottle broken before it was discarded. To enforce the rule, Corps officials patrolled the housing compounds inspecting garbage.

My job at the Corps of Engineers was as a clerk-typist at the lowest grade in the United States Civil Service. I worked in the office of the supervising engineers for the King Khalid Military City, a new city with a projected population of seventy thousand and a price tag of $7 billion that was being built on the great empty plain between Riyadh and the border of Iraq. As humble as my job was, no one who was alert ever had a job in Saudi Arabia that was so menial that there was nothing to learn. Between typing government forms, I filed, and as I filed I discovered a whole range of interesting things about the forces at work in Saudi Arabia. There was the constant problem of where to recruit all of the labor needed to build a city; how to get visas for all the laborers that were recruited, where to find the technical expertise to install the equipment purchased abroad; how to keep foreigners in the country once they arrived. I noted the fear that went through the Saudi military every time political upheaval erupted in one of the countries supplying labor to Saudi Arabia, especially if that country were Moslem. I saw evidence of the Corps' unending battle with contractors to keep their costs realistic even under the unbelievably high cost of construction in Saudi Arabia. I heard discussions about the sensitive issue of allowing contractors to pay the bribes necessary to keep Saudi partners and government officials happy and still stay within the dictates of U.S. law, which the Corps of Engineers was supposed to defend.

After a few months with the Corps of Engineers, I had gotten my feet on the ground in the job market and decided it was time to move on. I had come to Saudi Arabia to learn. Having absorbed what was of interest to me at the Corps of Engineers, I needed to find a job that took me out into the city of Riyadh and away from the insulated community of American government employees.

After several weeks of being passed from woman to woman in the network of the labor black market, I heard about a contractor who needed someone to handle his correspondence. I called the number I was given and the voice at the other end said he would be right over and "by the way, my name is Tom Krogh." When the bell rang and I opened the door, a tall man, not yet·middle-aged, stood before me. He had shoulder-length red hair, noticeably thinning on the top, and a great long beard that made him look remarkably like Michelangelo's Moses. Tom was an American who had grown up in various corners of Africa, where his father was an international contractor. One of the early pioneers, Krogh had been working in Saudi Arabia off and on since the late 1960s. A marvelous character, he epitomized the autonomous entrepreneur, the commercial soldier of fortune, whom Saudi Arabia drew like a magnet during the oil boom. Holding a graduate degree in psychology, Tom had the most extraordinary talent for outmaneuvering the Saudis that I ever encountered.

In 1978 Tom Krogh was making a small fortune in an area of construction that he called "crisis management." Among the major problems a foreign company setting up business in Saudi Arabia faced was that most supplies and equipment were blocked in the ports. Furthermore, the jammed ports caused construction delays on new facilities, which compounded the already severe shortages of office space, housing, electricity, communication lines — everything needed to make modern business function. Western companies with fat Saudi contracts were desperate to secure any kind of office and housing accommodations. Shabby structures, thrown up for Saudi landlords, were leased to Western companies, which took whatever they could get. Often these were nonfunctional as leased. At this point, Tom entered to scour the local markets for whatever was available and then modify the bits and pieces into some Rube Goldberg contraption that would make everything work. His genius was handsomely rewarded by grateful clients.

When I went to work for Tom, he was problem solving for a major Western communications company with a multibillion-dollar contract with the Saudi government. The company had taken possession of a building for its Riyadh offices before discovering that it had no electrical supply. When showing the building, the sly Saudi owner had hung an electric bulb from a long extension cord that he ran out the door, down the street, and around the corner to the nearest building on the last street served by Riyadh electricity, and plugged it in. The housing compound the company had leased for its employees had snakes in the plumbing, air conditioners choked with dust, and a swimming pool with no source of water. Tom installed generators, fished the snakes out of the pipes, cleaned the air conditioners, and daily hauled in water in big Mercedes trucks to fill the pool.

Although I was hired to write contracts, I became a jack-of-all-trades while in Tom's employ. To avoid the visa hassles, he did not import his own labor. Rather, at sundown, he and I would bounce around Riyadh in his four-wheel-drive vehicle, a Pepsi case filled with cash on the seat between us, picking up laborers from their regular jobs to come work on Tom's projects (illegal under Saudi law). An immensely kind man, his reputation preceded him. He paid wages far above the regular scale and treated his workmen with respect. Soon we would have filled the car, delivered that group to the job site, and gone out again.

As well as Tom got on with his laborers, he was always having difficulty with his Saudi partner, whom he managed to change frequently. He called me one Thursday and told me he was going to have a showdown with the current partner at three o'clock that afternoon and he wanted me to go with him. I protested and said that he could not take a Western woman to a business meeting with a Saudi. He chuckled. ''That's the point,'' he said. When he picked me up, I was properly attired for meeting a Saudi man and nervous as a cat. No sooner had I gotten into the car than Tom said, "I have just appointed you as my lawyer." I looked at him in disbelief and cried, "Your lawyer! I don't know anything about law and certainly not Saudi law. You're out of your mind." He just smiled and said, "Don't worry. Just write down in legal language what I tell you to."

When we arrived at the meeting, the Saudi partner was there with his attorney, who claimed to be on the faculty of Riyadh University. The pair looked at me quizzically and then Tom introduced me as his attorney, who was there to negotiate on his behalf. The Saudis were dumbfounded. Seizing the moment, Tom took the initiative in the negotiations. Three hours later, we left. I had said nothing except to read out their points of agreement, which I had translated into a facsimile of legal jargon, and Tom had emerged with a new contract containing all his major demands.

Saudi Arabia in the late 1970s was like a giant boom town in which everyone was outrageously wheeling and dealing — Saudis and Westerners alike. Fantastic amounts of money were being spent as the Saudis, just emerging from their feudal past, seized the things their new-found wealth would buy. There had not been a rags-to-riches story like this since the Crusades awakened Europe from the Dark Ages and Venice, Genoa, and Florence became suddenly wealthy from Middle East trade. I was there and I was seeing it all. The next step was to report what I saw. Of course, this meant breaking another of Saudi Arabia's rules, that of censorship. At the same time as I was working at the Corps of Engineers and bouncing around Riyadh in Tom Krogh's truck, I was smuggling newspaper stories out of Saudi Arabia and publishing them under my new name, Michael Collins.

While I was working at the Corps of Engineers, I became acquainted with a delightful woman from California, whose husband worked for the Stanford Research Institute of Menlo Park. SRI had a team of economists in the country who were doing studies in preparation for Saudi Arabia's Third Development Plan, a five-year blueprint for economic and social development. As the preliminary work was nearing completion, the various sections written by different economists had to be edited to a common style to be published as the final plan. SRI's choice for senior editor was a woman from the company's headquarters in California. The Saudis rejected the choice because she was a female. Her replacement was not due in the country for several months. Meanwhile, the initial editing had to go on. I was approached about the job by my friend's husband, who knew from social gatherings that I had done some writing in the United States and that I also knew the basic terminology of development economics. Would I be interested in applying, being aware that, as a woman, I might be turned down? he asked. I wrote a résumé, submitted it to SRI, and got the job. I won out for several reasons. Having a woman as assistant editor, whose name would not be connected with the plan, was more palatable to the Saudis than having a woman as senior editor. The planning minister, somewhat of a revolutionary in his thinking, was a strong advocate of using women in the work force. But more than anything else, I was already in the country and housed, and therefore much less expensive than someone who had to be brought in from the United States or the United Kingdom. I went to work in Saudi Arabia's Ministry of Planning as an employee of SRI, not the Saudi government — a firm distinction demanded by the Saudis.

It is a credit to former King Faisal that Saudi Arabia even had a central planning unit before the oil bonanza hit in 1973. Yet even the far-sighted Faisal, in his grand plans for his kingdom, had to contend with Saudi Arabia's climate and topography and a population fiercely resistant to change.

Saudi Arabia is the largest country in the world with no major rivers and few streams. The Rub al-Khali, which encompasses the southeastern one-fifth of the kingdom, is the most arid desert on earth. Before oil was produced in sizable quantities, life was sustained by farming the oases and by herding animals — camels, goats, and the Nedji sheep, a breed that can live on as little as thirty liters of water a year. In the early twentieth century, eastern and central Arabia had little to trade with the outside world. Their exports consisted of dates and Arabian horses, in great demand by the British for use by its Indian army. Taxes on camel caravans moving goods from ports on the Arabian Gulf* to the Levant provided a little revenue for Abdul Aziz during the early days of his kingdom. Camel trading with the caravans supplemented the meager subsistence of the Bedouin tribes. The tax on pilgrims making the *hajj* to Mecca provided Abdul Aziz's paltry treasury its major source of income. None of these produced much. The Saudis existed from hand to mouth.

Even though oil production accelerated after the Second World War, Saudi Arabia remained a backward, agrarian economy. Slavery was not abolished until 1962, and the first paved road connecting Jeddah to Riyadh was not finished until 1967. Of the Saudis employed in 1970, 727,000 were engaged in agriculture, 91,000 in trade, and less than 17,000 in oil production or associated refining. In spite of twenty-six years of oil production prior to 1970, its impact on the way people lived was minimal. Only about 40 percent of all people employed worked in jobs that could be considered even remotely associated with a modern economy, and of this number many were expatriates. But as oil production continued to increase, bringing in ever-growing revenues, King Faisal recognized that Saudi Arabia must expand and modernize the structure of its economy. Therefore, in 1968, he created the Central Planning Organization, the forerunner of the present Ministry of Planning. It was under its direction that Western economists from SRI drew up Saudi Arabia's first five-year economic development plan for the years 1970 to 1975.

The first plan concentrated on building a basic infrastructure for Saudi Arabia and laying the foundations for an educational system. Resources were directed to the urban areas: Jeddah, al-Khobar, and Ri-

---

*The great body of water that separates the Arabian Peninsula from Iran has commonly been called the Persian Gulf in the West. The Saudis have always insisted that it is the Arabian Gulf. Since the oil boom and the 1979 Iranian revolution, the name Arabian Gulf has grown in usage, particularly in the Western press.

yadh. The approximately 440,000 working Saudis living in rural areas who had low incomes and followed a traditional lifestyle would be unaffected. Since these people had none of the skills needed to build a modern state and the government was fearful of treading on their religious fundamentalism and way of life, the political decision was made to leave the rural areas alone. Even primary education by-passed the rural areas so that by 1974, 70 percent of the total Saudi population was illiterate, and only 13 percent could be considered "educated."

When the plan was completed, it called for a total expenditure of SR 41.3 billion, or $9.1 billion over the five years from 1970 to 1975. The gap between the assumptions the plan was based on and the reality of a world short of oil soon became evident.

In the second year of the First Development Plan, King Faisal and his oil minister Sheikh Ahmed Zaki Yamani recognized the growing importance of imported oil to the economies of the industrialized countries. In 1971 Faisal demanded changes in Saudi Arabia's one-sided agreement with ARAMCO. Under this agreement, Saudi Arabia was paid 50 percent of ARAMCO's profits in exchange for its crude oil. Wanting a better deal and sensing latent power over ARAMCO, Faisal dispatched Yamani to the Organization of Petroleum Exporting Countries (OPEC). Since 1960 OPEC, a loose, impotent alliance of oil producers, had been exploring ways to force the oil companies to accept its members' direct participation in the ownership and, thereby, in the profits of the companies. Afraid of outright nationalization, ARAMCO agreed to give Saudi Arabia 20-percent participation in the company in early 1972.

With part ownership of the oil company and ever-increasing sales of Saudi oil, by the end of 1972 Saudi Arabia's earnings exceeded the kingdom's ability to absorb the money. Budget allocations rose 70 percent over the preceding year. In fiscal year 1972–73,* the budget was raised by another $3.8 million, but not all of the allocations for either year were spent. The economy was so undeveloped that it was impossible to disperse money in these quantities through the existing system, so excess revenues were turned into gold and foreign reserves.

In October 1973, the forces of supply and demand for oil and the political goals of Saudi Arabia and the other Arab oil producers merged

---

* Saudi Arabia's fiscal year runs from 1 Rajab to 30 Jumad II of the Hijrah calendar. See Chapter 4.

in the oil embargo against countries friendly to Israel. Production was cut to support Egypt's war against Israel, and a world that had become subservient to OPEC's oil proved its willingness to pay for it. Saudi Arabia's revenues skyrocketed. The rural population, no longer content to stay outside the economy, began to migrate to the cities. Between 1963 and 1974, Riyadh's population jumped from 159,000 to 667,000, Jeddah's from 147,000 to 561,000, and smaller cities like al-Hufuf, Taif, and Medina doubled in size.

On the heels of the oil embargo, Saudi Arabia's rulers made the decision to meet the world's demand for oil by raising its production and to use the revenues for a gigantic economic development plan that would thrust the kingdom into the twentieth century. They had to start from scratch. Just how far the kingdom had to go is demonstrated by the fact that the tallest building in Riyadh in 1974 was the water tower. Money was poured into the infant economy. Budget surpluses (allocations over expenditures) were $6.75 billion in 1973–74 and $19.1 billion in 1974 75. National income grew 44 percent in real terms between 1973 and 1975. The price increases imposed by OPEC gave Saudi Arabia a per capita income that ranked it among the world's largest economies. But the people possessed none of the basic skills to build a modern country.

The kingdom launched the Second Economic Development Plan in 1975 with a whole new set of opportunities and problems. In a country caught up in the euphoria of its newfound wealth, an alternative development strategy that emphasized low production to conserve resources, slower economic growth, and more limited social change had few advocates. Although Saudi Arabia had the money to make every citizen a ward of the state, King Faisal was ideologically opposed to diverting oil revenues into a grand welfare scheme. The enrichment of citizens as an end in itself was not, in his eyes, the goal of development; rather, he believed all Saudis should be assured an adequate standard of living, with anything beyond that the reward of individual effort and achievement.

The second plan sought to vastly broaden the development of the physical infrastructure and to seriously tackle problems of education, health, and housing. Specifically, the plan sought to relieve port congestion and build highways and airports to promote the movement of people and goods.

The problem of port congestion was a nightmare. In the autumn of

1975, 130 ships were waiting at anchor in Jeddah on the west coast, and Dammam on the east coast. By the end of December, there were 200 ships sitting in ports, facing delays of months to reach the docks to unload. Not only were these delays frustrating, they were costly. Shipping lines imposed surcharges on their freight bills of 50 to 250 percent to take cargo to Saudi Arabia. Additional demurrage charges of $3,000 to $5,000 were frequently billed to shippers. By 1976 port congestion was adding an estimated 40 percent to the cost of imports. Moreover, progress on whole construction projects stopped for lack of supplies while laborers sat collecting their wages.

When I was traveling in Italy several years after the great port jam, I met an Italian seaman named Phillip who told me about being stranded aboard the ship *Portia* in the port of Jeddah. The *Portia,* carrying Carrara marble and expensive French perfume, lay at anchor in the oppressive, humid heat and stark ugliness of Jeddah from October 1976 to June 1977. In eight months, Phillip left the ship only twice — it was too expensive. The local Saudis were enterprising enough to turn a handsome profit from stranded seamen, charging $10 each way for the boat from ship to shore and $20 for the round-trip taxi ride to town. Once he reached Jeddah, there was nothing to do. Verging on madness from boredom, Phillip tried to quit but could not because under the terms of his visa he was forbidden to leave Saudi Arabia before his ship. The Italian ambassador had no authority to intervene in his behalf since the ship sailed under the Panamanian flag. The *Portia* was eventually unloaded and Phillip never went to sea again.

The ports were finally unclogged by the creation of the General Ports Authority under the direction of Faiz Badr, one of the true heroes of the period. The greatest secret of his success was that, as a Saudi, he was able to deal more effectively with the inner workings of Saudi Arabia than the Western management companies that he replaced. A major problem of the ports was that once cargo was unloaded, it sat on the docks while merchants and contractors scrambled to secure the ground transportation to move their goods. But more often, importers were just overcome by inertia. Badr gave his compatriots a deadline and threatened to auction off their goods if they were not moved from the docks on time. This would never have been tolerated from a Westerner.

The costs that port congestion added to goods and materials was only one of the factors that accounted for the exorbitant expenses of doing business in Saudi Arabia. The early development projects carried extremely high prices because each site had to build its own infrastructure. KFSH, for example, had its own power plant and water purification system. To build the King Khalid Military City, a functioning town had to be created to service construction crews before work on the actual city began.

As a result of the harsh climate and the shoddy workmanship of the time, most buildings seemed temporary. The average life span for a building in Saudi Arabia in the 1970s was seven years: buildings constructed in 1973 were being replaced in 1980. Consequently, Riyadh lacked a feeling of permanence. It was as though the city could slip right back into the desert if the pace of construction slowed.

Trying to integrate utilities that were in place when the building boom began required the expenditure of huge sums of money. Riyadh spent $208 million standardizing its electrical system before expansion could even begin. In 1978 so many new drivers drove into electrical poles that the government was forced to spend another $400 million to put the lines underground to keep the electricity that was available flowing.

Costs were also increased by the rush the Saudis put on nonessential projects. The elaborate conference center in Riyadh, built to host inter-Arab meetings, was built and furnished in eleven months.

And there was always the problem of over-consumption. Dan had two electron microscopes in his department, with no one who knew how to use them. The Saudis were constantly drawn to the technically sophisticated or the outwardly glamorous while ignoring the substantive, such as personnel or maintenance, that make things work.

To circumvent lurking economic traps, contracts were bid at high enough levels that delays, shortages of critical materials, visa problems, unavailable labor, transportation delays, high salaries demanded by Westerners, harsh penalty clauses in contracts covering completion schedules, commissions to Saudi agents, and the government's own failure to pay its bills on time could be covered and still ensure the contractor a handsome profit.

All of these factors, plus the vast amounts of money being thrown into an infant economic system, resulted in high rates of inflation. The government's official figures claimed inflation in fiscal 1975–76 was 31.5 percent. No one inside or outside the government actually believed that it was that low. Estimates by bankers and diplomats put the figure somewhere between 40 to 50 percent and as high as 70 percent if rents were calculated in. To lessen the impact on the average Saudi citizen, the government subsidized flour, rice, sugar, lamb, milk, milk products, vegetable oils, and medicine. Taxes were all but eliminated when customs duties were removed from most imports, the excise tax on petroleum was abolished, and road taxes ended. The causes of inflation were perhaps unique to the Saudi economy. Real income was dependent on Saudi Arabia's ability to import goods and services rather than on its ability to produce many goods and services other than crude oil. To control inflation, spending under the Second Development Plan was slowed substantially by either drawing out the completion dates on projects or eliminating them altogether. Revenues from oil sales were kept abroad, the money released into the Saudi economy as it could be absorbed.

Foreign labor increasingly emerged as the problem that would be the most difficult to solve. In 1975 foreigners were working in all economic sectors, particularly in services, construction, trade, and finance. What disturbed the social planners was that while this large number of foreigners was working, segments of the Saudi population remained severely underemployed. One of the early adjustments in the Second Plan was a drive to limit expatriate manpower to a growth rate of 1.2 percent annually, rather than the 7 percent officials estimated.

The Second Development Plan spent $3.61 billion between 1975 and mid-1980. Additional expenditures on behalf of the Ministry of Finance and special road, railway, and electric projects reached another $2.45 billion. The results were spectacular.

Electricity had been provided for 4.1 million people. Seven thousand elementary and secondary schools were built, putting 1.1 million Saudi boys and girls in school. Desalination plants were producing 73 million gallons of drinking water a day in a country that had sought water long before it sought oil. The ports had been cleared and now had a capacity of 22.7 million tons a year. Two hundred thousand housing units were built. To diversify the economy, the government had pumped $25 billion into the non-oil private sector and achieved a growth rate of 15 percent. Employment grew at an annual rate of 4.8 percent.

By 1980 the average Saudi family had an income that ranged between $588 and $2059 per month, not including the value of the government's various social welfare programs.

In the Second Development Plan, the urban population benefited the most from economic growth. Wealth was spread by insuring that companies with part or total Saudi ownership won government contracts. The number of Saudi millionaires grew rapidly, mainly among those who were engaged in some kind of private business activity when the economy boomed in the 1974–77 period. But the easiest way to become a millionaire was to engage in buying and selling land. It was not unusual for the value of a plot of land bought one day to more than double a week later. Those who owned the land were usually members of the royal family or nonroyals who were close to the al-Sauds through marriage or through favors extended to it in years past. The Saudis who benefited the least from economic growth were the Bedouins. As the Second Plan wound down, there was little but praise for the economic managers. The Second Development Plan built Saudi Arabia's basic infrastructure. The Third Development Plan had to make it work.

I arrived at the Ministry of Planning as work on the Third Plan was nearing completion. The ministry was housed in a squat, modern two-story building on University Street in the Maalaz district. Its importance in the bureaucratic hierarchy was announced by a fountain and palm trees at the entrance.

One of the early adjustments to my sex that SRI was forced to make was how to get me to work. For a while I was driven by a rather lovable old curmudgeon named Ellis Conrad, who had spent seven bitter years in Saudi Arabia as a development economist. Every morning on our way to work, he fretted about his irregular heart beat, haunted by the specter of a colleague who had dropped dead at Ellis's dinner table on his first night in Saudi Arabia. When we arrived at the ministry, I was delivered to the rear of the building to scurry in the back door before anyone saw me. As I hurried down the long, narrow hall to my office, clutching my long skirt above my ankles, my eyes darted from side to side, watching for any Saudi who might unexpectedly emerge from one of the doors. When I reached my office, I slid in, closed the door, and locked it. I shared quarters with Mira, an Egyptian translator. Upstairs were three female secretaries — a Lebanese, an Egyptian, and an Indian — hidden in their own cubicles. Mira and I stayed locked in our office for the day, from 7:30 A.M. to 2:30 P.M. The only time either of us could leave was to go to the rest room, which was back down that long hall. The procedure was to open the office door just far enough to get my head through, look up and down the hall to make sure no one was there, dash to the rest room, and dash back, locking the door once more behind me. Under no circumstances was I to cross the bright red carpet that ran through the lobby and up the main staircase, bisecting the second floor. On my side of that forbidding carpet was the office of the assistant deputy minister, who knew of my presence in the ministry; on the other side was the office of the other assistant deputy minister, who was vehement in his opposition to women being anywhere but in seclusion at home, and was, evidently, kept in ignorance about the presence of women in his ministry.

There was a certain degree of game playing among both Saudi officials and the Western consulting companies working for the ministry about whether the women they employed were there or not. This created a constant air of tension for the women. I was dumbfounded when I was summoned one day to a meeting of the staff of Western consultants with the assistant deputy minister, the one on my side of the building. I carefully checked my clothing to make sure my arms and legs were covered. At the last moment, I borrowed a scarf which I wound around my neck to fill up the gap in my blouse. When I entered the large conference room, the chair at the head of a huge table was empty. The deputy minister had not yet arrived. I hugged the backs of the high, ornate Spanish style chairs as I crept along to the very end of the table and slithered into the last seat. No one acknowledged my presence. Finally, the deputy minister arrived, and the meeting proceeded as if I were not there. After about thirty minutes, the minister grew bored and left. The meeting ended and I returned to my office without having spoken to a soul, still not sure why my presence had been requested.

Life at the ministry moved on smoothly until the approach of Ramadan, the Moslem month of fasting, when Saudi Arabia goes into an annual spasm of religious fervor. Suddenly rumors flew through the halls and offices that the labor minister had called the planning minister to warn him to remove all female employees from the building because there was to be a raid. The secretaries, the translator, and I were hastily packed up and moved to a villa several blocks from the ministry, where SRI housed its staff on temporary assignment in Riyadh. There we were stowed behind the locked steel gate in the cement-block wall that surrounded what appeared to be an ordinary house in a residential neighborhood. Our working accommodations were comfortable enough, but the separation from the men we worked with complicated things enormously. I was particularly frustrated. As I edited what the economists had written, it was vital that I understood exactly what they were saying. If I had a question, my only means of contacting them was by telephone. Most of the time the telephone either did not work or was not being answered by the Saudi who ran the switchboard at the ministry because it was prayer time, or tea time, or simply was not convenient. When I was finally able to ring through, the person I needed to talk with usually had to come see me, which meant leaving the air-conditioned comfort of the ministry to drive to the villa in his oven-hot car. Before being admitted, he would have to ring a prearranged code on the bell at the gate.

Both the Lebanese and Egyptian secretaries I worked with soon left, to be replaced by two Western women, English and Canadian. Mira, the translator, left also and was replaced by a tall, thin Syrian girl named Hessa. Unlike any of the previous Moslem women, Hessa arrived at work swathed in a veil and an *abaaya*. She was a devout Moslem, who every day rose from her desk at prayer time, did the ritual washings in the bathroom, then covered her head with a black scarf, spread out her *abaaya*, faced Mecca, and knelt for prayers while the activity of the office continued around her. Then we found out that her father worked for the Ministry of the Interior, the parent organization of the secret police. Although all working women lived with the vague fear that they would be caught, the anxiety was largely subconscious until forcefully aroused into raging paranoia by seemingly suspicious events. Toward the end of Hessa's first week at SRI, when we were all still eyeing one another, a high beeping sound went off in her purse. She quickly shut it off and went on with her work. That was it — we knew she was spying on us. We would be sent home and our husbands hauled into court at any moment. The atmosphere in the villa was so tense that the Westerners were afraid to talk to one another for fear of what Hessa's recording device might be picking up.

Early one afternoon, Adele, the Canadian secretary, stopped typing and said, "I smell something burning." At that moment, a voltage regulator, installed to protect electric typewriters from frequent and strong power surges, burst into flames. As the cheap, dirty carpet where the regulator sat smoldered, we frantically searched the villa for a fire extinguisher, but failed to find one. Shirley, the English secretary, cried, "Let's call the fire department!" Fear crossed Hessa's face at the same moment that I realized that we could not call the fire department because the fire department would bring the police. The only thing to do short of letting the villa burn down was to race upstairs to the men's kitchen and grab every container we could find and then fill them with sand to smother the flames. The three Westerners plus Hessa, who was looking less and less like an Interior Ministry spy, formed a fire brigade line. Scooping up the sand in the garden in saucepans and a flour canister, we passed them hand to hand until the fire was out. Glowing in the camaraderie of our triumph, I asked Hessa why she had looked so frightened when Shirley had suggested calling the fire department. She said, "I was afraid the authorities would catch me working!" The mysterious electronic gadget in her purse turned out to be a small clock given to her by an aunt.

Though confined to my cubicle in the Ministry of Planning or concealed behind the locked gate at the villa, I had a view of Saudi Arabia that was panoramic. The reams of paper crossing my desk from almost every ministry gave me an inside look at the government's structure, philosophy, development strategy, and spending priorities at the height of the oil boom.

Saudi Arabia's Third Development Plan, to span the years 1980 to 1985, was perhaps the most ambitious ever undertaken by a country. The Third Plan was in preparation when Saudi Arabia was at the peak of its confidence. Oil production was 8 to 9 million barrels a day, the price of the benchmark Saudi Arabian light crude was $26 a barrel and climbing, the fallout of the Iranian revolution had not hit with its full impact, and there was little concern about a major oil glut on the horizon. In this atmosphere, Saudi Arabia was prepared to move on into the next phase of its development.

The Third Plan was a $234.4 billion scheme to complete the process of Saudi Arabia's progression into the industrialized world. To cover the financial requirements of the plan, oil policy would allow petroleum reserves to be lifted at a rate that would generate sufficient revenue for development. In other words, oil production would follow revenue demands. It was projected that Saudi Arabia needed to produce 5 million barrels of oil a day to sell at $18 per barrel to pay for the Third Development Plan, a level of revenue easily achieved under conditions current at the time.

Basically the plan was a wish book put together by government ministers whose aspirations were restricted only by the rather arbitrary spending and labor ceilings imposed on them by the Ministry of Planning.

Although the plan was ambitious, there was no reason to question its basic philosophy. As in the previous two plans, government spending was consistent with the goals established for the overall plan, even though in both the First and Second plans some individual projects were more heavily funded or drawn out or eliminated altogether to adjust for changes in revenues or priorities. Economically, the plan was the vital link between the oil sector and the rest of the economy. Since all oil revenues accrued directly to the government, the only way that individual citizens could benefit from the oil boom was through the government's budget and spending decisions. Politically, the plan was crucial to the House of Saud, which depended on the generous distribution of oil revenues to keep its subjects satisfied.

Born in a time when all things seemed possible, the various programs that constituted the plan ran the gamut from the $30 billion petrochemical complexes at Jubail and Yanbu to a $1.9 million program to teach the Saudis how to mail a letter. When the plan was finished, it included something for everyone: highways, schools, airports, vocational training, housing, subsidies on food and utilities, desalination plants, and a morgue for every village. Inspired by nationalism, the government continued the process begun in 1976 of buying out the American oil companies that had founded and run ARAMCO for thirty years. There was even confidence that a projected oil glut in the mid-1980s would not cause Saudi Arabia any problems. The vast reserves that Saudi Arabia was accumulating abroad would be tapped to prevent a severe disruption of the economy until the next oil shortage hit the globe shortly after 1990, when Saudi Arabia would once again dominate the world's oil markets.

Regardless of the Saudis' buoyant mood, there were severe limitations on planning. The inertia and inexperience of most government ministries left Western economists with incomplete data at best. The air of intrigue and secrecy that characterized all government agencies made frank discussions of priorities impossible. In most ministries, the Saudis themselves did not know what needed to be done, when it needed to be done, or if it should be done at all. Moreover, there was no basic data on which to base assumptions and projections. The problem of gathering population statistics is an example of how underlying cultural factors made planning in the kingdom so difficult. Saudi Arabia has never had a census, nor will it in the foreseeable future. For security reasons, the government is extremely tight-lipped about the kingdom's sparse population. Preferring illusion to fact, the government overestimates the population while choosing to remain ignorant of what it actually is. Furthermore, there is among the Saudis a strong cultural tradition that closes a man's house to prying eyes, including those of prying census takers. And finally, the discipline needed to gather data on which to base statistics is wholly absent in the society and, therefore, in most government departments. Consequently, much of the data on which the Third Plan was built, as with the Second, was conjecture on the part of the Westerners trying to plan for the Saudis. Nevertheless, Saudi Arabia's ambitions, if not its planning, were impressive.

The Third Plan departed from its predecessors in several ways. While the first two plans concentrated on building an infrastructure, the Third Plan was to move on to industrialization, make agriculture self-sufficient, expand social services, limit the growth of the bureaucracy, and distribute the wealth of the country more evenly among the people. Looming over all of these goals was a determination on the part of those in power to limit the number of foreign workers in the country by putting the Saudis into the work force and mechanizing everything possible.

In the Third Plan, the government seriously sought to diversify the economy by expanding into industries that utilize the natural gas that is the by-product of crude oil production. Industrialization was intended to maximize Saudi Arabia's advantage as the possessor of the world's largest oil reserves. Instead of producing only crude oil, the kingdom was to move downstream into refining and petrochemicals, processing gas either as an energy source or as a chemical feedstock, and developing energy-intensive industries such as metal smelting, as well as adding industries that are ancillary to oil production and its by-products.

The cornerstone of Saudi Arabia's industrialization was to be the creation of two complete cities containing petrochemical plants, Jubail, on the Arabian Gulf north of Dammam, and Yanbu, on the Red Sea west of Medina. Under the supervision of the Royal Commission for Jubail and Yanbu, created by King Khalid in 1975, the sites by the Third Plan were being cleared and construction had begun. As relieving port congestion had been the major goal of the Second Plan, industrialization would be the superstar of the Third Plan.*

---

*What the Saudis have actually spent at Jubail and Yanbu can only be surmised because of the various sources of funding, government figures that are notoriously unreliable, the modification

Jubail, on the east coast, was by the early 1980s the largest construction project in the world. Among its plants, the only non-oil-related industries were a direct-reduction steel mill, which would provide 850,000 tons per year of steel reinforcing bars for use by contractors in the kingdom, and an aluminum smelter. For the rest of Jubail, plans called for production of a variety of petrochemicals using ethane as a feedstock, as well as an oil refinery that would produce 250,000 barrels per day (bpd).

Yanbu, on the west coast, would have another 250,000-bpd oil refinery, geared to exports to Europe, a 170,000-bpd refinery for domestic needs, an ethylene-based petrochemical facility, a natural gas liquids processing complex, and an export terminal for the 1.4 million bpd of crude oil delivered to Yanbu via the cross-country pipelines from the oil fields in the Eastern Province.

Other pipelines that would link Jubail and Yanbu to the kingdom's oil fields and associated natural gas collectors represented the biggest infrastructure project of all. The natural gas collection system alone could use more than 3 billion cubic feet per day of associated gas, which previously had been disposed of by burning.

Construction of Jubail and Yanbu proceeded even though the environment for industry, beyond cheap energy sources, was bleak. The extra capital and operating costs required by the plants, the need to pay and house expatriate managers and technicians, and the constant problem of recruiting an adequate labor force tended to neutralize Saudi Arabia's advantage of access to plentiful and cheap oil and gas. Some experts predicted that these higher costs would cause Saudi Arabia's products to lose their competitive price advantage in world markets.

The critics' arguments that Saudi petrochemicals could not find a market were met with scorn. The Saudis were smug if not arrogant in their conviction that Saudi Arabia could divert part of its petroleum resources into a petrochemical industry whose markets would be insured by the West's dependence on Saudi oil. Operating in the days of worldwide oil shortages, Saudi Arabia announced that it would use oil quotas to force industrialized countries not only to buy Saudi products but to transfer technology and invest in the Saudi industrial complexes as joint venture partners. The Japanese were a prime target of the pol-

---

of the overall plans necessitated by sharply decreased oil revenues after 1982, and the large outstanding debts that the government still owes to contractors on the projects. At the time of the Third Development Plan, the final cost of Jubail alone was projected to be as much as $40 billion.

icy. After Mitsubishi Gas Chemical became a major backer of the methanol project at Jubail in 1980, it was announced that Saudi Arabia would supply Japan with 3,800 extra barrels of crude oil a day in 1981, with that amount increasing as work on the plant at Jubail progressed. Furthermore, a Saudi government official was quoted by the Saudi press as saying that foreign oil companies would be entitled to 500 barrels of oil per day for every $1 million they invested in Saudi Arabia. And it might not be long, Planning Minister Hisham Nazer warned, before a reduction in the high cost of technology transfer would become a condition under which OPEC countries continued to supply crude oil to the industrialized nations. And in one isolated incident of hyperbole, Western countries were threatened with having to impose tours of duty in Saudi Arabia on their technically qualified citizens as a condition for continued oil supplies.

The success of Saudi Arabia's industries seemed almost guaranteed as long as the West was so dependent on Saudi oil. As with technology and investment, access to the industrialized world's chemical markets would be gained by linking future sales of crude oil to the sale of Saudi petrochemicals. Various government officials broadly hinted that crude oil supplies for the West might well depend on access to Western markets for the petrochemicals, fertilizers, refined petroleum distillates and liquid petroleum gases, which formed the backbone of the entire industrialization program.

The Saudis were less haughty about their agricultural program. With access to cheap fertilizers to be produced by its industries and large underground water reservoirs, Saudi Arabia had a surprising capacity to increase its agricultural yield and lessen its dependence on food imports.

Agricultural policy rested primarily on setting up large farms financed by private capital, which the government would provide with infrastructure and subsidies. Although large commercial farms were an important component in the agricultural plan, its core was the creation of a system of cooperatives among small farmers to increase production and cut costs. Prior to 1980, agriculture was producing 1 percent of the gross national product (GNP) and employing close to one-half of the population. Saudi Arabia's development strategy was to make agriculture more productive so Saudi manpower could be shifted from the agricultural sector to the new industrial sector.

The government provided every incentive for agriculture. Land was either free, as in the case of wheat farms, or could be bought with long-term, interest-free loans. For seed and equipment purchases, the government provided up to 50 percent of the cost, with interest-free loans available to farmers for the remainder of the purchase price. Pesticides and spraying equipment were provided free, as were veterinarian services. Irrigation water was heavily subsidized and the cost to farmers covered by more interest-free loans. The government then bought the farmers' produce at highly subsidized prices. For a while, the Grain Silos and Flour Mills Organization was buying farmers' wheat crops at double the price of imported wheat.

Dairy production was another of the priority agricultural projects. As one Saudi businessman engaged in the agricultural boom said, "You can even import livestock by plane and make money." And that is just what they did. Dairy farmers air freighted cows in from the United States at a cost of $2,300 per cow, which the Ministry of Agriculture paid. Because of the traffic in Holsteins, Trans-Med Airlines, operating out of Beirut, was, for a time, one of the most profitable airlines in the world.

Regardless of all the incentives, farming Saudi Arabia's desert was not easy. Just preparing the soil was arduous. Special plows that would turn up the soil from sixteen inches deep had to be imported. Interimco Projects Engineering from Ontario, Canada, introduced mechanized "rock pickers" to clear the rock-strewn fields. Water had to be delivered to the land either through irrigation channels or by pumping it from underground wells to large sprinklers on wheels that rotate around the fields in circles, spraying water at the rate of 1000 to 1250 gallons per minute.

With an average of only 10 centimeters of rainfall a year, Saudi Arabia gets most of its water from underground reservoirs called aquifers, which are filled with fossil water. Fossil water, up to ten thousand years old, is like oil — a nonrenewable resource. The Third Plan projected that by the year 1997 agriculture would be using almost all the water available from deep aquifers, and by the year 2000, agriculture would be expected to consume 73.9 percent of all available water in the kingdom.

There were alternative water sources but all were expensive. The government has spent $5.29 billion on desalination plants since 1969, yet desalination even now supplies the kingdom with only 1 percent of its water. The Saline Water Conversion Corporation, the government

agency responsible for the desalination plants, says that the real cost
of desalinated water is about $2.00 per cubic meter. Depending on the
section of the country, most agriculture is at least partially or totally
dependent on desalinated water. But in this period of supreme confidence, the problem of water seemed manageable. Studies of cloud
seeding and importing water by pipeline were commissioned. Water
might be brought in by tanker. And there was talk of converting icebergs to usable water. While this seemed like one of the more outrageous stories of the oil boom, a hydrologist working for the al-Hassa
Irrigation and Drainage Authority told me that the infamous plan for
towing icebergs from the Antarctic to Saudi Arabia would actually
produce sizable amounts of water for Saudi Arabia at a much lower
cost than desalination.

Despite the problems, agriculture showed some success by the end
of the 1970s. Totally self-sufficient dairy farms, primarily run by Irish
expatriates, were doing everything from growing feed to bottling milk.
Saudi Arabia was marching toward self-sufficiency in wheat, chickens, and eggs. Date processing would one day send Saudi Arabia's
dates, reputed to be the best in the world, into stores in California,
where they would compete with California's own domestic date
production.

The Saudis engaged in economic planning continued to look at the
successes of their development plans and ignore the underlying problems. It seemed that little could go wrong. Even the riches of King
Solomon opened to Saudi Arabia. The Mahd al-Dhahab gold mine
northwest of Mecca, believed by historians to be the source of Solomon's gold, was being explored during the period of the Third Development Plan. Scheduled to open in mid-1987, the mine is expected to
produce approximately 120,000 tons of ore and two to three tons of
gold bullion. Additional mineral surveys discovered gold in at least
150 other locations in the kingdom, as well as deposits of zinc and
copper in commercial quantities.

The level of activity on the mammoth construction projects (where
so much of the wealth of both the entrepreneurial class and the foreign
business interests was made) was phenomenal. When the government
was experiencing large budget surpluses, there was a strong incentive
to increase spending. As a result, the number of projects proposed in
the kingdom's budgets exceeded the number that were carefully planned.
Projects were almost always more elaborate and costly than needed.

The amounts of money being both profitably invested and totally squandered were staggering. When I was adding up the figures for Saudia Airlines' expenditures for equipment purchases, route expansion, and added operating costs during the Third Plan, I had to send out for a new calculator with more places on the display panel to total the projected losses.

Who devised and executed some of the expenditures was always a mystery. Street work in Riyadh, for instance, was never-ending. The street that ran in front of the King Faisal Specialist Hospital was first paved in 1975. In the following years, it was dug up for electrical lines, repaved, dug up for sewers, repaved, dug up for storm sewers, repaved, dug up for curbs and a center median, repaved. When I left Riyadh in 1984, it was being dug up again to redesign the storm sewers. Every time Riyadh was hit by one of its rare rainstorms, the street flooded because the drains had been set in the sidewalk, ten inches above the street. Road construction was so constant that the inevitable joke appeared: "Saudi Arabia built 100,000 kilometers of roads last year. The kingdom now has a total of 20,000 kilometers of paved roads."

This building, tearing up, and rebuilding served a necessary political and economic function during the booming seventies. Members of the royal family all had concessions on various development projects or public works. Princes owned construction companies and building supply establishments and often were labor brokers or represented equipment companies exporting to Saudi Arabia. Government development activity kept them rich. But the mechanism reached beyond the royal family and the enormously rich merchant princes such as Adnan Khashoggi and Gaith Pharon. Distribution of Saudi Arabia's vast wealth was based on the "trickle down" mechanism. Every Saudi who was engaged in business either as an owner or an employee participated. In the rapidly expanding economy, the employee became rich by taking his commissions from suppliers, whose cost he passed on to his employer, who in turn passed on that cost plus his profit to the golden goose, the government of Saudi Arabia. The system worked well in distributing wealth as long as the boom continued. Those in power believed that the system was serving its purpose of developing an integrated, modern economy. They believed that once the boom eased, the free enterprise system that had been so carefully nurtured during the years of plenty would, in turn, invest in the non-oil sector of the economy, creating its own economic base from which to continue to prosper. But the economy was diversifying, not by private investment, much of which was being sent to foreign bank accounts, but by government spending. Diversification was being subsidized by government, funded by oil revenues, and sustained by government purchases of its output, the cost of which reflected the existing system of commissions within every business organization. Paradoxically, even the government's attempts to transform farming in Saudi Arabia by extending loans and grants to small farmers with the object of aiding their mechanization and modernization were instrumental in the preservation of a subsistence-based traditional rural sector. Loans and grants taken by farmers were spent on consumption, not investment. Government loans became income to farmers. They alleviated the need to work, and the farms themselves were allowed to stagnate or decline further. The government had no choice but to continue to spend to keep the domestic economy intact. But of all the problems plaguing development planning for Saudi Arabia, the problem of labor was the most serious. As early as 1980, the director general of the Western Region Labor Office for the Ministry of Labor and Social Affairs believed that between 70 and 75 percent of the total work force was non-Saudi. The unofficial but more-often quoted figure was that the labor force contained one foreign worker for every Saudi in the adult population.

It was originally thought that foreign manpower demands would level off in the Third Plan period. This assumption was based on the fact that more Saudis were being educated and could move into technical and administrative positions and that the relatively labor-intensive construction industry would run out of things to build. It was with the decision to press ahead with the industrialization of Saudi Arabia that all of the previous assumptions died. The increasing emphasis on industry required both people to build factories and people to work in them. Huge numbers of foreigners would be needed for construction of the petrochemical complexes at Jubail and Yanbu alone.

No matter what the estimates of manpower needs were in 1980, they were bound to be higher when the various projects then being constructed actually went into operation. The Second Development Plan envisaged a total foreign work force of 812,000 by 1980. But by 1980, some estimates placed the number of foreign workers already in the country at close to two million. As an indication of the number of foreigners compared to Saudis in the economy, the usual small industrial plant functioning in 1980 likely did not have a single Saudi employed. Most plants were managed by Westerners and staffed by Oriental laborers, who were increasingly becoming a factor in the work force.

Unfortunately, a significant reduction of foreign manpower proved impossible no matter how much the planners wanted it. The number of workers required simply to keep what the Saudis had already built functioning was enormous, yet new projects continued to be completed that demanded even more manpower. For instance, the total personnel required to maintain the vital desalination plants of the Saline Water Conversion Corporation was estimated to rise from 1240 people in 1980 to 5269 people by 1985. The mammoth new Riyadh and Jeddah international airports would need an additional 1810 people when the two facilities became fully functional. But even this figure was deceptively small since it did not include employees of contracted companies, airline and military personnel, passport and customs control, or maintenance. The same held true in sector after sector of the economy Saudi Arabia simply did not have enough of its own people to meet its manpower needs. When the government tried to mechanize, it only produced another problem — maintenance. Alarmed by the country's insatiable appetite for labor, the government decided to limit as much as possible the number of expatriate employees. The reduction of foreign manpower came to rank along with industrialization and agriculture as a major goal of the Third Development Plan. The Ministry of Planning adopted two criteria for judging every development project: cost in dollars and cost in manpower. Of the two, the cost in manpower was of greater concern. The fear was that at some point the foreigners could no longer be contained and would spill out their corrupting influences on Saudi life.

In its development planning, the House of Saud sought to give Saudi Arabia the façade, if not the substance, of a modern country. Under the direction of Western consultants and Western contractors, everything from sewers to universities, from a banking system to a sophisticated telecommunications system, was built from scratch. Saudi Arabia was being remolded by the Westerners hired to develop the country to the Westerners' own perceptions of modernization. In advocating the wisdom of their plans, Westerners often pushed for changes in Saudi society that they deemed necessary to enable the country to support the advances made by economic development. Some of the Westerners' plans, such as the expansion of female education, cut to the heart of the Saudis' most sacred traditions. And all was being done under the auspices of the House of Saud.

The House of Saud was torn by its desire to be seen as a modern, progressive regime and its need to preserve Saudi Arabia's culture. In attempting to do both, the al-Sauds performed a delicate and dangerous balancing act. Starting with King Faisal, the rulers pushed the country ahead. Yet every move made in education, labor, health care, housing, and welfare had to outwardly conform to the strictures of Islam. For making it all work depended on preserving the Islamic traditions of Saudi Arabia.

4

Servants of God

THE GREAT GATE of the Grand Mosque of Mecca dominates a broad plain lying between the barren, scruffy hills of western Saudi Arabia. Standing at the center of the mosque's immense courtyard is the Kaaba,* a crude stone structure draped with an enormous black cloth intricately embroidered with sayings from the Koran. Here is the epicenter of the Islamic faith, the point to which all Moslems turn in prayer five times a day. I never saw the Kaaba. I am Christian and barred, as are all non-Moslems, from the holy cities of Mecca and Medina. Only once did I test the prohibition.

I was coaxing my exceedingly reluctant husband as we turned off the broad new highway between Riyadh and Jeddah and drove toward Mecca. Immediately billboard-size blue and white signs in both Arabic and English appeared along the road, warning non-Moslems to turn back. As we drew closer to Mecca, I saw a mixed group of religious authorities, dressed in traditional *thobes* and cloaks, and Saudi policemen, in Western-style uniforms of olive green, lounging in a small wooden building adjacent to the road. When they saw us, they jumped to their feet and dashed out. The religious elders excitedly waved their arms and shouted *"Wagif! Wagif!"* ("Stop!") while the policemen furiously blew on their shrill whistles. I realized that we had gone too far, but by then it was too late to turn around. We were forced off the road by one of the angry policemen, who was immediately joined by the others. Each yelled and gestured at us with a passion only a Saudi can muster. At last the policeman who appeared to be in charge col-

---

Kaaba means "a square structure."

lected the SR 300 fine (about $100) and sent us, shaken, back toward Jeddah.

This experience at the portal of Mecca is highly symbolic of the relationship between the believer and the infidel in Saudi Arabia. For throughout Saudi society, the great dividing line between the Saudis and the Westerners is religion. Islam for the Saudis is more than a theology, it is an entire way of life. Religion is the central force of their existence. Religion is life and life religion. Such an intense theology immensely complicates the Saudis' accommodation to modernization.

Islam, always a powerful force, exercises a deeper hold on the people of Saudi Arabia than on the Moslems of perhaps any other country. The religion of Mohammed rose out of the Arabian Peninsula, a product of the desert culture that ruled the peninsula for centuries before the coming of the Prophet. For the people of the peninsula, the symbiotic relationship between Islam and their civilization has ebbed from time to time but has never broken. Islam as practiced in Saudi Arabia remains today as it did at the time of Mohammed, a reflection of Arabia and of the pure Arab.

Islam was born in the seventh century A.D. in Mecca. The religion emerged from a period of conflict within Meccan society that was remarkably similar to the stress now tearing at Saudi Arabia — new wealth versus traditional values. Located halfway down Saudi Arabia's west coast, forty-eight miles inland from the Red Sea, Mecca was a convenient stopping place for the fabled camel caravans that transported goods from India and Central Africa to Egypt and Palestine, where they were fed into the pipeline of trade to the Mediterranean and the crumbling Roman Empire. The merchants of Mecca thrived from this trade. To promote business, they formed joint stock companies and dominated an annual trade fair at Ukaz, near Mecca. In stark contrast to the austere life of the desert people around Mecca, Ukaz brought together hundreds of merchants, actors, gamblers, prostitutes, and poets in a great festival of vice for the sole purpose of promoting business.

Removed from the influences of urban areas like Mecca, the desert Arab still clung to the old values of desert life: honor, bravery, hospitality, and the sacredness of family and tribe. Haunted by a primitive religion, the Bedouin was engulfed by a swarm of spirits, or *jinn*. Responding sporadically to ill-defined rituals, he worshiped the *jinn* at a series of places containing sacred stones. The center of this stone worship was in Mecca, controlled, as was trade, by the city's merchants. But as intimidated as he was by the *jinn*, the Bedouin's real religion was his belief in the immortality of the tribe and the near spiritual affinity and protection it spread over its members.

By the end of the sixth century, a great gulf had erupted in Meccan society between the ethical system of the Bedouins and the wealth and decadence that gripped Mecca itself, especially its ruling classes. The fair at Ukaz characterized the decline in the values prized by the desert Arab and the ascendancy of the new age of materialism. In pursuit of wealth, the tribal system had broken down into clans, all warring against one another. Life was a cycle of vengeance as an attack on any clan member was an attack on all and every act of reprisal was followed by yet another act of revenge. Into this social disruption Abdulqasim Mohammed ibn Abdullah ibn Abd al-Muttalib ibn Hashim was born in A.D. 570 or 571. Orphaned at the age of six, he passed to the care of his grandfather, the respected custodian of the Kaaba, who claimed to be a descendent of Ishmael, the son of Abraham and Hagar.

When Mohammed was about forty and married to a rich widow of Mecca, he began to retreat into the desert for long periods to meditate on the sins of Meccan society. During these meditations, he claimed God was revealing a new religion to him. His revelations were written down by his followers, for he never learned to read or write, and collected into the Koran, the fundamental source of Islamic doctrine. Soon he began to attract followers. Like every successful preacher, Mohammed gave voice and form to the restiveness of his time. He gathered in the young who were shut out of the councils of power. He denounced the quest for wealth, attracting the poor. He rid the Bedouin of the dreaded *jinn*. He restored the honor of the family while uniting his followers in the great tribe of believers.

Fired with religious fervor, the followers of Mohammed poured out of the Arabian Peninsula to spread their newfound religion. Before they were depleted, they had established Islam from Persia (Iran) to southern Spain. No longer purely Arab, the world of Islam became pluralistic and polyglot almost overnight. Whole peoples, ancient languages, and traditions that were beyond the scope of anything known in Arabia meshed into the whole. The basic tenets of Mohammed's religion and the cultural dictates of the Arabs became infiltrated by alien ideas.

The successful expansion of Islam was accomplished under the first four caliphs, or successors to Mohammed. Bakr, Umar, Uthman, and Ali had all known Mohammed personally and each was successively selected as caliph by the elders of Medina. But in an expanded empire with conflicting rivalries, the ability of the religious authorities in far-off Arabia to choose the leader eventually collapsed. In 661, Muawiyah, the governor of Syria, challenged Ali for the caliphate. When Ali was assassinated, control of the caliphate passed forever from the hands of Mohammed's followers in Medina. Shocked by their loss of power and hostile to the foreigners now in control, the Arabs of the peninsula withdrew from the concerns of empire and retreated into their own traditions. The Persian segment of Ali's supporters reacted to his murder by renouncing the main body of Islam to become Shiites, or followers of Ali. The Islamic nation split. The more orthodox Sunnis claimed to follow the way of the Prophet while the Shiites incorporated martyrdom, saints, and a priesthood into the simplicity of Mohammed's teachings about the unitary relationship between God and man. The failure of the Medina leadership to break with the main body of Islam over the death of Ali was representative of the conflict between the culture of the worldly Persians and that of the parochial Arabs of the peninsula. But it was Sufism, an Islamic sect that preached mysticism, that caused Mohammed ibn Abdul-Wahhab, a mid-eighteenth-century itinerant preacher in north-central Arabia, to cry for a return to the true teachings of Mohammed and the re-Arabization of Islam. Abdul-Wahhab leapt backward across medieval theologians and legalists. His theology banished the thought of the Sufis and thundered with the call to return to the purity of Mohammed's teachings, untainted by exposure to foreign influences. Mohammed ibn Abdul-Wahhab, in essence, restored Arab cultural values as the standard by which a Moslem was measured.

Early in his wanderings across the Nejd, Abdul-Wahhab came to Diriyah, a village located on a large and fertile *wadi** east of Riyadh. There he converted the local ruler Abdul Aziz al-Saud** to his teachings and joined the *sheikh*'s court. The house that Abdul Aziz gave to Abdul-Wahhab still stands among the ruins of Diriyah. A large house

---

*A dry river bed.
**This was the first Abdul Aziz. Abdul Aziz II unified Saudi Arabia and founded the present House of Saud.

by the standards of an Arab village, it sits on a steep incline opposite the old mosque and dominates the approach to the town, now nearly deserted. I often climbed that hill and wandered among the crumbling walls. In the rear, the pillars of the courtyard extend upward to the sky, its blue unblurred by pollution, its calm undisturbed by material progress. As I sat in the stillness of that courtyard, leaning against the mud wall, the stubble of the straw bonding prickling my back, I sometimes sensed the presence and the force of Abdul-Wahhab.

Although a powerful religious revivalist, Abdul-Wahhab, in the hands of an al-Saud, also became a political force. Abdul Aziz, under unceasing pressure from neighboring tribes who coveted his territory and his water supply, seized Abdul-Wahhab's religious revival as his own. Fired by a religious renewal that banished all things foreign from Islam, the tribes of the Nejd under the leadership of Abdul Aziz became the army of Wahhabism. Fed by its triumph in driving the heretical Shiites out of Mecca, the Wahhabis turned toward the east. By the end of the eighteenth century, they had reached the gates of Baghdad. There the mission clashed with the political reality of the Ottoman Empire, whose sultan also claimed the title of Protector of the Holy Places. In 1811, the Ottomans executed Abdul Aziz and sent the Wahhabis back to Diriyah. Subdued but not beaten, the Wahhabis rose up again in the early twentieth century. The second Abdul Aziz, exiled to Kuwait by the al-Rashid family, rivals to the al-Sauds in Diriyah, returned to his ancestral home to unify the Bedouins and the townsmen of the Nejd. Together they destroyed Abdul Aziz's enemies and drove the decadent Sherif Hussein from Mecca. In 1932 Abdul Aziz declared the present state of Saudi Arabia, founded on the religious principles of the Wahhabis. Thus the House of Saud tied itself inexorably to the religious fundamentalists.

Abdul Aziz was able to unite and rule the fiercely independent Bedouins and the more numerous townsmen through an ingenious combination of piety and patronage. In all things, the king was the protector and defender of the faith. Through the philosophy of Wahhabism, he cultivated a unique political system that totally integrated all aspects of life, religious and secular, into one. Today as in the time of Abdul Aziz, the Wahhabi state admits no distinction between the body of religious beliefs and the political system.

Islam lends itself to a system that is both religious and secular. For Mohammed created not just a religion but an entire way of life that is built on three sources. At the core is the Koran, the revealed word of God.* Second is the Sunna, a body of words and deeds of the Prophet remembered and recorded by his followers, which with the Koran is incorporated into a body of law called *sharia*. The *sharia* is both the constitution and the legal system of Saudi Arabia, covering social, commercial, domestic, criminal, and political affairs. The third source of Mohammed's wisdom is the *hadith*, a written record of Mohammed's pronouncements. On these three authorities, both the society and political system of Saudi Arabia function.

Islam is a revealed religion, with a Prophet and a complete set of rules. It is neither philosophical nor speculative. It regulates not only religious beliefs and rituals but also every aspect of a believer's daily life, from the number of times he should pray to how he should wash after sexual intercourse. Islam as practiced in Saudi Arabia remains demanding in its rituals, inflexible in its attitudes, and intolerant of those who deviate from the way of the Prophet. The Saudis possess the mentality of true believers, regarding other Moslems as inferior and non-Moslems as infidels. These convictions manifest themselves in the theory of government propagated by the House of Saud. Saudi Arabia is in essence a hybrid theocracy — a monarchy built on and maintained by a strict adherence to the religious rules set down by Mohammed for Arabia fourteen centuries ago. The link between religion and the state is seen everywhere. Emblazoned in white across a green field on the flag of Saudi Arabia is the Islamic statement of faith: "There is no god but God." Government documents begin, "In the name of Allah, the Compassionate, the Merciful." To the world, the House of Saud continually, through word and deed, pronounces itself the guardian of the Islamic holy places and, within the kingdom, defends its existence by being the most visible leader of the faith, reigning over the enforcement of its rituals.

Religious law and public morals are enforced by the Committee for the Protection of Virtue and the Prevention of Vice. The *matawain*,** or religious police, were created by Abdul Aziz while his kingdom was still in its infancy. After seizing Mecca from Sherif Hussein in 1924, Abdul Aziz sent *matawain* missionaries into the Bedouin settle-

---

*Allah of the Moslems, God of the Christians, and Yahweh of the Jews are the same deity.
**Matawain* is the plural of *matawah*, an enforcer of religious law. All *matawain* are part of the Committee for the Protection of Virtue and the Prevention of Vice.

ments of the Nejd. Their mission was to coax the Bedouins to give up their nomadic ways and settle in religious communities. Under its religious façade, the mission of the *matawain* was in reality political: to put the Bedouins under the control of Abdul Aziz.

Most of the original *matawain* were ignorant zealots. Although the body is still largely staffed by fanatics, a surprising number of foreign-educated younger men, perhaps disillusioned with what they see as the decadence of the West, return to Saudi Arabia to join the ranks. The *matawain* today have coalesced into a group of vigilantes with an increasingly sophisticated bureaucracy. The government has little control over its membership or its actions. A *matawah* is not appointed but rather rises up, by virtue of his piety, through the ranks of the local mosque. The Committee for the Protection of Virtue and the Prevention of Vice is a genuine grass-roots organization and an important component of the backbone of the House of Saud's political support — the religious fundamentalists. Therefore, it has tremendous power. Although mostly free of political control by the House of Saud, the religious organization is largely dependent on government financing since the practice of Wahhabism does not include contributions to the local mosque. But the committee does not approach the government as a suppliant. Highly sophisticated in the budget process, the organization hires its own professional budget consultants, often Western. A friend of mine who sat in on the budgetary meeting for the Third Development Plan told me that the committee's requests for money were masterful presentations to be envied by any bureaucracy. When the erect and imperious committee members entered the hearings with their gold-trimmed black *bishts* ("cloaks") draped from their shoulders, they seemed to fill the room with their aura. Rather than basing their petition for funds on emotional appeals to the charitable instincts of the budget managers, the committee's consultants unveiled color charts and handed out bound folders showing objectives, justifications for various requests for money, and documentation of the organization's current activities. These elaborate presentations were probably not necessary since no one in the bureaucracy — and especially not the Western consultants to the Ministry of Planning — had the courage to challenge the data or assumptions of the religious leaders. If a request failed to meet planning guidelines, the whole package was pushed into the bureaucratic pipeline for someone else to confront. In the end, the *matawain* got what they wanted.

Although there is no way of knowing just how much money the *matawain* garner from government coffers for salaries, mosque construction, purchase of Korans, educational functions, and so on, it is a significant amount. But unlike most other public agencies, there is never any hint of impropriety in how they handle their funds. Corruption goes against the faith and the practice of these men. Intolerant, bigoted, and arrogant they may be, but no one can accuse them of dishonesty.

The sophisticated bureaucratic side of the *matawain* was something that I never saw on the streets. The self-appointed foot soldiers who patrol the streets are, for the most part, uneducated, often poor, and fanatic defenders of the faith.

The *matawain* literally keep watch over the public's morals. It sometimes seemed to me there was a *matawah* on every corner. He needed no identification other than his straggly beard dipped in henna and the camel whip he carried in his grubby hand. At least two were always parked on folding chairs at the entrance to the women's *souqs*. At prayer time, others walked the streets shouting *"salaah"* ("prayer") and rapping on windows ordering shops to close.

Through its political power, the *matawain* keep foreign books and magazines they find objectionable out of the kingdom. Offensive advertising is controlled by a legion of manual laborers armed with ink pots and brushes, who leaf through imported magazines, painting out pictures of women and ads for alcohol. Photo-developing labs are periodically raided to see that they are not printing pictures that fail to pass the *matawain*'s rigid Wahhabi standards. Almost any subject is a target — pictures of statues, temples, religious celebrations, beach scenes, party pictures, or a male and female embracing. Westerners seldom send a prize roll of film to the processor. To protect themselves, developers will only print the pictures they know will pass censorship, if a *matawah* has not already seized the whole roll. For a stiff surcharge, the Falcon lab would develop film for anxious customers during the night for even the *matawain* went to bed.

All Westerners have a healthy respect for if not downright fear of the *matawain*. It is they who keep Western women in the publicly prescribed dress, for a Western woman who ventures out in a knee-length skirt risks a whipping on her legs with a *matawah*'s camel whip. The *matawain* forbid women to ride a bicycle or jog. An unmarried man and woman riding in the same car together risk being arrested by the *matawain* and taken to one of their special jails, where they will be harangued about their loose morals. In Riyadh, almost every Westerner runs afoul of a *matawah* at some time. The most unpleasant encounter I ever had was in the *souq* in the oasis town of al-Kharj.

On a hot Friday morning, my friend Jane Walker and I entered the old covered market. We milled through a collection of Bedouin women squatting on the ground, selling hand-spun yarn of wool and camel hair and crude yogurt bags made from the whole skin of a goat with the neck left open and rawhide cords tied around the ragged ends of the severed legs. I was in a long skirt, a short-sleeve but modest T-shirt, and had my hair covered with a scarf. I had a camera, securely snapped shut in its case, slung over my shoulder. Suddenly out of nowhere a *matawah* swooped down on me like a bird of prey. Screaming insults, he grabbed my arm, dragged me to the back door of the *souq*, and threw me into the alley with the debris from the market. As I picked myself up, totally dazed, a young Saudi stepped up, pointed at my camera, and said, "Go to your car!" Dutifully, I went to the car, left the camera, and returned to the *souq*. Back through the yarn, the spices, and the yogurt bags, I reached the spot where I had been previously. To my astonishment, I was attacked again by the same man. He charged at me through the crowd, screaming a torrent of Arabic. He grabbed me by the fleshy part of my upper arm and pinched hard, leaving a large black bruise. He then swung me around and grabbed the other arm, squeezing my flesh between his coarse fingers. Before I could comprehend what was happening, I was back out in the alley, staring into a pile of severed sheeps' heads, their fixed eyes staring back at me. As the *matawah*'s verbal harangue continued, I realized that it was not my camera but my short sleeves that had offended this keeper of the public morals.

The *matawain* are obsessed with controlling the influence of heathen Westerners. To guard the young against deviation from Wahhabism, the government is under continual pressure to keep movie theaters and other recreational activities out of the kingdom and to limit the number of Saudis who are allowed to go abroad to study. There is acute apprehension that even pleasure travel abroad, which the Saudis enthusiastically embraced with the oil boom, will undermine the Islamic tenets. Any place outside the hallowed borders of Saudi Arabia is considered wracked with sin. One religious leader deplored the foreign contamination of the young by saying that Saudis leave the kingdom to "go to dens of iniquity such as Bangkok, Paris, London, and Omaha."

At the root of the *matawain*'s rigidity is their belief that to be a devout Moslem is to be guided by rules. In the face of the onslaught of wealth, materialism, foreign influences, and the ever-escalating press of change, the *matawain* stand in defense of a way of life. They are there to enforce the rules that have measured life in Saudi Arabia since Mohammed.

Islam is built on five pillars of faith: the profession of Allah as the one great God, prayer, fasting, *zakat* ("charity"), and the pilgrimage to Mecca. All command an important place in the religious and political life of Saudi Arabia.

The rhythm of daily life is set by the five prayer times: sunrise, midday, midafternoon, sundown, and one hour after sundown. By 4:30 A.M. many mornings, I was awakened from a deep sleep by the unmistakable *"Allahu Akbar"* ("God is great") reverberating from the neighborhood mosque. As I was groaning and turning over in my bed, the devout Moslem was plowing through the street in disheveled *gutra* and sandaled feet to pray with his brother believers at the nearest mosque. From the first call to the last, the day is punctuated by prayer.

The morning hours are the time when the most business can be accomplished. I loved the humming activity in the *souqs* during the morning. Noisy trucks laden with fresh vegetables honked their horns as they moved through the crowd of shoppers in the square just off of the Medina road. The money changer on the corner riffled through Saudi riyals, dollar bills, pound notes, and Swiss francs in his small office crowded with customers. Tea boys scurried between other offices carrying trays filled with miniature cups of sweet hot tea. The women, huddled in their own area of the market, haggled over the prices of nuts and spices. Then as midday approached, there was a noticeable lessening of activity. Metal shutters clanged down over store fronts, dust covers were thrown over vegetables, and women left for home as an eerie calm fell over the cityscape just before the call to prayer went out from the mosque. As the centuries-old chant washed over nearby al-Margab Square, men crowded around the long row of water spigots at the mosque to perform their ablutions — the washing of the face, nostrils, ears, hands, and feet before entering the presence of God in prayer.

The stillness of midday remains through the afternoon while the population, well fed, lies down to sleep. Somewhere between three and four in the afternoon, depending on the time of year, the *muezzin* calls the third prayer of the day. Sleep ceases, prayers are said either at home or at the mosque, and the men leave once again for their shops and offices. What commerce or business has not been accomplished in the morning possibly can be done before the fourth and longest period of prayer, the sunset prayer when everything else once again ceases. Facing Mecca, the men, led by the oldest or most respected in the group, surrender to the will of God. Perhaps because of the time of day, this is the most dramatic of the prayer times. One of the most profound moments I experienced in Saudi Arabia was during one evening at sunset. As I walked across the hospital grounds into a stiff west wind, I came upon a group at prayer. Mecca is west from Riyadh, causing the worshipers to face into the setting sun, its orange light heightened and diffused by the millions of dust particles in the air. The men were kneeling, their heads bowed to the ground. A lone woman stood apart, erect, her head held high, the wind whipping her veil and *abaaya* as she prayed. They were performing the same ritual that has been performed in Saudi Arabia for the last millennium and a half. An hour later, these same people, dispersed to other places, would fall down again in the direction of Mecca to end their day of ritual with the final prayers.

The scene of men kneeling in prayer is an integral part of everyday life in Saudi Arabia. I walked around groups of men at prayer in the airports. The horse races on Monday afternoons in the winter never began until the jockeys, the stable boys, and the assembled royalty observed the afternoon prayers. But it was at the great annual camel race that I saw man best overcome his surroundings in order to bow down before God. As I milled through the big camp especially set up for the race on the plain outside of Riyadh, I was buffeted by hundreds of people leading cantankerous camels to and from the track. Coffee pots were boiling on a hundred fires, while small Toyota pickups filled with feed for the camels careened through the grounds. And then the call for midafternoon prayers went out. Men hurriedly staked their camels and gathered together. With silent consent, one man stepped forward to be the leader. Quickly the others lined up in rows behind him with no distinction drawn by wealth or social class. In the midst of incredible activity, they faced Mecca, knelt, and touched their foreheads to the crusty earth in submission.

The non-Moslem necessarily became involved in prayer times because by Saudi law everything must close during the prayers. It was never enough for a merchant to refuse to admit anyone into his place of business during prayer time; everyone who was in the store was forced out on the sidewalk. As we sat there, the shades with which most places of business were equipped were drawn and the lights doused until the prayer period ended thirty to forty-five minutes later.

To avoid these interruptions, all errands and shopping must be done between about 8:00 and 11:30 A.M., 4:00 and 6:00 P.M., 6:30 and 7:30 P.M., or after the last prayer call. To help the faithful meet their religious obligations and the shoppers to prepare themselves, the daily newspapers publish the times of the prayers. Every day is different, as is every city in the country, according to the precise time of sunrise and sunset. The hour between the fourth and fifth prayers has been dubbed the "prayer window" by the expatriates. The end of the workday is a prime time to shop. As soon as the sunset prayers ended, I would dash out to the supermarket, race through, grabbing bread and milk, and then charge through the check-out stand before I was caught in the final prayer call.

Actually the *muezzin* no longer calls the prayers. As with so much else in Saudi Arabia, prayer call has been mechanized. In the old days, the *muezzin* would laboriously climb the steps of the mosque five times a day, every day, to call out the faithful. I once heard a *muezzin* call the prayers in rural Egypt. No amount of electronic equipment can draw up emotions in the same way as the low, penetrating sound that comes from deep in the throat of a *muezzin* standing alone on a minaret. But what the prayer call in Saudi Arabia may lack in emotion, it makes up for in volume. The blast from the loudspeakers is so deafening that Westerners often choose where to live by whether it is downwind or upwind from the mosque. On Fridays, some mosques broadcast the entire service over their loudspeakers. The thundering fundamentalist Protestant of the United States Bible Belt could never match the emotion and volume of an *imam* (the spiritual leader of the community) on a good Friday.

The Moslem does not view prayer as a petition for the favors of God. Nor is it communication with God. Rather, prayer is a ritual that recognizes the power of God, while communal prayer, wherever it is performed, affirms the brotherhood of believers. Prayer is the celebration of the unity of a great tribe held together by its submission to Allah and its obedience to his teachings. Prayer affirms the equality of believers, a concept especially strong within the Wahhabi sect. In conforming to the dictates of Abdul-Wahhab, all Saudi men dress alike as a statement of this equality in the eyes of God. The king's *thobe* may be made of silk and the shopkeeper's of cotton, but their simple, unadorned garments make them brothers before God. It is this statement of unity and equality that makes prayer not only a ritual but a deep emotional experience for a Saudi. During Ramadan, the month of fasting and another of the five pillars of Islam, a Moslem's prayers take on added meaning.

Ramadan is observed in the ninth month of the Hijrah calendar.* By tradition, this is the month in which the first Koranic verses were revealed to Mohammed. Its significance is further heightened by the fact that it was during Ramadan that Mohammed's armies consolidated their first important military successes in the Battle of Badr in 624. Throughout Ramadan, a Moslem fasts from the early morning hours when it becomes light enough to tell a white thread from a black thread, until it is too dark to distinguish between the two. Ramadan is the holiest time of the year, when a Moslem struggles through self-sacrifice to master his worldly concerns, encourage compassion, and foster within the Islamic community a collective sense of conforming to God's commands.

For the devout, Ramadan can be a rigorous exercise in self-discipline. During the daylight hours, which in the latitude of Riyadh or Jeddah can last up to sixteen hours, an observant Moslem abstains from food, drink, and sex. An elaborate set of rules defines what constitutes the breaking of the fast, which in turn requires additional penance. According to Moslem scholars, actions that invalidate the fast are eating, drinking, smoking, or having sexual intercourse during daylight hours. Also included are "deliberately causing oneself to vomit; beginning of menstruation or post-childbirth bleeding even at the last moment before sunset; ejaculation for reasons other than sexual intercourse (e.g., kissing or hugging one's wife)."** So faithful to the restrictions are some of the old, ultra-religious men that they will not break their fast even to swallow their own saliva or to take vital medication.

Ramadan radically alters the pace of daily life. No one knows ex-

---

*The Hijrah calendar is a lunar calendar in which one year is approximately twelve days shorter than that of the Gregorian calendar. See Chapter 9 for its present application in Saudi Arabia.
**Saudi Gazette, June 23, 1984.

actly when Ramadan will begin since it depends on the visual sighting of the new moon, but Moslem and Westerner alike view its approach with nervous anticipation. (Westerners often define their time in Saudi Arabia by the number of Ramadans they have experienced). The week before the expected new moon, the Supreme Judicial Council publishes public notices calling on any citizen who sights the new moon "to approach the nearest court to testify to witnessing the event." If the court agrees, the spotter is rewarded with a generous cash award. Every year for several days before the projected start of Ramadan, I awakened at sunrise to listen for the sound of the cannon that announced the beginning of the fast. The Ramadan cannon, a relic that I suspected was left over from Lawrence of Arabia's raids on the Turks during the First World War, was hauled out of storage every year and installed in front of a dirty square canvas tent on an empty field fronting Intercontinental Road. It was faithfully tended by two men, who, for some unexplained reason, always fired the weapon straight at the passing traffic. Every morning at first light, the cannon was fired to mark the beginning of the day's fasting. It was fired again at sunset to mark the end of the fast and signal that the *iftar*, the meal breaking the fast, could begin. Families would then gather around laden tables to eat and celebrate through most of the night. A second large meal, the *saool*, was served at about 3:00 A.M., in preparation for sunrise. Then almost everyone went to bed and stayed there through much of the day, for during Ramadan day and night are reversed.

At midmorning of one typical Ramadan day, I wandered the streets of downtown Riyadh. Unlike the bustle of ordinary mornings, a deathlike stillness hung over Tamari Street. Shops were padlocked. The few dealers in the gold *souqs* who had opened their shops dozed behind their counters. The black African women who usually clustered on the street selling soft drinks were gone. Across the square from where Tamari Street meets the clock tower, the seldom seen poor of Saudi Arabia gathered near the main mosque, waiting for their measure of charity from their more prosperous Moslem brothers. The obligation to pay *zakat*, or alms tax, another pillar of faith, is often tied to Ramadan. Although the Koran does not specify the amount or when it should be paid, many Saudis distribute money and also food during Ramadan. In order to make the poor available to the pious, the tough restrictions imposed on beggars by the Bureau of Beggar Control are lifted for the month. As I walked by the mosque, I saw men sitting on the broken pavement of the sidewalk, leaning against the stone wall of the low, square building, their crutches clutched in their hands. Others, in ragged clothes, slept on thin blankets spread out on the sidewalk or under the thin foliage of the nearby trees. A few women with dirty, tattered children gathered around them sat in the shade on the opposite side of the building. This quiet would last until the end of the final prayer call, when the deserted streets would again come alive. Like nocturnal animals, people would emerge from their homes to make merry or simply to restock their depleted pantry shelves for the following night's feasting.

One of the deepening conflicts between the traditionalists and the more religiously lax Saudis is that Ramadan is becoming less a period of deprivation and more a time of merrymaking in the name of religion. Over the years that I spent in Saudi Arabia, I saw Ramadan increasingly become the occasion for lavish entertaining or complete escape from the kingdom. While the devout fasted and prayed, large numbers of the well-to-do left for the pleasure spots of Europe. When these escapees were members of the royal family, it created a political problem. Of the three kings since the oil boom, only King Faisal succeeded in keeping most members of the royal family in the kingdom during Ramadan. The absence of even some of the more prominent members of the royal family is distasteful to the people, for Ramadan commands a special reverence for all Moslems. There is the belief among the Saudis that not only the conduct of pious people but the conduct of the general population is affected in a positive way by Ramadan. Attendance at prayers at the mosques increases, the level of charity rises, and, according to the statistics of Riyadh's Crime Department, the already low rate of crime drops. "There was a crime drop in Riyadh during this year's holy fasting month of Ramadan for the Moslems. . . . Only five youngsters went to jail for harassing women in various markets and public parks. Another 112 young people were imprisoned for hot-rodding their cars. . . . A total of 59 persons were caught red handed while eating when they should have been fasting."*

Arrests for eating are common since public observance of the fast is mandatory for non-Moslems as well as Moslems. All restaurants and other eating establishments remain closed during the hours of the fast.

---

*Arab News, August 16, 1982.

Non-Moslems who eat or drink in the presence of Moslems risk subjection to the camel whips or the jails of the *matawain*. This means that Westerners away from their homes must either do without food and water or plan ahead. Because of the danger of dehydration, any foray out in public during Ramadan required provisioning. When I went out, I would freeze water in a slender plastic bottle which I then put inside a heavy sock and hid in the bottom of the basket that I used for shopping. The problem then became how to get to the water without being seen. I remember hiding in an alleyway in Baatha with my friend Kathy Bows one hot Ramadan morning to steal a drink of water. While I hugged the corner of an old, decaying building, watching for a *matawah*, Kathy fished the bottle from the basket, unscrewed the cap, and gulped down a quick drink. We quickly switched places to give me a turn at the cold, reviving liquid.

Essentially very little is accomplished during Ramadan. Under Saudi labor law, Moslems are not required to work more than six hours a day. Government offices do not open until 10:00 A.M. and close at 3:00 P.M. But whether or not anyone is there during that time is another matter: in the middle of one Ramadan day, my superior at the Ministry of Planning found himself totally alone in the ministry building. In addition, during the 1970s, the already short food supplies dwindled even further because few ships were unloaded in the ports. At the end of that first Ramadan I spent in Saudi Arabia, only one bony, freezer-burned chicken was left in the market when the month ended.

Yet the Westerners are caught up in the festive aspects of Ramadan as well. Workloads are light and schedules are thrown to the winds. And like the Saudis, the Westerners more often than not prowl the streets until 1:00 A.M. Life goes on in this vein until everyone begins to look for the new moon heralding the beginning of the month of Shawwal and the five-day feast, or Eid al-Fitr, marking the end of Ramadan. Following the *eid*, the Ramadan cannon is rolled into storage until next year and life returns to normal until the *hajj*, the other great religious event of the year.

The *hajj*, or pilgrimage to Mecca, occurs two months after Ramadan, by the Hijrah calendar. Every year during the month of Dhul-Hijjah, an incredible one and a half to two million Moslems from around the world descend on Saudi Arabia to perform the pilgrimage, a ritual begun by Abraham and affirmed by Mohammed 1400 years ago. During the *hajj*, the holy city of Mecca becomes an immense caldron of humanity, black, brown, yellow, and white. The entire government of Saudi Arabia closes down for a ten-day period, most non-Moslems attempt to leave the country on vacation, and life stands suspended as the pilgrims perform their rituals. For the Moslem, the *hajj* is a profound statement of his devotion to God, a rejection of sin, and a celebration of the brotherhood of all Moslems.

The *hajj* is also a marvel of logistics and endurance. At the height of the *hajj*, planes bearing pilgrims wrapped in the *ihram*, a simple white seamless garment, land at the Jeddah airport at the rate of one per minute. The arrivees are taken from the plane and shuttled into the special *hajj* terminal, a massive structure that sits just beyond the main terminal at Jeddah, where the all-important *hajj* visas are checked before the pilgrims can enter Saudi Arabia and undertake religious rites. The pilgrims are accommodated in everything from luxury hotels to tents. During much of the *hajj*, all two million pilgrims congregate within an area called the Holy Haram, which extends in an elongated shape three miles to the northeast and eighteen miles to the southeast from the mosque at Mecca. The Plain of Arafat, located within the Holy Haram, becomes a sea of white tents. Food, water, medical services, and sanitation facilities have to be provided and the maze of traffic kept under some control. After completing their rituals, the *hajjis,* or pilgrims, will have been transported, most en masse, on a 120-mile, six-day trip from Jeddah to the holy sites and back again. As in all aspects of Islam, the rituals of the *hajj* are exactly prescribed. The highlights are the throwing of stones at Mina, which symbolizes the driving out of sin; drinking from the Zamzam well, by tradition the well that saved Hagar and Ishmael from death; prayer on the Plain of Arafat; and, as the culmination, the Eid al-Adha.

The Eid al-Adha, the Feast of Sacrifice, takes place on the tenth day of Dhul-Hijjah, following the prayers at Arafat. As part of the ritual of the *hajj*, every pilgrim who can afford it sacrifices an animal to share with the poor. Moslems around the world participate in the same ritual, which, as other aspects of Islam, affirms the brotherhood of believers. When we lived at Doctors' Villas #4, I heard a commotion outside my window on the morning of the *eid*. Looking down I saw the Tabahs, our Palestinian neighbors, hanging a live goat up on a red and white metal swing set in front of their house. When it was tightly secured, Majid deftly slit the throat, letting the bright red blood drain into the dry sand. The children in the compound were fascinated. As they gathered around, Majid severed the goat's tail and handed it to Colin as the oldest male of the group. The animal hung there for several hours before it was cut down and taken into the house to become the main dish of the *eid*. In proper Moslem tradition, the Tabahs delivered pieces of it to their Western neighbors, perhaps not the poor but certainly the spiritually less fortunate.

Most of the *hajjis* who come to Mecca are making their first trip out of their native land. Although kings, presidents, wealthy businessmen, and religious scholars are among the pilgrims, most are simple people who saved all their lives for the chance to make the pilgrimage to Mecca. They pour off of the planes and boats knowing no language but their own and with no experience in international travel. To ease the confusion, groups are organized by language and assigned guides, who stay with the group throughout the *hajj* to instruct the pilgrims in the proper performance of the religious rituals. In recent years, tour companies operating out of Pakistan, Indonesia, and other countries with large Moslem populations provide their clients total package tours consisting of air fare, accommodations, and religious instruction.

The large number of pilgrims now coming to Saudi Arabia is due to the advent of air travel, which revolutionized the *hajj* beginning in the 1950s. In past centuries, the trip was made by ship, horse, camel, or on foot. Some who left for Mecca as children returned as adults. Many others who left their homes never returned. The Hijaz railroad from Damascus to Mecca was the first convenience built to ease the rigors of the trip. Unfortunately, before it could be used the First World War intervened and the rail line was destroyed by Arab guerrillas led by T. E. Lawrence, the legendary Lawrence of Arabia. It was never rebuilt. Wreckage of one of the trains is still strewn across the desert in northwest Saudi Arabia. Even a few years ago, thousands of pilgrims came by car. Before security concerns forced the government to channel most pilgrims in and out of Saudi Arabia by air, caravans of cars drove from Iraq, Iran, and Syria across the breadth of Saudi Arabia to Mecca.

Vehicles came through Riyadh, their horns blowing and green *hajj* flags flapping from their antennas, so loaded with people and possessions that their rear bumpers just cleared the road. Every year there was an area outside of Riyadh that was designated as the "*hajj* camp," where the government provided tents for the pilgrims. Just as their ancestors did, the *hajjis* brought rugs from their homelands to sell in order to finance their pilgrimage. The Oriental rug enthusiasts among the Western community yearly stampeded the camp in search of treasures. The *hajjis* had learned to merchandise. Rather than bringing the family heirlooms, they loaded their cars with machine-made carpets, which they pawned off on gullible Westerners as examples of their country's or tribe's finest craft. Bargaining was fierce and difficult since Arabic was not always sufficient and none of us knew a word of Afghani or Urdu. Not being particularly fond of Oriental rugs, I usually wandered among the canvas tents, where the women cooked over small gas heaters and the children played or slept on blankets or rugs spread out on the hard ground. In different years, I found both of my *hajj* camp rugs among the pilgrims' tents. One is a large tribal rug dyed with vegetable dyes, probably from somewhere on the border between Iran and Afghanistan. It is greatly worn and has small, carefully darned holes where the embers from countless campfires have fallen and burned through. The other is a Bedouin weaving from the Hadramaut, the southeastern part of the Arabian Peninsula that borders the Rub al-Khali, where rug weaving among the Bedouins is a dying, if not already dead, art. The sellers were amazed that I had rejected their new merchandise in favor of these dirty weavings dragged from their tents. Not believing their good fortune, they were anxious to sell. Often when I look at my much-loved rugs, I laugh to think how generously I must have added to those *hajjis'* funds for Mecca.

Just as the stampede to Mecca gradually accelerates, the *hajj* season winds down. The cars wander back through Riyadh. Congestion at the airport declines as the pilgrims, many carrying small plastic jerry cans of water from the Zamzam well, bundle themselves and their possessions back on planes for the trip home.

The credit for the security of the pilgrims and the relative ease of the *hajj* today goes to the House of Saud. Pilgrims were shamefully pillaged and exploited until Abdul Aziz ibn Saud won control of Mecca and personally undertook to guarantee their safety. Every Saudi king since Abdul Aziz, with the exception of Saud, has been identified with some aspect of the *hajj*. Just as King Faisal expanded the Grand Mosque at Mecca and King Khalid presided over its completion, the present king, Fahd, has announced plans for a major renovation and enlargement of the Prophet's mosque at Medina. Within the bureaucracy, the minister of Pilgrimage and Endowments holds the same cabinet rank as the minister of Petroleum or Foreign Affairs. Every year the ministry oversees the spending of more than $50 million for the *hajj*. And every year the government continues to pour enormous sums into the *hajj* for everything from mosques to road construction to public telephones to Zamzam water for the pilgrims.

Why does Saudi Arabia go to such extraordinary lengths to stage the *hajj?* In simple terms, it is a gigantic public relations venture, ensuring that the kingdom retains its image as protector of Islam's holy places. Former King Faisal, as well as being truly devout, grasped the significance of the *hajj* in the modern nation-state system. Saudi Arabia's oil wealth freed the House of Saud from its dependence on revenues from the pilgrims' fees to run the government. After 1973 the House of Saud was in the position to turn the celebration of Moslem brotherhood into status for Saudi Arabia. And it has succeeded. Symbolically, the *hajj* has become enormously important to both Saudi Arabia and to the House of Saud. For a country with vast reserves of a vital natural resource and threatened by inadequately defended borders and an insignificant population, the prestige attached to being head of the "Islamic nation" pays important dividends in the world arena. During the *hajj,* the Saudis host dozens of well-known but widely divergent pilgrims. One year President Zia ul-Haq of Pakistan and Indian film star Dilip Kumar were officially received the same day. Entire delegations from Islamic countries from Djibouti to Indonesia file past leading members of the House of Saud, the self-proclaimed guardian of Islam's holy sites, to pay homage. And each year following the *hajj,* hundreds of cables of thanks from foreign governments flood into the kingdom in gratitude for the Saudis' hospitality. With the mantle of Islam wrapped tightly around itself, the House of Saud has embraced the *hajj* as the ultimate symbol of the power and the universality of Islam. At the same time, the rulers, in the name of Wahhabism, fight a rear-guard action against the infusion of other religions, especially Christianity, into the rigorously controlled confines of the kingdom.

5

Living with Islam

THE LOW, DISTANT HILLS were barely visible through the dust-laden sky as I stood gazing out of the window of the new (unbelievably modern by Riyadh standards) Hyatt Regency Hotel in Jeddah. According to the round paper prayer compass stuck to the top of the air-conditioning unit that ran beneath the glass expanse of the window, Mecca was beyond those hills, separated from me by the barriers that the Saudis impose between the believer and the infidel. In my hand was another phenomenon of the frontier days in Saudi Arabia, a hotel service directory. As I leafed through the listings of airline and embassy telephone numbers and descriptions of points of local interest, two sentences that I had seen printed in many other places caught my attention as if I had never seen them before. "Islam is the official religion of Saudi Arabia. Churches of other religious denominations do not exist in the kingdom." Perhaps it was the Western tenor of my surroundings that gave new emphasis to the repressive nature of Saudi Arabia's restrictions on other religions. Simply stated, there is a total prohibition of the open practice of any religion other than Islam within the Kingdom of Saudi Arabia.

Whether the Saudis publicly recognize it as such, the level of intolerance demonstrated by the Wahhabis is vastly greater than that found in other sects of Islam. Historically, the Wahhabis isolated themselves in their perceived purity. They rejected foreign ideas and foreigners themselves to such an extent that to travel the Nejd in the nineteenth century was to invite death at the hands of religious fanatics. So enraged were the people when Gertrude Bell, the intrepid British Arabist, arrived in Hail in 1913 that she was allowed to leave unharmed only by the grace of being a woman. As late as the 1940s, the British explorer Wilfred Thesiger was forced to skirt the territories claimed by especially zealous tribes of the Hadramaut, who would kill any infidel who broached their boundaries. In the early 1950s, the increasing numbers of Westerners brought in to develop the oil industry were confined in their own town in the Eastern Province to keep them out of sight in order to protect Abdul Aziz from the wrath of the pious. Yet the Saudis do not see this as intolerance. Dr. Mujahid al-Sawwa, an Oxford-educated former professor of Islamic law and comparative religion, speaks for those in the kingdom who regard themselves as enlightened: "Islam believes in religious tolerance. You just have to practice your religion in private." *

The inability of not just the Saudis but all Moslems to accept other religious groups has always puzzled Westerners. There is a school of thought among Western experts on Islam that postulates that there is a great binary division between Islam and the West that is impossible to broach. According to the anthropologist Claude Lévi-Strauss,

> [Islam] is based not so much on revealed truth as on an inability to establish links with the outside world. . . . [Moslems are] incapable of tolerating the existence of others as others. The only means they have of protecting themselves against doubt and humiliation is the "negativization" of others, considered as witnesses to a different faith and a different way of life. . . . The truth is that contact with non-Moslems distresses Moslems.**

For those of us who lived with the Saudis, their particular hostility to other religious groups seems to express a great fear that somehow the beliefs and the legalisms of Wahhabism will not stand up to examination by or exposure to other ideas. In reality, religious intolerance is another form of the Saudis' all-consuming need to preserve their honor and their traditions.

While in some respects a revolutionary, Mohammed largely reflected the pure Arab culture of the Arabian Peninsula. Few of his rules and practices have changed significantly since his time. Saudi Arabia's

---

*Atlanta Constitution, May 25, 1985.
**Quoted in Fouad Ajami, The Arab Predicament: Arab Political Thought and Practice Since 1967 (Cambridge: Cambridge University Press, 1981), p. 16.

religious tyrants claim nothing has changed, and furthermore they are determined to see that whatever accommodations Saudi Arabia makes to modernization do not undercut the tenets of their very existence. Much of the history of Saudi Arabia since 1974 involves the House of Saud's attempts to force Westerners to conform to the Saudis' religious dictates and, at the same time, to make some politically acceptable concessions to its Western work force's own religious needs in order to recruit and hold its technical expertise.

The religious issue is greatly complicated by the House of Saud's own agenda for modernization, which in itself is in conflict with the royal family's long-time political needs. The House of Saud was built on religion and sustained by political stability. The peace Abdul Aziz brought between the warring tribes contributed to the interests of those outside Wahhabism and added their acquiescence to the kingdom of the al-Sauds. But the devoutly religious were the core of the House of Saud's support. How far the leadership could stray from Wahhabi doctrine has never been seriously tested. Through the reign of King Faisal, the innovations that were introduced into the society were tenuous until the leadership felt secure in their acceptance, or at least toleration. As the House of Saud became swept up in the oil boom, the constraints of religion began to seriously clash with the goals of modernization. Fearful of revolt, a fear justified by the religious uprising in Mecca in late 1979, the House of Saud probed at the religious issue but never directly challenged it.

How to address the religious bigotry of the Saudis while catering to the religious demands of the Westerners constitutes a whole chapter in the annals of the oil boom. It is only one of the many ongoing conflicts between tradition and progress that continue to grip the kingdom. The religious question represents the broader struggle of Saudi Arabia to come to terms with the twentieth century, a century in which God's special providence pumped from beneath the sands of its desert no longer permits the Saudis to remain isolated in their own intolerance.

As Islam orders the life of the Saudis, Islam impinges on basic aspects of the foreigner's life. Religion regulated our days. It governed what we ate. It controlled our behavior. It determined, to a large extent, our recreational activities. Those who could not or would not adjust went home.

The panoply of prohibitions on non-Moslems at times causes serious and expensive problems for foreign contractors. Bell Canada, responsible for the kingdom's telephone system, maintains offices in both holy cities of Mecca and Medina. Since the cities are barred to Christians and other non-Moslems, the company is plagued with the problem of trying to match an employee's skills with his religion to keep the in-town offices functioning. Since it is seldom able to keep them fully staffed with Moslems, auxiliary offices and housing compounds for non-Moslem employees are maintained on the outskirts of the cities. These people live in a type of exile, for they cannot enter either city. To shop for food, the women living near Mecca take a bus to Jeddah, an hour away, several times a week. For the employees in Medina, more than 300 miles from the nearest accessible large town, the company maintains a general store and operates a grueling once-a-week shopping excursion to Jeddah.

The Westerner who succeeds in enjoying life in Saudia Arabia under the conditions imposed by the Wahhabis does so by honing a keen sense of humor. For me, life was a quest for any situation that, no matter how frustrating or infuriating, might enter the annals of oil-boom comedy. Among the classic tales circulating among the expatriates was the story about the first modern hotel built in Mecca. The structure was designed by a Western architectural firm, but when building actually began, the Saudis, it is said, refused to allow the supervising architect into the city. Instead they insisted that he stand on a hill outside of town and direct the work through a telescope. And then there was the word play involving the Saudi weekend. Since the Moslem day of rest is Friday, the weekend is Thursday and Friday. On Wednesday afternoon the Westerners gather to celebrate "TAIW" — "Thank Allah It's Wednesday." But few instances of life in the Moslem theocracy gave me as much pleasure as the tug of war over "near beer." Of all the stories that I was sending out of Saudi Arabia at the time, the roller coaster fortunes of imitation beer was my favorite.

Saudi Arabia's prohibition on alcohol includes wine, cider, and beer as well as hair tonic, ordinary rubbing alcohol, alcohol-based insect repellent, and medications containing alcohol. When large numbers of German workers began to arrive in Saudi Arabia in the late 1970s, the Saudis faced yet another problem of bringing Islam and modernization into some kind of equilibrium. The ban on beer severely hindered the recruiting efforts of German companies and threatened to hobble some of the Saudis' favorite construction companies. To placate the Germans while at the same time protecting the Islamic purity of the kingdom, enterprising beer companies, who had been eager to break into the rich Saudi economy, came up with the idea of near beer. The non-alcoholic brew approximated the taste if not the kick of beer. During the spring and early summer of 1979, Schlitz staged a massive ad campaign aimed at the expatriate market, claiming that the taste of beer could now be purchased in the kingdom. Large, colorfully painted delivery trucks, precious in this period of shortages, were put on the road. The supermarkets that catered to Western tastes cleared their shelves to receive shipments. With everything in place, Schlitz, along with the Swiss brewer Moussy, sat back waiting to rake in their profits. As predicted, cash registers happily rang as the expatriates lined up to buy.

In August the religious authorities struck back. Under pressure from the Wahhabi fundamentalists, the government banned nonalcoholic beers, "wines" (fruit juice in a fancy foil-wrapped bottle) and "champagnes" (carbonated grape juice). The reason: consumers might imagine intoxication precipitated by a taste reminiscent of alcohol. Perhaps it was more than reminiscent. Some, primarily manual laborers, were lacing their pseudo-beer with cologne, the only product containing significant amounts of alcohol that was sold in the country. Consequently, the jail population markedly rose on weekends, and by Saturday empty lots in the major cities were strewn with an exotic array of empty beer and cologne bottles.

All distribution ceased and the shelves of the supermarkets were stripped of beer. But then the back-pedaling began. The Saudi merchants, partners in the companies distributing and selling the beer, were unwilling to sit still while something as lucrative as the beer trade was taken from them. The elaborate network of family and tribal connections went into action, taking the entrepreneurs' complaints directly to the king. Within two weeks of the ban, the government announced that merchants would be allowed to sell their current stocks and then near beer was to disappear. Well, it did, for a while. As a result of the mysterious back room sparring matches that are always going on between the government, the merchants, and the religious authorities, near beer was kept under wraps for about a year and then slowly began to reappear in supermarkets. By now the incident is long forgotten, and the Germans continue to drink their near beer and build their buildings, the merchants go on ringing up their sales, and the religious authorities enjoy whatever tradeoff they received from withdrawing their objection to look-alike beer.

As entertaining as the episode was for the expatriates, it was yet

another serious dilemma for the House of Saud, which often finds itself
hostage to the intolerance of the Wahhabis. This intolerance of all
things beyond their own strictly defined bounds of Islam has made
even something as esoteric as archaeology a point of serious strife
between the progressives in the government and the religious establishment. Archaeologists are stymied in their attempts to excavate the almost untapped treasure trove of ancient sites in Saudi Arabia by the
refusal of the powerful religious leaders to allow any attention to be
focused on the *jahiliyah,* the "ignorant days" before the revelations
of Islam. As late as 1969, the government maintained a total ban on
all excavations of the pre-Islamic era, a concession some claim was
made in return for the religious leaders' acquiescence to economic
modernization. Then in 1973, a young Western-trained archaeologist
named Abdullah H. Masry was appointed director of Antiquities and
Museums by King Faisal. By patience, endurance, and consummate
political skill, Masry has done a remarkable job of restoring at least
some of the Saudis' pre-Islamic past. He persuaded the government to
pour millions of dollars into the exploration of hundreds of archaeological sites in an effort to unearth and preserve relics of the past. He
established a small but expertly done museum on one of Riyadh's main
thoroughfares and has overseen the construction of others around the
kingdom. Masry continues to succeed largely because he ties his archaeology projects back into religion and the distrust of infidels. One
of Masry's archaeology students at the University of Riyadh summed
up the philosophy when he said, "The Koran has many references to
the ancient cultures. We must study this history to see how they lived.
European archaeologists have given the wrong impression of our people. We want to make a correction. We want to write our own history
by ourselves." *

The archaeologists in Saudi Arabia have been successful in getting
money and recognition because their work tends to counter the Saudis'
image in the West as a tribe of ultrarich Bedouins with no cultural
roots. But because of the deep political dispute between Israel and the
Arabs, impossible obstacles remain to archaeological research that might
turn up evidence of a long-ago Jewish presence in Saudi Arabia. A
British archaeologist working on the eleventh century A.D. Nabatean

---

*Robert Reinhold, "Uncovering Arabia's Past," *New York Times Magazine,* August 23, 1981,
p. 18.

ruins at Madain Saleh for Saudi Arabia's Department of Antiquities told me that Saudi Arabia has the last major unexplored sites of Biblical-era archaeology. Unfortunately, among the few artifacts unearthed are inscriptions in what appears to be ancient Hebrew. Since it is politically vital both domestically and within the Arab world for Saudi Arabia to distance itself as much as possible from Israel and the Jews, everything remains buried. Unable to bury the Jews, the Saudis simply refuse to allow them in the country.

Islam, meaning "submission to the will of God," * followed Judaism and Christianity as the last of the three great monotheistic religions. At the very core of Islam is the concept of Allah, the one great God, the same God of Jews and Christians. The belief in the oneness of God dominates the theology of Islam, for Mohammed's great message was the direct relationship between God and man. In Islam, unlike Judaism and Christianity, there are no synagogues or churches, only places to pray. There is no priesthood. There are no sacraments. In orthodox Islam, there is no central doctrinal authority, for no man or institution stands between the believer and God.

Mohammed had a limited knowledge of the scriptures of both the Jews and the Christians and incorporated parts of them, modified to fit the Arabs' own culture, into Islam. From the very beginning of his revelations, Mohammed saw Islam as the culmination of both the teachings of Christ and the beliefs of Judaism, which in the end would supplement both. Jesus is recognized as a prophet in Islam. Certain commandments about charity and love of fellow believers have their roots in Christian theology. Mohammed's descriptions of paradise as the reward of the believer parallel the Christian heaven. But it was from Judaism that many of Mohammed's basic tenets came. Midday prayers, facing Jerusalem to pray, fast days, and Friday sabbath were all Jewish in origin. Mohammed took the concepts and changed the rituals. Moslems pray five times a day including midday, face Mecca rather than Jerusalem, observe a whole month of fasting rather than one day, and begin the sabbath at midday on Friday rather than sundown. Even Jerusalem remained critically important in Islamic theology. According to Islamic belief, Mohammed was transported in a vision from Mecca to Jerusalem. There a winged horse stood atop the remaining wall of King Solomon's temple to bear Mohammed to heaven

---

* A Moslem is one who submits.

before returning him to his bed in Mecca. On the site of his ascent now stands the al-Aqsa mosque, the third holy site in Islam, while in its shadow the Jews of the world come to pray at the Wailing Wall, the same wall on which Mohammed's horse stood.

Even the Kaaba is tied directly to Jewish tradition. The existing Kaaba is believed to be the tenth such structure on the spot. Again according to doctrine, the first was built by the angels at the dawn of Earth. The second was constructed by Adam, father of man; the third by Adam's son Seth; and the fourth by Abraham (the father of all Moslems) and his son Ishmael. The present Kaaba is believed to have been built by the followers of Mohammed in A.D. 696.

Identical to its predecessors, the crude stone structure is forty feet long, thirty-five feet wide, and approximately fifty feet high. Imbedded in the exterior southeast corner, five feet from the ground, is the sacred Black Stone, the only specific object of veneration at the Kaaba. Seven inches in diameter, mounted in a silver frame, the Black Stone is presumed to have been part of the Kaaba since the time of Abraham. Among the theories about its origins is that it is a meteorite sent down from heaven at the time of Abraham. Regardless of its source, it has come to symbolize God's promise to the Moslems.

Jews, Christians, and Moslems all recognize the Abraham story in Genesis. Abraham through his faithfulness to the one God is the symbol in all three monotheistic religions of the perfect oneness between the heart of God and the heart of man. It is in God's promise to Abraham's descendants where Jews and Moslems differ.

Abraham's wife Sarah had no children. In old age, she gave her Egyptian maid Hagar to Abraham as a wife. When Hagar conceived a child, Sarah in a fit of jealous rage sent her into the desert. God dispatched an angel to Hagar while she was in the wilderness, who told her to return to Abraham, where she would be delivered of a son. Ishmael was born to Hagar and Abraham when the patriarch was eighty-six years old.

Thirteen years later, God again came to Abraham. Sarah, many years past child-bearing age, would birth a son who would be called Isaac. God promised Isaac would become the father of nations and that Ishmael would beget twelve princes and also establish a great nation. Isaac remained with his father in the Hebrew nation. In Moslem tradition, Sarah forced Ishmael and his mother to once again leave Abraham's household to wander in the wilderness near the present city of

Mecca. When they were near death, God led them to the waters of the Zamzam well. Thus saved, Ishmael became the father of the Arab nation.

The very seeds of the Arab-Israeli dispute that has raged in the Middle East for much of this century lie in the Abraham story. To the Moslems, God's covenant is with their ancestor, Ishmael. To the Jews, God's covenant is with their ancestor, Isaac.

Yet the Moslems' conflicts with the Jews always have had more political than theological overtones and date to the earliest days of Islam. The Prophet exiled to Medina by his struggles with the Quraish, the tribe that dominated Meccan commerce and controlled the lucrative traffic in pilgrimages to the Kaaba, appealed to the Jews to support him. The Jews were willing to forge a political alliance but refused to accept an Arab as a prophet. Mohammed, furious at his rejection, increasingly saw Islam less as an extension of Judaism and more as an "Arabized" creed, rising out of Arab culture and tradition.

Despite Mohammed's rejection by the Jews, Jews are still recognized as "people of the book," loosely meaning monotheists. The current hostilities between Jews and Moslems stem from the creation of Israel in 1948 and its territorial expansion in 1967. Saudi Arabia, like the other Arab states, has never recognized the loss of Arab land to the Jewish state. To the Arabs, Israel is a threatening pawn of Western imperialism sitting on sacred Arab land. To keep its credentials high with its Arab brothers, Saudi Arabia does its share of verbal posturing on the part of the Palestinians. Maps in Saudi Arabia designate Israel as Palestine. Jerusalem is al-Quds. And the al-Aqsa mosque is the recipient of abundant pledges to wrest it from the grasp of Israel by *jihad,* or holy war.

Since it is politically vital both domestically and within the Arab world for Saudi Arabia to distance itself as much as possible from Israel, all Jews and any Christian whose passport bears an Israeli visa are banned from the kingdom. That is, unless a Saudi high enough in the government or with the right connections wants a particular person for a particular job; then arrangements, as always, can be made. The few Jews that I came across working in the kingdom were almost always there on short-term assignments. All observed an oath of silence about both their religion and ethnic group. I met several other people who I thought might be Jews, but according to the expatriates' code of honor I never asked.

Politics aside, Judaism, in one important aspect, is held in higher esteem than Christianity by the Saudis. Unlike Judaism and Islam, Christianity smacks of polytheism because of the Christian doctrine of the Trinity. The whole central theme of Islam is the oneness of God. The prayer call declares that "God is great, God is great. I testify that there is no god but God." Obviously, in such a doctrine, there is no room for a savior, both all-human and all-divine, or for some ephemeral concept of a holy spirit dwelling in the trees, the sky, and the human heart.

In the days of innocence, when the few Westerners in Saudi Arabia were clustered in the ARAMCO compounds in the Eastern Province, the issue of the religious rights of foreigners was handled by confining the heretics and denying them any visible organized religious activity. It was a manageable problem until the boom decade scattered more and more Christian families across the kingdom. Many sought a Christian community, especially at Christmas time.

Christmas was always the most difficult time of the year for Western expatriates. Even for those of us who thrived on life in the kingdom, Christmas brought the dull, painful ache of homesickness. To make things worse, until the 1980s, expatriates were forbidden any kind of Christmas ornaments to moderate our loneliness. It was not only the religious symbols of Christmas that were banned but the nonreligious trappings, such as colored lights, tinsel, and Santa Claus. So stringent were the rules about Christmas decorations that in 1978 the U.S. Army Corps of Engineers issued the following bulletin for its employees:

CHRISTMAS DECORATIONS: All employees are reminded that Christmas decorations may not be placed on the outside of any building, nor may they be placed inside a building in such a manner that they can be seen from outside. In this matter, as in many, cultural discretion and common sense must take precedence over personal desires.

I will never forget our first Christmas in Saudi Arabia. The temperature was 85 degrees and the mosque down the street had just installed a new loudspeaker so the prayer call was coming in especially loud. The few presents around our "Christmas tree" (desert weeds stuck in a pail of sand) were wrapped in an assortment of grocery bags colored with crayons and some aluminum insulation from an air-conditioning duct. On Christmas eve, Colin hung his Christmas stocking from the evaporative cooler. Christmas day itself was dreadful. There was no contact with our families at home. The few international telephone lines out of Saudi Arabia at the time had been inundated for two weeks by Westerners calling home. We all worked that day because it was a normal day in Moslem Saudi Arabia. As the sun went down, Westerners gathered for Christmas dinner. The group we joined happened to be largely Canadian. The same food we ate on a daily basis was made festive by a little extra seasoning and the addition of some dates or oranges for decoration. There were no turkeys available in the kingdom, but someone with connections at the Army Corps of Engineers arrived bearing a ham, which to us was as precious as frankincense or myrrh. As we ate and traded stories of Christmases past, an x-ray technician triumphantly appeared with an electronic keyboard and launched us into song writing. What emerged was a new rendition of "I'm Dreaming of a White Christmas." It went something like this: "I'm dreaming of a bleak Christmas, with every prayer call I hear. Where the date palms bristle, above desert thistle, and sheep bleat, in the heat." Bad as it was, we thought it was enormously funny at the time. Flushed with success, we went on to rewrite " 'Twas the Night Before Christmas" with the reindeer becoming camels named Abdullah, Hamid, Nazer, Hisham, Said, Hassan, Bandar, and Muhsin.

Despite the restrictions surrounding Christmas celebrations, the fortunes of the Christians actually had improved by the time I arrived in Saudi Arabia. It had taken a former governor from the heart of the Southern Bible Belt of the United States to win some concessions for the Christians from the Saudi government. John West, ex-governor of South Carolina, was appointed U.S. ambassador to Saudi Arabia in 1977 by the newly elected Jimmy Carter. To say West was an unknown quantity when he arrived in Saudi Arabia is an understatement. The professional diplomats were horrified that Saudi Arabia's major ally was forcing a back-slapping, hand-pressing Southern politician on the austere Saudis. Despite the predictions of disaster, the jovial West, seasoned by years on the campaign trail, applied just the right amount of graciousness and diffidence to charm his hosts. Accustomed to religious politics in his home state, West was less hesitant than his predecessors had been to approach the Saudis about the plight of the Christians in the kingdom. Using his access to King Khalid to speak on behalf of the Christians, West is said to have told the king that Americans had great respect for Islam and he was sure that the king, in turn, had respect for Christianity. Furthermore, because the Saudis were such religious people, he knew that they wanted to attract morally upright people to their labor force and that this was greatly hindered by the government's ban on religious activity for non-Moslems. To his credit, King Khalid, exhibiting a great deal of courage in risking the rage of the religious zealots, agreed to allow a loose, clandestine organization of Christians to function in the kingdom. The rules were strict and the government warned that any deviation would result in withdrawal of the privilege.

The ground rules were: there could be no public organization that even faintly resembled a church; there could be no publicity connected with any religious function; there could be no proselytizing among either Moslems or non-Moslems; the availability of Christian religious groups could not be used in recruiting Western labor, nor could new employees be informed of the existence of Christian worship by an employer. In return, the Christians could meet as long as the purpose of their meetings did not become known to the Saudi population. The Christians were permitted to bring in ministers for the major cities of Riyadh, Jeddah, and Dhahran. For the political purposes of the House of Saud, the visa for the Protestant minister in Riyadh listed him as an employee of Lockheed, and the Catholic priest was officially a social worker with the British consulate. The ministers and priests in the three major cities were circuit riders for Christians living on outlying construction sites. Rather than using horses, though, they used airplanes provided by private companies.

By 1978 the Christian community was in full swing, or at least as active as it could be under the rules. I had been in Saudi Arabia for several weeks before word filtered through about when and where the Christians met. In Riyadh the Protestants were housed in a combination basketball court and movie theater for U.S. military personnel training the Saudi Arabian National Guard (SANG), located not far from the King Faisal hospital. The Catholics held mass in the British diplomatic facilities. "Keep a low profile" was the watchword. Since the SANG compound in Riyadh was on a main thoroughfare in sight of a large mosque, we had to park on side streets and come in the back gates so the religious authorities would not become unduly curious about the presence of a large number of cars. Photocopied maps giving directions to the services carried no heading and were passed between interested parties like state secrets passing between spies. Church bulletins handed out at the door were collected following the service to be burned. When an attempt was made to compile a directory of participants, many refused to have their names listed for fear of reprisals if the list got into the hands of the Saudis.

The Christian community in Saudi Arabia may well have reached its zenith at Christmas of 1978. In January 1979, the shah of Iran went into exile and the fortunes of the Christians in Saudi Arabia fell with him. Fear of repercussions from the "Islamic revival" touched off by Khomeini's victory haunted the House of Saud. As fear of the Shiites escalated so did fear of the Christians. The House of Saud increasingly came to see any religious activity other than that of the Moslems as political subversion. Modifying the comfortable understanding that the Christians had with Prince Salman, governor of Riyadh, the Ministry of the Interior moved in to supervise the Christians.

The problems of the Christians were not entirely a result of the Islamic revolution in Iran. The Christians, knowingly and unknowingly, brought on some of their problems themselves. On the Easter Sunday following Khomeini's triumph in Iran, the Catholics in Riyadh held a sunrise communion service behind the concrete wall of a Corps of Engineers facility off of Pepsi Road. They assumed they were hidden and, therefore, safe. But what the priest failed to anticipate was the Saudi in an adjoining two-story house who, upon rising for morning prayers, was greeted at his bedroom window by the Eucharist. It did not take long for the news of this affront to Islam to reach the religious authorities, who went directly to the king.

Shortly, the first ruling against the Christians in Riyadh came down. Permission for the Christian Fellowship to meet was suspended. To circumvent the ruling, the congregation broke up into small groups, which secretly met in people's homes presided over by laymen. To keep the authorities confused, we met at a different villa or compound every week. Appropriately called "the Catacombs," these clandestine gatherings ended after a few months when we were allowed to resume activities as a united congregation at the Lockheed compound on the outskirts of Riyadh until more problems developed.

By Christmas of 1979, six weeks after religious opponents of the royal family took over the Grand Mosque at Mecca, the Christians were once against caught in the crossfire of religious politics in Saudi Arabia. In Riyadh, Lockheed withdrew the use of its compound. Although never confirmed or denied, rumor was that an official in the

Ministry of Defense and Aviation had threatened Lockheed with the loss of its contracts if Christian church services continued to be held on company premises. The fellowships in both Dhahran and Jeddah, previously immune from the problems the Riyadh group faced, began to confront similar restrictions. The clergymen were allowed to stay in the kingdom, but for the congregation it was back to the Catacombs. That is where we remained until I left Saudi Arabia in the late spring of 1980.

The unpredictable relationship between the Christians and the government of Saudi Arabia, intimidated by its own religious right, was a tug of war. Rules were laid down. The Christians accepted the restraints and then often breached them, either through overconfidence or error. But more often, government policy zigged and zagged through the minefield of the House of Saud's own political agenda. The erratic nature of the government's attitude toward the Christians appeared to be the height of hypocrisy to the Westerners. For the House of Saud, it was another exercise in balancing the demands of religion against the goals of modernization. It was a game that the House of Saud played well. Historically, the royal family has maintained the support of the Moslem fundamentalists by staunchly defending Saudi Arabia's traditional values and placating the religious establishment with grants and favors while gradually pushing the country in the direction of modernization. The technique that has been used time and time again when government policy and religious dictates clash is to initially accede to the demands of the religious power structure and then either divert attention to some other issue or cause the religious leaders to lose something they want.

The classic example of this process in operation was Abdul Aziz's tobacco tax. When Abdul Aziz took Mecca in 1924, the Wahhabis demanded that he banish tobacco sales, a major source of revenue for the merchants and, therefore, a source of taxes for the king. He did as the *ulema** demanded. But the following year when the religious leaders appeared for their annual stipends, Abdul Aziz informed them that since the tobacco tax was no longer coming into his coffers he could no longer pay them their allowances. As if by magic, tobacco appeared

---

*The *ulema* is the hierarchy of the religious establishment. Made up of the most noted and respected religious scholars in Saudi Arabia, the *ulema* regulates religious matters and issues rulings on legal questions. The power and symbolism of the *ulema* is such that the king holds highly publicized meetings with the group on a weekly basis.

once more in the markets. In the case of the Christians, the on-again off-again status of their right of religious expression was a practical way for the House of Saud both to cater to the religious establishment and to avoid social conflict with Saudi Arabia's vital Western work force. It was the House of Saud's own unique way of insuring that modernization continued, while at the same time protecting the traditional values of its people and its own political survival.

In spite of the efforts of the rulers, the breakneck pace of modernization after centuries of rigid adherence to the traditions of the Wahhabi sect of Islam was fraying the Saudi social fabric. During the 1970s, the House of Saud was sending young Saudi men to the West to study everything from business administration to physics. Grand schemes for economic development were coming out of the government planning bureaus. Upper- and middle-class Saudis traveled around the world. Any prospect of a bitter fallout from Saudi Arabia's bold moves to embrace the material benefits of the outside world was little imagined. It was all still too new and exciting. The small signs of disillusionment that were appearing were overwhelmed by consumerism and the excitement of acquiring automobiles, jewelry, luxury houses, and shopping centers — the trappings of modernization. Even Islam was being commercialized by the new rising Saudi entrepreneurs. Advertising and sales gimmicks related to Islam increased every year. "Congratulations on your Pilgrimage. Ask for your gift from Citizen when you buy a Citizen Watch." Ramadan one year was ushered in by this ad: "For the blessed season of the Holy Month of Ramadan, good news for the citizens. The arrival of new models of the multipurpose cleaning systems by Filter Queen. Generous discounts during Ramadan." The Salch bin Mahfouz Establishment of Jeddah sold a clock in the shape of a miniature mosque that announced the prayer calls. At the appropriate time the clock's two minarets lighted up and a recording by the late Sheikh Abdul Basit Abdul Samad called the prayers. A sophisticated honing device for locating Mecca was introduced one year during the *hajj*. According to its inventor, the Marsad Makkah could obtain the true azimuth of Mecca within seconds after the user programmed in a code and arched the instrument in the air above his head until he heard a distinct clicking sound. The slab-shaped instrument was available in two models: the standard version of polished chrome with gold edges, and the luxury model, studded in diamonds, with an emerald at the end of the directional arrow.

While most of the population was sampling the materialism of the

West and some of the Saudi entrepreneurs were exploiting Islam, Sheikh Abdul Aziz ibn Baz, the blind president of the Islamic University of Medina and a major power in the religious establishment, remained the major spokesman for the other side of Saudi Arabia, the religious fundamentalists. Baz, who is the most public authority on Islamic law, has changed little since he declared in 1966 that the sun revolves around the earth. In an essay written to refute the heresy of the theory of the solar system taught at Riyadh University, Baz said: "Hence I say the Holy Koran, the Prophet's teaching, the majority of Islamic scientists, and the actual fact all prove that the sun is running in its orbit, as Almighty God ordained, and that the earth is fixed and stable, spread out by God for his mankind and made a bed and cradle for them, fixed down firmly by mountains lest it shake." *

Amid the tinsel of progress, the soul of Saudi Arabia remained with Sheikh Baz. Although not necessarily sharing the *sheikh*'s mentality, the newly Western-educated elite continued to accept Islam as the central focus of life, contributing to the power that Islam holds over the people of Saudi Arabia. Development was perceived in the physical sense and with the understanding that physical progress would not alter the force of Islam in the minds and hearts of the Saudis. A Saudi's emotional identification with Islam is rooted in the fact that Islam is not just a religion, it is a civilization and a culture; it is fundamental to a Saudi's perception of who he is and what his world is about. Even with their exposure to foreign influences, the Saudis held tenaciously to their traditions defined by religion. This reality created a situation in which every move toward modernization made by the government had to be justified in religious terms.

There is among the religious fundamentalists an all-consuming fear, which exists to a lesser degree among most Saudis, that foreign influences are breaking down this dominant position of religion in Saudi society. What the Saudis most fear from Westernization is not so much that it will cause people to abandon Islam in favor of Christianity but that, in an increasingly secular world, religion will take a secondary place in society as it has in the West. The religious leaders want Saudi Arabia to return to its insular existence, where their precepts are unchallenged by conflicting philosophies and practices. At the end of the

---

*Quoted in David Holden and Richard Johns, *The House of Saud* (London: Holt, Rinehart and Winston, 1981), p. 262.

1970s, the general population was ambivalent not about its own society but rather about what Saudi Arabia's contact with the West might mean to its way of life.

Just how much Western ideas and Western ways were seeping into Saudi society was not clear. In fact, the oil boom had instilled in the Saudis a new pride. There was a reawakening to the possibility of a true renaissance, a society opened and enriched by the new, as the Moslems in their early days of glory had been enriched by the knowledge acquired through their conquests. But Saudi Arabia had never really participated in the zenith of the Islamic empire. As contact with foreign peoples increased, they retreated farther into their own culture, behind the legalisms of Islam. Except for pockets of enlightenment, the Saudis remained unshakable in their isolation until the last part of the twentieth century. As if suffering a repeated curse, they then faced once again, as they had in the age of the Islamic empire, the dilemma of how to respond to foreign ways. During the oil boom, Saudi Arabia was characterized by the struggle to apply its own concept of Islam, as defined by Abdul-Wahhab, to the modern world.

For its political survival, it was vital for the House of Saud to stay identified with Islam through this struggle. Unlike the shah of Iran, Saudi Arabia's rulers, Faisal and Khalid, protected themselves from becoming victims of a revolutionary movement for a return to an Islamic state. The House of Saud's safety was to be found in promoting religious orthodoxy. Saudi Arabia, in relation to an Islamic state, was never allowed to leave the point to which Iran, through revolution, returned in 1979. Even at the height of the oil boom, the regime protected itself from another "cleansing of the faith" like that of the Wahhabi movement of the eighteenth century. Keeping government and religion intertwined ensured against the rise of a rival political movement drawing its strength from religious orthodoxy. Never was protection of the faith separated from any public decision. Seemingly innocuous decisions were carefully undertaken and defended. For example, the government's public announcement that a series of national parks would open in the Assir sought to reassure the population. "Planners expect these projects can be implemented with a minimum of impact on the country's social values." It was with this attitude that the House of Saud presided over modernization, warily walking the fine line between progress and the preservation of the Saudis' sacred traditions.

6

Bedouin Pride

IT WAS ONE of those wonderful mornings at the end of summer when the intense heat has waned and the pristine blue of the sky arches uncluttered into space. Standing near the clock tower across the street from the open square in front of Riyadh's main mosque, I was watching the scene on the street, drinking in my surroundings. It was just before the noon prayer call. Men on their way to the mosque streamed in front of me. I gazed at the passing parade of worshipers as they hurried along, some fingering their plastic prayer beads, others crossing and uncrossing the ends of their *gutras* in absent gestures as they walked. Abruptly, my attention focused on one man in the crowd. He was dressed like all the rest, in sandals and a white *thobe*. But beneath the sheer white *gutra* held in place by the familiar black *agal* was a moon-shaped face with yellow skin, Mongoloid features, and a thin, scraggly beard hanging from the tip of his chin. In all of his physical characteristics he was Chinese. Only his clothing identified him as a Saudi.

There is in Saudi Arabia a segment of the population, its size undetermined by any official or even vaguely accurate count, that is non-Arab. It is composed primarily of immigrants from Africa, some former slaves, and *hajjis* who came to Mecca on the pilgrimage and never left again. The man who caught my attention so forcefully was probably a descendant of Chinese Moslems who have lived in the kingdom for unknown generations and who stay segregated in their own community. While sharing the Saudis' religion and dress, this man, like all non-Arabs, would always remain outside of the Saudi social and political system, which is structured on the ancient tribes of the Arabian Peninsula. Although Saudi Arabia's population is a heterogeneous mix from the five' great geographic areas, the Hijaz, the Assir, the al-Hassa, the north, and the Nejd, a true Saudi is an Arab inextricably bound to an ancient past, with his heritage, and his whole sense of being, tied to the pure Arab's desert culture. As I traveled through the major topographical areas of Saudi Arabia, it became clear that each of the various regions had taken on its own special characteristics in the broader context of Arab culture.

The Western Province, or the Hijaz, runs north and south along the Red Sea and west to the escarpment that rises up to the plateau of Saudi Arabia's interior. Containing the port of Jeddah and the holy cities of Mecca and Medina, the Hijaz has always been influenced by foreign cultures and is one of only a few limited areas in Saudi Arabia ever subject to foreign domination. As the gateway for the *hajj*, Jeddah early developed into a commercial center that attracted immigrants from across the peninsula. Along with the pilgrims who remained after the *hajj*, they settled into the ethnic mosaic of the western coastal area. Geographically included in the Hijaz is the Tihama, the coastal lowlands southwest of Jeddah. Here descendants of Africans migrating from east Africa have all but taken the Tihama from the Arab population. Everything I saw in the Tihama was distinct — the colorful clothing, the thatch roof dwellings, and the absence of repressive religion. Government policy, backed by a visible military presence, tries unsuccessfully to confine the Africans to the lowland plains and away from the Arab population. But their presence in all parts of Saudi Arabia continues to grow. African women are hawkers on Riyadh's streets, men are personal servants to well-to-do Saudis, and the most infamous person in Riyadh, the public executioner, is an enormous black man.

In the mountains south of the Hijaz is the Assir, culturally a part of Yemen but annexed to Saudi Arabia by Abdul Aziz. Its topography is startlingly different from the rest of Saudi Arabia. Rugged mountains covered with pine trees rise from the coastal plain. Even in the hottest part of summer, its high altitude keeps the climate delightfully cool, so much so that from early June until mid-October, the royal family moves to the mountain city of Taif, taking the government with them. There they race their horses in the late afternoon, eat the abundant agricultural produce of the area, and hold the native Yemenis at a safe distance.

Across the peninsula from Taif is the flat, intensely humid Eastern

Province, or the al-Hassa. The area was once known for its palm groves and pearling industry, but oil is now its primary output. All of Saudi Arabia's proven petroleum reserves are located in the al-Hassa and the adjacent Rub al-Khali. Because of its economic importance, the al-Hassa has a vibrancy absent in other parts of Saudi Arabia. When I came to the kingdom, the al-Hassa, almost as a symbol of its vibrancy, was aflame with flared gas from hundreds of wells producing seven million barrels of oil a day. I remember riding the train across the flat, gray sands of the coastal plain and seeing the energy of Saudi Arabia freely burning into the skies while the world begged for its oil. Today, in a new statement of the al-Hassa's importance, that gas is collected for use in the petrochemical industry at Jubail.

Like any coastal area, the al-Hassa has traditionally been exposed to the diverse lifestyles of townsmen, farmers, fishermen, and desert nomads who wander in and out in search of grazing lands. In addition, the Eastern Province, more than any area of Saudi Arabia, has felt the impact of change brought on by the birth of the oil industry in 1938. The oil industry has, in fact, made such inroads into the traditional way of life that in the al-Hassa tribal patterns have crumbled and the past is very difficult to study.

Arching across the vacant northern frontier of Saudi Arabia, connecting the Hijaz with the al-Hassa, are the provinces of Jawf, Hail, and the Northern Frontier. The north is actually an extension of the Syrian desert, where the sparse grass, steppe vegetation, and numerous *wadis* provide support for nomadic and seminomadic people. There is an atmosphere in this high, empty area broken by ranges of low hills that somehow always made me feel terribly alone. Perhaps it is because the north is alone. It is the beneficiary of neither ports, produce, petroleum, nor political power. Hail, one of its few sizable towns, remains a stronghold of Arab tradition and serves only as the gateway to the geographical and political center of Saudi Arabia, the Nejd.

The Nejd, lying on a plateau that rises between the two coasts, is the heartland of Saudi Arabia. As the tribal homeland of the royal family, the Nejd is the political center of the kingdom. The al-Saud dynasty began in the vast oasis of Diriyah, an area lush enough to sustain life through the intense summer heat. The numerous springs and extensive date palm groves supported settled agricultural communities whose populations far outnumbered that of the nomads. The townsmen and the nomads of the Nejd are descended from mixed northern and southern Arabian stock. Their remoteness from the non-Arab immigrants of the coastal areas resulted in a purity of race matched nowhere else on the peninsula. The haughty Nejdis regard themselves as the aristocrats of the Arab race, the pious and conservative protectors of Arab ideals. People, ideas, lifestyles — everything outside of their own communities traditionally is regarded as impious, impure, and infidel. Until the 1970s, the Nejd to a remarkable extent succeeded in shutting out alien influences. Righteous and secure, they were content until the foreigners arrived, drawing a reluctant people into the world.

Regionalism, reenforced by decades of rule by separate entities or no government at all, created social and cultural gaps between the various regions of the Arabian Peninsula. But none of these divisions is as great as the chasm that exists between the ways of the townspeople and the ways of the desert dwellers. The arrogance of the town Arab is exceeded only by the arrogance of the nomads. Yet I found in the nomads the same purity of spirit and intense independence that has immortalized them throughout the centuries. Their ability to reject all that threatens to entrap them and to endure with equanimity the brutality of the desert is what captured the imagination of Westerners like T. E. Lawrence and Pasha Glubb (Sir John Bagot Glubb). Although often irritated by the town Arab's assumption of superior airs, I found it fascinating to watch the nomad with even more offensive manners challenge any man who dared stand in his way. It was as if he knew that his ideals still hover in the heart of every Saudi.

The legendarily tough and fiercely independent nomads of the Arabian Peninsula are called Bedouins, a French derivative of an Arabic word meaning "an inhabitant of the desert." For centuries the Bedouins alone dominated the vast, empty wasteland of the Arabian Peninsula. Through civilization after civilization, it was the Bedouin with his superhuman ability to survive who not only controlled but characterized the desert.

Nowhere in the world was there such a continuity as in the Arabian desert. Here Semitic nomads . . . must have herded their flocks before the Pyramids were built or the Flood wiped out all traces of man in the Euphrates valley. Successive civilizations rose and fell around the desert's edge: . . . Egypt of the Pharaohs; Sumeria, Babylonia, Assyria; the Hebrews, the Phoenicians; Greeks and Romans; the Persians; the

Muslim Empire of the Arabs, and finally the Turks. They lasted a few
hundred or a thousand years and vanished; new races were evolved and
later disappeared; religions rose and fell; men changed, adapting themselves to a changing world; but in the desert the nomad tribes lived on,
the pattern of their lives but little changed over this enormous span of
time.*

The Bedouin lived on almost nothing. What meager cash he did
scrape together came from transporting goods across the desert or selling camels to those who did. Camels were the mainstay of the Bedouin. They were transport, commerce, and, when they died, food.
Uniquely suited to the desert, a camel could go without water for five
days in summer and twenty-five in winter. For its owners, it provided
milk for food, dung for fuel, and urine for hair tonic or a bath to keep
the flies away from the baby. The Bedouins survived the ravages of
nature in tents woven by the women from the odorous hair of family
goats. Meat from their sheep was the staple of their diet. To increase
their life-sustaining herds, tribe raided tribe under sacred rules that
spoke of medieval forms of fidelity and warfare.** They had nothing
except a great sneering pride in who they were.

And then it all changed within a few short years. The Bedouins
became victims of mechanization. After the First World War, the
products of technology — cars, airplanes, and radio — undermined
the Bedouins' advantage in the desert. No longer could a Bedouin tribe
stage a raid against those who sought to control it and then disappear
unpursued into the desert. No longer were the Bedouin tribes able to
blackmail governments for their good behavior, levy tolls on travelers,
or extract tributes from villages. But above all, mechanical transport
destroyed the Bedouin economy. No longer was there any demand for
their only cash crop, camels. Yet the Bedouins still survive. Continuing to live in tightly knit groups of family and tribe, they drift in and
out of Saudi Arabia's towns and cities, an object of public scorn.

For centuries in hundreds of towns such as al-Hotghat, the mud-
walled settlement in Wadi Hanifa, the town Arabs were traders whose
only contact with the Bedouins was in pursuit of commerce. In the
coffee houses, there was endless ridicule of the Bedouin for everything

---

*Wilfred Thesiger, *Arabian Sands* (New York: E. P. Dutton, 1959), pp. 77–78.
**The system of chivalry is believed by some to have been carried to Europe from the Arabs
during the Crusades.

he did, including the way he prayed. Yet the emotional intensity of the desert nomad irrefutably imposed its ideals on the towns. Urbanized Saudis look back on the Bedouin and endow him with almost super-human traits that transform him into an idealized giant. But at the same time, Saudis of the city, especially the young and educated, delight in poking fun at the Bedouin, especially in the presence of a Westerner, and claim that they themselves never step foot outside the limits of the city. In the age of petroleum, the Bedouin is both the archetypical hero and comic buffoon of Saudi society. This conflicting set of attitudes, the Bedouin as hero and the Bedouin as fool, is another of the many conflicts within the Saudi psyche. Psychologically, the Bedouin rep-resents to the present-day Saudi what the Western cowboy folk hero represents to an American. And like Americans, the Saudis have cre-ated from the Bedouin, idealized as a desert warrior, a powerful pro-totype that influences their value system and their patterns of behavior. No matter how much the various geographic regions of Saudi Arabia may differ or how far a Saudi is removed from the desert, the Bedouin ethos is the bedrock of the culture.

Just how many Bedouins are left in Saudi Arabia is an open ques-tion. A study done in the early 1980s suggested that perhaps 5 percent of the Saudi population remains wholly nomadic. But this figure is grossly misleading. A Bedouin can no longer be defined by a nomadic lifestyle. The demarcation line between the sedentary and the nomadic population is fluid, for the Bedouins themselves can be nomadic, semi-nomadic, or settled. It is the strength of the Bedouin mentality that is important for the classification of a Saudi as Bedouin or a town Arab rather than the way he lives. Under this criterion, the Bedouins consti-tute a significant part of the Saudi population.

How well have the Bedouins adjusted to the age of development in Saudi Arabia? There are Bedouins working in the oil fields, in busi-ness, and in the bureaucracy, and there are Bedouins still herding cam-els. There are Bedouins living in the heart of Riyadh and there are Bedouins still living in tents. Most Western academicians claim that the Bedouins have not adapted well to modernization, are trapped be-tween their traditional past and the unknown future, and survive eco-nomically on government handouts. On one level all this is true. The Bedouins have been deeply affected by modernization. There is an ongoing struggle to merge the material benefits of modernization with the Bedouins' traditional lifestyle. Although they travel by plane now, the Bedouins still have a nomadic attitude about the amount and kinds of luggage they carry. When a Bedouin gets on an airplane, he checks battered suitcases, cardboard boxes, and his bedroll. As compartment luggage, he carries a cloth sack filled with food and his portable cooking stove.

For those Bedouins who still choose to live in tents, the clutter of development has moved into their camps. Before the oil boom, a nomadic family's spartan belongings consisted of coffee pots, cooking utensils, some rugs on which to sleep, and a few articles of extra clothing. The Bedouin family now has sewing machines, radios, insulated coolers, aluminum cots, and garishly painted tin trunks imported from Yemen. Abandoned campsites are no longer marked by the blackened stones of the campfire but are littered with punctured tires, empty oil drums, plastic bags, and rusting tin cans.

But on another level, the Bedouin psyche is less torn by development than that of the town Arabs. The Bedouins are so secure in their perception of themselves that they have an amazing ability to accept the things they choose from development and reject the rest. Every day I saw Bedouins manipulate their environment to suit their desires. A graphic example of this occurred along one of the valleys west of Riyadh. As we crested a rise on the roadless desert, Dan was forced to swerve our Nissan Patrol sharply left to avoid a dump truck creeping up the other side. Below, an army of trucks and heavy earth-moving equipment was loudly chewing at the desert floor between massive steel towers that would carry high power lines to villages throughout the valley. In the midst of all this construction activity, a lone figure stood serenely. It was a Bedouin, his leathery feet stuck in traditional sandals, his ragged *gutra* dropping down the back of his loose, soiled *thobe*, his staff clutched in his horny hand. Oblivious to the noise around him, he stood watch over his flock of Nejdi sheep, pulling at the spotty vegetation that had survived the onslaught of progress.

Of all the Saudis, the Bedouins are the least willing to interact with Westerners. There was seldom any banter between Bedouins and Westerners in the *souqs*, and Bedouin camps in the desert were armed fortresses closed to outsiders. Yet even if the Bedouins refused to accept foreigners, they did accept the most advanced medical treatment as a matter of course. One of the most interesting aspects of being associated with the tertiary care center for Saudi Arabia was seeing the cross-section of people who came through the hospital. Every day I could observe the Bedouins interacting with modernization on the most personal level. I often saw veiled women, their hands patterned and painted with henna, *abaayas* covering their loudly striped polyester dresses, squatting outside the door of the x-ray department, waiting for a CT scan. But it was the time I spent in an isolated Bedouin camp to celebrate a tribal member's recovery from a kidney transplant that confirmed in my mind that the Bedouins have emotionally survived the oil boom better than is generally acknowledged.

It was seven o'clock in the morning when those of us invited to the camp excitedly gathered at the gate of the hospital. All of us realized that this was special, for few Westerners ever had the opportunity to enter a Bedouin camp. Mohammed, our guide, arrived in a new Chevrolet Caprice, which he probably had purchased with a government grant to dig a well or with a bonus from the National Guard, where he served as a part-time soldier. With him in the lead, our little caravan proceeded north out of Riyadh, through Darma, northwest into the province of Gasim, on through obscure towns and settlements, and out into the high northern desert. After four hours, the Chevrolet abruptly turned off the road, seemingly in the middle of nowhere, and bounced across the rough terrain. As we crested a sandy incline, the camp spread out before us. A long, black goat-hair tent open in the front, through which goats were wandering in and out, stood at the center. In front a campfire burned, warming the traditional coffee pot. Scattered across the camp area was a collection of Toyota and Datsun pickups and a square canvas tent. As we pulled to a stop, old and young men, some with ammunition belts strapped across their chests, veiled women, and a multitude of children tumbled out of the tents to greet us. The men of our party were escorted toward the big tent while we women were separated out and taken to the smaller tent. There we were entertained by the camp women and all the children. In the ritual of hospitality, a small handleless cup of pale green coffee spiced with cardamom was thrust in my hand as soon as I was seated on a machine-made Oriental rug imported from Bulgaria. A boy of about four, thick yellow mucous running from his nose, shyly reached into an aluminum tin buzzing with flies and pulled out a sticky date, which he thrust at me in his dirty hand. I gingerly took the date, passed its sand-coated skin across my lips, and chewed its sweet meat. I was intensely curious about life in the camp. From where I sat I was able to look out through a slit where the sides of the tent joined. Directly in my line of vision was the men's tent. Through its open front, I saw the men sitting in a circle while a young man in his late teens moved from one to the other pouring coffee from an obviously new brass pot of the kind the Saudis imported in great quantities from Pakistan. Leaping out of this montage was a roll of paper towels imported directly from the West, which dangled from the side of the tent on a strand of rope.

By midafternoon, the lamb roasting in an oven made from an oil drum buried in the sand was done. The men lifted the meat up on heavy metal skewers and laid it on a metal tray that was at least two feet in diameter. Dining was reserved for the guests. When we were joined by the Western men, the Bedouin women disappeared. With great ceremony, our hosts set down before us a great steaming tray of lamb and rice. Only the choicest pieces of meat were presented. There were tender neck joints and large chunks of the leg, and lying on top of the wrinkled stomach with its fuzzlike villi was the skull with the brain encased. Loaves of flat Arabic bread were handed around, which we used to scoop up the rice and lamb from the communal plate. It was one of the best meals I have ever eaten. When we finished, the tray was removed and taken to the Bedouin men in the main tent. When they finished, their scraps went to the women.

The Bedouin women reentered the guest tent carrying piles of quilts and mattresses made from cotton wadding, which they rolled out on the ground so we could rest. With the goats temporarily shooed away, I reclined on a square bolster pillow and talked to the women hidden behind their veils. I asked the wife of the transplant patient how her husband happened to know about the availability of transplant surgery. Obviously puzzled about my lack of knowledge of basic facts, she said, "From his brother. He had a transplant at the Military Hospital last year." Sitting in that tent, looking out on the patient, his brother who had donated the kidney, and the young, bright, highly trained Western surgeon who was comfortably talking with them, I thought that out of the boom decade the Bedouins may have survived the best. Perhaps it is because in the tumultuous days of Saudi Arabia's awakening to the outside world, the Bedouins never doubted their superiority. When the Westerners came with their machines and their different way of life, the Bedouin was able to gather in a share of the new consumer goods purchased with government money. He could choose to send his sons to school and on into the modern economy, or he could choose, without shame, to remain what he had always been — a Bedouin.

Clustered in family or tribe, the Bedouins refuse to surrender to outside authority. Their support can be bought but their loyalty is anchored in the family. In the past, each desert family was alone, separated from the rest of society by the sparseness of the vegetation needed to support the animals on which their very lives depended. From this isolation in family units there developed over many centuries an intense feeling that an individual had no protection beyond that of the family. Of the various values the Bedouins have bestowed on modern Saudi Arabia, the primacy of the family is among the most important.

Saudis live in large extended families. It is one of their significant differences from Western culture that, for the Saudis, the concept of individuality is absent. A Saudi sees himself in the context of his family and, to a lesser degree, the tribe. His duty is never to himself but to the group. Within the family, there is a strong sense of patrilineal descent, for a man is considered to be a descendant only of his father and his paternal grandfather but never his mother or maternal grandfather. He belongs only to his father's group, which claims his entire, undivided loyalty. This is why the most sought-after marriages are first cousin marriages between children of brothers. By sharing the same grandfather, the all-important group solidarity is ensured.

There is within the family a rigid hierarchy made up of the male members of the family in descending order of age. The oldest male member decides what is in the best interests of the family and dictates the role each individual is to play in the group's general goal. For the individual, this determines whom he marries, where he lives, whether he pursues an education, and what his occupation is. I never became accustomed to the answer I often got from young Saudis, male and female, to my question "Are you going abroad to study?" The response was, "I do not know. My father has not decided."

This idea is anathema to Westerners steeped in the intense individualism of Western society. But to a Saudi, the absence of any independent choice is in no way perceived as doing damage to the individual. The docile acceptance of decisions made by the patriarch results from the way the Saudi family perceives itself in relation to the rest of the world. The world outside the family is viewed as an inimical place, where a family must be ready to defend itself even against its neighbor. In the last part of the twentieth century, even educated Saudis harbor a deep fear of the world outside the home. Well-to-do families live in houses clustered together in compounds that are walled off from the rest of the world. Modest homes and the new apartment houses are built with small windows that seem to shut out everyone but those admitted through the iron gate or locked metal door that stands in front of all Saudi dwellings. So insulated is the family that Saudi social life is markedly different from that of other Middle Easterners. A pattern of socializing among village women is absent. The men do frequent the coffee houses on occasion, but otherwise there is almost no social infrastructure for cultural reenforcement through festivals, dances, or drama. Socializing among Saudis is almost exclusively within the kinship group. As a result, without the support and approval of his family, a Saudi is lost. With no other alternative, a Saudi willingly pays the price for family support — the strict conformity to the group's demands.

The Saudis are obsessed with the protection of the family. I, like all Westerners, found it almost impossible to become a friend, in the Western sense of the term, with a Saudi. Acquaintances, no matter how long enduring, never seem to blossom into deep, intimate friendship. An educated Saudi may collect a few foreigners, Arab and Western, as minor diversions but not as true friends. Even with other Saudis, they do not often form close friendships. So much of a person's energy is consumed by the family that there is little left to expend on others. Only on rare occasions is a Westerner ever admitted to a family gathering (as opposed to women's gatherings). The few family functions that I attended were largely those of Saudis whose roots were in the Hijaz or the al-Hassa, or who had studied abroad. For most of the population, outsiders, even Saudis, are seldom invited into any family other than their own.

One of the characteristics of this group life is the apparent absence of a need to be alone. A Saudi is constantly surrounded by mobs of children and relatives. There is no privacy. It is as if there is an unspoken fear of being alone. I was forever amazed at the size of the entourage that surrounded patients in the hospital. It was the rare patient who did not have at least one relative staying in the hospital as a sitter, who turned the patient's room into a hospitality suite to entertain the stream of family members who came to visit. The Saudi family is the source of both excessive interference and complete security. For the Saudi,

every [family] member interferes in his life to steer or mislead him. He may not make decisions without consulting his near relatives and the senior members of the group. He lives in a compact organization in which everyone knows everyone else's business. His every utterance or deed goes through the censorship exercised by his group. He is constantly subjected to the value judgments that are passed on all his words and actions.*

Yet in all of its meddling, the family never leaves a member in need. Traditionally, the extended family system has taken care of the problems of the needy, the sick, the handicapped, and the aged. The family cares for the divorced or widowed woman and her orphaned children, as well as maiden aunts, aged uncles, unemployed nephews, and so on. A blood relative left in material or physical need is a personal disgrace to the rest of the family. And unlike in the West, nepotism is a virtue. Intolerable shame would fall on any Saudi who refused to give a job to a relative.

Beyond the family is the tribe. Today the strength of tribal identification is in a state of flux. Those who by attitude remain Bedouin identify with a tribe in which all members are in some degree kinsmen since they are descended from a common ancestor. But beyond the Bedouins, the strength of tribal loyalties among townsmen and urbanites varies widely. Active tribal affiliations do not exist for much of the population. Yet kinship remains such an important link in the structure of the society that, in the absence of any documentary evidence, it has to be assumed that the tribal mystique, if not the form, still exists for most Saudis. The tribe serves the same function as the family in ensuring group solidarity or striving for status in the community. And it is the foremost vehicle for revenge against those who would slight its honor. The tribe is, in many ways, an elaborate extension of the family unit.

Traditionally an individual's loyalty to the tribe is first and foremost based on the bonds of common bloodlines. The closer the relationship, the stronger is the loyalty an individual feels for his fellow tribesmen. A man instinctively supports his fellow tribesmen under any form of attack. These ties of loyalty were crucial in the past, since the family and tribe provided an individual his only protection. There was no central authority because organized government with a military force required surplus food, impossible in a subsistence environment. The tribe, therefore, was the most complex political structure that could be

---

*Raphael Patai, *The Arab Mind* (New York: Charles Scribner's Sons, 1976), p. 284.

supported by the sparse resources available. And within the tribe, group cohesion was the key to survival. Each member's commitment to group solidarity was the supreme value of life. A Saudi continues to support his kinsman in any quarrel with an outsider irrespective of the question of right or wrong. A famous Arab proverb says, "I and my brothers against my cousin; I and my cousin against the stranger." Group revenge in the event a relative has been killed is imperative because his death has caused each family member to suffer in the diminution of his group's strength. The need for relatives to avenge the death of one of their members carries over into village life and complicates the attempts of government to be the arbiter of justice. Even if a murderer is caught, sentenced to death, and executed by a governmental authority, the responsibility of the victim's kin to avenge his death has not been relieved. To fulfill the Arab proverb "Blood demands blood," the Saudi government permits the relatives of the victim's *khamsa* (a man's kin group, composed of all male relatives who are removed from him by no more than five male links) to publicly behead the murderer convicted in the courts.

There remain hundreds of tribes and subtribes scattered across Saudi Arabia. Abdul Aziz strove to integrate the kingdom's tribes into a national political structure. His early religious message was in reality a vehicle to knit Saudi Arabia into a single state rather than a collection of independent political entities. Allegiance was fickle. The desert bred into man the need to be free. In all matters of power and politics, Bedouin values were intensely personal. They recognized neither settled administrations nor national borders until tamed by Abdul Aziz through a combination of religion, marriage, bribery, and punishment. But the House of Saud has never controlled the tribes through nationalism or loyalty, only through rewards. Despite the House of Saud's ongoing campaign over the last fifty years to end tribalism in the interest of nationalism and Islamic solidarity, family and tribe remain a potent force in Saudi society.

The importance of each individual tribe is derived from the combination of its size, military power, geographic location, form of livelihood, character, orientation of leadership, progeny, and religious outlook.* Abdul Aziz used the tribal leaders, or *sheikhs,* as the major

---

*Among the most important tribes are the Aanaza, from which the al-Sauds claim to originate, Harb, Utaybah, al-Murrah, Shammar, and Mutayr, and the Qahtan, the largest in terms of num-

channel of communications and favors between the government and the people. During the reign of King Faisal, the tribes provided a form of local government. After the oil boom, tribal membership provided a Saudi citizen with *prima facie* evidence of his claim to the rights and privileges of Saudi citizenship. Membership in a tribe was valuable, for it gained a Saudi entrance into the local school system, gave him access to government health facilities, assured him, if he chose, the privilege of going abroad to study at government expense, and even warranted the issuance of a passport. The *sheikhs* still command a privileged place in Saudi Arabia's economic and political order.

When the oil boom hit, Sheikh Hamed Hassan al-Mutlaq combined business interests in gold shops and money-changing establishments in Riyadh with his traditional duties as leader of a tribe located south of Riyadh. Rejecting the rural life in the euphoria of the boom, he moved his wife and five daughters to Riyadh and housed them in one of the few architecturally well-designed houses I was ever in in Saudi Arabia. Located in a good but not the most prestigious section of the city, the house was a California contemporary, furnished in an odd combination of Oriental and art deco. The decor also contained the only example of the Saudis' past that I ever saw incorporated in the homes of the upper class. On each side of the wide steps that led up from the cavernous entry hall to the dining room were two magnificent old camel saddles made of dark, highly polished wood, with white sheepskins thrown over them. The *sheikh*, who was in his sixties and thus could adopt a somewhat relaxed style with foreign women, brushed aside my compliment on his saddles, saying, "The old ways." He was more intent on showing me the reception room in which he conducted tribal business. Leading me to the end of the entry hall, he threw open tall french doors that led into a separate section of the house. Stepping inside, he proudly presented a room that was at least fifty feet long and thirty feet wide. The high ceiling supported a massive crystal chandelier, and the floor was covered with a very large but not very good quality Oriental rug. The walls were completely lined with spindly chairs and overstuffed settees covered in brocade and trimmed with heavy fringe. In front of these were low tables, where the male mem-

bers. Important but slightly less significant are the Ruwala, Dawasir, Manasir, Munjaha, Yam, Ghamid, Shahram, al-Jahadilah, Juhaynah, Balt, Huwaytat, Bani Hajir, Bani Khalid, Quraysh, al-Rashid, Aajman, and Awazim.

bers of the *sheikh*'s tribe could place their tea and coffee cups and dispose of their date pits. Decorated entirely in red, it was a room worthy of an Oriental potentate. What transpired in this room located in an urban center of approximately a million people was not much different from what had transpired in the *sheikh*'s mud-walled village house or his tent in the desert. Members of the tribe come to the *sheikh* to settle disputes. They come to solicit his intercession with the royal family, as they did in Abdul Aziz's time, to get anything from a truck to a multimillion-dollar contract with the government. Most of all they come to be together, to reaffirm the ties of blood and tribe, to state their unity against outside forces.

For most of the population born before World War II, tribal affiliation has remained an important symbol, identifying their membership in Saudi society. But for the younger generation, the ambitious development programs and administrative machinery of Riyadh and the individual governates have drawn the tribal population and its leaders closer into the government's orbit. Growing numbers of Saudis have migrated away from the villages to the urban areas and, in the process, have migrated from the authority of the tribal *sheikhs*. Although tribalism certainly declined as a result of the enormous resources that accrued to the central government and the building of a bureaucracy, through which the royal family sought to dispense government benefits and services rather than through the tribe, the importance of various tribes remains visible. The House of Saud keeps the leaders of the Ahl al-Sheikh, the Alireza and al-Rashid, defined more as extended families than tribes, close to the king. The Manasir, al-Murrah, Shammar, Aanaza, Ruwala, and the Huwaytat are the bedrock of the military and political strength of the National Guard or are influential beyond Saudi Arabia's border into Syria and Iraq.

Among the reasons that the power of the tribes diminished after Abdul Aziz became king and even more so after 1973 is that tribal law can only work in conditions of anarchy and breaks down in conditions of stability. Left without the need for his tribe's protection, a man can more successfully reject its decisions. One of the great debates of the oil boom is whether tribalism has been permanently replaced, as some claim, by nationalism, or whether, as others claim, the Saudis will revert to their tribal roots if economic conditions no longer permit the House of Saud to deliver what the Saudi perceives as his just measure of the kingdom's wealth.

As important as the tribes remain, it is the family far more than tribe on which the structural foundation of Saudi Arabia rests. The family is the means by which lineage is maintained, social cohesiveness is reinforced, and the structural integrity of Saudi Arabia from the Bedouins all the way up through the royal family is enhanced. This splintering of society into kinship groups intent on retaining their group cohesiveness has always been the great challenge to any political system that seeks to weld together a kingdom.

Beyond the structures of family and tribe, the Saudis' Bedouin ancestors have left the modern-day Saudi with much of his value system. Soiled as the Bedouin may be by materialism generated by oil money and development, belittled as he may be by the more sophisticated urban dwellers, it is the Bedouin's idealized values of courage, bravery, hospitality, and honor that underlie all of Saudi society — urban, rural, and nomadic. Courage can best be defined by the ability to endure deprivation, withstand physical pain, or suffer emotional stress without showing signs of suffering. In other words, it is stoicism. Bravery, on the other hand, is a man's willingness to risk his life for the group. Both increase an individual's standing in the eyes of his peers, thereby reflecting the honor and strength of his group. Courage and bravery are regarded as important attributes among the Saudis, who, divided into families and tribes, are characteristically conflict prone. In the past, when the tribal wars raged, there was perpetual tension. A tribe that felt threatened needed, in turn, to threaten. Therefore, fighting and revenge both became highly esteemed values in the society. But the Bedouins for all their famed exploits were less than fearless warriors. Tribal warfare involved little more than hit-and-run raids. There was no shame in attacking a weaker group. Aggression in any form — with empty guns, broken swords, or sticks and stones — was considered manly. Retreat was always in order if the tide of battle turned, for there was no glory in fighting to the last man. Westerners seldom understood this. William Shakespear, a young captain in the Indian Army sent out by the British in 1910 to make contact with Abdul Aziz, was killed when he stood to defend the al-Saud's cannon while the rest of the Bedouin army beat a hasty retreat.

The major weapon in the Saudis' intertribal warfare was not arms but language. And language remains the weapon of choice. In reality, fear of violence is one of the striking characteristics of the modern-day Saudi. It takes spending some time in the kingdom to realize this. On the streets I saw hundreds of shouting matches in which the antagonists appeared to be ready to draw arms. At car accidents, the crowds of spectators who gathered quickly turned into participants. Clustered around the wrecked cars, everyone screamed, waved his arms, gesticulated, and yelled ominous threats. But I never saw one Saudi strike another. Just as ancient tribes hurled insults at each other believing that the insult, true or false, caused the recipient grievous harm, the modern Saudi still uses language as a mode of aggression. The government, like its citizens, carries the rhetoric of confrontation to great heights. Saudi Arabia will vocally condemn the state of Israel in the most vehement terms, but in the long history of the Arab-Israeli wars it has sent only its dollars into battle.

Like courage and bravery, the legendary generosity of Arab hospitality ultimately serves the one great goal of Bedouin life, the strengthening of the group. To extend hospitality increases a man's standing among his peers and reflects favorably on his family, bolstering its standing in the community. The function of hospitality is to add to the reputation of the giver, not necessarily to benefit the recipient. To increase his status, a Saudi will bear crippling expense in the name of hospitality. In the late 1940s there was a revered Bedouin who wandered the Eastern Province in rags because he had killed all his camels to feed his guests.

Hospitality is an elaborate ritual, presided over and controlled by the host. Like all rituals, it follows exacting rules. Although the Saudis who invited me into their homes were warm and generous people, as a guest I often felt possessed by my host. On entering the house, I was obliged to drink at least one but never more than three cups of coffee, followed by one but never more than three cups of tea. And the table of my Saudi host was always filled with more food than could be consumed in a week. The host, rather than eating with his guests, actually stands opposite them and watches their every move as they eat. I once attended a lavish dinner party at a *sheikh*'s house. The dining table seated thirty-two people and was shaped like a horseshoe. The *sheikh* stood in the middle, watching every bite that went into our mouths. As soon as one thing was eaten, something else was put in its place. It is an offense, a slight show of disrespect, to stop eating before the host allows dinner to cease.

The ritual of hospitality is a crucial part of a Saudi's hierarchy of values and extends to whoever is in his care. One night while I was waiting for a plane at the Riyadh airport, an Indian walked into the international departure lounge handcuffed to his Saudi guard. Fascinated, I watched as the prisoner was politely seated and his handcuffs carefully removed. Sitting comfortably, he was left alone while his guard went to get tea. When he returned with the steaming cups, the Saudi solicitously served his prisoner his tea and then waited until he had finished before he drank his own cup. The ceremony completed, the handcuffs were put back on and the man marched to his plane to be deported back to India.

A successful show of courage, bravery, and hospitality is necessary for any Saudi who means to protect his honor. The concept of honor, or preserving "face," is the most compelling characteristic of the Saudi psyche and the most difficult aspect of the Saudi personality for the Westerner to fathom. In Western culture, there is no psychological imperative that approaches a Saudi's concern about how others see him. Preservation of honor is paramount in the behavior of the whole society. Everything that a Saudi does is to protect his image. As a result, life is ruled by the tyranny of saving face.

Honor is a mystical concept that takes many forms. For instance, a man's honor demands that he have pure Arab blood. A man's virility, confirmed by the number of sons he fathers, is an important part of his honor. Hospitality and generosity bestow honor. A man is honored or dishonored by the type of work he does.

One's honor determines one's image. The key to saving face is the assiduous avoidance of shame. Shame is not to be confused with guilt. Shame destroys self-respect, but guilt, primarily because it is a matter between a person and his conscience, does not. While the burden of guilt is interior, the burden of shame is exterior, in other words, "What will people say?" In Saudi culture, shame, because it is exterior, is a much heavier burden to bear than guilt.

This oppressive fear of shame accounts for the difference between the Saudis' puritan behavior within the kingdom and their often outrageous behavior abroad. The reports of lavish sexual orgies indulged in by Saudis in London, Miami, Los Angeles, Paris, and even places like Denver is part of the folklore of the oil boom. The Western press turned out a stream of these stories each set in a different hotel and in a different city. The basic scenario was that a prince or wealthy merchant came to town, rented the entire floor of a hotel, set up an elaborate bar, expropriated room service, hired a bevy of call girls, and partied nonstop for a week, departing only after having spent thousands of dollars and leaving the hotel in shambles. Conversely, the strict code of deportment followed by this same Saudi at home is primarily calculated to impress those around him. A Saudi obeys social requirements not so much because he has a deep-seated belief in them but because to gain self-respect he must conform outwardly to the ethics of society. A Saudi's behavior is controlled not by the interior forces of right and wrong but by who is going to see it. To complicate his burden, honor is not individual; it is the collective property of the family. If one member of the family brings disgrace, it descends to everyone. Therefore, a male adult makes sure that his own behavior is impeccable in the sense of preserving outward appearances.

Few Westerners, I think, can truly appreciate what a terrible burden a Saudi places on himself. The old Bedouin proverb sums it up: "Even if I have to see the worm of hunger emerge from my mouth, I shall not debase myself." Like the proud Bedouin who commanded his family to tie his camel foodless to his grave so that it might soon follow him to the other world and save him from the social disgrace of going on foot to paradise, the Saudi builds all sorts of defenses around himself to make sure that he too will not be disgraced.

A Saudi's refusal to be humbled extends to the most mundane events of daily life. If two trucks, each driven by a Saudi, meet on a narrow street, neither will back up until a policeman armed with a night stick arrives to force one to give ground. Or if a Saudi who is sitting in his car blocks someone trying to get out of a parking space, he will not yield one inch until he is forced into a verbal battle by the driver of the other car and the assembled pedestrians. And the government, in the name of Saudi honor, engages in all sorts of games to ensure that the people and the country will not be humiliated. Its most effective game, of course, is to keep the foreign press out of the kingdom.

The relationship between the Saudis and their Western work force is greatly complicated by the Saudis' need to preserve face. Most Westerners find that the never-ending tension that ensues from the Saudis' careful protection of their honor creates difficult and often impossible working situations. To survive in Saudi Arabia, a Westerner has always to be alert to situations that might embarrass his Saudi employer. The Westerners who are most successful in dealing with the Saudis are those who are able to balance a tricky combination of flattery, subservience, and authority.

To begin with, a Saudi employer, loving exaggerated flattery, usually will regard intellectual honesty in the form of criticism as a personal insult. Although no one likes bad news, when a Westerner presents a business problem to his Saudi partner, he must first flatter the Saudi's business acumen before he delivers the unpleasant facts. And when these facts are laid out, they must be presented in such a way as to reflect on the incompetence of anyone but the Saudi. For there is a strong cultural inclination for a Saudi to place the blame for his mistakes and failures on others. Transferring responsibility to others makes it easier to justify a potentially embarrassing situation. Cost what it may, one must defend one's public image. Teachers who were brought in to instruct the Saudis in English found that most, like students everywhere, wanted to succeed without the necessary toil. The difference is that when a Saudi fails he never accepts the responsibility but blames it on "bad luck," the unfairness of the teacher, the difficulty of the material, and, in the end, the will of Allah. Teachers told me that students take great pains to hide their failures from their family and friends. Although this is a universal truth, it is the intensity of the need to hide shortcomings and failures in order to preserve appearances and save self-respect that sets the Saudis apart.

Subservience to the Saudi employer is an an unavoidable consequence of the fact that the Saudi controls the money with which the Westerner's expertise is purchased. A Westerner who wants to retain his self-respect as well as his job can politely engage in the ceremonies demanded by the Saudi's ego and still maintain his freedom by setting limits on the conditions under which he will provide his services. Maintaining a fine line between subservience and integrity, a Westerner has to be sufficiently humble but firm enough to win the Saudi's esteem. A Saudi respects a Westerner's authority if it is meted out in such a way as not to humiliate him. But a Saudi who senses that a Westerner is in a weakened position often delights in "getting him" if for no other reason than to prove his own superiority. The jail population always includes a number of foreigners who have failed to grasp the importance of keeping their employers' egos satisfied.

The need to preserve each Saudi's honor may be the single biggest obstacle to the development of a modern economy. Pride hampers routine functions, a condition that Westerners find exasperating. In any joint project, the Saudi's goal is to maintain his honor, while the Westerner's goal is to complete a task. These differing objectives create conditions for endless conflict. A Saudi dentist, one of the people trained during the boom, could not sit at his desk to write up his patient charts because his desk chair was on the other side of the room and he refused to engage in the labor needed to move it. When he was asked why, he replied, "What if one of my patients saw me?" In despair, one young Westerner told me that he had just lost a multimillion *riyal* contract that he had spent six months negotiating. Neither party would humble himself to go to the other's office or a neutral place to sign the papers. One of the most angry Westerners I ever encountered was an SRI consultant who was working on an important aspect of the petroleum industry for the Third Development Plan. He had spent weeks juggling figures supplied by the Ministry of Petroleum and Minerals. No matter how many times the data was verified or manipulated, it made no sense. After a stormy confrontation, the Saudi who had given him the information reluctantly confessed that the numbers were wrong, but since they had been signed and certified by the deputy minister they could not be changed without causing the minister intolerable loss of face.

It is, perhaps more than anything else, the decision-making process involving the Saudis and their Western advisers that results in so much disorganization in Saudi Arabia. Saudis are so obsessed with their pride that most postpone making a decision because of a terrible fear that it might be wrong. This characteristic of the Saudi psyche paralyzes decision-making and raises a serious question about the Saudis' ultimate ability to manage an economy that they have structured in the mode of the West. Decisions are delayed until options have disappeared. When a decision is finally forced, a Saudi tends to act on the impulse of the moment. There is little discrimination or sense of proportion in the action taken, or little consideration of the consequences. In my world at the Ministry of Planning, projects would be in limbo for weeks, waiting for decisions to come down from Saudi officials. And then suddenly work that should have taken a month at a reasonable pace had to be completed within a week. Time after time I saw decisions made in government and in business that had predictable consequences. As an example, a government decree might be issued denying Westerners the right to bring their teenage children into the kingdom. When recruitment then began to dry up, there would be utter surprise among the decision-makers, who would grudgingly rescind the ruling. This mentality is one of the major reasons why life in Saudi Arabia has such a rollercoaster quality about it.

Although the Westerners endlessly lament their relations with the Saudis, the Saudis suffer far greater psychological stress from their preoccupation with their honor than do the Westerners. The glorious oil boom was in reality immensely threatening to the Saudis. With inadequate education and skills, a tiny elite was called on in 1973 to manage the largest infusion of wealth and the most rapid change thrust on any country in modern history. Within a few years, this core of managers was supplemented by a new foreign-educated middle class that entered business or fleshed out the bureaucracy. With few exceptions, those who came home to assume high-level jobs still lacked the experience or sophistication to function efficiently in a world dominated by Western-style institutions and mechanisms. They had no choice but to recognize their inadequacies publicly and hire the expertise Saudi Arabia needed. A Saudi possessing any education rapidly moved from being solely a member of family and tribe, proud in his sense of who and what he was, to being a cog in a new economic system dependent on foreigners. In the Saudi psyche, the Westerner rose up as a person whose superior technological skills threatened to shame him. As a defense against humiliation, most Westerners were kept in a position of servitude. For his part, the Westerner looked on the Saudi not as a person struggling with his past and his future at the same time but as an arrogant taskmaster, intellectually and culturally inferior to his Western work force. As haughty as the Saudis are, there is blatant arrogance on the part of the Westerner who sees the Saudi as unable and unwilling to manage his own country and deserving of the high prices that the Westerner charges to do his work for him.

During the boom times, the Saudi's sense of honor was saved by the level of wealth pouring into Saudi Arabia. No matter how inferior or belittled he might feel, he retained his dignity through the copious amounts of money that he could squander on impressing his peers. The Westerner might know how to untangle the maze of international finance or be able to construct a chemical plant, but the Saudi saw himself as controlling a major share of the world's wealth. He could remain proud, master of his servants. As the boom ebbs and hostilities mount, both Westerners and Saudis remain trapped in the web of Saudi pride. Westerners are infuriated by it, Saudi men are paralyzed by it, and their women are imprisoned by it.

7

The Shackles of Sex

A CRUDE CARDBOARD SIGN hung over the outside door of the barren, unkempt departure lounge in the Riyadh airport. Bold letters in both Arabic and English scrawled across its face read: "Women and Families." Custom decreed that every time I took a flight in Saudi Arabia I was required to stand before that door. So once again I found myself huddled with a throng of black-veiled women. As we waited for the boarding call, their men prowled the perimeter of the group, barking orders like sheep dogs. At last the special bus for women arrived to ferry us to the airplane. When the guard threw open the door, I was caught up in the herd of women being stampeded aboard by the ever-watchful men. Over several years and innumerable flights, I never adjusted to this practice of being singled out and separated from the rest of humanity by reason of my sex.

This particular night, as the half-loaded bus lumbered down the tarmac toward Saudia Airlines' green and white L-1011, I reflected once again on the gross discrimination against women in Saudi society. I was jolted out of my reverie when the bus shuddered to a stop among the glaring beams of the giant floodlights and the frenzied activity around the plane. As soon as the bus door opened, the usual frantic scramble to board commenced. Suitcases, baby strollers, and bulky bundles of bedding, the ordinary baggage of a traveling Saudi, were tossed, scooted, and pushed as impatient men steered their women along. Gripping my hand luggage and gathering my long skirt around me, I was pushed by the crowd behind me into the noise of whining engines and the noxious smell of exhaust fumes. A Saudia employee, armed with a walkie-talkie in one hand and an airline schedule in the other, excitedly flagged us over to the boarding ramp and hurried us up the steps. Struggling on the ramp in front of me was a heavyset woman of indeterminate age. Her progress was stymied by her long dress, which she grasped in one hand, while with the other hand she desperately clutched the black *abaaya* around her for fear it might fall from her shoulder to expose her fully clothed body to the eyes of a man. Arduously she felt her way up each step with the toe of her pink plastic sandal, for the heavy veil over her face obscured the light. Suddenly all progress ceased as the shoe slipped from her foot, leaving her stranded. Her husband, standing at the top of the stairs, screamed *"yellah!"* ("come on, hurry up!"), never making the slightest move to help his wife, immobilized by the archaic dress code imposed on her by him and his fellow men.

Saudi women are victims of a set of rigid traditions that celebrate a godlike superiority of men and hold women responsible for their mystical honor. It is a society in which women are little more than chattels. Denied many basic human rights, responding time after time to society's demand to reproduce, haunted by the fear of a second wife, spending her time in the emptiness of shopping and tea parties, a woman exists to serve men. During my four years in Saudi Arabia, I watched with feelings of pain and anger how Saudi women live, I talked with them, I wrote about them, and I publicly suffered many of the same indignities that they suffer. Out of these experiences I learned to care deeply for these women, and, as a woman, I developed a deep empathy with them. In no other facet of Saudi culture have the shock waves of modernization struck as strongly as they have for women. And in no other area is the potential fallout from development so difficult to evaluate. On the surface women have reaped enormous benefits from the opening of Saudi Arabia to the outside world. Yet, beyond the new educational opportunities, women themselves appear unwilling to struggle for their stake in the new society. From a Western point of view, women show an alarming obedience to the basic presuppositions of the Saudis' traditional culture. Although there are pockets of resistance, the vast majority of women continue to accept their imprisonment at the hands of men.

Tradition commands this position of near imprisonment for women because Arab ethics revolve around a single focal point: the personal honor of the man. And the most important factor on which the preservation of a man's vaunted honor depends is the sexual behavior of the women for whom he is responsible, his daughters and his sisters. Re-

sponsibility for his wife's sexual behavior resides not with him but
with her male relations. Men live in terror that their women will commit a sexual offense. So exacting are the rules that a woman can lose
her sexual honor by doing something as seemingly chaste as sitting
next to a man on an airplane. And once lost, her sexual honor can
never be regained. Beneath this exaggerated apprehension surrounding
a woman's honor, in truth, it is the man's honor that is at stake. *Sharaf,*
or the honor of a man in his own eyes and the eyes of his peers,
depends almost entirely on the *ird,* or sexual honor, of the females of
his family. It is as if a man's honor is buried in the vaginas of his
women, for a woman's violation of her chastity is a violation of the
honor of her men. In a kinship culture such as Saudi Arabia, family
bonds are so strong that all members — fathers, brothers, cousins —
suffer from the dishonorable act of any one of them. Her indiscretion
is their dishonor. For the men to regain their honor, the offending
member of the family must be severed from the group.

Sensitivity to the *ird* is so great that an entire way of life has been
built around it. Saudi society is structured to keep a woman within
strictly defined limits that make it difficult if not impossible for her to
lose her sexual virtue. Beginning even before the onset of puberty and
continuing until death, a woman is protected by societal arrangements
decreed and policed by men.

The Saudis' preoccupation with female sexual chastity has become
an obsession, explaining many of the baffling social practices that confront foreigners in the country. The veil is the most obvious. There are
others. A traditional Saudi woman does not go out alone. She speaks
to no man other than her husband or blood kin. She seldom leaves her
house unless she has the permission of the senior male of the family.
She cannot travel outside Saudi Arabia without the written permission
of the senior male member of her family. The precisely circumscribed
role of each sex is so complete that Saudi society, in important aspects,
is defined by the way in which it treats its women.

Over the centuries, women were physically confined to protect their
chastity. Abdul-Wahhab's old house in Diriyah lays out in mud and
stone the conditions in which Saudi women of the eighteenth and nineteenth centuries lived. The house is perhaps a little more grand but still
typical of the basic design of the home of a well-to-do village dweller.
As I crouched through the low doorway that fronts on the dirt street
running through the settlement, the temperature instantly cooled by at

least twenty degrees as the thick mud walls absorbed the pounding rays of the sun. The bare simplicity of the old receiving room is much as it must have been in the mid-1700s, when travelers from the high plateau of the Nejd came to sit at the feet of Mohammed ibn Abdul-Wahhab. The men's area, fronting the street, is a rambling collection of meeting rooms, bedrooms, and storage areas where most of the activity of the house and all of the contact with the outside world occurred. In Abdul-Wahhab's time or even in the time of the second Abdul Aziz, I, as a woman, would never have been permitted there. These rooms were reserved for the men's exclusive use. Women were banished to their quarters in the back of the house.

Built around its own interior courtyard, which allowed the women and children to get some sunlight and air but screened them from the life of the house, were the rooms shared by the women of the house and their female servants. This was the *hareem*. Hollywood has imprinted on the Western mind an image of the *hareem*, commonly translated into English as "harem," as a stable of concubines. In truth, the *hareem* is simply the women's quarters. For the women of Abdul-Wahhab, this is where they lived their lives in seclusion. They were not allowed to shop in the *souqs* or venture out for a walk. As I stood in one of those cramped, windowless bedrooms, looking out into the walled courtyard, a feeling of utter depression washed over me when I thought about any woman who had been confined there. She entered as a bride and, except for the one day a year when her husband allowed her to visit the *hareem* of another family, left when she died.

That was the eighteenth century; what about the twentieth century? The basic layout of a family house was still very much the same in the period following World War II. Marianne Alireza is an American who married a member of one of Saudi Arabia's most distinguished families while he was a student in California. She was brought back to the Alirezas' old tabby house in the sleepy backwater seaport of Jeddah in 1948, veiled, and relegated to the *hareem* as any other Saudi wife. The family's living quarters were upstairs and the offices of the family business were downstairs. I once heard Marianne Alireza describe the wooden bridge with enclosed sides above the courtyard that connected the opposite corners of the house. The bridge's construction enabled the women of the family to pass from one wing of the house to the other without showing themselves to the men working below. When the women wanted to come into the garden, it took a massive organizing effort to remove all the men working there. Once the men were moved out, trusted family servants were posted at the doors as guards to chase away any man who might wander in unaware that the women of the house were present. Even following the oil boom, the Saudis continued to build houses that accommodated the separation of the sexes. The Saudi-style house that I lived in during 1978–79 had a large balcony above the entrance, on which the women of the house, separated from the men, could entertain their friends. A friend of mine lived in a house in al-Khobar that had two front doors and two living rooms, one for men and one for women.

The purpose of keeping women in seclusion is to protect their chastity and their value. For the worth of a woman in Saudi culture is as breeding stock to increase the size and the strength of her husband's family. Regardless of the education, travel, and career opportunities that came with the oil boom, a woman's life is still largely spent penned up like a valuable mare, her pure bloodlines protected from contamination until it is time for mating with a male who has been chosen by her family.

Women succumb to their lot largely because of the overpowering hierarchy of sexes in Saudi culture. Society decrees the privileged status of males and the inferior position of females from birth. A man's honor resides not only in the sexual honor of the females of his family but in the number of sons he sires. No Saudi experiences more joy than at the birth of a son, for a son is the supreme statement of a Saudi male's virility. The society's preoccupation with male children is so inbred that the birth of a girl often results in nothing but shame for the mother and anger for the father. A mother can become so upset by the birth of a daughter that she will refuse to see the baby for several days. The father's initial disappointment in a daughter is replaced at puberty by anxiety over whether or not she will violate the moral code, bringing disgrace on her father and his entire family. In all relationships between fathers and daughters, both affectionate and distant, looms the unspoken fear that she is a danger to the honor of her father.

The importance of sons goes back to the days of tribal war. Traditionally, when a girl married she left the house of her family and went to that of her husband's. Her offspring contributed to the strength not of her own group but his. This is why the birth of a son was always greeted with such jubilation. He would grow up to become part of the group and would marry, bringing a wife and more sons to his family. A daughter, on the other hand, was a liability. She consumed scarce food, could not defend the camp, and would eventually leave, taking her precious fertility with her. Over the centuries, it became imperative to a woman's position within her family and for her own self-esteem to bear sons. In some tribes still, a woman is not given a prestigious name until she produces a son. No matter how many girls she might have, she remains known as, for example, Nura bint ("daughter of") Hamid. But on the birth of a son, she becomes Nura umm ("mother of") Abdullah, or simply umm Abdullah, "mother of Abdullah."

The society's approach to and methods of rearing males and females is so different that there are no Arabic equivalents for the English words "baby," "infant," or "child." *Awalad,* or children, for example, is actually the plural of *walad,* meaning male child. The typical male attitude toward women as primarily sex objects whose destiny is to serve and obey men is instilled early, even before the weaning process begins. For instance, boys are breast-fed much longer than girls, often for as long as two to three years. And all breast-feeding of a boy child is demand feeding. In the *hareem,* I saw little boys who were old enough to speak in complete sentences walk up to their mothers and demand to be breast-fed. Within seconds, the child was gathered up in his mother's arms, where he blissfully lay stroking her breast as he nursed. From the Saudi women I knew, I suspected that rather than feeling victimized by her child the mother received great satisfaction from this long nursing period. Through nursing, a woman can fulfill the culture's demand that she give intensive pampering to her sons, and at the same time she can enjoy prolonged intimacy with a male, something she does not have with her husband nor will she have with her child beyond the age of about four.

The pampering of a male child is not solely the preserve of the mother. All of the women in the *hareem* participate. It is common practice for the women of the *hareem* to pacify baby boys by fondling their genitals. As with breast-feeding, this continues so long that the child carries into adult life memories of women stroking his penis. A Saudi boy comes to believe very early in childhood that women are there to provide for his pleasure. As a result, "The association of the mother, and women in general, with erotic pleasure is something that Arab male infants experience and that predisposes them to accept the stereotype of the woman as primarily a sexual object and a creature who cannot resist sexual temptation."*

---

*Raphael Patai, *The Arab Mind* (New York: Charles Scribner's Sons, 1976), p. 32.

Girls, unlike boys, are weaned by the time they are one to two years old. Within a few months of weaning, a female begins to internalize her role as a woman: a subordinate with little personal worth and subservient to the whims and desires of the men who will dominate her life. So ingrained is this attitude that by the age of four or five a girl requires little discipline compared to a boy and by eight or nine is already taking on the role of mother. In the *hareem*, it was fascinating to watch the little girls of all social classes compete with each other over the care of a young male child. Both the upper-class girls, dressed in lacy frocks, gold earrings through their pierced ears, and a hint of make-up on their faces, and the Bedouin girls, who wore dirty dresses of velveteen or polyester, behaved the same toward young boys. Each would pursue toddling little boys to caress them, brush their hair, or play with them, all the while looking over her shoulder toward the adults for nods of approval.

Ironically, even though girls experience a far less nurturing relationship with their mothers, growing up for girls is probably less traumatic than it is for boys. No matter how a girl is treated, she experiences a certain security from always staying in the woman's world. Boys, on the other hand, are forced to make the painful transition from the hovering, adoring world of their mothers to the demanding world of their fathers. They are two worlds that stand in stark contrast. In his mother's world, a boy is constantly catered to, humored, and generally kept happy by women both younger and older than he. In his father's world, which he enters permanently by the age of seven, he must conform to the hierarchy of males determined by the rule of seniority. This rigid social order is dominated by older men with younger men ranked by age working their way up the ladder, while lagging behind, forbidden to put a foot on even the bottom rung, are all women, regardless of age or position. A boy learns quickly to live up to his father's expectations, to pattern his life to his wishes, and to obey his commands. The male personality that eventually emerges reflects the strictly ordered society of the man's world in which it developed.

Women survive by totally placing themselves in the hands of men. It is in this basic relationship of master and servant that a woman's physical needs are met. Emotionally she draws her strength from other women, from her place in the family, from her image of herself as a prized possession, and, after marriage, from her role as a mother. Restlessness is repressed. Obedience is security.

The man's absolute authority over the women in his family is maintained through fear — the fear of physical brutality, the fear of economic insecurity, and, above all, the fear of being alone, severed from the security of the family. Girls are brought up to fear their fathers. When they marry, they fear their husbands. If they are widowed or divorced, they fear their brothers, brothers-in-law, or sons. There is always a man to fear and the fear is real. I once sat in the women's quarters of a modest house of a traditional family near Khurays, halfway between Riyadh and Dammam, nervously fingering the camera that I always carried with me. The presence of cameras around Saudis is always touchy, for few Saudis will ever permit their picture to be taken.* With great trepidation, I asked my host if I could take pictures of his family. He said I could photograph the children but not the women. With that injunction, the men left the *hareem* and I was left alone with the women and children. Putting aside my 35-mm Olympus, I propped a Polaroid camera on my lap while I studied the light and decided how to pose the children. The women stood at the door, looking out at the retreating men. When they were safely out of sight, the women with childlike exuberance repeatedly pointed at the Polaroid and then at themselves. Perplexed, I told them that the men had said no. Like giggling schoolgirls, the women posted the mother of four as a lookout to warn of the approach of the men. The others threw back their veils, merrily posed, and gestured to me to take their pictures. As each print came out of the camera, the subject snatched it and quickly stuffed it into the bodice of her dress. The Polaroid film was rapidly exhausted, forcing me to switch to 35-mm film. No one understood why no more pictures were appearing. When I explained that the remaining pictures would be dispatched to them as soon as they were developed, looks of what can only be described as terror crossed their faces. Fortunately, an Iraqi friend was with me who could translate the rapid and, to me, garbled conversation. After several min-

---

*For many years, Wahhabis believed that photographs violated Mohammed's injunction against the artistic representation of the human figure. It was not until Abdul Aziz began to allow himself to be photographed that the most religious among the Wahhabis became less fearful that the camera would capture their souls. Today a Saudi's refusal to have his picture taken has more to do with his honor than his soul. The camera summons forth great apprehension about looking foolish or appearing as an object of ridicule to a Westerner. Women are seldom photographed by anyone outside the family and then, with some exceptions in the Western Province, never without their veils.

utes, she said that the women told her that under no circumstances was I to send back any pictures of them. They wanted the pictures of the children but. if any woman appeared, even in the background, of any one of them, I was to throw it away. Increasingly puzzled, I asked why. My translator lowered her head and quietly said that if the men found out about the women's disobedience, they would be beaten.*

The repressive superiority of men and the servile inferiority of women is so impressed into the subconscious of both males and females that it exerts a profound influence on the overall social order. It is from the typical child-rearing practices combined with the highly structured social order that a girl enters adulthood with an image of herself as little more than a sex object, dependent on the whims and at the mercy of the men in her life. Consequently, women see themselves primarily as erotic objects to be pursued. This perception of themselves is reinforced by the *hareem* environment, where the various attentions of women cause little boys to develop a wholly erotic attitude toward females. After these heavy doses of sexuality, both males and females are then burdened with the sanctity of female chastity and the threat it poses to male honor. In an attempt to protect families from dishonor, parents and other authority figures ingrain in the Saudi child the concept of the sinfulness of sex, and the repressive atmosphere of the society as a whole constantly reinforces the idea. Out of these primitive attitudes about sex and sexuality, males and females emerge with their whole approach to life rooted in a warped outlook on sex and on each other. The woman's image of herself as an erotic object to be pursued, combined with the male's fantasy that all women are sex-craved creatures, results in a society obsessed with sex. Sex is such a taboo that it is, ironically, the prime preoccupation of the culture. As a result, the air is charged with a sexual tension that engulfs all women, Saudi and Western. Underlying even the most casual encounter between a Saudi man and woman is the assumption of intense and uncontrollable sexuality. Most Saudis actually fear that any man and woman of suitable ages will be irresistibly driven to having sexual intercourse even if they have never seen each other before and regardless of the consequences.

Yet the responsibility for a dishonorable sexual act is hung around the neck of women. In the Saudi mind, the sexual drives of women can only be controlled, and their fathers, therefore, protected from

---

*The prevalence of physical abuse varies widely according to social class. See Chapter 8.

dishonor, by a strict code of conduct that prevents both women and men from being exposed to erotic temptation. An intricate system of restrictions has been devised to protect society from indiscretions resulting from the threatening sexuality of women. The sexuality of the male is seldom discussed expressly, for the strong sex drive of men is socially acceptable. Instead, society decrees that women are to be policed to protect their chastity from their own sexual urges, and relieves men of the responsibility for the violation of a woman's *ird*.

The paradox is that in policing the freedom of women in their families, men impose an enormously heavy burden on themselves. They are victimized by their own system. As an example, women are forbidden to drive, as a way of controlling their movements. This throws the problem of logistics on the men. Men commonly do the grocery shopping. They frequently find themselves accompanying their wives, sisters, or daughters to the *souqs* or the boutiques. The man of the family must do most of the errands and take care of all of the family business. These are inconveniences. But it is the psychic energy that is expended to uphold tradition and to protect a man's image among his peers that so drains the energies of Saudi men. I once wrote a story about the strict prohibition on women driving in Saudi Arabia that gives perhaps more insight into the weight of tradition and male anxiety about the behavior of women than it says about the issue of driving a car. In response to male concerns, King Saud issued a royal decree in 1957 that banned women from driving. Nonetheless, women drivers are not illegal in the strict sense of the term. The operation of a motor vehicle is not included in the *sharia,* the Islamic body of law. It is tradition, a far greater force than the rules of kings, that prevents women from driving. The comments of the men I interviewed for the story would be comical were it not for the underlying tragedy of Saudi society. All freely admitted that there is nothing in religious law prohibiting women from driving. But all defended the ban, on the hallowed grounds of tradition. One of those interviewed was a Moslem scholar who resides in Mecca. "To say that for the woman to drive a car is forbidden [in the *sharia*] there is no evidence." And then he went on to say, "For a woman to drive in the present social circumstances in the kingdom, I will not advise it nor will I take the responsibility to do so." Captain Ghali al-Badr, the head of the Jeddah Traffic Bureau, confirmed that nothing in the legal code prevented municipalities from issuing a driver's license to a woman. But he was careful to point out numerous "practical" obstacles to women drivers. "Suppose she has a flat tire. Would she get out and repair it herself? No doubt that such things will force her to remove the veil from her face, and that does not agree with our Islamic tradition.'' He went on to discuss the problem that would be created by accidents or traffic violations in the strict social system where no woman is allowed to talk to any man other than her husband or a male relative. Captain al-Badr, in obvious distress, said, ''How do we bring her out of her car to take a report in order to prove her innocent or guilty?''

The strength of tradition and what it does to women in Saudi Arabia is perhaps best illustrated by what was said by the chairman of the sociology department of the King Abdul Aziz University. His comments confirm that the attitudes toward women are not confined to the uneducated class but permeate every social and educational level. ''Women driving in our Saudi society is undesirable for our social habits as it contradicts with the Saudi traditions.'' He had no solution to the transportation problem. He insisted that it is simply better for a woman visiting or shopping to be accompanied by her husband, brother, or son. He was liberal enough to admit that hiring a car and driver would be acceptable if the woman rode in the family car and not in a public conveyance such as a bus or a taxi. But the idea of a woman's riding in the same car with a nonrelative was strongly refuted by a religious scholar who said, ''To let women ride alone in cars with a strange driver, I will not accept for my daughters nor for anybody's daughter.'' So men continue to shepherd their women through life to ensure that their own honor does not fall before these supposedly sex-crazed creatures.

The whole dress code for women is designed so that a woman cannot sexually arouse a man whom she casually passes on the street. Women are layered with long petticoats under floor-length dresses with long sleeves and high necks. They are then cloaked in the *abaaya*, under which is a tightly tied scarf covering their hair, and finally veiled. Of all of the garments that a Saudi woman is thrust into, it is the veil that is the least understood in the West. Assumed to be a dictate of Islam, the veil is actually a product of the culture, not of the religion. In the Koran, Mohammed in his instructions on female dress said, ''And I say to the believing women that they should lower their gaze and guard their modesty.'' * Through the Prophet's teachings, a list of

* Sura 24:31.

parts of the female anatomy emerged that are *aurat,* things that cannot be shown. A woman's hair but not her face is *aurat.* Traditional Moslem women, especially in the Middle East, bind their heads in an array of scarves or knitted head wraps that conceal every wisp of hair. Even in Saudi Arabia, covered hair, not the veil, is the universal standard. But it is the veil that has stamped its imprint on a whole culture.

The origin of the veil in Saudi Arabia is unknown. Face veiling in the Middle East is recorded as far back as the Assyrians (1500 B.C.), followed by a brief revival about the time of the Crusades. The most accepted theory about the specific veiling practices in Saudi Arabia is that when the eastern coastal areas were under Turkish control, women of high social standing wore veils, probably to protect their complexions against the brutality of the desert sun. The desire for status — an overpowering emotional need among Arabs — decreed, therefore, that every woman wear a veil so everyone could lay claim to being upper class. Another theory is that when Bedouin tribes made war on each other and raided the livestock of the rival tribe, the women were veiled so that the beautiful ones would not be carried off with the goats. Others say Bedouin women were such fierce fighters in these raids that, by a code of desert chivalry, women were veiled as a form of identity and kept out of battle so the intrepid men were spared the risk of fighting them.

Regardless of the veil's origins, today few Saudi women are allowed by their men outside the house without a veil. The rule applies to women in all social classes, from those sharing the back of a pickup truck with shaggy sheep to those stepping from limousines at chic boutiques. In public, women lose all personality and individuality to become so many black blobs gliding down the street. Each is covered in black, her face masked behind impenetrable black gauze. In the eyes of a Westerner, the veil is starkly symbolic of woman's subservience to man in all areas of Saudi life. It sets the tone of a woman's confinement and states her total dependence on the male members of her family, who regulate her ability to function as a member of society.

To further protect the female's *ird,* Saudi society has devised an elaborate system of sexual segregation. By the age of seven, boys spend their time in the man's world, girls in the woman's world. All public facilities are segregated. There are boys schools and girls schools, men's waiting rooms and women's waiting rooms, a women's door and a men's door to the respective sections on public buses, with a steel wall separating the two. In Riyadh's Baatha gold *souqs*, some shops are reserved for women customers only, some for men, and others for "families." Christian Dior on Nassiriah Street has a men's department and a women's department, each with its own door and divided by an impenetrable wall. Even as a Western woman, I always had to be aware of my place. When I arrived in Riyadh, the Intercontinental Hotel had the only restaurant in the city that would serve women. Although other eating establishments gradually opened up (only to be closed periodically by the *matawain*), the underlying message to women was always there: Your presence is a danger to men. The few Western-style fast food places that began to creep into the coastal areas in the late 1970s tried to accommodate women by walling off a section of the dining area for their use. In the coastal cities, going to the Dairy Queen with a group of women was one of my few forms of entertainment. Because we were not allowed to stand in line with the men, our food was handed to us from the side of the counter, and then balancing hamburgers, Pepsis, and french fries, we parted the heavy drapes hung over the doorway and disappeared into the women's section to eat. I learned to accept these indignities with a certain equanimity. But periodically I went into a rage. I stumbled onto a Jeddah pizza parlor that had posted a sign outside saying, "Ladies are requested not to come inside this restaurant. If you want to order, wait outside and we will serve you."

This system of strict sexual segregation and the Saudis' desire for modernization are in constant conflict. Early in the oil boom, it became apparent that women as well as men were acquiring great wealth and property. Under the law of the *sharia*, a woman has the right to inherit property as well as retain as personal property the dowry she receives when she is married.* But a woman was immobilized in the management of her assets by her inability, among other things, to enter a bank. A tenuous truce between tradition and progress was struck when the first women's banks were opened in 1980 by the al-Rajhi Establishment for Currency Exchange, in a flurry of publicity about the forging of modernization within the sanctity of religion. A few months after the women's banks opened in Riyadh, I rode in the women's section of the public bus to the National Commercial Bank on Nassiriah Street.

---

* A woman does not share in her husband's property except through the legally stated share she can inherit. "Do not give the feeble-minded the property with which Allah has entrusted you for their support; but maintain and clothe them with its proceeds. . . ." Sura 4:2.

I found its women's bank tucked behind and to the side of the parent company. As I rounded the corner, a uniformed policeman standing with a Saudi in a traditional *thobe* curiously watched while I crossed the open courtyard that separated the bank from the street. When I reached the building and opened the heavy glass outer door, I was immediately confronted by the guard stationed in the small foyer for the purpose of repelling any man who might come on the premises. Silently he nodded for me to pass. I followed two black-clad women through an archway draped with heavy damask into the main part of the bank. Just beyond the drape, hanging like shrouds from a chrome hall tree, were the symbols of women in Saudi Arabia: black veils and *abaayas*. Except for the tightly closed and darkly curtained windows that protect the women from the view of men and the all-female composition of the staff, it looked like any other bank.

At the time that the women's banks were founded, voices of doom rumbled over the kingdom. An unnamed bank official said women's banks would "have dangerous reperoussions on society and women themselves, for they would be departing a realm where they find natural safety."* But by 1983, the regional manager of the western zone for the al-Rajhi Establishment was one of many who touted the progressive nature of the idea. "It's the Arabian custom that women don't go in public places where men are. This is the Islamic religion. The second thing is that women who are divorced or widowed and have their own wealth should not have to hire someone to run their businesses. With us, they can look after it themselves."** The al-Rajhi Establishment, like the banks, goes to extraordinary lengths to maintain the all-female character of its women's bank. A woman audits the female branches and the guards at the door are married to women working inside, so that papers delivered to the bank can be passed from man to wife and then on to the branch manager. As one bank official said, "We take great care in these things."

Most officials of the banks with facilities for women agree that many of their customers are attracted to their banks because they do not want their husbands to know how much money they actually have. All of the banks that offer services to women say that most of their customers' accounts are kept in savings. In the women's bank of the Saudi-

---

* *Saudi Gazette*, April 28, 1980.
** Quoted in Jane Alford [Sandra Mackey], "Saudi Banks Experiment with Branches for Women," *Atlanta Constitution*, November 6, 1983.

British Bank in Jeddah, an average of 80 percent of deposits are in savings. The primary reason is that women have little use for checking accounts since many shops and businesses will not accept a check from a woman. Businessmen who do accept checks from women often have difficulty in cashing them. One jeweler took as payment from a princess a check on the women's branch of his own bank. His bank refused to cash it. When he took it to the women's bank, he was refused admittance. Finally that ever-present guard took the check and passed it to his wife inside, who cashed it and passed the money back to her husband, who in turn gave it to the merchant. Most of the banks will not make personal loans to women, although they do make rare loans for entrepreneurial enterprises. And in spite of the rosy forecasts that greeted the establishment of women's banks, they have not proved profitable. Even the ones that are showing a profit admit that it is small. Most of the branches are regarded as "customer service" and have been written off as revenue producers by their parent companies. The profit problem appears to lie with the women themselves. It seems that Saudi women are hesitant about breaking out of their traditional role and still depend on men to do their banking for them. One official of the Saudi-Cairo Bank said, "It is amazing. We are doing all these things to facilitate things for them, but many still prefer to do things the traditional way and have more faith in the men's banks."

The reluctance of women to experiment with the few opportunities afforded to them is not surprising. Although on the surface it appears that Saudi women have made significant strides since the oil boom began, many of these are superficial. Education, banking, access to public transportation, and job opportunities are still rooted in strong traditional values. Women as well as men largely uphold sexual segregation. The severe shortage of women teachers for female students at the university level, for instance, has forced modern innovation to uphold ancient social practices. The universities do, at times, use men teachers for women's classes, but all such instruction is done via closed-circuit television so that the teacher and the students never meet face to face. The King Abdul Aziz University in Jeddah uses a microwave system of communications, which it considers an "improved media tool for the girl students, who cannot be taught by male professors in the normal face-to-face classroom method." *

---

*Arab News, December 12, 1982.

The long-standing prohibition against women working in Saudi Arabia has its roots in the strict segregation of the sexes. Under Saudi law, women may work only in capacities in which they can serve women exclusively — as doctors or paramedics, teachers, or in a few other special situations where there is no physical contact with men. There are currently approximately fifteen thousand women working in government jobs in highly restricted areas. One of the privileged few is a woman named Jameela. I met her at one of the endless women's teas that are a constant of Saudi social life. She is tall, with striking good looks still gracing her in middle age, highly intelligent, and commands a great presence. She is employed by the government as the supervisor of six female secondary schools in one of the kingdom's major cities. In describing her job, she told me that she visits schools under her jurisdiction to ensure that the government's education policy is being carried out and to solve problems. It is a middle management job and is hers, rather than a man's, because as a female she can enter the girls schools. With a heavy sigh, she said she has risen as high as she can go in her career. The next step would put her into a policymaking role in the overall educational system, which would require that she work with men. Reflecting the general level of frustration of the minuscule cadre of career women, she spoke with indignation about the absurdity of her situation. In conducting any business with her superiors (all men) she must either write a letter or speak to them over the telephone. A personal conference between the two can never take place, and her superior can never go into the schools under his authority because in doing so he would step across the sacred line of male-female exclusiveness.

Theoretically, a woman in present-day Saudi Arabia can hold any job in which she does not come into contact with men. The Ministry of Planning under Hisham Nazer, one of the few Saudis in government who favors using women in the work force, has prepared for women employees. A whole section of the ministry building has been set aside for females, properly separated from the areas used by men. It now waits for authorization from the ruling hierarchy to put women to work.

Even if the House of Saud wanted to significantly alter the position of women, it is almost powerless to do so. In the Saudi political system, public policy is, like women, hamstrung by tradition. And tradition all but shuts women out of the economic and political system. Traditionalists claim that they oppose women in business and politics not so much because of women's perceived abilities or inabilities but because they could not retain their chastity. The *majlis,* or audience with the king, the major avenue for the ordinary Saudi to take his grievances to the ruler, is closed to women because the king is a man. Traditionalists argue that women could never be allowed to vote because they would have to mix with men in the polling places. It is a flimsy argument that covers the basic attitude of men toward women. Always returning to the Koran to back up his assumptions, a traditionalist quotes Mohammed: "In truth, the woman, because of her femininity is tempted to abandon the path of reason and measure." *

While the government of Saudi Arabia proudly proclaims to the world that in a few short years it has moved from its medieval past into the modern world, events continue to confirm that the kingdom is still inextricably tied to its tribal origins.

Always alert to a good story, I was intrigued by rumors circulating around the hospital about a mother and a new baby who were being kept under guard by the hospital's security department. Making the rounds of my contacts, I soon learned that no one knew or was willing to tell me anything of substance. It was not until a year later, when I was able to surreptitiously obtain a copy of the security department's records, that I knew the whole tragic story.

A twenty-year-old unmarried Saudi woman, accompanied by her mother and a male relative, appeared at the hospital's emergency room complaining of severe abdominal pain. Her mother told the doctor that her daughter had been suffering from a stomach tumor for several months. As soon as the girl was examined, she was rushed to the delivery room, where she gave birth to a healthy baby boy. When her mother and the male relative, assumed to be her brother, were told that the girl had delivered a baby, they were outraged and demanded that the medical staff kill both mother and baby with lethal injections of drugs. Totally perplexed, the medical staff called into the melee a Western-educated Saudi woman who was a social worker at the hospital. Intervening on behalf of the patient, she persuaded doctors to tell the family that a "mistake" had been made. The child actually had been delivered by another woman while the daughter was in the operating room having the troublesome tumor removed. Seemingly calmed by the new information, the family left and the medical records were clamped under tight security.

*Patai, *The Arab Mind,* p. 127.

But the episode was far from over. The mother and her son, now strengthened by several other family members, returned. Among them was a man who had at one time been a medical resident at the hospital. He had gained access to the guarded records and reported to the family that the girl had, indeed, had a baby. New threats of death against the mother and child erupted, making it necessary to place hospital guards around the clock at the mother's room and the nursery. During the following days, various law enforcement agencies and government officials were dragged into the case. The office of the governor of Riyadh conducted an investigation and, it is assumed, would have liked to have quietly whisked the mother and child out of the country before the story found its way into the Western press, tarnishing the government's progressive image. But by this time the local police were involved at the insistence of the family. Unable to intervene in family issues, the government hierarchy allowed the wheels of tribal justice to grind on. Five days after the baby was born, the hospital surrendered the mother and child to the local police. The police, in turn, handed them over to the waiting family, which took them home where its own justice would be dispensed.

The punishment for fornication is the same as for adultery: death. Both are acts of sexual dishonor that reflect on the honor of the female's family. In the case of adultery, the female's family is much more damaged than her husband because it is her male relatives and not her husband who are responsible for her behavior and her dishonor. Therefore, it becomes their duty, not her husband's, to punish the adulterous woman. The mores of society simply do not force the wronged husband to carry around the shame that falls on the adulteress's family. For in the eyes of society, the wronged husband's honor has not suffered in the same sense as the honor of the woman's family. Her family has been shamed; her husband has only been smudged. He escapes the burden of shame because society considers it demeaning for him to admit that a wife's frailty could move him to any emotion warmer than contempt. If he does demand blood revenge from his wife's sexual partner, it is because his property rights in her exclusive sexual services have suffered irreparable damage. A traditional Saudi will likely kill his wife's lover, and the culture and the law will exonerate him.

The purpose of punishment for adultery by the woman's family members, like so much else in the culture, is to maintain group cohesion. In the patrilineal family structure of Saudi Arabia, the patriarch of the group jealously guards his control over the life of its members.

This right is not abdicated when a daughter marries. If the wronged husband were allowed to punish her adultery, the woman's family would, in essence, surrender control over one of its members to an outsider, weakening the control that the patriarch exerts over the rest of its members. In the Western view, a person can neither legally nor morally be held responsible for the acts of another. But in societies where kinship is as important as it is in Saudi Arabia, all family members suffer from the dishonorable act of any one of them. Killing daughters who have disgraced the family is known as *urf,* traditional local law. While Islamic law protects society from the sin of adultery, it is tribal law that restores the honor of the family.

The most celebrated case of the patriarch avenging the family honor was the July 1977 public executions of Princess Mishaal bint Fahd bin Mohammed and her lover Khalid Muhallal. The incident was graphically dramatized in the television docudrama *Death of a Princess,* which became a cause célèbre and dealt the House of Saud's carefully cultivated progressive image a severe blow. The princess was a great-niece of King Khalid and Muhallal was the nephew of General Ali Shaer, the Saudi ambassador to Lebanon. Few of the facts have been confirmed, and so the episode continues to whirl in contradictions. Apparently, the princess was married and the mother of a small child. Muhallal is believed to have been a student at the University of Riyadh. Unable to marry, the pair is purported to have fled from Riyadh to Jeddah, where they spent several days at a seaside hotel and then attempted to flee the country with the princess disguised as a man. Apprehended at the airport, Princess Mishaal was returned to her family. The head of that family was Prince Mohammed, older brother of King Khalid, who had renounced the succession in 1965. Mohammed was an arch traditionalist and a real power within the inner circle of the senior princes. As the king's senior brother and a man known for his temper and strength of personality, he possessed enormous political power within the royal family. For Mishaal's adultery, Mohammed insisted on his right to sever this offending member from his family for the shame she had brought on his house. To set an example to other women in the family who might be tempted into similar deviate behavior, Mohammed demanded a public execution. Horrified at the prospect of the foreign publicity that might result from such an action, Khalid refused and pushed for the executions to be carried out behind a palace wall, far from the public eyes. But the king was unable to resist the demands of his brother entirely. The punishments were finally carried out in a Jeddah parking lot instead of the public square and on Saturday rather than Friday, the official day for public executions. No public announcement was made following the deaths, as in state executions, and no identification of the victims was made. The whole episode might well have quietly joined the league of legends that surround the royal family if a British expatriate with a nose for money to be made in the exposé press had not happened along with a small camera concealed in a cigarette pack. As he took pictures, Princess Mishaal was shot six times in the head, while her lover was beheaded with five hacking blows to the neck, probably performed by the princess's husband or a member of her family rather than by a public executioner.

When British television aired the infamous *Death of a Princess*, the government of Saudi Arabia went on the offensive. I read story after story in the Saudi press that claimed the whole episode was an attack on Islam, the usual argument when something detrimental to the Saudis' image hits the foreign press. To demonstrate Saudi Arabia's displeasure with the British for allowing the program to air, the government asked the British ambassador, James Craig, to leave the kingdom on April 23, and he was not allowed to return until August 26. Various recriminations were meted out to British expatriates in Saudi Arabia. These ranged from the loss of contracts to the segregation of British citizens from the other passengers on incoming London flights. The British passengers were then forced to wait until everyone else had cleared customs before they were allowed to proceed. A deluge of anger and verbal abuse descended on all Westerners, who took it in stride while desperately trying to smuggle videotapes of the movie into the country. The government's ongoing public argument with the foreign press was that the punishment for adultery is clearly stated in the *sharia* and, therefore, the charge that the due process of law was not carried out in the case of the princess and her lover was unfounded. The point missed by the critics was that there was no need for a trial. It was tribal law and not religious law that had been invoked. Under tribal custom, Prince Mohammed as the senior member of his family had every right to kill any woman in the family who violated her *ird* in order to restore the honor of the family. The executions were a matter of his honor, not a matter of the *sharia* courts.

The struggle between Mohammed, the traditionalist, and King Khalid and the progressives in the royal family over Princess Mishaal is symbolic of the struggle over women in Saudi Arabia since the oil embargo brought the kingdom to world attention. The advances that economic development have brought to women are largely due to government policy that aims to replace the image of Saudi Arabia as the backwater of the Middle East with the image of a respected country that has managed to forge its future while preserving its past. It is an image that has been cultivated for Western, not domestic, consumption. How much an individual woman benefits from the programs of education and the few job opportunities depends on her family. It is the senior male of the family who decides whether or not a girl can sample the very limited freedoms now being extended to Saudi women. The family is sacrosanct, an institution with which no government will interfere. Despite the limited advances, women continue to be trapped in an exaggerated male mystique, sanctified by a culture thousands of years old and extending back centuries before the Prophet, that decrees that women exist solely to serve men. In the bustle of the boom days in Saudi Arabia, every day I saw busloads of young women winding their way to and from school. Sitting side by side, row behind row, the passengers were veiled and covered in the *abaaya*. Like draped, lifeless forms, they pursued an education not to open their minds or to prepare them for a career but to make them more suitable wives. For the supreme achievement for any Saudi woman is to marry and bear sons.

8

Mysteries of the Hareem

AS HE STOPPED the car in front of a large villa in the Sulaminia district of Riyadh, the driver barked *"henna"* ("here"), motioning for me to get out. Stepping from the car, I quickly crossed the narrow sidewalk and passed through the gate to the house. Ignoring the front door, I turned left and walked through the darkened garden toward a hidden side entrance. A servant, apparently watching for me, immediately opened the door. I entered a long hall that led directly to the inner recesses of the *hareem*. It was dimly lit by a single low-wattage bulb encircled in an ornate gold filigree fixture that hung by a frayed cord from the high ceiling. The distinct aroma of coffee spiced with cardamom led me on toward a large sitting room at the end of the passageway. When I entered, I saw that most of the other guests had already arrived for the all-women party, the standard form of female entertainment in Saudi Arabia. The women, with small cups of tea balanced in front of them, were reclining on large armless sofas covered in elaborate brocade and scattered with small pillows. Each woman was dressed ostentatiously in silk, satin, or organdy, which billowed into a large, full skirt covered with ruffles, sequins, or heavy metallic thread. The hostess, seeing me in the doorway, came forward to extend her greetings. Clasping me by the shoulders, she lightly brushed her lips across each of my cheeks in the traditional greeting before she introduced me to the other women. With the exception of a sprinkling of minor princesses, all were upper middle class and most were probably related in some way.

Another servant, this one carrying a heavy silver pot, appeared to pour green coffee into small, handleless porcelain cups embellished with heavy clusters of grapes outlined in thick gold leaf. Soon the hostess passed around expensive chocolates wrapped in pink or lavender foil and heaped in a graceful swan-shaped bowl. She was followed by yet another servant, carrying a large incense burner, about twenty inches high, made from teakwood and covered with deep, rich brass. When the burner was passed to Princess Nahela, who was sitting next to me, she fanned the sweet-smelling smoke toward her face with several sharp flicks of her wrist. Lifting her long hair, she held one side and then the other over the burner, allowing the smoke to penetrate each strand. In a far corner of the room, the women of a three-piece band were softly beating their drums and chanting the dull, repetitious melody of an Arabic song.

From time to time, one of the younger women rose to dance to the pulsating beat of the drums. Slowly and seductively she moved to the rhythm of the beat and finally ended her dance by writhing her body and making her long hair fly out behind her and then wrap around her head. Elsewhere two more women slowly danced together, while other women passively sat, sensually stroking their thick, ebony hair.

The evening wore on with conversation about jewelry, clothes, children, travel, obstetricians, and, most of all, sex. In the *hareem,* all of the prohibitions that hover over life outside its walls seem to dissolve as these otherwise puritanical women endlessly discuss sex in exquisite detail. But despite their erotic discussions, all of these women wore the characteristic look of the modern Saudi woman — the look of incredible boredom. For like most Saudi women, they had little to do but wait. A woman waits to be married; then she waits for the next time she will have a sexual union with her husband; then she waits for her next child to be born; and finally she waits for old age, when, relieved of her childbearing duties, she assumes a place of honor within her family. Saudi women have been profoundly shaken by the oil boom; but in no other segment of the population is it as difficult to judge what internal conflicts are present as a result.

Issues such as education, rebellion against the veil, and hostility toward the repressive attitudes of men are not often discussed. Women are so dominated by the expectations of family and the need for peer approval that feelings of rebellion, if they exist, are kept under tight rein.

The way a woman lives her life today depends largely on her social class. Lower-class women are almost untouched by modernization except in their material expectations. They live in ignorance because their husbands and fathers refuse to allow them any education. They continue to tend their families, exhibit fear of the men in their lives, and worry about their fertility. All that development has done for them is to give them some gold bracelets, a few baubles, and maybe somewhat better health care. Otherwise, life for them is much as it always was.

Upper-class women, including those in the royal family, can escape the conditions that the sexual system imposes on women by spending time abroad. I know one princess, midway up in the hierarchy of the royal family, who refuses to live in Saudi Arabia. Except for visits with her family in Medina, she spends her time in Europe and California, where she lives a Western lifestyle. When she is in the kingdom, she conforms. But even her conformity has the stamp of Westernization on it. Discreetly woven into the silk of her $700 *abaaya* and veil are the initials of Dior.

Wealthy women spend incredible amounts of time and money on clothing both in Saudi Arabia and Europe. Outside the kingdom they wear chic designer clothes, but within the kingdom they wear dresses that are a cross between those of Marie Antoinette and Scarlett O'Hara. Known by the expatriates as Cinderella dresses, they are stocked in quantity by every clothing store, including the designer shops, and sold at outrageous prices. I saw a dress at Riyadh's Center for Modern Design that was fashioned from greenish yellow silk. It had a tight bodice attached to a hooped skirt adorned with purple sequins, ribbons, and garlands of artificial flowers and sold for $3928. The wealthy also import Oriental seamstresses to make their clothes and often boast that they never wear a dress more than once. Even when the ports were the most congested and the consumer markets had almost no wares, the fabric shops were overflowing with chiffon and fine satins, gold and silver lamé, lace, embroidery, rhinestones, and beads to keep the newly rich women of Saudi Arabia dressed like circus ponies.

Other than shopping, upper-class women have absolutely nothing to do. The servants clean the house, cook, do the grocery shopping, and care for the children. One acquaintance of mine had seven servants to take care of a family of three. She claimed to be perfectly happy and pitied those of us who find fulfillment in physical labor. But are these women really happy? An English nanny in an influential Saudi family once told me that she left her job because of the acute depression she suffered seeing the emptiness of Saudi women's lives. Their days are long and the quickest way to get through them is to sleep. Few upper-class women rise before noon and some sleep until five in the afternoon. When they are not sleeping, they watch videotapes, most of which are brought in from the United States. As might be expected, there are drug and alcohol problems within the upper classes that extend into the palaces of the most powerful. An addicted woman is generally left alone unless her problem becomes known, threatening to create a political issue or cause embarrassment for her family. Such was the case of the rejected wife of one of the highest ranking princes, who came into the hospital one night under the influence of drugs and threatened anyone who got in her way with a gun. She finally collapsed and was taken away by a special contingent of police, never to be seen at the hospital again. Like other women with similar problems, she was probably sent abroad or kept at home under the watchful eye of trusted servants.

But the future of women in Saudi Arabia does not lie with the wealthy. It is the new middle class that has experienced the greatest psychological impact from development and it is there that much of the limited rebellion that is occurring is to be found. The women who most acutely suffer the pains of change are those who have lived abroad either as students or with their student husbands. Almost all speak a second and sometimes a third language. Returned to Saudi society, they float between two worlds. Since the King Faisal hospital was the most Westernized institution in Riyadh, women patients, dressed in traditional garb, entered the examining rooms of male physicians. Without hesitation, however, they removed their veils, allowing the doctor to examine them while they comfortably conversed in perfect English. Then they donned their veils again and emerged once more into the sea of black-clad women.

The current state of middle-class women in society is mixed. Like other women, most are relegated to the house in their traditional roles. Some are more liberated. Increasingly, with the support of their husbands, middle-class women are no longer wearing veils. (This is true more of the coastal areas than Riyadh.) Birth control is becoming more widely accepted. A growing number of urbanized women have jobs in education or medicine. And some women are going into business, primarily as shop owners. One of the few attempts to preserve traditional crafts in the kingdom has been undertaken by a woman in al-Khobar who sells authentic weavings and other handcrafts. With the approval of her husband, she has discarded her veil, hired a driver, and scours the countryside for Arabian antiques and Bedouin jewelry. She clearly states that she has been able to do what she wants only because she has the permission and support of her husband and father. Even with the liberties she has assumed, she still functions within her family. As it is for the vast majority of women, her willingness to grasp the opportunities that have opened up as a result of development depends on how damaging she perceives it to be to her family relationships. Those who do have jobs regard them as secondary to their primary role in a rigid family structure. For among Saudi women, there is a basic acceptance of the role religion and society have decreed for them, that of wife and mother.

The worth of women in the traditional Arabian tribal society was as bearers of children, who would supplement the strength and, therefore, the survival of the group. In the harsh environment of the desert, life spans were short, disease rampant, and infant mortality high. Tribes survived by raiding their rivals for their animals, pasturelands, and water. Protection depended on numbers, demanding high birth rates from fertile females. In religion, Mohammed coupled the tribe's need for a woman to reproduce with a set of stern dictates on a woman's position in Islamic society.

Mohammed's highly structured social order based on the family seems to betray an underlying bias against women. From a Western point of view, the Koran's specific references to women belittles them, especially in their relationships with men. In Sura 4:34, Mohammed said:

Men have authority over women because Allah has made the one superior to the other, and because they spend their wealth to maintain them. They guard their unseen parts because Allah has guarded them. As for those from whom you fear disobedience, admonish them and send them to beds apart and beat them.

It is through these claims to the superiority of men that the Koran ratifies the traditional roles of men and women in society. Men are to hunt and trade while women are to keep the house and tend to the children. Men are strong and free; women, because of their femininity, are weak, dependent upon men and available for their use upon demand. "Women are your fields. Go, then, into your fields as you please." *

---

*Sura 2:223.

In Islam, as with traditional society, woman's supreme task is to produce and care for children. In theory this should bless and strengthen her because it is through her that God has chosen to bestow children on men. Yet a woman is somehow tainted by the reproductive process. A woman's menstrual cycle condemns her as unclean, preventing her from entering a mosque. And menstruation is viewed as so weakening a woman that she is granted concessions in her religious duties. For example, menstruating women are excused from fasting during Ramadan.

Islamic theologians view the rigid roles assigned to each sex as a simple recognition that each sex is best suited to fulfilling specific functions in the life of the family and, beyond that, in the social structure of the Moslem community. As one contemporary Islamic scholar said, "Islam has given women the status which is most suitable to them and has provided them with the necessary care and protection which is due to them in order that they would be able to contribute to the life of the family and the life of society to the best of their ability." He went on to say that Allah has never chosen a woman as a prophet because the role He has assigned to prophets is best filled by men.

> . . . Each one of [the prophets] had a mammoth task which required him to give of his abilities and talents more than anyone can give to his work. To ask a woman to do that when she has to look after her family, is to assign to her a burden which is far too heavy. . . . What sort of an example of a happy family life would a woman prophet give if she were to abandon her family duties in order to discharge her message the duties of which are greater by far than the duties of a prime minister in a country like India or Britain?*

No matter how archaic the status of women appears, Mohammed did go a long way in giving women some protection over their status in the tribal hierarchy of the time. Women were granted legal rights. The Koran and the *hadith* both laid down rules ensuring women a respectable and dignified status that had been denied to them previously. The Koran explicitly states that Moslem women are not servants, chattels, or playthings. Their equality in seeking to serve God is guaranteed, and no ancestral Eve is held responsible for the imperfections of mankind. "We shall reward the steadfast according to their noblest deeds. Be they men or women, those that embrace the faith

---

Arab News, February 10, 1984.

and do what is right we will surely grant a happy life.''* What has been assigned to women to achieve a happy life is to tend the home and family.

Because ancient traditions have made a woman the repository of group strength and Islam has made her subservient to men and the protector of the family, Saudi attitudes toward marriage are vastly different from what they are in the West. The philosophy of marriage in the West emphasizes individual choice and personal fulfillment. In Saudi culture, the purpose of marriage is never the happiness of the individual but rather the good of the group and the perpetuation of its interests. A Saudi never expects to experience the romance and ecstasy of courtship and marriage that a Westerner does because love, if it develops, comes after marriage, not before.

Marriages are arranged. Although there is some breaking away from tradition, most marriages remain an alliance between families. The ideal union is a marriage of first cousins. By marrying a cousin, a man's daughter, instead of leaving his family to add to the population of another, becomes the wife of his brother's son, consolidating the two families and increasing the benefits to both. As a result of centuries of consanguineous marriage, the Saudi population is a vast laboratory of genetic defects. The problems extend from the lowliest peasant to the royal family. Congenital heart defects, hip displacements, an exotic array of endocrine abnormalities, and strabismus, a muscular disorder of the eyes, are a mere sampling of the range and variety of inherited disorders. Among the educated Saudis whom I knew there is an awareness of the problem of consanguineous marriages but little willingness to alter the practice. The prevailing attitude is that the benefits of marriage within the family far outweigh the risks.

Girls are considered marriageable from the time they reach puberty. The lower class marries very young. The ages for marriage and first pregnancy on Tarut Island, off the east coast, were published in a rare study on women that I unearthed from a library. In the group as a whole, the mean age for marriage was fourteen, with the first pregnancy occurring at sixteen. Out of 193 girls, 3 married as young as ten.** Among the Bedouins and the rural poor, a girl can be the second

---

*Sura 16:97.
**M. Akram Bhatty, M.D., Hishm al-Sibai, and Surindar M. Marwah, M.D., "A Survey of Mother and Child Care in the Saudi Community in Rabaiyah, Tarut Island," *Saudi Medical Journal* 4 (January 1983): 37.

of two wives, married to a man older than her father, the mother of several children, and suffering from severe depression by the age of eighteen. But according to the norm, most girls marry somewhere between sixteen and eighteen and boys anywhere from about sixteen to twenty, ages regarded as optimum for reproduction.

Girls on the marriage market are like prime breeding stock on the block. The right girl can be a valuable commodity on the market, for, like all good breeders, the groom's family is shopping for bloodlines to perpetuate the pure strains of his family. The bride's family, knowing the worth of its stock, will negotiate the best possible marriage contract in terms of money and family connections. When agreement is reached, a marriage contract is drawn up that clearly states what the groom is to bestow on the bride. This bride price is usually paid in jewelry. Before the oil boom, brides were adorned with heavy, low-grade silver jewelry peddled throughout the peninsula by craftsmen from Yemen and surrounding areas. Now it is primarily the Western expatriates who collect the Bedouin jewelry, which the Saudis have rejected. Today's brides receive 21 karat gold coins strung together to make breastplates that reach from shoulder to shoulder and drop to the navel, accompanied by a matching ring, bracelet, and large earrings. I never went to the gold *souqs* without seeing young men shopping for their brides. At the height of the oil boom, they came weighed down with grocery bags full of *riyals,* which they traded for gaudy jewelry. All were packaged in flashy velvet presentation boxes to be laid out before the bride, the bride's family, and all of the guests as testimony to the worth of the bride and the wealth of the groom. This jewelry becomes the exclusive property of the bride and is, in essence, her alimony if she is divorced.

In addition to perpetuating the family, the other purpose of marriage is to legalize sex. Sheikh Abdul Aziz ibn Baz proclaims that marriage shields young people from vice and the whims of passion that can lead them to all that is forbidden. "Marriage makes our young people lead a decent life".* Because no family gives a daughter in marriage for nothing, the poor can become desperate in seeking wives for their sons. Sheikh Baz has established a fund to supply gifts to needy Saudis marrying for the first time. The fund, his favorite charity, is supported by donations from wealthy Saudis. In 1983 it spent $21.2 million, with the *sheikh* making a public plea for several million more. Under the terms of the grant, any certified needy Saudi receives about $7200, which can be used for the bride price. The only requirements other than need are that both the groom and the bride are Saudis and that the *imam* from the mosque nearest to the groom's home will testify that the groom performs collective prayers.

In any marriage negotiation, a girl does have the right to refuse her family's choice, but that seldom happens. Because girls are raised with such a strong sense of existing for the good of the group and with such fear of the men in their lives, it takes an extremely strong person to reject the choice of her family. Therefore most girls docilely accept the choice of their parents.

A young Saudi woman sees her wedding as the affirmation of her maturity and the most important day in her life. Marriage is her reason for being, the ritual that will allow her to fulfill her ultimate destiny, that of mother.

Wedding celebrations, attended only by female guests, are held in the evening in the bride's home, or, for the wealthy, in the posh new hotels. A wedding can consume the net worth of the bride's family, for her father, to retain his honor, must stage a ceremony as elaborate as he can muster. I spent many hours drinking coffee and tea, nibbling from baskets of candy and nuts, and fanning myself with the smoke of burning incense as I waited for a bride to arrive. Especially among the upper classes, weddings are the occasion for intense competition between the guests over clothes and jewelry. The women preen and strut before each other like peacocks, eyeing what everyone else is wearing. The men celebrate elsewhere, casually sipping their own supply of tea and coffee and never seeing the bridal couple. The festivities having started about 9:00 P.M., the wedding party eventually arrives about 11:30. The bride and groom, accompanied by several of his closest relatives, slowly proceed through the guests, displaying to everyone how much the father spent on the dress and how much jewelry the groom bequeathed as the bride price. They then take their seats on a flower-decked platform to receive the congratulations of the guests. After greeting the last guest, they depart. Once the wedding is over, the quest to produce sons for the family begins.

The need for males to ensure the tribe's survival had a certain rationality in its day. Even now the need for one son as a form of social security in old age can be argued. But the male ego has intruded beyond even this rationalization. A man must father children to claim any respect among his peers, but to father sons in great numbers gives him honor and proves his virility. There are few scenes of Saudi arrogance that surpass a male strutting down the street followed by several sons, who in turn are followed at a respectable distance by his wife. And psychologically, Saudi men never let loose of the need to produce sons. Typically, a seventy-two-year-old man admitted his sixteen-year-old-wife of one year to the hospital's fertility clinic, obsessed with her failure to become pregnant. It is this tremendous desire for sons that puts such enormous demands on women's bodies and psyches.

Science has failed to penetrate the minds of Saudi males. Only the most educated and sophisticated men, whether they accept it or not, know that the sex of the child is determined by the male. The failure to produce sons is laid squarely at the feet of the female. A woman who has only daughters is not much better off than a childless wife. Divorce is not only a threat but often a reality and bears upon all social classes. An acquaintance of mine described accompanying one of the wives of a prince, highly placed in government, on a falcon hunting expedition far into the northern desert. During the entire two-week trip, the princess sat in her ornate, custom-built recreational vehicle and constantly talked about her anxiety that she had had five daughters and no sons. She was frantic to conceive. In the middle of the desert, she spent all her time with her dressmaker, who produced a new garment almost daily, and her hairdresser, who curled, combed and scented the princess's hair, in case the prince might come to her.

But as difficult as is the plight of women who are constantly called on to bear more and more children, it is the barren woman who really suffers. In the case of the middle class, it means almost certain divorce. The alternative, if the husband is particularly fond of his sterile wife, is for him to choose instead to take a second wife. This can prove more difficult for the barren wife than divorce. Because of her childless state, the first wife is humiliated in her relationship with her husband and the second wife, especially if the second wife bears him a child. In addition, she also becomes an object of pity within the female social circles, where women spend the majority of their time. Children are the major status symbol for a woman and one she uses to establish her position with her peers. At a tea one afternoon at an Arab friend's house, I observed a small porcelain-skinned figure huddled in the corner of a heavy, overstuffed sofa, her pale skin and high cheekbones highlighted by her heavy black hair, drawn into a soft knot on top of her head. She seemed cowered by all the chatter about children, one of the chosen topics of conversation at these women's gatherings. Soon she made her excuses, kissed her hostess on both cheeks, put on her *abaaya* and veil, and quietly left. No sooner had she closed the front door than my hostess began earnestly to explain to me with compassion that the woman had been married for eleven years and had never conceived. She had consulted specialists in the United States, had had surgery in Europe, and was now desperately taking high doses of experimental fertility drugs. Through all of this, her husband's sisters constantly nagged him to take a second wife, which he had so far refused to do. The hostess's final comment to me was, "It is remarkable that he continues to tolerate the situation. He must love her."

With the pressures to reproduce and society's general preoccupation with sexual behavior, sex dominates a marital relationship as it dominates all relations between men and women. Western women who suffer frequent and blatant sexual advances on the streets come to believe that Saudi men are sex-craved and thrive on stories that confirm this belief. There were many such stories. One jolly little middle-aged man proudly told his doctor that he had sex with all three of his wives every night. An eighty-year-old man continually sought treatment for his impotence. But perhaps the best account came from a nurse on the cardiac surgery ward. One evening while she was checking the progress of the day's postoperative patients, she threw back the curtain surrounding one of the beds and found a patient's husband indulging himself in sexual intercourse with his near-comatose wife.

Saudi men are obsessed with sex largely because it is so forbidden but also because male sexual prowess is among the highest values in the society. Although female chastity is paramount outside of marriage, in marriage sex is encouraged. In the marriage bed, everything is allowed. "The knowledge that nobody sees what is being done, and that therefore anything can be done with impunity, breaks through the repressions and inhibitions." *

But just as there is a dichotomy of strict female chastity outside of the *hareem* and a preoccupation with sex inside the *hareem*, there is an equally strong contrast between the frank openness about sex in general terms and the obsessive concealment of bedroom specifics.

---

*Raphael Patai, *The Arab Mind* (New York: Charles Scribner's Sons, 1976), p. 138.

The individual sexual habits of Saudi couples is more sensitive and private than in the West. But at the same time, the outright honesty about the pleasures of sex remain. H. St. John Philby, the Western confidant of Abdul Aziz, described how casually the king got up from lunch with his male entourage, excused himself to go to the *hareem,* and then returned shortly with no indication of embarrassment. Black-shrouded women cluster around display windows in the new shopping malls to admire and chatter about the prominent exhibition of lingerie in the style of Fredericks of Hollywood. And under all of the black garb, women sport underwear that belongs in a Paris brothel.

The general assumption about Saudi sexual practices is that for them intercourse is frequent and quick. The rapidness of the sexual act is certainly the norm among the Bedouins and in joint families sharing limited living space. Tents and communal living provide little privacy. Sex is almost a furtive act, usually performed from the rear with both parties fully clothed. How little personal intimacy is involved was demonstrated by a patient Dan once had, a Bedouin woman who appeared with large blue circles distributed over her body. Unable to elicit from the patient how long they had been present, he asked her husband when he first noticed them. Confused by being questioned about such a subject, the husband said that he never knew they were there since he had never seen his wife undressed. The practice of staying dressed during intercourse may explain why the absence of pubic hair is believed to be sexually stimulating. Bedouin women pull out their pubic hair with a mixture of sugar and water, while upper-class men shave theirs with expensive razors.

Since men place such importance on their prowess and women so highly prize their sexuality, illicit sex is almost bound to follow. But considering the severe punishment for sexual dishonor, where and how often women work out their sexual fantasies is a dark and dangerous secret. Saudi women do carry on discreet flirtations with men. One of the points made in *Death of a Princess* was that affluent Saudi women cruise the roads in their chauffeur-driven limousines looking for interesting men. It is true that, before it became a major transportation artery from the Arabian Gulf to Riyadh, the Dammam Road was the scene of princesses out for the sport of it, leering at men. A few affluent female adolescents boasted to Westerners about going to Bahrain, the island state off Saudi Arabia's eastern coast and the "den of iniquity" for the whole gulf, to find attractive men. And it is not uncommon for upper-class women to proposition foreigners working in the country. Foreigners are probably chosen because both the chance of being accepted and the chance of being caught are reduced when the intended partner of illicit sex is not a Saudi. I knew young Lebanese male nurses who refused to be left alone with a Saudi woman for a moment because they were terrified that the women's sexual advances would result in deportation at best or an appointment with the public executioner at worst. Whether or not these women carry through with their propositions or their quests for sex partners becomes another question. No doubt some do. During my first two years in Saudi Arabia, all public beauty parlors in Riyadh were closed because, according to rumor, they were being used by women for clandestine meetings with possible lovers. Boutiques are closely patrolled by the *matawain* to ensure that they are in the business of clothes and not sex. During my second period of residency in Riyadh, a woman was stabbed to death by her husband as she walked through the back door of a supermarket after meeting her lover. And three Filipinos were beheaded in rather obscure circumstances, the speculation being that they were sexually involved with some member of the royal family. Other than these instances, I saw little evidence that seriously suggested that Saudi women often venture outside the strict confines to which the protection of their chastity sentences them. The risks inherent in extramarital affairs for women are far too great for many of them to cross the line. Female flirtations and hints of sexual indiscretion are, in all probability, an arena in which women can play out their sexual fantasies. The men, on the other hand, have their own outlet for their sexual fantasies: the flesh markets of Bangkok.

In the mid-1970s, London was rampant with examples of the sexual binges engaged in by Saudi men. Soon the playgrounds of the rich spread out from London to the French Riviera, the Costa del Sol, and on into staid Switzerland. The Swiss, having endured the most recent onslaught of the ultrarich, ultranaughty Saudis, have developed a certain sympathy with anyone who strikes back. The courts once allowed a Swiss prostitute to escape with a murder sentence of only eight and a half years for castrating a Saudi diplomat with a pair of scissors. But Europe faded for many except the very rich, who could afford the steep fees for hotels and prostitutes. For the less rich, Bangkok plugged into the petrodollars by offering beautiful, demure, and submissive girls for a fraction of the cost of London or Geneva. So the stampede for easy sex moved to the Far East, and the Saudis' reputation for sinning in the excess went with them.

With their sexual exploits abroad, Saudi men are bringing home new and virulent strains of venereal disease. The rates of gonorrhea especially are increasing rapidly. Although no statistics are kept by politically astute health officials, gynecologists report that the incidence of venereal disease has increased dramatically over the last decade. According to one physician, when he came to Saudi Arabia in 1979 there was essentially no gonorrhea. Now he sees six to eight cases a month in an elite population. Among the victims he saw was the wife of one of the royal family's black sheep princes, who was infected with a highly resistant strain of gonorrhea endemic to southern Thailand. She was finally cured with massive doses of medication. She emerged from the ordeal with little emotional trauma, for venereal disease among married women is not, as yet, a sensitive problem for them. Few women really understand what they have or how it is transmitted and are, therefore, relieved of any social stigma attached to the disease.

The impact of a man's sexual exploits on a Saudi marriage is clouded, and the attitude of the offended party obviously differs from one individual to another. Extramarital sexual relations can be divided into categories, some of which do not fall under the all-consuming ban on adultery. Under the laws of Islam and the rules of Saudi society, a married man is permitted to have sex with his legally allowed limit of four wives plus concubines or women not under the jurisdiction of another man and still not be guilty of adultery. A man is guilty of adultery only if the woman with whom he has sex has herself committed an act of sexual dishonor. In other words, she is responsible for his sin. Although Abdul Aziz openly maintained a complete household of concubines, a Saudi man today is not likely to maintain a mistress in a house of her own. Most Saudis with mistresses use the sexual services of an Asian or African house servant, maintain a Western mistress outside Saudi Arabia, or, as the ultrarich do, staff their private airplanes with a whole crew of beautiful girls. Much of any wife's attitude about "other women" depends largely on whether or not she maintains her position of respect in her husband's household.

Beyond the unanswered questions about heterosexual practices is the other question: how much homosexuality is there? Behavior patterns, if viewed from Western cultural norms, indicate homosexual acts may be prevalent among a significant percentage of the population. Loving relationships between men, even strictly heterosexual men, are more common than loving relationships with women. Men seldom walk down the street together without holding hands or physically touching. The long hours of conversation that characterize Saudi social life take place only in either all-male or all-female groups. Greetings are always extended by kissing. How these physical relationships translate into overt sexual acts is difficult to judge. Men, in their long hours together, are not believed to engage in group sex, nor are their social gatherings an excuse for homosexual activities. Adolescent boys practice group sex but its incidence may be no more than in Western culture. The significant difference that distinguishes Saudi adolescent sex from that in Western culture is that masturbation is rejected in group situations and in private as psychologically repugnant to those who practice it. To the Saudi, masturbation is far more shameful than taking a prostitute because of its inference about a man's virility. The Saudis share with the Turks the attitude that an active homosexual role is compatible with virile masculinity. The performance of the active role in the homosexual act is an assertion of one's aggressive masculine superiority. But the acceptance of the passive role is demeaning because it puts a man into a submissive, female role. The same parallels can be drawn with masturbation. When a man has intercourse, even with a prostitute, he is performing a masculine act. When he masturbates, he is implying his inability to perform the active sex act, inviting the contempt of his male peers.

There are marked ambiguities regarding homosexuality in Saudi society. There is a fairly consistent opinion among the medical experts that I talked to that bisexuality is more common than it is in the West. But it appears that almost no men choose to live a strictly homosexual lifestyle. Although homosexual acts are expressly forbidden by the Koran* and therefore illegal, society gives little attention to the issue. There seems to be widespread acceptance of occasional sexual acts between men as being neither sinful nor seriously damaging to a man's image, as long as the act is performed in private — and only within his own society. It is when a Saudi man becomes sexually involved with a Westerner that the authorities intervene. During my time in Saudi Arabia, there were at least two incidents, one in Riyadh and one in al-Khobar, where a number of known or suspected Western homo-

---

*Sura 26:165.

sexuals were rounded up and deported on twenty-four-hours notice because young Saudis had been seen frequenting their living quarters. And like other forms of illicit sex, homosexual relationships are often carried on abroad.

Despite the various deviations, most sex stays within marriage, where a woman produces one child after another. Contraception was technically illegal until 1980, but every brand of European and American birth control pill was openly available in the pharmacies. The legal ban on contraception was the government's verification of Mohammed's words that Allah blesses the righteous with many children and of the culture's demand that great numbers of children be produced. The government never sought to forbid birth control, only to placate the traditionalists. Birth control is now becoming more widely accepted among the educated women but only after an adequate number of children have been produced. I remember sitting at dinner in a restaurant one night with a Saudi couple expecting their fifth child. The wife, fluent in English, sat silently while her husband pressed Dan about every form of birth control available. She remained silent because the decision to limit their family would be made by her husband. This is true even among Western wives of Saudis. An American I knew was allowed to get her first IUD only after bearing seven children.

The emotional attitude toward, if not actual rejection of, birth control is a reaction to the threat that any limitation of a woman's fertility poses to the cultural imperative to reproduce. The decision to have a Caesarean section is fraught with fear for the possible consequences it might have on a woman's fertility. Only the most educated and enlightened women or their husbands will permit Caesarean sections to be done. The possible sacrifice of the life of the mother or child is less threatening than the fear that a surviving woman might in the future be barren.

Since men and women who approach marriage carry exaggerated taboos on male-female relationships, have little to say as to whom they marry, and, once married, find their lives consumed with fulfilling the needs of their extended families, one might not expect to find many "good" marriages in the Western sense. In any society, however, marriages are good or bad as judged by that society's norms. Because of the low level of expectation in Saudi marriages beyond the production of children, most are probably neither particularly good nor particularly bad. It was my experience that the majority of Saudi women seem willing to accept marriage as a practical arrangement to further the interests of their families and to provide themselves with security. From the viewpoint of a Westerner, I saw marriage as another way of institutionalizing the inferior position in which a woman is placed by a society that deems her little more than a convenience for her husband. Close relationships, if they develop at all, often come after a woman has gone through menopause, removing from the relationship the burden on both the husband and the wife to reproduce. A woman who has produced ten children is content to be left alone by her husband. The husband, since his wife can no longer conceive, is released from his obligation to beget as many children as possible and can approach his wife as a companion and not as a sex object.

Old age may well be the most satisfying period of a woman's life. After a lifetime of serving men, she is accorded great honor by her family. Sons revere their mothers. Younger women in the household fall under the authority of the matriarch. Her husband can become solicitous of her needs I will never forget the emaciated figure that I watched in the King Faisal hospital chemotherapy department. Her hair was gone. She slumped in a wheelchair for lack of strength to sit. Periodically she moaned with pain. Her husband, a Bedouin, stood behind the chair whispering comforting words into her ear and gently stroking her thin hand. He stopped only to keep a light blanket tucked around her legs. At the other end of the social scale, King Khalid and his wife also enjoyed a warm relationship. To an outsider, they appeared to revel in each other's company. The king was, above all, a kind man, not particularly fond of his position, and his wife was a traditional Saudi woman almost untouched by either her status or the changes that had descended on her country. They exhibited a playfulness and humor with each other that I saw between few other couples.

But for most women, married life is spent in the company of female relatives, waiting to be summoned to serve her husband. A woman has almost no control over her own life. Her husband makes all the decisions for the family. If she lives in a joint family, then she is under the authority of her mother-in-law or the wife of the oldest brother. If she is the youngest wife in a joint family, she is usually designated by the other women as charwoman, scullery maid, and baby sitter for the entire household, with no defense other than to await the arrival of someone her junior. There is in the society a general, although largely unspoken, knowledge that various types of wife abuse are common. It could be claimed that the entire marital hierarchy is a form of psychological abuse, which Saudi women accept as the way society should be structured. Late in the oil boom, the government, in its murky decision-making process, assumed a position of trying to improve the physical and emotional well-being of women. Recurring attacks on how men treat their wives appeared in the press. Perhaps because it undermined the unity of the family, the practice of men going abroad on vacation and leaving their wives and children in the kingdom came under particular scrutiny. The message was most often delivered in the form of cartoons in the kingdom's newspapers. One showed a man clutching a suitcase overflowing with money, standing over his pregnant wife and three weeping children, saying, "Now that's enough. I promise I will take you on an enjoyable tour of the city when I get back from Europe after three months."*

The most direct criticism of wife abuse came from Dr. Abdul Aziz Muhammad al-Nahari, writing in the Arabic-language newspaper *Al Bilad:*

> I cannot understand how marital life can proceed peacefully when the husband adopts the role of the all-powerful, domineering, and violent tyrant. . . . He exercises his might over a feeble woman, who tries to indulge him even at the cost of her health, her self-respect, and her humanity. He treats her as a child who still needs educating despite the presence of her children around her. He scolds and humiliates her. He may even turn into a criminal and a savage to slap her for the most trivial reason. . . . He has no regard for her as a human being nor as a housewife who relieves him of the task of bringing up their children and shouldering domestic responsibilities. . . . The passive attitude of the wife in condoning the maltreatment meted out to her may be the result of a similar treatment in her own family before marrying or that she was weakened by the loss of one or both parents, thus succumbing to persecution and humiliation. The husband shamelessly exploits this weakness and vents his complexes on her by subjecting her to excessive maltreatment whenever he can.**

Along with abuse, the possibility of divorce is accepted as part of the marital arrangement. And if it occurs, it is not regarded as evidence of a failed relationship, with all the accompanying guilt as in the West. Women constantly live with the possibility of divorce because it is so

Saudi Gazette, July 19, 1983.
**Reprinted from *Al Bilad* in the *Saudi Gazette*, April 19, 1984.

quick and easy for the husband. A man may divorce his wife by simply pronouncing three times: "I divorce you, I divorce you, I divorce you." His only obligation, aside from staying with a pregnant wife until after the birth of the baby, is to convey to his wife any property agreed upon in the marriage contract to be hers. The children of any union stay with the mother until the age of seven, when they become part of the father's family.

In extraordinary circumstances, it is possible for a woman to divorce her husband. A divorce order can be issued by the local *imam* on the grounds of the husband's failure to support his wife, excessive physical abuse, the husband's refusal to have sexual relations with his wife, or impotence. A woman may not divorce her husband on the grounds of polygamy. Because divorce is an assumption in marriage, there is no social stigma attached to it for either a man or a woman. Therefore, it is the threat of a second wife, more than divorce, that haunts most marriages. Divorce, more common than taking a second wife, may well be psychologically more palatable for a woman than suffering another wife.

Plural marriage on the Arabian Peninsula is older than Islam. As a practical man seeking to enlist converts, Mohammed was hardly in a position to abolish the custom outright, especially since he himself enjoyed a total of nine wives during his lifetime. Practically, though, polygamy was the solution to the problem of large numbers of widows and orphaned girls. The Koran sanctions polygamy, but in terms that seek to discourage the practice. Rather than forbidding plural marriages, Mohammed limited the maximum number of wives allowed to any man at any one time to four. And polygamy is permitted only to those who can treat all their wives equally.

> If you fear you cannot treat orphans [orphan girls], with fairness, then you marry other women who seem good to you: two, three, or four of them. But if you fear that you cannot maintain equality among them, marry one only or any slave girls you may own. This will make it easier for you to avoid injustice.*

A man with more than one wife must provide each with material possessions equal to those of another wife or wives, and he must further distribute his sexual favors equally among them.

The injunction to treat all wives equally is taken seriously. I once

---

* Sura 4:2.

saw an old Bedouin man squatted down in the Dirrah gold *souqs,* surrounded by four veiled wives huddled in a circle. In his hand, he clutched a large roll of SR 50 bills, which he was distributing one at a time around and around the circle. When he reached the end of the roll, each wife grabbed her share, stuffed it in her plastic purse, and scurried off to spend it with her favorite gold trader.

Because of economics and a new attitude among educated urbanites that the practice of polygamy is archaic, the instances of multiple marriages are rapidly declining. Yet Prince Abdullah, currently next in line for the throne, marries and divorces with equanimity. Seldom does he fail to have his full quota of four wives. Someone in his court recounted that the prince has had more than thirty wives, so many that one year during the *eid* at the end of Ramadan, the prince rented an entire hotel in Taif for a grand family reunion of his children and former wives.

Second wives are still socially acceptable in the more Westernized classes if the existing wife is ill and unable to fulfill her sexual obligations to her husband. Or if the existing wife is unable to bear children, it is incumbent upon the husband to seek a second wife. King Fahd currently has at least two wives. Fahd's first wife has long been a victim of kidney disease, allowing him to take a second wife and still retain his image as a progressive.

The complex relationships in the triangle of one man and two or more wives defies generalization. Few women experience the husband's taking a second wife as anything but devastating. Multiple wives are most often intensely competitive for the attentions of their husband, although they can, on rare occasions, become close friends and confidantes. In most situations, the second wife never suffers the same level of emotional stress as the first wife. Second wives are spared the same sense of rejection felt by the first wife. And, for some women, becoming a second wife is the only road to marriage. Such was the case of the daughter of a *sheikh,* pretty, well educated, employed, and somewhat emancipated because she had lived abroad, who agreed to become the second wife of an older man. She had all she needed to make an excellent marriage until her chances were ruined by a car accident that left her lame. Her deformity denied her certification as prime stock. As the daughter of a *sheikh,* she told me, she could only marry a Saudi of equal standing or a member of the royal family. With her accident, her marriage prospects evaporated, leaving her no apparent alternative but to become a second wife. The marriage lasted only a few days, however. She was almost immediately divorced, leaving her desolate. She is now back with her family, watching her six sisters be married off one at a time while she sits wondering if she will ever have another chance.

I knew other women who developed severe psychosomatic disorders associated with a second wife. One was middle-aged, the first of three wives, who spent seven months bedridden with arthritis. The disease was not severe enough to incapacitate her, yet she refused to walk. In talking with her, I found that when she first became ill her husband promised not to take another new wife until she was well again. In another instance, the advent of a second wife not in her own marriage but in her sister's was enough to incapacitate a woman. Three sisters, all in their thirties, were married to three brothers. When one of the brothers took a second wife, his first wife adjusted to the situation but one of her sisters did not. She became emotionally paralyzed by the fear that her own husband might also take another wife. Consequently, she developed excruciating headaches and became extremely dependent on her husband. With him always at her side, she moved from one specialist to another, trying to find relief for her physical symptoms without ever coming to grips with the emotional root of her problem.

The status of women in Saudi Arabia was already a collage of conflicting values and practices by 1980. The pattern of competing forces in which women were tangled had been established. In the ensuing years, the conflict between the thrust of change and the pull of tradition has done nothing but escalate.

Much of the evolution in the position of women is due to the wide availability of female education that came with the oil boom. And education remains the field in which women have experienced the most real progress. Prompted by the late King Faisal's wife Iffat, the Dar al-Hanan and the Nassif schools for girls were opened in Jeddah in 1957. State schools soon followed, but not without the unremitting opposition of the religious fundamentalists. The opening of the girls school in Buraydah in 1960 forced King Faisal to call out armed troops to control protesters. Much has changed. Today schooling for girls has become widely accepted as a way of improving a girl's chances for a good marriage.* Education is open to any Saudi female whose family

---

*From the perspective of fathers with marriageable daughters, there was an alarming tendency for Saudis sent abroad to study early in the oil boom to return home with a foreign wife. In the

will permit it. By now even the arch-conservative Sheikh Abdul Aziz ibn Baz is calling for girls to pursue an education. It seems he wants every Saudi girl to be either an educated housewife so she can teach her children the Koran or an obstetrician/gynecologist who will uphold Islamic tenets by ensuring that female patients have female doctors. But he will only go so far in the emancipation of women. When the government announced that it was instituting a training program for girls to work in both the male and female wards of the King Khalid University Hospital in Riyadh, the *sheikh* said that a mixed staff would be inconsistent with the Koranic injunction "aimed at keeping the society away from temptation and corruption." *

The bottom line for any Saudi female seeking an education is the impact it will have on her primary responsibility: her role as wife and mother. Reporting on a graduation ceremony awarding diplomas in gynecology, the *Arab News* said, "The Saudi government was extending every facility to Saudi female doctors to carry on their duties in a way which does not affect their marital life." **

The education of women has had predictable consequences, which the government tries to contain. In the early seventies, the need for educated Saudis to fill jobs created by the demands of development won for some women the right to study abroad. It soon became apparent that university graduates returning home brought with them dangerous ideas about how women in Saudi Arabia should live. So the government, reacting to the concerns of Saudi males and the religious uprising in Mecca, announced in 1980 that "women university graduates will not be allowed to go abroad to study for Masters or PhD degrees in future. . . ." †

A second problem is where to put these educated women. With education, the boredom factor amplifies, presenting a menacing possibility that women will violate their sexual chastity for lack of anything else to do. Constructive outlets are being pursued. The government sponsors a group of charitable organizations for women, the Saudi

---

late 1970s, the government attacked the problem in two ways: regulations forbidding a Saudi to marry a foreigner and still retain his benefits as a Saudi citizen were enforced, and the number of university places open to women were greatly increased, to make Saudi girls more desirable as wives for the newly educated men.

*Arab News, April 18, 1984.
**Arab News, March 2, 1984.
†Saudi Gazette, March 4, 1980.

version of the Junior League. If a woman chooses a career, she is largely restricted to the fields of medicine, education, or women's banking or becoming an entrepreneur who deals only with women. With the government easing the bonds on female employment, what men fear most is that the entrance of women into acceptable areas outside of the home will be like the nose of a camel in a tent: eventually the entire camel will move in, disrupting the life of its former occupants.

A third problem rising out of the boom was that few women were left unexposed to Western culture. Through education, television, foreign travel, or simply the presence of Western women in the kingdom, a whole new way of life unfolded before the eyes of Saudi women. At least some are questioning some aspects of Saudi Arabia's system of sexual authority. There were recurring rumors in Riyadh that both King Khalid and later King Fahd were being besieged by complaints from Saudi fathers and husbands about the increasingly restive females in their families. Rebels continue to rise among the women of Saudi Arabia, but their rebellion is of their own design, to fit their own culture. No Saudi is an individual first and a member of his group second. After centuries of the most severe sexual oppression, women may complain but few will openly defy the existing social order. They do pursue some subtle forms of rebellion. The women's section on a public bus is a small cubicle in the back, separated from the men's section by a heavy metal wall. On the back of the wall hangs the fare box, out of the sight and reach of the driver. The Saudi Arabian Public Transportation Company estimates that it loses about SR 4 million a year because women do not pay their fares and no man can touch them.

The overt acts associated with social change are largely the rejection of the veil and of strict seclusion, because women see these as prescribed by Saudi culture and not by Islam. Yet those who successfully throw off some of their shackles do so with the permission of their families. Those who rebel directly against patriarchal authority most often fail.

I had a friend who as a nurse spent several months working with a twenty-two-year-old girl hospitalized with anorexia nervosa. Her problem began when she finished secondary school and her brother, the forty-year-old head of the household, refused to let her go on to the university. To placate her, she was sent to visit her twin sister, who lived in the United States with her Saudi student husband. Exposure to the West only aggravated the situation. When the brother demanded that she return to Saudi Arabia, the girl became so depressed that she spent a year and a half in a psychiatric hospital in the United States before being brought back to Saudi Arabia. In Riyadh, her physical condition deteriorated, allowing her to use the King Faisal Specialist Hospital as a refuge. Her hostility toward her brother increasingly forced her to reject not only him but her whole culture. Because she is so alienated, she has no friends and refuses to accept a Saudi husband either of her brother's choice or of her own. What she wants she cannot have: escape from her family. When I last saw her, she sat in a hospital bed, her large, sad eyes emphasized by the extreme thinness of her face, staring into an untouched plate of food.

The issue of women's rights, as with so many other issues rising out of modernization, has caught Saudi Arabia's rulers between two powerful forces. On one hand are men backed up by the religious authorities who desperately fear what development might do to the subservient position of women. On the other hand are educated Saudi women, many of them occupying positions of influence in the royal family, who are being buffeted by an inescapable whirlwind of foreign influences. Women themselves fear many of the changes that are occurring. But once alien ideas were let loose in the society, it became difficult, if not impossible, for women to determine just how far they wanted the modifications to their unique way of life to go. How firmly women have actually set forth on the road to change is a great unanswered question. Men remain unchallenged in their exalted position. Their superiority is continually reaffirmed in all major areas of Saudi life, as well as in such minor instances as a newspaper report on the mental hospital in Taif: "In November, 139 patients were admitted to hospital, only ten of them men."*

At the root of the Saudis' struggle with the new role of women is the knowledge that it was the introduction of Western ideas into this, the most sensitive area of Saudi life, that has so disrupted age-old traditions. When I asked a one-time deputy minister of Planning what he thought was the single most negative feature of development, he immediately said, "What it has done to the family." This was really a statement that the changing position of women is the most threatening aspect of development. Much of the growing emotional rejection of the West among Saudi men is, in reality, the rejection of women

*Arab Times, June 28, 1983.

and the role they might play in a new social order. The confusion, hostility, and fear of men about their women manifests itself in their relations with Western women. Saudi men regard Western women on two levels. I experienced both. When they deal with a Western woman as a professional, it is as if she ceases to be a female and becomes a man for the purposes of conducting business. This same woman can then go out on the street and angrily be pushed into a gutter by some Saudi who decides that she is blocking his movement on the sidewalk. There is a contempt for Western women inside the kingdom that causes Saudi men to view them as prostitutes unless the women draw firm lines between themselves and any social relationships with Saudi men. Western women in the kingdom are warned repeatedly not to socialize with Saudi men. In the first place, the government frowns on it, thus causing problems for the woman's employer. But the protection of a woman's own safety demands prudence. There are endless stories about naive Western girls succumbing to the fast cars, lavish presents, and intrigue associated with a romance with a Saudi. One young woman ignored the warnings and went to a Saudi's apartment, where she was entertained with contraband alcohol. After getting her intoxicated, her companion summoned a group of his friends by telephone, offering them the opportunity to gang rape a Western woman. It is as if Saudi men see Western women as posing a deep threat to them. Consequently, they act out their anger in gestures meant to humiliate the same women they fear.

Less threatened than men, educated Saudi women seem more willing to make contacts with Westerners and to cultivate friendships as opposed to acquaintances. This seeking out of Westerners is perhaps symptomatic of an alienation they feel from their own culture. It is the general assumption among Western students of Saudi Arabia that women are trapped between two cultures. What women are thinking is impossible to know; one can only guess. With the Saudis' great concern about their image in the eyes of others, the government will hardly allow itself to be embarrassed by studies of women's attitudes, especially if such studies are done by Westerners. And no man will allow his women to be questioned about anything. Saudi women themselves tend to tell a listener what they think that person wants to hear rather than the truth. All of these factors combine to make conclusions about attitudes among Saudi females difficult. With this qualification, it is my feeling that educated Saudi women, even the ones who have lived in the West, are not as trapped between two cultures as many suspect.

Saudi women enjoy great confidence from an unflinching belief that their culture is far superior to that of the West. They may not be as restive as some think. I have had countless Saudi women shake their heads and click their tongues at me as they told me how much they pity Western women because we lack the security that Saudi women have within their families. The great majority of Saudi women are willing to accept their position within society in return for the guarantee of security that their traditions provide for them. They do not deny that they would like to see some changes in their society, but they want these changes within the context of their own culture. They resist forced alteration in their lives prompted by nothing more than the desire to appear Westernized. As the fascination with Westernization increasingly wears thin, Saudi women may become as ready as Saudi men to retreat back into their own culture.

But whether they realize it or not, Saudi women have been subconsciously and irrevocably changed by Western images. The greatest impact of the West on women may prove to be television. Most urban women sit in front of their video recorders six or more hours a day, watching Western movies. Will adolescent girls brought up on a steady diet of contraband movies such as *Endless Love* and *The Blue Lagoon* still accept an arranged marriage? How will the distorted picture of Western sexual practices affect a society obsessed with female chastity? Will Saudi women be disappointed in what they perceive as a Western style of life and then become even more hostile to the Westerners who imported heretical ideas and practices into their society? These are profound questions as women struggle to define their place in a new order, an order not necessarily chosen but one that has become fused with the physical development of Saudi Arabia.

For those who have chosen to break out of the mold imposed on women, the struggle is hard. One brilliant early morning I passed a girl on the sidewalk who I knew had rejected marriage for a career in medicine. As she briskly walked down the street on her way to work, her long brown dress wrapped around her legs, barely exposing the top of her Nike sneakers. Her hair was tightly wound in the traditional black scarf. Perched on her head over the restrictive scarf were earphones, the cord trailing across her bust to the Sony Walkman hooked to her belt. Here was the transitional woman, searching for a new identity, trapped in a traditional society.

9

Putting the Saudis to Work

"EVERY MAN A DRIVER!" was the early cry of affluence in Saudi Arabia, as government grappled with the problem of how to rapidly distribute the kingdom's copious wealth among its sparse population. Part of the answer was to put every Saudi man behind the wheel of a car. Bedouins became taxi drivers in the bright yellow Datsuns provided by the government under one of its many plans to make sheep herders into entrepreneurs. Peasants obtained Toyota pickups as part of farm subsidy programs. Shop owners bought Chevrolets with interest-free business expansion loans from the same generous government. So rapidly were Saudis turning into drivers that the Toyota dealership in Riyadh was forced to build a corral where Saudis could jump off their camels and into their shiny new cars.

Most Saudis had never been behind the wheel of a motorized vehicle before. In the absence of any licensing procedures, anyone who was able to careen forward while lying on the horn became a legal driver. Thousands of such ill-equipped motorists poured onto the roads to spread terror and desolation. There was such havoc on the streets that revolution, pestilence, and plague were minor concerns for the expatriates compared to the perils of traffic.

The number of ways a Saudi could wreck a car were astonishing. Whole cars disappeared into construction ditches. Small Japanese buses, popular for transporting immigrant workers, became marooned on eighteen-inch-high concrete road dividers placed on the major thoroughfares in a vain attempt to keep drivers on the right side of the road. I once saw two cars hit the same utility pole within seconds of each other. The first car smashed into the base, bending it at a ninety degree angle. The second car, barreling down the street oblivious to impending doom, collided straight on with the end of the angled pole, forcing the slender metal cylinder through the windshield and on through the back window. There the car floated, suspended on the swaying post above the vehicle that had originally struck it. The driver, unhurt, still gripped the wheel.

It was no safer to walk than ride in a car. In Jeddah, police records showed that 22 percent of all accidents were caused by drivers running down pedestrians. There were 17,000 cases of blood money paid to the families of victims of fatal car wrecks in 1976, and by 1977 an estimated 80,000 wrecked cars were piled on the city's streets.

In 1978 Riyadh had traffic lights at only four major intersections. Rather than contributing to public safety, the lights became signals for the Saudis to honk their horns while they blasted through the intersection. The embryonic traffic laws only added to the general bedlam. Drivers turning left out of the left-hand lane were required to yield to drivers turning left out of the right-hand lane. And with only a minuscule police force, boys barely able to see over the dashboard of a pickup could speed down the streets with their black-draped mothers squatting in the back with the livestock.

Traffic was a visible symbol of the organizational demands that rapid modernization had thrust on inadequate structures. Because urban areas were hardly more than market towns before the oil boom, they had been patched together with insufficient funds, borrowed technicians, and no planning. During the early part of the oil decade, when money was not a problem, it was easier to build a whole city from scratch than to try to integrate existing services. Riyadh's electrical system was part British, part French, and part American, none of which worked in concert. The primitive telephone system that existed had to be replaced before it could be expanded, causing delays in service of up to two years in some areas. When I lived in Doctors' Villas #4, the entire compound had a single telephone line, with an extension in each of ten houses. The electrical resistance was so great that the bells on the phones refused to ring, making it possible to call out but impossible to call in. The rare Riyadh telephone book that existed listed numbers by the name of the landlord and not the tenant. This eliminated all foreigners since only Saudis could own property. The telephone numbers of foreign government and commercial establishments were listed but freakishly arranged. The foreign consultants were under "O" for "organizations," Western Electric, Seimens, and British Leyland under "C" for "companies," while the United Nations and the Ford Foundation were under "E" for "establishments."

As for billing, the telephone office in al-Khobar was prohibited from sending out bills because of the absence of an adequate mail service. So when a customer's bill was due, the telephone was disconnected. But the failure to provide mail delivery was not totally the fault of the post office. In defense of his department, the mail supervisor in Jeddah announced, "We have plans to start door to door delivery of mail in Jeddah as soon as street naming is completed." * In the meantime, mail was picked up in one location, letters were mailed in another location, and stamps were purchased at a third.

Many of these problems occurred because modernization in Saudi Arabia was not evolving slowly, building its own mechanisms by trial and error. Rather, the Saudis were jerked from a society organized around the family or tribe, in which people had little regard for time and where few demands were put on individual performance, and shoved into twentieth-century systems of organization that had little relationship to Saudi culture and that were managed by Westerners. After erecting grand buildings, the Saudis' Western managers stood aside to shake their heads arrogantly and chuckle as the Saudis, still accustomed to their desert culture, tried to learn how to use them. Public institutions placed colorful, graphic diagrams above toilets that instructed the user to sit and not squat on the seat. When public phones were installed on the street, the Saudis would drive up on the sidewalk and lean out of their car windows to use them. In hospitals equipped with the latest technology, the first Arabic phrase its foreign staff learned was "Do not spit!"

The kingdom was forced almost overnight to create institutions, mechanisms, and procedures in every area of government and commerce just to cope with the distribution of its money. So much was thrown at the Saudis as the country struggled to create the rudimentary structures of a modern state that it is remarkable that the whole society did not rupture. It did not rupture in part because the Saudis refused to move too far away from their traditional way of life. As a result, de-

---

Arab News, February 6, 1984.

velopment plans as envisioned by the leadership in the House of Saud and its Western advisers were enormously complicated at every turn by deep-seated values and by a religion frozen in the past.

The monetary and banking systems represent a case in point. Throughout the history of Saudi Arabia, whether in the issuing of currency or the founding of a bank capable of performing international financial transactions, the mechanisms created by government had to balance the need for modernization with the Saudis' distrust of new ideas and the teachings of Islam. Abdul Aziz's monetary policy was able to stay within the confines of Islam. But after 1973, as more and more financial institutions were born and matured, his successors ruled on the side of modernization. The Western composition of the management of these organizations and their measured deviation from Islamic teaching, necessitated by the international character of banking in Saudi Arabia, became increasingly entrenched as the boom progressed.

Considering Saudi Arabia's present position in the international financial markets, it is difficult to realize that the kingdom did not issue its own currency until 1935.* Before that time, the government operated on gold sovereigns, and Saudi families relied on the heavy, ornate jewelry of low silver content given to brides and on Maria Theresa coins. These large silver coins were originally an Austrian currency, with an established quantity of high-grade silver. They were popular throughout the Middle East, some claim, because they bore a profile portrait of the empress, not merely unveiled but displaying a magnificently full bosom in a low-cut gown. Maria Theresa died in 1780, but the coins continued to be minted, carrying the date of her death. Shrewd Yemeni traders now counterfeit the coins for sale to gullible expatriates, but when I came to Saudi Arabia a few authentic Maria Theresa coins could still be found in the Bedouin *souqs*. Squatting on the dusty ground behind one of Riyadh's more odorous slaughterhouses, I spent many hours digging through the clutter of artifacts and junk to unearth Maria Theresa's image, sometimes as coinage and sometimes worked into the now abandoned Bedouin bridal jewelry. As serviceable as the

---

*The first *riyals* were actually issued in 1928. They were thick, chunky coins, whose value rested on their silver content, a concession to the religious authorities who believed that Islamic law forbade coins to circulate at a value above that of their metallic content. In 1935 Abdul Aziz was able to secure permission to issue a smaller *riyal*.

Maria Theresa coins were in backward Saudi Arabia, a currency and a banking system inevitably came to the kingdom.

For the first thirty years of Saudi Arabia's existence, there were no banking statutes and no foreign banks. The financial affairs of Jeddah's small European community were handled through the trading firm of Gellatly Hankey. During the yearly *hajj*, when foreign pilgrims came into the kingdom, the Dutch Bank and the Banque de l'Indochin et du Suez were allowed to operate seasonal offices. But any banking business a Saudi had was done through the money changers in the bazaar. In 1938, in the aftermath of the early oil concessions, Abdul Aziz allowed the money changers Mahfouz and Musa Kaki to open the National Commercial Bank.*

The Saudis' resistance to banks, enforced by the policies of the House of Saud, was rooted in the Koran's injunction against usury. Not only were banks in Saudi Arabia forbidden to charge interest, but it was considered unseemly for a country in which Islam's holiest sites are located to enter into financial arrangements with international institutions that made their living from loaning money at interest. And with the Saudis' xenophobia, there was a genuine fear among the rulers that the sheer economic power of Western banks, with their worldwide assets many times greater than those of Saudi Arabia, would make them impossible for the House of Saud to control.

But with the resumption of oil production after World War II, these attitudes and practices had to change. In 1950 the Saudi Arabian Monetary Agency (SAMA) replaced Abdul Aziz's treasurer, Abdullah al-Sulaiman, and the chest containing the national treasury that he stashed under his bed. One of the first problems to confront SAMA was how to store the government's money. Wildly escalating revenues that were $56.7 million in 1950 would reach $338.2 million by 1955. SAMA's vault, which measured seventy feet by seventy feet with an eight-foot ceiling, was already overflowing with silver *riyals* and gold sovereigns. To cope with the logistics of wealth, paper money had to be issued. The question was how. It would be extremely difficult to convince the people, most of whom acknowledged the sovereignty of the person of Abdul Aziz but had no concept of a nation-state, to accept

---

*Only the third wholly indigenous bank to be established in the entire Arab world between 1938 and 1950, the National Commercial Bank made enormous profits when the oil boom hit because it had had the foresight to set up Western-style banking facilities.

in payment paper issued by some mysterious entity. As in all innovative moves by the government, the change was tied to religion. During the *hajj* in 1953, Saudi Arabia issued its first paper money, not to the Saudis but to the pilgrims journeying to Mecca. The *hajjis'* money, brought from their home countries, was converted to paper pilgrim's receipts that could be exchanged for silver *riyals* or converted back to foreign currency by either the pilgrim or a Saudi. Once the principle of convertibility of paper money was established, paper *riyals* were introduced and their use gradually began to be accepted by most of the people.

No additional innovations were demanded until after the oil embargo. When oil revenues deluged the kingdom in 1974, Anwar Ali, a Pakistani, was SAMA's financial czar. Among the earliest of the foreign advisers, Ali had been brought in from the International Monetary Fund (IMF) in the 1950s by King Faisal for the purpose of cleaning up the kingdom's financial mess, brought on by overspending. Abhoring risk and loving liquidity, he invested SAMA's funds almost entirely in government securities and corporate bonds in the West. Ali was among the first to recognize that if Saudi Arabia were going to live and to prosper in the outside world, then strict adherence to Mohammed's prohibitions on interest would have to be modified. Using the euphemism "return," Ali ignored the act establishing SAMA that expressly forbid the agency to collect interest on its assets. As petroleum income rolled into SAMA, its traders switched on their Telex machines and wired banks in the international money markets for quotes on interest rates. They deposited where rates were the highest. A philosophy quickly developed among money managers and princes alike: if collecting interest is sinful, then make the highest return possible on that sin. Ali's philosophy remains the cornerstone of SAMA's operation.

During the financial frenzy of 1974 and 1975, SAMA's headquarters were located in a rustic converted apartment house near the airport in Jeddah. Outside, an old woman crouched on the steps selling nuts, which she measured out of a palm wood bowl with a tin cup, while inside, SAMA's hard-pressed staff was overseeing the local banking system, issuing Saudi Arabia's currency, opening letters of credit, paying the salaries of government employees, and managing the government's pension fund. This group of ten men controlled Saudi Arabia's billions of dollars in foreign reserves and had only recently shifted from posting its books manually to using simple bookkeeping machines.

With the eyes of the international financial markets focused on Saudi Arabia, SAMA appeared as just one vignette of how ill equipped the kingdom was to absorb its wealth. The domestic economy had so few enterprises that there was nowhere to invest even a fraction of the country's income. Only a handful of Saudis had the education or training to begin to administer the largess. Nor had any plans ever been on the board that would have prepared Saudi Arabia for this harvest of money. The sudden surge of income caught the Saudis by surprise. Oil revenues per capita were less than $300 in 1970, a year in which the government budget had experienced a small deficit. That same year officials were predicting that oil income would grow by a healthy, but not disruptive, 54 percent by 1975. As it turned out, income shot up an astonishing 1,900 percent.

By 1976, two years after oil prices skyrocketed, the Saudis were still debating their proper relationship with international financial institutions. There were still only fourteen foreign banks in Saudi Arabia, compared with forty in Abu Dhabi and fifty in Dubai, two of the city-states making up the United Arab Emirates, which commanded only a fraction of Saudi Arabia's income. Most of the foreign banks operating in Saudi Arabia were overwhelmingly managed by Westerners. Smarting under this Western domination of the banking system, all foreign banks were "Saudized" (stock sold to private Saudi citizens) between 1977 and 1980. Although the ownership passed to Saudis, the managers and much of the philosophy remained Western.

The necessity for these banks as well as the National Commercial Bank to survive financially corrupted the spirit if not the letter of Islamic law. Using the same principle as SAMA did in managing its assets, banks gave their borrowers interest-free loans that carried a "service charge" that matched going interest rates. Demand accounts received no income, but time and savings deposits earned a fixed "commission" in lieu of interest, a rate that was very low compared to overseas deposits. This caused other problems. Offshore banking in Bahrain, protected from Wahhabi purity and spurred by the movement of Middle Eastern banking interests out of war-torn Lebanon, mushroomed. In February 1980, while Saudi banks were paying commissions in the range of 5 to 6 percent, depositors could earn 17 percent in Bahrain. Consequently, people were borrowing from Saudi banks at relatively low rates and depositing money in Bahrain to earn high interest. As a result, Saudi Arabian banks suffered a cash shortage for domestic loans. Through various currency manipulations and a lowering of reserve requirements, SAMA alleviated some of the competition. But the basic situation remained. Islam restricted Saudi banks from competing effectively in money markets by forcing them to keep their interest charges, under whatever name, low enough to prevent an outcry from the religiously pure. For the less religiously pure, capital went abroad to seek haven in high-interest-bearing accounts.

While the banks endeavored to make a profit in Mohammed's world of no interest, the money changers remained an important part of the financial system. With the oil boom, they moved out of the *souqs* and expanded their businesses to include the newly arrived Westerners. Money changers were often located in the neighborhoods, operating out of storefronts and avoiding the pitfalls of usury by charging a simple fee for service. Their convenience and favorable exchange rates were the keys to their popularity.

Checks were pioneered by the banks and money changers but did not gain acceptance until well into the 1980s. (Checks are still not accepted by merchants in the *souqs*.) Purchases had to be paid for in cash, forcing everyone to either carry large sums of money or make frequent trips to the bank. Considering that a hundred *riyal* bill (about $28) was the largest denomination, the bulk involved in large transactions could be staggering. When we bought our first car, Dan carried the SR 24,000 to the dealer in a large brown grocery bag. My salary from Stanford Research Institute arrived as a stack of blue and white 100 *riyal* bills sealed in a fat envelope. The King Faisal hospital also paid in cash until it was forced to go to payroll checks by the number of trucks required to move the payroll from the government treasury to the hospital.

Using the money changers, the Westerners converted most of their *riyals* into their own currency to send home. The remainder was deposited as operating cash. The al-Rajhi Establishment for Currency Exchange, the largest of the money changing operations, was typical of most businesses in Saudi Arabia during the 1970s — overcapitalized, with a poorly equipped staff. My branch was located in the basement of the hospital, a location that protected it from the *matawain* and allowed it to admit women. A cavernous free-standing safe, its black paint chipped by age, stood in the middle of the cramped quarters. The safe door always stood open during the workday, exposing bundle upon bundle of *riyals,* dollars, pounds, francs, lire, rupees, and so on, tossed on top of each other in random order. The Egyptian bookkeeper, cramped in the corner behind the safe, thumbed through his great ledgers, posting his entries by hand. A Pakistani clerk pounded out money orders on an old Underwood manual typewriter, while his assistant slipped thin sheets of carbon paper in his receipt books. The only piece of modern banking equipment that the al-Rajhi possessed was a digital money counting machine. When I presented a withdrawal slip, manually verified in the ledger books, the Saudi cashier flexed his fingers, reached for a stack of *riyals,* ruffled one end with a quick motion of his thumb, squared the stack, and loaded his machine. The lighted digits clicked in rapid-fire order, counting hundreds of *riyals.* When the machine stopped, the money was unloaded and slapped on the counter. Flush with cash, I was prepared to function for another week in Saudi Arabia's supercharged economy.

As the arduous building of structures and mechanisms proceeded, customs and traditions within Saudi society that did not fit the models designed by Westerners added another dimension to the development process. As an example, the concept of record keeping was alien to the Saudis, creating great frustration for the Westerners putting their systems in place. Despite the emphasis that is placed on family in Saudi culture, a Saudi seldom has a family name. A man is simply known as Ahmed ibn Mohammed ibn Abdul (Ahmed son of Mohammed son of Abdul). Only the most important and established families, such as the al-Saud, al-Zamil, and al-Sheikh, claim a last name in the Western sense of the term. Furthermore, a woman does not assume her husband's name but remains Jameelah bint Hassan ibn Ahmed (Jameelah daughter of Hassan son of Ahmed). As the country modernized, the absence of last names created a bureaucratic nightmare in everything from school enrollments to social insurance records. There are probably thousands of Mohammed ibn Abdullahs presently in Saudi Arabia, with more being born each day. And with the absence of any address or other secondary means of clarification, people were left to stand on their names alone. Perhaps the most crucial area for matching a name with the right person is medical records. In its early days, the King Faisal Specialist Hospital realized that in one respect Orwell's 1984 had arrived in Saudi Arabia ten years early. Everyone had to be identified by number and number only. Every person who was registered as a patient was given an identification number embossed on a plastic card. As far as the hospital was concerned, that person did not exist without that number. It was stamped on charts, prescriptions, braces, and even attached to babies. So trained did the Saudis become to the system that we once received a greeting card from one of Dan's patients who had painstakingly printed out his name in the Roman alphabet and appended his patient identification number to it.

As the waves of change pounded the Saudis, forcing them to make all manner of accommodations to Western systems and structures, the government insisted that "the distinguishing mark of the Saudi approach to development is that its material and social objectives are derived from the ethical principles of Islam and the cultural values of Saudi society." * Tradition and progress were engaged in a titanic struggle to maintain an impossible equilibrium. Western advisers designed mechanisms that would allow Saudi Arabia to function the way the Saudis believed they wanted it to function, and the culture, dominated by Islam, rose up to do battle against the kingdom's quantum leap into the future.

One of the ways the government sought to keep Saudi Arabia on the path of tradition and religious orthodoxy was to ensure that the calendar continued to conform to Islam. Saudi Arabia functions on the Hijrah calendar, a lunar calendar that has no correlation with the Gregorian calendar. Hijrah in Arabic means "migration," or, more descriptively, "flight." The first day of the first year of the Hijrah calendar corresponds to July 15, A.D. 622, the date that Mohammed and his followers fled from Mecca to Medina to escape persecution at the hands of the Quraish. Counting from this date, Saudi Arabia is now in the first decade of the fifteenth century.

The Hijrah year, consisting of 354 days, is divided into twelve lunar months. One day is added to the last month eleven times in thirty years to make some accommodation to leap year. Therefore, on a thirty-year cycle, the Islamic calendar will be roughly just over two years shorter than the Gregorian calendar. Since each year is approximately twelve days shorter than the previous year, the seasons do not fall in the same Hijrah months from one year to the next. Proceeding through the cycle of the calendar, the *hajj* can take place in the gentle warmth of winter or the savage heat of summer.

---

*Kingdom of Saudi Arabia, Ministry of Planning, *Third Development Plan: 1400–1405, A H., 1980–1985, A D* (Riyadh, 1980), p. 3.

The major difficulty with the Hijrah calendar is its imprecision.* Tradition holds that a month or a year cannot begin until there is a visual sighting of the new moon, confirmed by religious authorities. This means that Ramadan 8 could fall either on Tuesday, June 21, or Wednesday, June 22, depending on what day the new moon was sighted. Therefore, printed calendars and schedules must list future events and holidays as "tentative" or "subject to official confirmation." And it is impossible to accurately translate Gregorian to Hijrah dates in the future. While I was at the Ministry of Planning, I spent a week and covered an entire wall with charts in an attempt to devise some standardized way to convert the completion dates of contracts, using the Gregorian calendar, to Hijrah dates two, three, or four years in the future. In the end, every date remained tentative within three or four days since the date the new moon would be sighted escaped faultless prediction. Because Saudi Arabia has to live with the outside world whether it wants to or not, most paperwork carries two dates, the Hijrah and the Gregorian. Government documents, contracts, and the mast heads of all newspapers read Saturday, March 10, 1984 and Jamad Al Thani 8, 1404.

The growing nationalism that came in the wake of the petrodollars, rather than causing a drift away from the Hijrah calendar, led to a more rigorous enforcement of the Hijrah system. This made the dual Hijrah-Gregorian calendar circulated by large companies the most popular advertising gimmick among expatriates. The only problem was that it would be at least two months into the new year before they came out since it was never possible to begin printing until the new moon was sighted at the beginning of Muharram, signaling the new year.

The Saudis' high-priced Western advisers sought to bring order to traffic, they refined and expanded the banking system and other mechanisms under the constraints of Islam, and they worked around the calendar. These were largely structural problems. It was when working relationships reached into the realm of the Saudis' psyche and values that the partnership bogged down. Beyond their inborn Bedouin arrogance, it was the Saudis' use of language, their concept of time, and their lack of organization that so frustrated their Western work force.

---

*Saudi Arabia is the only place I have ever worked where I checked the phase of the moon to see how long it was until payday.

Much of this frustration rose from how the Saudis and the Westerners talked to each other.

The role that formal poetry, prose, and oratory play in Saudi culture is totally alien to Western culture. Traditionally there is a strong attachment to language, originating in the spartan life of the Bedouin. The Bedouin poet was the repository of tribal history. He expressed the ideals of manliness, gallantry, bravery, loyalty, generosity, and independence of spirit. Through his beautiful language, he spoke the oral folk literature, the stories, proverbs, and genealogy of his people. Used with great virtuosity even by the illiterate, the richness of Arabic combined with its cadence transforms the language into an artistic instrument that provides great emotional satisfaction to both the speaker and the listener. The Saudis are so enamored by language that poetry can arise in the most curious situations. An old Bedouin man suffering from a chronic disease appeared in Dan's clinic, where he was examined and sent to the laboratory for tests. After being taken through the perplexing world of blood samples, x-rays, and unveiled Western women in white uniforms, he was told to report back to the hospital in a week for the results and medication. When he returned, he entered the examining room, paused at the door, and launched into a lengthy, perfectly constructed poem. Through verse after verse, he rocked back and forth as he recounted how he had been plagued by this dreadful disease for twenty years. Praise be to Allah, he came to the famous King Faisal Specialist Hospital. Now, a week later, he lamented he was not yet cured.

Among the Saudis, the skilled use of language commands the same prestige as virility. Language in the most mundane of circumstances becomes lofty and embellished with hyperbole. For example, the *Arab News*, reporting on an inspection of Jeddah made by an official of the Arabian Cleaning Enterprise, the company that collects trash, junk, and dead cats from the streets of the city, waxed eloquently: "Melk said that his drive during his brief stay through the most modern King Abdul Aziz International Airport and the lovely, modern, clean city amid the breathtaking architectural beauty of buildings, residential and commercial complexes and mosques, well-planned wide streets and gardens, was a unique experience to be remembered for a long time."*

Because of his love of language, a Saudi is swayed more by words

---

Arab News, March 15, 1984.

than ideas, and more by ideas than facts. The cultural propensity to say what sounds good, not what is necessarily true, causes untold problems for Westerners in every area, from foreign policy to simple contracts. For the Westerner, a simple yes or no is a definitive statement; for the Saudi, conditioned by exaggeration and overassertion, the understanding of a brief, simple statement is beyond his experience and capacity. The single word "yes" means to the Saudi only "perhaps." I saw many novice Western businessmen come out of meetings with Saudis believing that they had a contract, only to find that when it was time to sign the papers the Saudis' "yes" to the terms had only meant that they could still be discussed. Or as one weary businessman so aptly put it, "A signed contract is the signal for negotiations to begin." What many Westerners never learned was that a Saudi's eloquent exaggerations were never meant to be taken literally. Nor did the Saudi ever believe that what he said for effect was to be interpreted as fact.

Because the language is also a substitute for action, the Saudis and their Western economic planners were always at loggerheads over what the Saudis said their goals were and what their expectations actually were. When a Saudi verbally states a wish, intention, or demand, he expects it to bring about realization without any additional action. But when no action is forthcoming, there is no hue and cry, only the pleasure of making the statement once again. In reporting on Saudi Arabia, I trained myself to look at emphatic government statements not necessarily as policy but rather as exercises in mild polemics. It was only after an announcement had been repeated over months or even years that there was some expectation that what had been said repeatedly would at last become policy. I still view with wry amusement the columnists in the Western press who pontificate about the ramifications of an announcement the Saudi government has made about Saudi Arabia's firm stand on oil prices or its intention to fight a holy war. As for economic development, to plan a project was as good as achieving it. Many of the grandiose plans that rolled out of the ministries expressed some intention; they did not necessarily make a statement of action. The promise is the reality. The Saudi understood this, the Westerner never did.

The Saudis can function perfectly well within the parameters of their linguistic style. It is matters of organization and the concept of time that seriously hinder Saudi Arabia's attempts to turn the kingdom into an efficient, functioning machine. Schedules and completion times drawn up by the Saudis' Western advisers are most often ignored, for the Saudis never take them seriously. The Saudis see Westerners living under the tyranny of time, which they have every intention of avoiding. Unwilling to deal with time sequences or to concern themselves with precisely defined timing, the Saudis tend to float along, depending on the will of Allah. *Bukarah, in-shaalah* ("Tomorrow, God willing"), is more than a phrase, it is a state of mind. Procrastination permeates everything, from the local tailor shop to the airlines. Nothing infuriated me more than to arrive at the airport for a flight and to be told that it was not to leave as scheduled. When I asked the Saudia employee on the desk when the plane was expected to leave, the inevitable answer was "three days." Shrugging his shoulders at my protestations, he would say, "Same, same" — loosely translated to mean, "Today, tomorrow, next week — it is all the same."

Because of this attitude toward time, a Saudi cannot be depended on to plan ahead, keep appointments, or honor time commitments. The latitude the Saudis exercise in the realm of organization is a definitive characteristic of the country. An international hotel booking service has declared that the Saudis hold the record for "no shows" for reservations. The Ministry of Planning's move into its newly constructed building was delayed for months because no one had thought to order the furniture. And in 1978, in perhaps the most blatant example of procrastination, a newspaper reported that representatives of Saudi Arabia, Jordan, and Syria were just then meeting to discuss repair of the Hijaz railroad line from Damascus to Riyadh. Originally built by the Ottomans in the early 1900s, the railroad has been out of commission since it was blown up by Lawrence of Arabia in 1917.

Some claim that the Saudis' aversion to planning is rooted in their language. Arabic has no future tense. Perhaps it is true that language reflects cultural values, for the attitude regarding organization and time is buried deep in the Saudi psyche. It is a throwback to the Bedouin's deep love of freedom. To be on time, to plan for the future, means that a man is not master of himself but a slave to circumstances. During the 1970s and on into the 1980s, there appeared to be no serious recognition that these attitudes toward organization were inconsistent with the type of economic development the Saudis were pursuing. With big contracts at stake, few Western advisers were willing to risk telling the Saudis that their national character was not responsive to the demands of a complex economy or a program of industrialization. For the truth was that if the Saudis were to succeed in increasing the value of their raw petroleum products and diversifying their economy, the whole configuration of the national character would have to undergo modification. While the top echelon of government dreamed of industrialization and the Western planners and builders created the machinery to accomplish it, the Saudis themselves stubbornly resisted attempts to put them in the work force.

Wilfred Thesiger, the intrepid Arabian explorer, once said:

All that is best in the Arabs has come to them from the desert: their religious instinct, which has found expression in Islam; their sense of fellowship, which binds them as members of one faith; their pride of race; their generosity and sense of hospitality; their dignity and the regard which they have for the dignity of others as fellow human beings; their humour, their courage and patience, the language which they speak and their passionate love of poetry. But the Arabs are a race which produces its best only under conditions of extreme hardship and deteriorates progressively as living conditions become easier.*

The Saudis were pulled out of the desert by the oil boom and, like the Arabs of which Lawrence spoke, became dependent on a paternalistic welfare state and armies of foreign laborers. Like other values of the Saudis, the aversion to labor is also buried deep in the Bedouin tradition. Unlike in the West, achievement is not an important part of the Saudi value system. In a society where the maintenance of group cohesion is paramount, the drive for individual accomplishment is largely absent. But beyond the absence of ego satisfaction derived from labor, structured employment is in contradiction to almost every value a Saudi holds dear. Entering the work force compels a man to chose between the requirements of his job and the needs of his family. A job demands obedience to a set of rules made by men — an affront to God. Employment means a worker is expected to be in a certain place at a certain time, a restriction on his freedom of movement. An employee has to conform to the orders of those above him, a slight to his honor.

With the right title and working environment, a Saudi can partially accept these restraints if their administration is lax. It is physical labor

---

*Wilfred Thesiger, *Arabian Sands* (New York: E. P. Dutton, 1959), p. 82.

that is totally repugnant. A Saudi will accept a position but not a job. A Saudi will ring the cash register in his shop but he will not sweep the floor. A Saudi will drive a truck but he will not repair one. A Saudi will be a bureaucrat but never a plumber. This is the great problem of development in Saudi Arabia. The absence of the work ethic permeates all of Saudi Arabia's development ambitions and explains much of the kingdom's dependence on foreign labor.

All through the height of the oil boom, Saudi Arabia suffered acute labor shortages. Large numbers of foreign workers from both developed and underdeveloped countries were hired, while segments of the Saudi population were technically underemployed because they shunned the multitude of jobs available. As thousands of men were being brought into the kingdom to drive buses, man the post office, install telephones, and work as clerks, the reception desk of the Ministry of Information, an extremely low priority need, employed a cadre of young Saudis. With the demand for labor being met by foreigners, every time I went into the ministry I observed several members of Saudi Arabia's precious manpower reserve lounging on sofas, watching Popeye cartoons on television.

In 1980 there was one foreign worker for every adult Saudi in the population. Frightened by the number of foreign workers, the government publicly attacked the Saudis' prevailing attitudes about work. Minister of Planning Hisham Nazer repeatedly conveyed the government's hope that people's attitudes would change so that meaningful work, even of the blue collar variety, would be looked on with regard. In its goals for the Third Development Plan, the Ministry of Information stated: "One of the goals of [the] information services is to publicize the importance of labor as an activity with real religious and social value, in order to change the prevailing attitude toward certain trades and occupations which are held in low esteem.* By putting Saudis into the work force, the Third Development Plan hoped to limit expatriate manpower growth to a rate of 1.2 percent per year between 1975 and 1980, as compared with the standing estimate of an annual growth rate of 7 percent.

Putting the Saudis to work depended first on education and training. Human resource development had been a major part of every economic plan. The first plan allocated $882.3 million to manpower training; the

---

* Kingdom of Saudi Arabia, Ministry of Planning, *Third Development Plan,* p. 380.

second plan, $6.69 billion; and the third plan $10.58 billion. But it was with its much-touted program of "Saudization" that manpower training became the battle cry of the Third Plan. Determined to train Saudis in the skills that the kingdom now demanded, the government dreamed that the foreigner could be replaced. However, the goals of manpower training were doomed from the start. Teachers and facilities for training were not adequate for the enormous breadth of the government's aspirations. Most of all, training was hamstrung by the recurring reluctance of Saudis to work. Training statistics reflected the average Saudi's attitude toward acquiring a skill. During the Second Plan, the Presidency of Civil Aviation (PCA) instituted the Aeronautical Training Center in Jeddah. After employing twenty-three teachers to train air traffic controllers, seventy-four students enrolled for the course and only thirty finished. Registration for the next session of the same course attracted just thirty applicants. The Airway Training Facility, also run by the PCA, was staffed with twenty-seven teachers and had no students, while the Airport Maintenance Training Center employed eleven teachers and also had no students. Significantly, this was in the airline industry, a sector of the economy that is attractive to Saudis.

The record of vocational education is even more dismal. In an attempt to attract students into courses on welding, carpentry, refrigeration, car mechanics, electricity, and plumbing, the government during the Third Plan paid all educational expenses for the students and gave them a salary during training. To sweeten the attraction even further, graduates were promised a SR 200,000 ($58,823) interest-free loan to set up their own businesses. Yet there were few takers.

Providing suitable employment for its citizens and meeting the demands of wealth and modernization combined to cause the bureaucracy to mushroom during the 1970s. Government was everywhere — in agriculture, education, health, telecommunications, aviation, railroads, ports, housing, roads, judicial services, community development, even the Boy Scouts. Each activity commanded its own ministry, and each ministry contained dozens of departments and bureaus. Bedeviled by problems common to all bureaucracies, government assumed additional burdens imposed by inexperienced bureaucrats and the Saudis' own culture. The failure to do long-range planning was further corrupted by the demand for instant gratification that arose in both the government and the public. In behavior characteristic of the nouveau riche, bureaucratic judgments about projects to pursue and what to purchase were often guided by the desire for what was glamorous and impressive, not by what functioned. Furthermore, there was a strong tendency to believe that constructing a building built an institution. Few in government were willing to look beyond these physical structures to the critical need to develop qualified Saudi staffs who could make the institution function.

Even with a bureaucracy interlaced with hired Western experts, the Saudis became trapped in the personal relationships that govern their culture. Loyalties were to individuals and not to organizations. An organization became fixed in the Saudi mind as the person who ran it. Who got what in the way of services or government contracts in the private sector depended on who the recipient was and what connections he had. The fragile institutions that were in place became paralyzed and impotent because of "exceptions" to their functions or procedures constantly made to accommodate personal connections. Bureaucratic activity was not task oriented; likewise, effort was rewarded not on the basis of getting things done but rather on success in empire building achieved through trading favors. As a result, byzantine maneuvers for power among bureaucrats were ceaselessly paralyzing government functions. In the power game, there was an overriding resistance to the delegation of authority. The rare subordinate who was willing to risk his honor to make a decision was restrained since a mistake on his part might reflect unfavorably on the honor of the person in charge. Moreover, by delegating responsibility, the person in charge in effect surrendered power. But what occurred in the bureaucracy was only a reflection of decision-making at the top. Saudi Arabia's entire decision-making process was hamstrung by the senior princes. Any efficiency that might have developed in the bureaucracy was thwarted by the rulers, who so compartmentalized every function of government that no one except those at the core of power in the House of Saud ever had a grasp of the total picture.

In the bureaucracy, the government paid miserable salaries to lower-level civil servants and allowed promotion to be determined by family connections. Because of the low salaries, government employees were reduced to making most of their money by petty corruption, such as selling visas. Those higher up made considerably more in large-scale influence-peddling to foreign contractors. Consequently, every bureaucrat became some type of empire builder, protecting his own turf from the encroachment of others.

With all of the government's claims of Saudization, there was little movement toward an assumption of even limited responsibility by the Saudis, even within the upper reaches of the bureaucracy. The Westerners who were recruited to teach the Saudis the skills they lacked most often became surrogate administrators. I saw Saudis from mid-level administrators to deputy ministers loll behind desk plaques engraved with their names and titles, drinking tea while their Western counterparts labored through the tangle of demands, priorities, and politics within the government. Although much in these situations resulted from a culture that has no work ethic, much was also the result of Saudi officials' being unable to come to grips with the complexities of the outside world and the highly technological infrastructure being built in Saudi Arabia.

One of the basic reasons that Westerners played such an overwhelming part in Saudi Arabia's development efforts was that the international mechanisms of oil distribution and payment were almost entirely Western. The banks where the Saudis deposited their foreign reserves were either Western or were tied into the international banking community dominated by Western institutions. The technology the Saudis needed was Western. The highly trained people needed to operate that technology were in the West. Out of all of these Western sources and institutions, the Saudis came to believe that the path to all of their goals lay with Western methods and procedures. While endlessly claiming that development would proceed within the context of the culture, both government and business rushed headlong into recruiting Western expertise. The burgeoning bureaucracy on the outside appeared to be Saudi, made up of young men who had gone West very early in the boom and returned home to take dominant positions in government. But like construction and commerce, the nuts and bolts of government were in the hands of Westerners, who were putting together organizations based on Western philosophy and practice. And this Western expertise was committed to completing a job, not nurturing a technologically backward people into modernity while catering to their cultural norms.

Some of the Saudis' problems with institutions developed during the oil boom arose precisely because these structures were devised by Westerners on Western cultural values. One of the philosophies behind manpower training was that technological advancement and social change would be better accepted by the population if the changes were introduced by the Saudis themselves, not their foreign servants. But because of the lack of qualified Saudis, managing the process of modernization and transferring technology became a highly complex problem that entailed not just the desired goal but all intermediate steps needed to reach that goal. University graduates could not be turned out without an elementary school system. Computers were useless without electricity. Air service depended on maintenance, and so on. In most countries that experience a measured rate of development, organizational models largely parallel the established social structure of the country. Indigenous management that rises up in developing nations is accustomed to how that society functions. This did not happen in Saudi Arabia. The Westerners, fascinated with their organizational charts and efficiency studies, were not cognizant of how close to the desert the Saudis still were. When I arrived in Riyadh, large parts of the city were still mud-walled hovels. Much of the population was illiterate. Almost all were devoutly religious. Many saw no value in the headlong rush to development. Yet in the name of progress, government set lofty goals in every area of Saudi life and the Westerners implemented them. Impossible demands were placed on the average Saudi, and when he failed, condemnation from the army of Western advisers in the kingdom was poorly disguised. The attempts to develop Saudi Arabia without adequate concern for its religious and moral values gambled with the possibility that once the glamour wore off the Saudis might reject much of what had been thrust on them. This was the very reason that the leadership so tightly controlled social change, especially in the areas of religion and the position of women. Nevertheless, the Saudis increasingly saw modernization linked to the values and standards of the West. Modernization came to imply Westernization.

As Saudi Arabia moved on toward 1980, it was becoming clear that the nature of the changes occurring would at some point affect the ability of the royal family to rule. Economic development was steadily transforming the social structure by expanding the size and significance of a new, largely Western-educated middle class. For the time being, that class was satisfied with the material rewards descending on it. But the fundamental problem posed by this middle class was that it did not fit into the model by which the House of Saud had traditionally governed Saudi Arabia. Nor was it particularly enamored of the West. Often education in the West led to a stronger rejection of Western values among those who had experienced them than among those who had never been directly exposed. The nagging concerns about the nature of the political role that the middle class might seek or how its growing influence would affect the existing political framework was lost in the material gratifications of the oil boom. The House of Saud has always ruled not by sharing power but by serving as the patriarch of what might be described as the Saudi family. It is a system that ties the highest and lowest levels of society to its bosom but has no existing mechanism to draw in those in the emerging middle. But in the euphoria of the oil boom, it was a system that appeared to be highly successful.

10

The Royal Tribe

I GENTLY RAN my fingers across the polished surface of the door's wood paneling and inhaled the smell of the fine leather upholstery of the Rolls Royce in which I was riding. I was on my way to a royal wedding: the daughter of one of the handful of senior princes in the hierarchy of the House of Saud was marrying a great nephew of Abdul Aziz. It was a marriage arranged to strengthen the ties within the royal family, much as a marriage between cousins strengthens the tribe.

It was 9:00 P.M. when the car swung off Nassiriah Street onto Intercontinental Road. Almost immediately it slowed to take its place in line behind the other luxury automobiles waiting to go through the gates to King Faisal Hall, the building in which the grandiose royal weddings are staged. As the driver stopped at the foot of the broad steps that lead up to the entrance, a tall black man in a white *thobe* swung the car door open and I stepped out. There was an electric excitement in the air that I had seldom experienced among the dour Saudis. As soon as one car discharged its cargo of black-clad women, it pulled away to be replaced by another, while a crew of yelling, wildly gesturing traffic controllers directed the empty cars to parking places. To the right of where I stood, below the level of the sidewalk, was a secluded garden where the drivers who had already dispensed with their expensive vehicles gathered to beat drums and partake of the food provided by the bride's family.

Mounting the steps to the hall, I joined the veiled women streaming into the foyer. There, like the drivers outside, female servants were clustered, singing and dancing. I slowly worked my way through the crowd until I reached the entrance to the main hall, where the elaborate ritualistic exchange of greetings began. As I took the hand of the woman at the head of the receiving line, my eyes involuntarily riveted on her necklace. Covering the soft skin between her collar bones was a massive marquis-cut diamond. Radiating out from it, in groups of three, were smaller but no less perfect stones that completely encircled the princess's neck. Feeling somewhat embarrassed for staring, I moved on to shake hands with the next hostess. Her malformed arm, which denoted the prevalence of consanguineous marriage within the House of Saud, was encircled with a chunky emerald bracelet. On down the line, women were engulfed by rubies, sapphires, and more and more diamonds.

The hall itself was enormous. A peach-colored carpet, purchased especially for the wedding, ran down the length of the room, creating an aisle between dozens of spindly gilded chairs and two settees for the senior women of the family. To my left, at the front of the room, was a pole covered with dense bouquets of flowers, extending approximately twenty foot toward the ceiling. Thirty of these floral posts fanned out behind the platform where the bride and groom would sit to receive their wedding guests, and more flowers stood in great bunches on the stage. Calculating the price that fresh flowers flown in from Europe command in the Riyadh market, I estimated that the bride's father had spent over $100,000 on the floral arrangements alone. Behind me a group of professional women musicians played drums and a lone lute while they crooned the monotonous sounds of traditional Arabic wedding songs. Sixty servant girls, many of them Oriental, dressed in matching costumes passed coffee and tea in hand-painted cups and glasses that matched the peach color scheme of the wedding.

Between the time the wedding began and the bride made her appearance, approximately two and a half hours later, the bride's sisters and myriad cousins competitively pranced up and down the aisle in chic dresses directly out of the designer salons of Europe. Their children, held in check by their Western and Oriental nannies, wore velvet suits or long brocade dresses that ranged from exquisite to tacky. It was in this clothing that the gaps in generation and sophistication within the royal family were so noticeable. An aging daughter of Abdul Aziz sat splay-legged in her place of honor on a settee. She was dressed in a sleazy black dress that had a huge flower sporting several leaves worked in cheap sequins that climbed up her stout body. On her wide-set feet, accustomed only to sandals, were ill-fitting gold lamé shoes and anchored to her head by an elastic cord was a tight black net that plastered her thin hair to her scalp. In stark contrast was the daughter of former King Faisal, representing the elite branch of the family. Tall and slim like her father, she was striking in her perfectly tailored two-piece black dress, which subtly sparkled as the tiny rhinestones woven into the fabric caught the light when she walked. I was absorbed in watching all of these scenes around me, when I was startled upright in my chair by a series of high-pitched screams emanating from behind the tall doors to my right. Then a final primordial howl filled the hall, signaling the guests to click their tongues in the old Bedouin wedding ritual. The doors flung open and four heavy-set women in tight white satin dresses slit to the hip entered the room, beating hand-held drums. They were followed by four belly dancers balancing tall candelabras, each containing twelve lighted candles, on their heads. Astonished, I watched them wiggle their hips and writhe their bodies while precariously supporting their fiery headgear. They in turn were followed by six flower girls, who preceded the bride. The bride herself wore a Western-style dress with a great train, carried by two young girls. The procession of chanting drummers, shimmying belly dancers, flower girls, bride, and train bearers took twenty minutes to traverse the long room and reach the podium. As the dancers reached a frenzied climax, they were hurried away so the groom escorted by four of his relatives could enter the hall. It was approaching 1:00 A.M. when the bride and groom finished receiving the congratulations of the guests and the party moved into the adjacent Intercontinental Hotel for the wedding feast.

The dinner perpetuated the tribal patterns established by the reign of the first al-Saud king, Abdul Aziz. As in a great tribal gathering, every woman connected to the household of either the bride or the groom, noble or servant, was invited to participate in the celebration. But there was only one narrow door into the dining room, and Saudi impatience reared its head as servants and guests fought to get through the slender opening. Taken in tow by a teenage relative of the groom, I was finally stampeded into the dining hall. There, standing before me, was a towering twenty-layer wedding cake. Beyond the cake were long tables set with plates, glasses, cutlery, an assortment of food on burners, and bottles of apple juice straight off the supermarket shelf. Everyone from the highest to the lowliest sat down together. An old woman, who I assumed was a long-time family servant, sat across from me. She wore a massive gold breastplate, probably a gift from her employer, which completely covered her breasts and dropped down below her waist. Clutching a spoon near the bowl, she ravenously shoveled food into her mouth and proceeded to grind it between her toothless gums, letting it drool out the sides of her mouth. Choosing to look away, I saw another woman move down the dessert table methodically lifting the serving spoon from each dish, licking it, and then returning it to the bowl. I left my plate barely touched.

At 2:30 A.M., I was escorted back to the point where I originally had been dropped off early in the evening. The men in the garden were still singing as I stood waiting for the white Rolls Royce to work itself through the line of cars preceding it and pull to a stop. I said my goodbys, opened the back door, and gratefully sank into the soft leather seat for the drive home.

Royal weddings reflect many truths about the House of Saud: the lavishness of its lifestyle; the wide diversity within the family not only as to influence and position but levels of education and sophistication; the paternalism of the ruler toward the ruled that sustains the monarchy; and finally the competitiveness as well as the unity within the family.

Saudi Arabia's royal family numbers in excess of five thousand people and describes itself as "a highly privileged tribe that permeates every corner of the country." * The members of the family range from the suave and urbane foreign minister, Saud al-Faisal, to pimply adolescents in polyester suits. All claim the title of prince or princess and most demand the prerogatives of royalty.

The lifestyle of the upper levels of the House of Saud is opulent. Princes maintain huge households, travel abroad for weeks at a time, and think nothing of sending an airplane from Riyadh to Paris to pick someone up. One of former King Faisal's daughters includes twelve servants in her entourage when she travels. Prince Abdullah, not regarded as one of the more ostentatious princes, once spent $9 million decorating his palace in Riyadh. The major princes maintain fleets of cars, keep stables of valuable race horses, and spend hundreds of thousands of dollars a year on luxury items. The royals also expect everyone to cater to their whims. Members of the royal family bump ordinary passengers off airplanes. The politically astute Ajyad Makkah

---

*From advertisement purchased by Saudi Arabia in the *New York Times*, April 25, 1983.

Hotel in Mecca maintains two royal suites and forty-four princes' suites for the exclusive use of the royal family. The revolving restaurant on top of the Riyadh water tower is never used because it looks down into the garden of Princess Sara, King Faisal's favorite sister. And King Fahd's daughter Latifa refuses to sit in anything but a blue chair when she has her teeth cleaned.

The abundance of royalty is due to the sexual prowess and political needs of Abdul Aziz. He sired forty-five recorded sons by twenty-two different wives, representing most of the kingdom's major tribes. For the most part, these tribal wives remained with their families, elevated by the honor of raising a Saudi prince. The offspring of these sons then also became princes or princesses, breeding more titled offspring. To give some order to the system of royalty, the number of princes should have been restricted early, for even in Abdul Aziz's time perhaps one Saudi in five thousand was a prince. But that was and remains politically impossible.

Not every prince is ultrarich or commands real political power. To make any sense of the system, I divide the royal family into princes and "princelings." The inner circle of senior princes who actually run Saudi Arabia are in this position because of the combination of their proximity to Abdul Aziz, their abilities, their diligence, and their ambition.*

The next level of the royal family, still in the prince category, are those active in major business enterprises or in the second echelon of the bureaucracy or the military. Bandar ibn Sultan ibn Abdul Aziz, Saudi ambassador to the United States, is an example of this group of princes. The princelings, on the other hand, are far down the line of descendants of Abdul Aziz, on the fringe of the wealth, and have no power other than as a member of one or another of the power blocs in the family. There are hundreds of these hangers-on who manage to live off their limited access to the decision-makers. But they remain important in that they are al-Sauds, and no king can rule without the broad consent of the family.

The history of Saudi Arabia is the history of the House of Saud,

---

*The most visible members of the present power constellation are Fahd, the king; Abdullah, the crown prince and commander of the National Guard; Sultan, minister of Defense and Aviation; Naif, minister of the Interior; and Salman, governor of Riyadh.

divided into epochs by the personality and leadership qualities of each of the kings.

The al-Sauds were originally nothing more than tribal rulers of Diriyah, an oasis town in the Nejd. Their influence spread and contracted according to their successes in battle with other tribal chieftains. A moment of glory was reached in the early nineteenth century when the first Abdul Aziz merged politics and Wahhabism to build a short-lived empire that challenged the interests of the Ottoman Turks. But not only did the al-Sauds lose their empire to the Turks in 1818, they lost Diriyah itself. With their settlement razed by the cannons of a foreign army, the family moved their capital ten miles down Wadi Hanifa to Riyadh. Shortly thereafter the al-Sauds fell to fighting among themselves, when they were not under attack by their major rivals, the Rashids, rulers of the area to the north centered around Hail. By 1880 Riyadh was in chaos as rival Saud and Rashid factions fought bloody battles through the markets and alleys, hanging the losers by their necks from the battlements of the town. In 1890 the Rashids were strong enough to lay siege to Riyadh by cutting down its date palms and poisoning its wells. The al-Sauds' last supporters deserted their ruler, forcing Abdul Rahman ibn Faisal al-Saud to hide his ten-year-old son, Abdul Aziz, in a basket slung from a camel and flee Riyadh in the dark of night. The family was granted sanctuary in Kuwait. In 1901 the now grown Abdul Aziz, refusing to accept his father's resignation to defeat, put together an army of forty men and marched on Riyadh. In a combination of stealth and courage, he recaptured his father's capital for the al-Sauds and won a foothold for an empire.

Lifting the Wahhabi banner and brandishing the fire of evangelism, Abdul Aziz moved out of Riyadh to control the entire Nejd by 1912. In 1913 he drove the Turks from the al-Hassa. By 1921 he had conquered parts of the Assir and moved toward Mecca, Mohammed's holy city. Ruled by the effeminate and mad Sherif Hussein, a political convenience for British interests in the area, Mecca was the jewel that Abdul Aziz sought. Fired with religious fervor and the quest for booty, his dreaded Bedouin army swept down on the city. The terrified Sherif fled and Mecca surrendered to the Wahhabis. Sending his men ahead to destroy the Shiite shrines in the city, Abdul Aziz, dressed in the simple, seamless white *ihram*, entered the city on October 13, 1924,

---

*H. St. John Philby, *Arabia of the Wahhabis* (London: Constable, 1928), p. 108.

not as a conqueror but as a pilgrim. There he performed his rituals "with that mixture of humility before God and arrogance towards men so characteristic of the old Wahhabis."* Abdul Aziz's conquests were nearly complete. But it was not until 1932 that Abdul Aziz ibn Abdul Rahman ibn Faisal officially named his kingdom Saudi Arabia, or "Arabia of the Sauds."

The essence of the monarchy as forged by Abdul Aziz has survived. The government that he put in place was simple, direct, unorganized, and exceedingly democratic. He was a grand tribal *sheikh,* always accessible to his subjects. Regularly traveling his kingdom, camping at villages, he held court in a large tent, its sandy floor covered with Persian carpets and his state papers stored in wooden chests stacked in the corner. Yet Abdul Aziz was somewhat of a political genius. He did what no man before him had done: tied the quarrelsome, autonomous peoples of a major part of the Arabian Peninsula together in a nation-state. He did it by practicing the philosophy of one of his favorite quotations: "The chief of a tribe is its servant" — in Abdul Aziz's case, a servant always in need of money.

Although he lived a simple life, hundreds of people flocked to him daily with some demand or simply to be fed. A Palestinian pharmacist who joined the court in 1948 described for me what it was actually like. Wherever Abdul Aziz moved, the court, like some medieval circus, moved with him. With one visit to the king, a Saudi could file a complaint, get a meal, collect a dagger, a cloak, or a sack of sugar, dictate a marriage contract to a public scribe, have his ailments treated, and hear the Koran recited by the leading Wahhabi scholars.

In addition to his hospitality, Abdul Aziz's reign had heavy structural expenses. His political strength lay in the towns, not with the Bedouins. But to keep his kingdom intact, he had to control the fickle Bedouins. Therefore, in 1916 Abdul Aziz ordered the Bedouin tribes owing allegiance to him to give up herding and join the Ikhwan ("Brotherhood") communities that he established in the northern Nejd. But settling the Bedouins required infusions of Abdul Aziz's money. Regularly the *sheikhs* were brought to Riyadh in relays to receive both religious instruction and subsidies to keep their loyalty. The *sheikhs* in turn distributed the subsidies among their own tribesmen to retain their fidelity. As Abdul Aziz predicted, the tribes eventually became dependent on his central authority through their dependence on his gifts. For the townsmen, Abdul Aziz kept the peace, which promoted commerce. And like the Bedouins, the townsmen found that the demands that Abdul Aziz put on his subjects were light. They too received gifts from their monarch and paid few taxes.

To finance all of this, Abdul Aziz collected pilgrims' taxes and scrambled for handouts from the British, who were interested in protecting all approaches to the Suez Canal and their access to India. The state treasury was the king's private purse, and although Abdul Aziz doled money out to his subjects like an indulgent parent, he spent almost nothing on public works. Besides a few water wells, Abdul Aziz's major public works projects were the railroad from Dammam to Riyadh and a pier for pilgrims in Jeddah. He built a hospital in Riyadh and one in Taif but these were primarily for the royal family. Even after World War II, when he began to collect significant oil revenues, "it seemed never to occur to ibn Saud (Abdul Aziz) that his overflowing wealth laid any duty on him to give his people the amenities they lacked: a medical service, schools, sanitation, roads and public transport, or any kind of insurance less whimsical than his personal bounty."*

Between the time he seized Riyadh in 1901 and his death in 1953, Abdul Aziz experienced only one serious challenge to his rule: the Ikhwan rebellion in 1929. He survived largely because he had succeeded in establishing a personal relationship between himself and his subjects. No man or institution stood between the king and his people. For the emotions of every Saudi, those who loved him and those who feared him, were attached to the person of the king, not some impersonal bureaucracy.

Abdul Aziz, beloved patriarch of the Nejd, was a large man, scarred by numberless battles on the desert, and fabled for his virility. His mud palace still stands in central Riyadh just beyond the al-Masmak Fort, which he seized from the Rashids in his daring raid on Riyadh in 1901. The mud stucco structure, built in 1936, wraps around an open courtyard, where a massive date palm stands, a link between the past and the present. Whenever I entered the old palace, now painted an incongruous hospital green, with cheap inlaid glass windows shoddily installed, I could feel the aura of Abdul Aziz within its walls. There is his camel's saddle and a coat of mail that looks as if it belonged in

---

*David Howarth, *The Desert King: A Life of Ibn Saud* (Beirut: Continental Publications, 1964), p. 225.

medieval Europe, not the Arabian desert. In the anteroom to the king's salon, there is a large hearth cut into the stone floor, where countless fires boiled coffee for Abdul Aziz's guests.

The salon itself is a pitiful imitation of the grand salons of Versailles, a haunting reminder that there has always lurked in the House of Saud an attachment to things of the West. A rack of Abdul Aziz's rifles has been substituted for a coat of arms. Two undistinguished grandfather clocks stand in the corners. At the front of the room is the oversize Louis XIV–style chair, upholstered in a leopard print corduroy, where Abdul Aziz sat to receive his subjects. Next to the chair is the old-fashioned European-style crank telephone, whose technology so delighted the Bedouin king.

On the roof of the old palace is a promenade with rifle holes cut in its crenellated design. As I looked out on the collapsing mud walls of the *hareem,* my eye was drawn across the street to the unfinished palace that Abdul Aziz was building in 1953 when he died. The new palace is of that same, sad pseudo-Versailles style improbably set in the desert, which looks as out of place as Abdul Aziz would have looked if he had lived to occupy it.

Abdul Aziz set the line of succession before he died. As if he foresaw problems, he named Faisal, his second oldest son, to assist Saud, his oldest surviving son, whom he named king.

The system of rule that worked so well for Abdul Aziz was disastrous in the hands of Saud. He became a lackey for the people around him who were more clever and cunning than he. Basically Saud had no sense of what it meant to be king other than to toss coins to his waiting subjects when he left the pink-walled confines of his palace. He drank heavily and saw the monarchy as a symbol that allowed him to enjoy his rights of marriage,* to savor the plaudits of his subjects seeking money, and to squander the kingdom's ever-increasing oil revenues. Saud and his family set new records in consumption. When they traveled abroad, they bought everything from the complete stock of a store's linen department to a fleet of Cadillacs. In 1954, the year after he became king, Saud spent $50 million constructing palaces in Riyadh and Jeddah and claimed the $234.8 million dollars that Saudi Arabia realized from its oil sales as the king's personal income. The

---

* Saud fathered at least fifty-two sons and fifty-five daughters.

effectiveness of the fledgling bureaucracy established near the end of Abdul Aziz's reign collapsed in the waste, decadence, intrigue, and corruption that consumed Saud's court. In 1958 the House of Saud hit its lowest point when Saud's economic mismanagement had all but bankrupted the country and his flirtations with Egypt's revolutionary Gamal Abdul Nasser enraged his own family and every monarch in the Middle East.

Dissatisfaction with Saud brought into play the *ahl-aqd wal hal* ("those who tie and untie"), a group consisting of approximately one hundred of the most important princes and over sixty of the leading members of the *ulema*. Together the group sought to solve the problem of Saud ibn Abdul Aziz. For two years Saud's younger brother Faisal ruled in his name. Waste and corruption were stemmed. The treasury began to recover. But not all members of the family were satisfied, and much of the dissatisfaction involved money. Faisal was ruling the family as well as the country with a tight fist, stopping many royal perks. The cut in royal allowances, combined with the strong tradition of patri lineal descent in Arab families, returned Saud to the throne in 1960. By 1962 conditions were as bad as they had been in 1958. With a two billion Saudi *riyal* debt and an empty treasury, conditions demanded Faisal's return. But he was no longer willing to rule for Saud; he would return only as king. On March 29, 1964, the *ulema* issued a *fatwa*, or religious ruling, that declared Saud unfit to govern. The king went into exile and died in Greece in 1969. Although the deposition of Saud kept the family and the kingdom in turmoil for four years, in the end it was as if the House of Saud had exercised a mystical instinct for survival. Power, as if by osmosis, flowed to the family member most capable of exercising it.

Faisal tore down the walls of Nassiriah, the mini-city built by Saud for his family, claiming that they separated the king from his people. Only the main gate still stands, a reminder of the folly of Saud's monarchy. Hardly the reluctant heir to the throne who is so often portrayed, Faisal ordered Saud's portrait and any mention of him struck from public view. It was as if six years of history disappeared from the kingdom and the succession had gone from Abdul Aziz directly to Faisal.

Faisal is by far the most interesting of the post–Abdul Aziz kings. He was both the best educated and the most worldly wise of the al-Saud monarchs. Yet he embodied the old Wahhabi ideals of piety and devotion. He wisely understood the need to lead Saudi Arabia into the modern world while at the same time preserving the sanctity of its traditions. Adopting the classic position of an Islamic conservative, he shepherded his people backward into the future.

The Saudis both greatly respected and greatly feared Faisal. Living austerely himself, he put a stop to the ostentatious spending and unseemly behavior of the royal family. The construction of elaborate palaces ceased. He reduced allocations for the royal family. He banned the importation of Cadillacs because they represented the sumptuous living identified with Saud. And he, at last, separated the income of the nation from the income of the king. Upholding the authority of Islam in everything that he did, Faisal became revered as a leader who had restored the dignity of the monarchy and, reaching beyond the kingdom, promoted unity in the Arab world.

Faisal came to the throne in one major crisis — the deposition of a king — and died in another — assassination. On March 25, 1975, as he left a *majlis* (''audience'') with his subjects, he was shot by one of his nephews, Faisal ibn Musaaid. Theories as to a motive range from the assassin's alleged use of the drug LSD to radical political ideas absorbed in the West. The most accepted theory is that it was a revenge killing. The assassin's brother was killed in 1965 in a violent demonstration against Faisal's decision to inaugurate television in the kingdom. For his crime, Faisal ibn Musaaid was beheaded in Riyadh's Justice Square on June 18, 1975.

During the years that I was in Riyadh, a corpselike villa stood on the corner across the street from the hospital. Land all around was eaten up by construction, yet it still stood, half finished, a ghost crumbling a little more each year. Although the truth remains with the royal family, the widely accepted rumor is that this was the house being built by Musaaid ibn Abdul Aziz, father of the assassin, when Faisal was killed. It now stands as a symbol to all who would strike at the al-Sauds' chosen leader.

Like the presence of the other great figures of Saudi Arabia's history, Abdul-Wahhab and Abdul Aziz, the presence of Faisal still lingers over the kingdom. I could see the green slate roof of Faisal's al-Ma'ather palace from my window and could easily walk to its gate. Passing beneath the sycamore trees that line the long drive, I watched ordinary Saudi families sitting on mats spread out on the grass, enjoying the coolness of the shade. There was a tranquility here that became increasingly hard to find as Riyadh bustled and boomed. I had been there many times, but shortly before I left Saudi Arabia for the last time, I went back to that palace. Peace still reigned there. It was as if the spirit of Faisal continued to rule his flock.

The death of Faisal tested the unwritten, largely untested system of succession in the House of Saud. The order of succession set by Abdul Aziz in which Saud, the oldest son, became king, with Faisal, next oldest son, as his deputy established the precedent of the throne being passed from brother to brother rather than from father to son. The four successors of Abdul Aziz have all been brothers in order of age except for those who have stepped aside. But there is no firm line of succession. The throne is not inherited but bestowed after extensive consultations within the family and with the religious hierarchy. It is a system that has been little tested except in the periods of crisis surrounding the deposition of Saud and the assassination of Faisal. Although in these situations the family overcame internal bickering for the common good, the ill-defined system contains all of the elements of instability. As a result, anyone's claim to the crown is elusive.

When Faisal died, the next king by age should have been Mohammed.* But in the aftermath of Saud's removal from the throne, Mohammed renounced his place in the line of succession. The reasons remain locked within the family. Nicknamed "the father of two devils," Mohammed was a traditionalist, interested in Arabic poetry and possessed of a violent temper. The kingship may not have been acceptable to either Mohammed or the rest of the family, and certainly by 1975, when the family was currying its progressive image, Mohammed represented a throwback to the past. For what had been happening within the House of Saud during the reign of Faisal was that future candidates for king were working their way up the hierarchy through the bureaucracy. The major princes, such as Fahd, Abdullah, Sultan, and Naif, all held important governmental posts. Yet on the death of Faisal, the family and the *ulema* were not yet ready to switch to a technocrat king nurtured within the bureaucracy. So a deal was struck between rival factions of the family and with the religious leaders. Khalid, the oldest brother following Mohammed, became king. Then Naif and Saad, the next two oldest sons of Abdul Aziz following Khalid, stepped aside, allowing Fahd to assume a new title, crown

---

*This is the same Mohammed who had Princess Mishaal executed.

prince.* Khalid, known to be in poor health, was an interim king, chosen to allow the family time to chart its course for the future.

As it turned out, he proved to be an excellent choice. During his seven years on the throne, Khalid reigned and Fahd ruled. Khalid had the demeanor of a true *sheikh,* a kind, generous, pious man, whose bearing was regal but not haughty. He exhibited great patience with his subjects and chose to spend his happiest hours on the desert with his beloved Bedouins. Hundreds flocked to his weekly *majlis,* and, like his father, he sometimes shared his dinner with a thousand of his male subjects. He lived rather simply and seemed removed from the royal scramble for a percentage of government contracts. Khalid could preside over Saudi Arabia's great strides toward modernization and remain untainted by the stigma of Westernization because he was so much himself a Saudi. I remember seeing Khalid leaving the horse races late one winter afternoon. In the middle of his excited retinue, he quietly stood, his cane supporting the weight of a hip replaced in 1977. Lacking the charisma of Abdul Aziz, the decadence of Saud, and the authority of Faisal, he was a perfect father figure, one perhaps taken aback by the excitement around him. Because of his personal characteristics and the economic ability to take care of the needs and wishes of his subjects, the al-Sauds' unique political system hummed along under the tutelage of Khalid.

Faisal's moves toward modernization, especially after the 1973 oil embargo, left the basic mechanisms by which the House of Saud ruled remarkably intact. It was Faisal who made the decision to create an elaborate welfare state rather than bring the people into the political process. The monarchy remained, as it was under Abdul Aziz, a highly personalized relationship between the ruler and the ruled, a relationship now girded by enormous sums of money. This unique method by which it ruled preserved the position of wealth and privilege that the House of Saud enjoyed.

During the heyday of the oil boom, I weekly saw King Khalid ibn Abdul Aziz al-Saud on television, standing unprotected by guards or seated behind an improbable Louis XIV desk, receiving his guests at his *majlis.* Except for the serving boys dispensing endless cups of highly sweetened tea, it was impossible to separate the monarch's entourage

---

*Since 1953 Fahd had held the offices of minister of Education, minister of the Interior, and second deputy premier.

from the suppliants. All were scattered out on ornate French brocade sofas, dressed in the universal Saudi costume of white *thobe* and *gutra*. True, some *thobes* were whiter and newer than others and some of the waiting men chose to sit rather than sprawl, but within the king's chambers all were received with equal respect and hospitality. Unlike the isolated splendor of the court of the former shah of Iran, Saudi Arabia's monarchs have followed the Bedouin traditions. As with the tribal *sheikh*, the lowliest peasant still regards access to his king as his inherent right. The king, in turn, recognizes that he retains the allegiance of his followers only as long as he is responsive to their needs. Historically, this has been the strength of the House of Saud. For in reality, the absolute monarchy of the al-Sauds has been more akin to ward politics than despotism. Like skillful politicians the rulers play one group against another in a population defined by conflicting interests. These groups are then reunited under the king, himself defined by the multiple roles he fills. For the uninitiated, the whole exercise appears to be a rerun of "Who's on First." But this is a highly sophisticated game with high stakes, which has succeeded because of the nature of the Saudi social structure. Saudi society molds itself by first dividing vertically into classes and then dividing again, horizontally, into regional interests and tribal structures. In other words, every Saudi defines himself by his economic class, kinship group, and geographic region. Consequently, no individual or group ever has a single interest that is not blunted by a competing interest. Politics as practiced by the House of Saud, therefore, is a shell game where the pea of royal patronage and favors is rapidly shifted between classes, regions, and tribes in such a way as to keep at least two of the three roles in which every individual perceives himself satisfied at any given time.

The class structure is dominated by the royal family, composed of the direct descendants of Abdul Aziz. Next in order are the Juffalis, Alirezas, and other great merchant families, who rival the royal family in wealth but not in power. Then, dropping precipitously on the ladder of riches and influence, is the growing middle class, largely comprised of small traders, white collar clerks, and junior civil servants, who form the rapidly expanding urban society. Since few Saudis will accept positions as manual laborers or even as blue collar workers, there is virtually no Saudi working class in the cities. Therefore, the rural peasants and the nomads are at the bottom of the ladder financially, but not in terms of political influence.

Each of these social classes identifies itself by shared economic interests. But in Saudi Arabia, class interests are often superseded by regional interests, which range from the zealous enforcement of religious rules to the regional development of water sources. Because the Hijaz, the al-Hassa, the Assir, the north, and the Nejd each has a distinct way of life, each is in competition with the others for political power that infringes on purely class interests.

But then these regions further divide into an expanded tribal system, which the House of Saud has tied to the king through the emirate system.* There are two types of tribes in the al-Sauds' political constellation. First there is the traditional kinship group, such as the influential Utaibah tribe of the Nejd, and then there are political "tribes," such as the peasants of the Assir. It is this second type of tribe that is the most complex of all the kingdom's social groupings. It is also the weakest. For a "political tribe" to exercise power, it must bring together people with a common economic interest who live in the same geographic area and share the same way of life.

With these myriad political divisions, the House of Saud rules by addressing itself in any situation to whichever identity the disgruntled element of the population is attaching its loyalty to at that particular moment: class, region, or tribe. The system works because for a Saudi each of these identities is clear-cut and seldom comes into conflict with the others. A Hijazi merchant, for instance, selling his silks and velvets in a smart shop in Jeddah would never find himself in a showdown with a rural peasant of the Shahram tribe who farms the hills of the Assir. His class does not put demands on the same economic resources, his regional interests do not put demands on the same natural resources, and the tribe to which each belongs has neither a common demand nor a past dispute. With the multitude of groups in the kingdom, they are seldom thrown into competition with one another over resources or policy. The genius of the ruling family has been to keep it that way. The king's main function is not to rule by decree but to forge a consensus within and among all of these groups, plus the *ulema* and the royal family, before making government policy. As a result, the government of Saudi Arabia is characterized by endless consulta-

---

*This is the system of local rule. Originally based on the alliance between the king and the *sheikhs*, it now encompasses the fledgling system of municipal government headed by local mayors.

tion between the rulers and all facets of society. No mater how critical, no decisions are made before the all-important consensus is reached. This precludes rapid responses or innovations for any problem, no matter how urgent it might be. Western advisers trying to develop everything from primary education to petrochemical industries are driven to distraction by a government that stalls rather than moves. In one instance, while architects and builders waited, construction of the hospital for the King Saud University's medical school was halted for several years. Before work could proceed, a consensus had to be reached on whether or not it was acceptable for male and female students to share the same x-ray and laboratory facilities. What the Westerners on this project, whose complaints I listened to endlessly, failed to grasp was that this glacial movement of the decision-making process was essential in maintaining political stability and would not be hurried for the convenience of the Westerners.

Early in the oil boom, the first wrinkles in the House of Saud's time-honored political formula began to appear. Like a menacing time machine, development was creating changes that could not be controlled and threatened to outstrip the consensus process. In the realm of religious orthodoxy, for example, the more progressive urbanites were becoming restless with the overwhelming power of the *ulema*. In the rural areas, on the other hand, people still demanded a strict Wahhabi-style state. In the pressures of the oil boom, if the consultations necessary to achieve consensus dragged on interminably, the progressives were dissatisfied; but if they proceeded too fast, the traditionalists became disaffected. It was in these circumstances that the House of Saud manipulated the three-pronged nature of interest groups. Deftly using a tit-for-tat approach, it gave something to one interest group while taking something else away to satisfy another group. With the House of Saud in control of petroleum revenues and government spending, the rulers were in a position to take care of their own interests. While the Third Development Plan was being formulated, there were loud complaints from rural interests about both the economic and political thrust of government being aimed at the decadent cities. To deal with the conflict, the government continued to pour money into Riyadh but sent more *matawain* into the streets to visibly enforce the observance of prayer time among the urbanites. In addition, the Ministry of Municipalities and Rural Administration (MOMRA) was instructed to provide every rural settlement in the kingdom something immediate and tangible. When I was working on MOMRA's massive submission for the Third Plan, I noticed that morgues were being built in many communities, while others were given only a fence around the cemetery to keep out the wild desert dogs. When I asked why, I was told that the settlements designated for morgues had received fences in the Second Plan. Those designated for fences under the Third Plan would get morgues under the Fourth Plan and those settlements with morgues would move on to slaughterhouses.

But splintering the population into interest groups is only one part of the formula with which the House of Saud rules. The other part is constructed on the wide range of religious, traditional, and secular roles on which the king bases his authority.

The king is first and foremost the *emir*. A position described in the Koran, an *emir* is a local ruler of either a village or a tribe, who commands his position by possessing enough power to ensure that the Islamic code of laws is enforced within his community. Abdul Aziz began his career as the *emir* of Riyadh after he seized the town by force of arms. After uniting Saudi Arabia and declaring himself king, he assumed another religious title, that of *imam*, or "law giver." Although monarchy is not addressed in Islamic theology, the wily Abdul Aziz adopted the title of *imam* to imbue his rule with a certain religious legitimacy.

In addition to these religious roles, Abdul Aziz also became the *"sheikh* among *sheikhs."* Under the old Arab tribal system, the *sheikh* was responsible for settling disputes within the community. Like the *emir*, his authority was established by his prowess at war and existed only as long as he could demonstrate his control over others. Abdul Aziz once again established the pattern of applying old practices to a new concept. The idea of a nation-state on the Arabian Peninsula was more Western than Arab. By adopting the posture of a *sheikh* ruling a tribe, Abdul Aziz succeeded in creating an image with which the people, still tied to village, tribe, and family, could identify. Although the assumption of the title of king was a break with tradition, the actual combining of the roles of *emir, imam,* and *sheikh* had long been practiced on a tribal level. So it was as the enforcer of Islamic law and the *sheikh* of the tribe that Abdul Aziz and his successors ruled until the oil boom made it necessary for the king to adopt roles not associated with tribal rule.

Modernization has demanded that the king also become head of a bureaucracy and the commander in chief of the armed forces, functions unknown in tribal practice.* Being king of Saudi Arabia is not easy. To rule, the king must control all of the sources of his power and authority. As chief *emir*, he has to maintain the support of local leaders. As *imam*, he must protect religious orthodoxy to keep the support of the *ulema*. As *sheikh*, he has to command the loyalty of the tribes. As premier and commander in chief, he has to manage the bureaucracy and retain the loyalty of the military. In all, it is an incredible balancing act, but one which the House of Saud has managed well.

At the heart of the al-Sauds' success is a government structured in such a way that almost every individual has ready access to those in power. To prove their religious orthodoxy, Saudi kings are highly visible leaders of the faithful. Every king with the exception of Saud has been identified with major projects in the holy cities. Just as King Faisal spent $300 million expanding the Grand Mosque at Mecca and King Khalid spent another $300 million completing it, Fahd has financed a major renovation and enlargement of the Prophet's mosque at Medina. A *hajj* season seldom passes that the king does not go to Mecca to kiss the Black Stone. And every year some high-ranking member of the family is present for the washing of the Kaaba.

There is a golden road between the crown and the tribal *sheikhs*, paved with gracious hospitality, various economic rewards, and direct entree to the king. But access to the king is not limited to the *ulema* and the *sheikhs*. At the king's weekly *majlis*, his lowliest subjects kiss his cheeks, then his nose, and finally his shoulder as they press their crumpled pieces of paper with their requests on his majesty. And every Saudi realistically expects the king to deliver.

In the physical absence of the king, members of the royal family are scattered around the kingdom as local officials, personal representatives of the king. Prince Khalid al-Faisal, governor of the Assir, once said, "If you can't put them [the people] in touch with a ministry or other authority, you may have to help them yourself."** In fact, it

---

*There is a crucial division of the power of the armed forces into the National Guard and the more conventional military forces under the authority of the Ministry of Defense and Aviation. The National Guard is recruited from the tribes and so is an institution that ties the tribes to the House of Saud. The army, navy, and air force are largely recruited from the urban areas or from people with no strong identity with the tribal system of the Nejd. See Chapter 14.
**Quoted in David Holden and Richard Johns, *The House of Saud* (London: Holt, Rinehart and Winston, 1981), p. 462.

seemed during the golden days of the boom that almost every Saudi had a patron prince through family and tribal connections or simply as a servant in a royal household. On behalf of his wards, the prince interceded with the bureaucracy, doled out emergency cash, arranged admittance to the hospital, helped pay bride prices, and so on.

Despite the labors of his deputies, ultimately it is the king, as the *sheikh* of *sheikhs*, who is responsible for seeing that all in his flock prosper. Through the reign of Khalid, the king was still very much like a Bedouin *sheikh*. He was the first among equals in a society where every man is intensely independent. His authority depended not on institutions but on his skills in handling men. And like the Bedouins, all Saudis believed that the king was responsible for all — good or bad — that befell them.

With great political skill, the House of Saud came through the 1970s with its political machinery intact in spite of the 1979 uprising of religious fundamentalists in Mecca. Through the tumult, their sources of power remained the emirate system, the National Guard, and the Ministry of Defense and Aviation. The regime could stay in power as long as it controlled two of these three major power centers. Into Fahd's reign, which began in 1982, power was distributed evenly enough so that Saudi Arabia remained relatively stable, because the major segments of society continued to exercise their will through one of the channels of influence open to most Saudi citizens.

Although the Bedouin were poor, they were extremely powerful through their ties with the National Guard, the emirate system, and a king who had great affection for them. Approaching the Bedouin in loyalty to the king was the peasant class, which made up 40 percent of the population. They were also tied to the crown through the emirate system. As beneficiaries of land distribution and generous subsidies from the government, they had little to quarrel about. The antagonisms they harbored were directed at the bureaucracy, which irritated them, and the urban merchants, who they believed cheated them. As long as they perceived the kingdom's religious orthodoxy continuing, they remained placid. The professional military remained loyal through the position afforded them by their rulers. They were well paid, granted generous fringe benefits, and enjoyed a position that approached in status the knights of medieval Europe. That left the urban classes. Most were employed as traders, where the government ensured that they did fairly well financially. No income or property taxes were levied. Commercial trade was limited to Saudis, protecting them from competition from foreigners. And the government guaranteed access to generous interest-free loans for business and financing for houses. Of all of the Saudis, it was the lower-level civil servants who were probably the most discontent. They were educated, and so had rising expectations, but they had no power base through the military, the emirates, or even the ministries, a situation little noted by the usually astute House of Saud.

The government ministries still have little political power, but they do contain the expertise necessary to keep the machinery of government operating. In 1953, shortly before he died, Abdul Aziz established the rudiments of government structure by creating the Majlis al Wuzara (Council of Ministers). Before the oil embargo, the Council was composed almost entirely of sons of Abdul Aziz and Islamic theologians. Then in October 1975, to accommodate the Western-educated, urban middle class, the number of positions on the Council of Ministers was increased from fourteen to twenty with only eight of the positions being held by princes and two by Islamic leaders. The rest were staffed by rising technocrats.

The power of the ministries, and, therefore, their influence within the Council of Ministers, grew with national wealth as their technical know-how became critical in keeping Saudi Arabia functioning. But the premiership and the pivotal portfolios of the ministries of Defense, Interior, and Foreign Affairs, as well as the National Guard and the governorships of the important provinces, stayed in the hands of the royal family. For all of their ability, training, and reputation, the ministers remained managers, not policymakers. That was left to the king and the senior princes.* The ministers have influence in that they have input into the consensus process, but if no consensus emerges or if the interests of the royal family come into focus, the decision rests with the king and a handful of his brothers. During the reign of Khalid, this inner circle, the core of power, was made up of Fahd, Abdullah, Sultan, Naif, Miteib, Salman, and the elder Mohammed.

Throughout the reign of Khalid, the bureaucracy was held in line by

---

*In their decisions, the interests of the approximately thirty-member Council of the Ulema and the equally large Council of Princes who represent the broad interests of the royal family play a prominent role. The Council of Ministers is another, coming together in the tent of the *sheikh*, a place in which to express opinions that go into the consensus process. There is no fixed system for reaching any decision but rather a series of consultations from which decisions emerge.

the same mechanisms that held other segments of the population together. Those in the upper levels had their access to power through
family or tribal connections. Those in the lower levels collected the
financial rewards of Saudi citizenship and cashed in on opportunities
for petty graft afforded by their government jobs.

The royal family appeared to be protecting itself from its enemies,
but the question remained whether or not it could protect itself from
its own corruption and internal rivalries. When oil prices skyrocketed,
members of the royal family became wealthy in a variety of ways. In
the 1960s, a tight-fisted King Faisal distributed vast amounts of arid,
empty desert land among his family as a way of placating their demands for a share in the kingdom's resources without allowing them
to dip into the government's treasury. Neither Faisal nor the grumbling
princes could possibly have foreseen the explosion of real estate values
that would follow the oil embargo. A hectare of land, which was worth
perhaps $3 when it was distributed, could command $6,000 by 1980.
And the demand for land came from everywhere — for roads, airports, residential housing, pipelines, universities, sewage treatment facilities, power stations. Even now when the government wants to build
something, a prince is usually there to demand top price for his real
estate.

A second source of wealth for members of the royal family is patronage. The major ministries and the armed forces are staffed with
members of the royal family. For every purchase that the government
makes, the princes who negotiate the contract receive their cut. Such
a system is ripe for abuse. A prince I know has made millions of
dollars buying equipment for the air wing of the Saudi army. Consequently, in ministry after ministry, purchases are often determined not
by need but by who is on the receiving end of the commissions.

The third major way for members of the royal family to acquire
wealth is by becoming the legally required Saudi partners of foreign
construction and service companies doing business in the kingdom. All
of the major international construction companies, such as Blount and
Bechtel, have members of the royal family as business partners who
procure the government contracts for the company and then collect a
percentage of the profits. Or companies doing business with the government can be totally Saudi owned. Two of King Fahd's sons own
management companies that the government hires to manage certain
of its hospitals. Often, as I bumped over a road being repaved for the

sixth time, I wondered which prince had the concession on road work in Riyadh.

The royal percentage takers are everywhere. Probably the most avaricious member of the royal family is another of Fahd's sons, Mohammed. Owner of Al Bilad, the holding company for his many interests, Mohammed began getting rich from contracts with the Ministry of Posts and Telecommunications (PTT) when he was only twenty-five years old. In 1977 his greed became public when American ambassador William Porter, speaking for American, Japanese, West German, and French companies cut out of a deal with PTT, complained about a contract that Mohammed engineered between the Saudi government and a consortium headed by N. V. Phillips, the Dutch electronics concern, and L. M. Ericcson, the Swedish telephone company. Phillips' price was about five times that which the Western consultants hired by PTT estimated it would cost. Retreating from the public exposure, the government canceled the contract. It has been estimated that if it had gone through, Mohammed would have received a commission of 20 percent of the total cost, or $1.3 billion.

Almost all deals involving members of the royal family are simple contractual arrangements between the ministries and privately owned (or, perhaps more aptly, "princely" owned) companies. A direct cut from Saudi oil revenues is the special and highly secret purview of only a very select number of princes, whose deals rarely come to light. The *Wall Street Journal* reported that in November 1980 Saudi Arabia ordered one of the four American oil companies that formed the old ARAMCO consortium to begin selling 140,000 barrels a day of Saudi crude to a mysterious buyer in Japan called "Petromonde." The official agreement with Saudi Arabia called for the Japanese firm to pay $32 a barrel, but word soon leaked out from Japan that Petromonde would resell the oil to Japanese refiners for $34.63 per barrel. The extra $2.63 a barrel represented a "commission" that would net the dealer $368,200 a day, or $11 million a month. International oil industry investigators soon learned that Petromonde was not a Japanese company at all but a London-based concern with the same London telephone and telex numbers as Al Bilad. Discovered, embarrassed Saudi officials canceled yet another of Mohammed ibn Fahd's deals.

The Petromonde case came as close as anything to documenting the payment of large commissions to members of the Saudi royal family to obtain Saudi oil during the days of oil shortages. Known as "princely oil,'' it provided staggering amounts of money to selected members of the House of Saud and represents one of the components of the glue that holds the royal family together. Prominent princes expect a big share of the kingdom's wealth, which goes into their private fortunes and supports an intricate system of private patronage. Among the major beneficiaries of the system was the ubiquitous Prince Mohammed ibn Abdul Aziz (d. 1983), the older brother of kings Khalid and Fahd. When he renounced his place in the succession to the throne, Mohammed is said to have been allowed to allocate a share of Petromin's oil* in return for under-the-table commissions from his agents, who then contacted buyers. One deal turned down by an American company could have netted the prince $1.2 million a day.

The sacrosanct oil resources of Saudi Arabia are better protected from the financial manipulations of the royal family than other areas of the Saudi economy. While oil shortages lasted, only the highest ranking members of the family ever had access to oil deals, and then only those involving a small percentage of total production. During the boom, there were too many other less politically sensitive ways for people of privilege to make money. Besides land, joint ventures, and government contracts, there was income from capital invested abroad and an inside track on currency manipulations from the Saudi Arabian Monetary Agency, which controlled the value of the Saudi *riyal*.

This widespread corruption in the royal family generated little hostility directly toward the family during Khalid's reign. Censorship removed press scrutiny. There was a certain acceptance of corruption in the royal family as long as everyone else got a fair share of the pie. Furthermore, within the values of the culture, most people, from the poorest Bedouin to the richest merchant, consider anyone who does not use his position to enrich himself and his relatives as a fool. But most of all, educated Saudis blamed corruption on the influences of the West that arrived with the oil boom. Abdul Aziz had made no secret of distributing money as a way of maintaining loyalty among the princes and potential rivals. But the amounts of money involved were generally small. Saudis like to believe that big payoffs were not part of the scheme until the arrival of droves of Westerners hustling to capitalize on Saudi Arabia's riches. As one Saudi economist told a

---

*Petromin as originally created was in charge of the development of petroleum and minerals. Its role has now been reduced to the regulation and distribution of oil for domestic consumption.

Western journalist, "If there's a corruption problem in Saudi Arabia, it's because you taught us how." *

Access to large sums of money is a major source of competition between factions of the royal family. Other threats to family solidarity arise from conflicting values, the pace of modernization, rivalries between branches of the family, and the pure ego satisfaction of being considered important. The House of Saud always has two faces: conflict and unity. Constantly beset by varying degrees of infighting, the al-Sauds have twice fallen from family infighting (1865–66 and 1881). But the present dynasty has lasted in an unbroken line through the deposition of one king, the assassination of another, the natural deaths of two, and the orderly succession of the fifth — an admirable record for politically turbulent Arabia. Although rivalries exist over power and policy, the family motto could be "In unity there is strength." Although I have heard women in the family snarl at the mention of some prince's name, there is a general recognition within the family of the interests of all and an accommodation of all.

Perhaps how the family operates can be demonstrated by their fondness for horse racing, the family's favorite sport. During the winter months of January and February, the princes gather on Monday afternoon following the third prayer call to pit their European- and North American–bred horses against each other at the Equestrian Club in the Malaaz district of Riyadh. From time to time, I was allowed to attend. Over several years, as the upper class became more comfortable with Westerners, my place moved from the lower side bleachers to a seat directly behind the royal box. From there I watched the descendants of Abdul Aziz sip tea and calmly watch each other's horses. There was no excitement, no cheering, for there was really no contest. The winner of the major races is decided on a rotating basis.

One afternoon a son of Prince Abdullah arrived just prior to the last race. With him were his two young daughters, carefully coiffured, wearing matching silk dresses that brushed the tops of their patent leather shoes. Predictably, his horse won. Holding his daughters' hands, the prince moved to the track and proudly lifted the trophy above his head while photographers snapped his picture. That evening on television, I saw a rerun of the race. When the horses rounded the last turn, the jockeys reined in their horses, allowing the horse of the victorious prince to thunder across the finish line. Next week, it would be someone else's turn to win.

Yet the hostilities between the competing power groups within the family have been a poorly kept secret. Every time Khalid was felled by another bout of poor health, the question of the succession rattled through the kingdom. Like the urban-rural split of the population, the royal family splits between the progressives and the traditionalists. During Khalid's reign, the progressives, often viewed as overly Westernized, were led by Crown Prince Fahd. The traditionalists were led by Abdullah. Khalid formed the bridge between the two. But the progressives were the major power bloc in the family because of the tenor of the times and their organized strength within the family itself. Fahd is a Sudairi as well as an al-Saud, giving him an added power base in one of Saudi Arabia's most powerful families. The crafty Abdul Aziz married a Sudairi in appreciation of this political fact and produced seven sons by her. By 1980 the Sudairi brothers controlled the ministries of Defense and the Interior, the governorship of Riyadh, and the deputy governorship of Mecca, and Fahd reigned as crown prince.

Abdullah, commander of the National Guard and second deputy premier, represented the conservative, tribal interests in the kingdom. His Bedouin inclinations and multiple wives were a severe embarrassment to the progressive elements of the family, who craved the respect of foreign leaders and the international press. Abdullah expounded the rhetoric of a strong nationalist, a stance at odds with the pro-American policy of Fahd and his brothers. Among the Saudi public, Abdullah's pronounced stutter was considered a severe handicap in speaking to his subjects, who regard the poetic use of the language as the mark of a true *sheikh*. There was intense speculation about whether or not Abdullah would be chosen crown prince on the death of Khalid and even more doubt that he would ever become king.

It was during the late 1970s that the infamous "Sudairi Seven" were suspected of plotting to set up their own line of monarchs. When Khalid died, so the scenario went, Abdullah, a half brother and the next oldest son of Abdul Aziz after Fahd, would be dealt out and the title of crown prince would go to Sultan, minister of Defense and Aviation.

Watching the various elements in the royal family jockey for power was a favorite spectator sport in Riyadh. For me, it was part of my job as journalist. The obstacles to political reporting in Saudi Arabia rank with those in the Soviet Union. In the murky, devious realm of royal politics, all decisions are made behind closed doors. Since secrecy is a way of life, there are no leaks and nuances are the only way to judge who is on top. Among the methods I used were to keep count of how many times Fahd's picture as opposed to Abdullah's appeared on the front page of the *Arab News*. As I might have viewed events at the Kremlin, I watched who was sent on foreign missions, who was chosen to appear at ceremonial functions, who was absent or who appeared at public functions of groups outside any person's constituency. I kept track of who was out of the country when important decisions were announced or who was absenting himself from the kingdom for a long vacation. I had one distinct advantage over other reporters: I had access to certain aspects of the royal family's health care. So byzantine is the court of the al-Sauds that the pecking order, who was up and who was down, was often reflected in whether the mother of a new royal baby was put in a room, a suite, or given an entire floor. Or I noted how many guards were assigned to each royal patient, how many cars were in the entourage when the patient arrived at the hospital, who commanded the most nurses, who received the most flowers. When King Khalid was in the hospital after an overdose of bromides almost killed him, I watched to see which princes and ministers were admitted to see him, how often they came, and how long they stayed.

During Khalid's reign, Abdullah's picture was largely absent from the newspaper. He made almost all his public appearances with the National Guard. His palace was southwest of the city, on the road to al-Kharj, not clustered with those of his brothers. His wives came to the hospital, had their babies, and went home. And the only time I saw him as a patient, he was walking bare headed toward an examining room in one of those humiliating hospital gowns that stopped short of his knobby knees. Only one security guard preceded him, and the director of the hospital, marching behind, bore his folded clothes.

Fahd and Abdullah as individuals were not as important in the political alignment as the power bases they represented. The House of Saud reflects the same conflict that divides Saudi society itself: the promise of progress and the pull of tradition. If both Fahd and Abdullah were to die, the conflict between their supporting groups would remain.

Although the progressive branch of the family was dominant during Khalid's reign, the power centers were sufficiently controlled by opposing factions to protect Abdullah and his conservative bloc. He con-

trolled the vital National Guard, commanded some support in the emirate system, and was highly respected among the tribes. With the family
secure against unmanageable infighting and the apparent success of
King Khalid's checkbook monarchy, all seemed well within the House
of Saud. But in the process of modernization and the increasing Westernization of those in power, the old system had begun to crack. One
of those cracks erupted in November 1979, at the apex of the oil boom.

II

There Was No Tomorrow

I HAD JUST TAKEN the short cut between the employees' dining room and the front entrance of the hospital. On reaching the lobby, which looked more like the reception area of a fine hotel than a hospital, I saw an old bearded man stiffly shuffling past the lapis lazuli mosaic portrait of King Faisal. Pausing to peer at the diamond flecks in the former king's eyes, the aging peasant, his old fashioned *thobe* hitting his legs just below mid-calf, hobbled toward the front door. Suddenly he stopped. Leaning his cane against the wall, he raised his arms above his head, exposing the clear plastic indentification strip attached to the wrist of hospitalized patients. In the measured cadence of Arabic poetry, he loudly praised Allah, the doctors, the nurses, and King Khalid for his recovery. This old man, poor and illiterate, standing in the center of opulent surroundings provided by his monarch, demonstrated how successful the House of Saud has been in tying the population to a personal relationship with their rulers through the generosity of the king. The oil boom allowed that generosity to reach undreamed of heights.

The oil boom made the Saudis rich. They were not only statistically rich, as reckoned by dividing oil revenues by the number of people, but also in the sense that the Saudis commanded high disposable incomes and lived in one of the world's most benevolent welfare states. Huge oil revenues coupled with Saudi Arabia's small population enabled the House of Saud to give every Saudi citizen a share of prosperity on a scale few rulers have ever matched. Through careful management, there would have been enough money to make every citizen a ward of the state. King Faisal early rejected this idea, choosing instead to press the Saudis into the work force while cushioning them against serious need with grants, loans, subsidies, and government services. By 1980 this combination was providing a per capita income from employment of almost $2500 a month, supplemented by a pantheon of government programs that added another 29 percent to personal income.

The wide-ranging benefits of Saudi citizenship began with the tax system. To stay in power, the House of Saud historically has collected taxes from the Saudis themselves only when it was essential for the kingdom to survive. Like any restriction on their freedom as men, the Saudis not only abhor taxes but question any government's right to collect them. The prevailing attitude is summed up in the statement issued by the Ikhwan in its dispute with Abdul Aziz over the tobacco tax in 1927. "Taxes, we have ruled, are completely illegal and it is the king's duty to remit them, but if he refuses to do so we do not feel it permissible to break up Moslem unity and revolt against him solely on this account."* To everyone's delight, oil income after 1973 relieved the government of the need to supplement its income from pilgrims' receipts and limited oil revenues with taxes. The flimsy tax code crumbled. There remained some indirect taxes, such as modest and selective customs duties, a tariff of 20 percent on the few items produced locally, and a poorly administered social security tax on wages. The only direct tax Saudis were asked to pay, which they ignored more often than they remitted, was the religiously mandated *zakat,* or alms tax. Otherwise Saudi Arabia was tax free.

Not only did the citizens pay little or nothing into the government, there were elaborate mechanisms in every sector of the economy for distributing wealth to Saudi nationals. The agricultural sector is representative of how the system of distributing wealth worked.

The government declared increased agricultural production as a major goal of economic development and designated enormous sums of money for farming. Through his long-time ties with the royal family, a local *sheikh* exerted his influence to gain access to those funds which farmers in his area could use to buy farm equipment. This same *sheikh* then became the representative of a Saudi company that distributed foreign-manufactured farm machinery. The distributing agent and his

---

*Quoted in Christine Moss Helms, *The Cohesion of Saudi Arabia: Evolution of Political Identity* (London: Croom Helm, 1981), p. 169.

foreign partners, accompanied by the *sheikh,* went into the *sheikh*'s locality and sold each farmer tractors and plows. On signing the contract, the local farmer received a document from the equipment company certifying that he had contracted to purchase $100,000 in farm equipment. The farmer, often escorted by the *sheikh,* took the document to the Ministry of Agriculture to be officially stamped. From there it went to the bank, which paid the equipment manufacturer his full amount. The government reimbursed the bank 50 percent of the price or $50,000 and guaranteed an interest-free loan to the farmer that covered the rest of the purchase price. It was a game in which everybody won, including the foreign manufacturers. The Saudi distributing agent sold his foreign-manufactured product at a handsome profit. The *sheikh* received his share of the distributor's profits. The farmer had $100,000 worth of farm equipment for no money down and a $50,000 interest-free loan, which he in all probability would never repay. The bank eventually realized its capital plus "service fees." And the House of Saud reaped the political benefits of keeping its citizens happy without being forced to share political power.

It was in this interrelationship between government grants and contracts with Saudi owned or sponsored business that the middle class began to rise. It was a class the House of Saud deliberately created for several reasons. The birth of an entrepreneurial class was a way to bring Saudis, some of whom lacked connections through tribal or village structures, into the new economic system presided over by the House of Saud. The more progressive elements in the royal family also saw it as a way to lessen their domination by the religious fundamentalists. Yet the rise of the middle class was ultimately due to the crucial fact that the skills and services of educated Saudis were essential if Saudi Arabia were to modernize. Unless Saudi Arabia could produce its own managers and technicians, it would be forever dependent on its hated foreign work force.

As young Saudis were drawn into the new economic order and as they moved from their tribal locations into the urban areas, the network of the royal family, the *sheikh,* and the people, the vital composition of the al-Sauds' political formula, also began to weaken. The centralization of government and the weaning away of people from their tribal identities by growing Saudi nationalism were looked on with favor by the House of Saud. The leadership, with the possible exception of Abdullah, perceived that Saudi Arabia was moving forward in orderly fashion. The task of the royal family was to continue to provide for the economic well-being of its flock to see that progress continued. Saudi citizenship, restricted, with rare exceptions, to those born of a Saudi father, created its own aristocracy. Benefits accruing to these citizens seemed endless. "The council [of ministers] agreed that the state will pay the cost of transport of any Saudi national who dies abroad or will pay his burial cost if his family requests so." * Jobs in the civil service, the army, and the police, as well as jobs driving taxis, were set aside for Saudi nationals. In all other jobs, Saudi nationals had first choice — in fact were implored to take jobs that would otherwise have to be filled by foreigners.

As a way of mitigating the high rates of inflation generated by the oil boom, an elaborate system of subsidies evolved during the mid-1970s. Between fiscal year 1975–76 and the end of fiscal year 1982–83, the government of Saudi Arabia spent $12.9 billion on a whole range of direct subsidies. Food subsidies alone consumed $3.3 billion, while another $1.9 billion went to reduce the cost of electricity for individuals and businesses. Interest-free loans for real estate, industrial development, agriculture, construction, hotels, hospitals, and bakeries amounted to another $31.6 billion. And while the rest of the world was paying record-high prices for gasoline, those of us in Saudi Arabia paid 18 cents a gallon.

King Khalid's own pet project was to move all Saudis out of tents and hovels into permanent housing. To meet the goal, rush housing projects were instituted in Jeddah, al-Khobar, and Riyadh. Impressive high-rise apartment complexes with open areas, playgrounds for children, schools, retail space, and mosques rose on accelerated schedules. Building forged ahead despite the warnings by both Western advisers and some Saudis in government that the lower classes, who were mostly rural, would never live in high-rise apartments. They were too small to accommodate the joint families in which most of these people lived and there was no place to keep their livestock. Khalid, determined to provide housing for everyone as fast as possible, refused to listen. The three projects cost over $295 million each, and four years after they were completed not one apartment was occupied.

Individual family housing was more successful. I often drove through the town of Nassim, just on the outskirts of Riyadh. The town did not

---

*Arab News, January 25, 1984.

exist when I arrived in Saudi Arabia. The land where it now stands was parceled out by the government to low-income men, and the Real Estate Development Fund provided the loans to build square concrete-block houses. But in Nassim, like numbers of towns on the fringe of a metropolis, many people who had drifted in from the desert and small towns still lived in shacks constructed of packing cases. Some were still clinging to their nomadic roots and migrated to the cities for brief periods of time. Others had taken land grants and building funds from the government and built houses that they then rented to foreigners. Living on the rental proceeds, they were relieved of the need to take a job.

The Real Estate Development Fund was open to all Saudis, not just the poor. Any Saudi could qualify for a twenty-five-year interest- and fee-free loan to cover 70 percent of the cost of a house. There was a two-year grace period between the time the house was completed and the first payment was due. If the borrower repaid the loan a year before it was due, he was granted a 10 percent discount on the total of the loan. If the loan was repaid on time, he got another 20 percent discount. And anyone could get a loan whether he needed a house or not. Like the residents of Nassim, enterprising Saudis who had access to land became real estate tycoons by borrowing money, building houses, and renting them out to foreigners.

Then there were the education programs. All education was free. The government paid tuition and for books and clothes. Those enrolled in higher education programs — technical, religious, or academic — were paid monthly stipends, which increased in value as a student advanced in school. Within the kingdom's own system of higher education, a student was granted twelve subsidized years to complete an undergraduate degree. The elite, Saudis who qualified to study abroad, had all their expenses paid and received a salary of approximately $12,000 a year while in school.*

Health care at government hospitals was either free or provided at absurdly low fees. This included medication, dental care, wheelchairs, crutches, and so on. Patients with unique problems who could not be treated within the kingdom were sent abroad accompanied by at least

---

*Students on government-funded education programs were required to return to Saudi Arabia to work for the government for the same number of years that they studied abroad. In 1984 this rule was altered to allow foreign-educated Saudis to enter the private sector.

one family member, with the government paying all expenses.

The list of handouts went on and on, and the Saudis quickly learned how to apply traditional patterns of family and tribal connections to gain a share in the largess. Of all the government programs, it was the system of social security that was the most alien to traditional Saudi culture. The General Organization of Social Insurance, started by King Faisal in 1962, was greatly expanded during the oil boom. In instituting the system, Faisal said that the social security system was designed "to make the State fully responsible for the support of the aged, the disabled, orphans, and women who have no means of support."* It was revolutionary in that it moved government into areas that previously had been the sole responsibility of the joint family system. By 1980 social assistance was going to families of prisoners, the sick, the poor, the temporarily needy, and victims of natural disasters. To make sure that the recipients understood that the money came through the graciousness of the king, special committees in Taif on occasion delivered the money personally.

As primitive as this method of distribution appears, there was no easy solution to Saudi Arabia's dilemma of too much money. By the nature of the al-Saud monarchy, the plenitude had to be spread among the people just as Abdul Aziz and his tribal predecessors had spread their meager resources. But the immediate outcome of all of this generosity was that the Saudi people learned to expect that income was delivered, not earned. Needs and desires were satisfied by plugging into the pipeline of special favors distributed by persons in power. Work continued to be held in low esteem. Saudi Arabia's promise was the pleasure of the moment.

In 1979, with oil revenues pouring in at the rate of $65 billion a year, $180 million a day, and $7 million an hour, Saudi Arabia was like a great feast to which everyone had been invited. Conspicuous consumption was rampant. Anything that could be forced through the clogged ports would sell. A group of enterprising merchandisers from Denmark, Sweden, Finland, and Norway turned a North Sea ferry into a luxurious floating exhibition called Scan-Arab 80 and steamed into Jeddah. On board were racks of $12,000 fox fur coats and even costlier minks and sables, a 1927 vintage Cadillac, complete services of Swed-

---

*Quoted in Willard A. Beling, ed., *King Faisal and the Modernization of Saudi Arabia* (London: Croom Helm, 1980), p. 22.

ish Rorstran porcelain initialed in gold, and handloomed carpets with verses from the Koran emblazoned across them. So eager were the Saudis to buy, traffic to the pier where the boat was docked was backed up bumper to bumper for a mile.

The parameters of good taste exploded as the Saudis embellished their homes with items so gaudy as to defy description. Typical was a suite of furniture consisting of a settee, coffee table, standing screen, sideboard, and mirror that sported fanned peacock tails incrusted with dense inlaid mother-of-pearl and turned wooden knobs on each piece. There were clam-shaped Fiberglas bathtubs flecked with gold, covered by canopies upholstered in fake fur with crystal chandeliers dangling from the center and wired for stereophonic sound. The Saudis imported absurd Venetian glass light fixtures heavily laden with designs of fruit intertwined with drooping purple irises. Pseudo-fountains, molded of black plastic with sprays of thin plastic threads propelled by a motor and illuminated by colored lights, went into their foyers. There were telephones four feet tall, carved from wood covered in gold leaf with a picture of the Mona Lisa gazing from the center of the dial.

I once had dinner at the home of a *sheikh* where the floors were covered with exquisite silk Niyain rugs and price tags hung from all the lamps and furniture so his friends could see how much everything had cost.

Many of the cars that clogged the streets carried the yellow grease marks wiped on by customs officials at the port of Dammam and a weathered price sheet on the back side window, both confirmations that the owner was driving a new, not a secondhand car. Princes bought and quickly cast off a vast array of automobiles. At the used car *souq,* some Canadian friends of mine bought a reproduction Stutz Bearcat with a mink-lined trunk, which had belonged to Prince Naif.

The wealth was preposterous. A servant once offered me a towel and a liter bottle of Chanel No. 5 to wash my hands. A gold dealer sat in an open-front shop on Tamari selling kilo (2.2 pounds) bars of gold out of a dirty glass case, tossing his receipts into an old wooden box.

Electric hookahs and fine jewelry often shared the same display space. Despite the Wahhabi injunction against men wearing jewelry, Saudis were buying matched sets that included a gold watch, the face of which was incrusted with pavé diamonds, a ring, pen, pencil, and set of prayer beads. Out of curiosity, I once asked a clerk in an exclusive store on

Wassir Street how much one of these ensembles cost. His caustic reply
was, "Too much for you."

But the real national obsession was Kleenex box holders. No Saudi
room was complete without an elaborate container for tissues crafted
in everything from porcelain to chrome to gold filigree to acrylic. They
sat on coffee tables, dominated the accouterments attending an international conference, and graced the king's limousine. This enshrine-
ment of the disposable somehow made a profound statement about the
philosophy that permeated Saudi Arabia during the oil boom.

The Westerners consumed along with the Saudis, just more mod-
estly. With large discretionary incomes and little to buy, Westerners
gobbled up duty-free Japanese cameras, watches, and stereo equipment. Armed with *riyals,* which the kids called "rats," Westerners hit
the *souqs* on the weekends to see what else had made its way into
Saudi Arabia. But it was gold that was the irresistible attraction. One
of the major gold markets in Riyadh was in the old Dirrah *souq,* near
the clock tower. Dirrah was an authentic Oriental bazaar, a bastion of
traditional Saudi market life. Under the broad tin roof, dirt-floor stalls
were jumbled together along narrow, winding aisles. There was always something exhilarating about entering Dirrah's dark confines
spotlighted by bare electric bulbs dangling from frayed cords, smelling
the pungent aroma of the spices overlaid with the heavy, mysterious
fragrance of incense burning in the old wooden containers. The aisles
were always crowded, an important aspect of the ambience of the *souq.*

Merchants selling the same items clustered together. Coming in off
the Tamari Street side, the fabric dealers were first. Lengths of bright
cloth hung from wires strung between the posts defining each shop.
Buttons and thread were thrown into big baskets sitting before the single counter cluttered with lace and other bric-a-brac. Farther on were
the underwear merchants. The big boxer shorts that Saudi men wear
under their *thobes* were pinned to misshapen hangers that overlapped
each other up a rickety wall. On past these were the spice dealers, who
as a result of the boom had added laundry detergent and Pepsi to their
inventory. Then there were the cosmetic and perfume dealers, always
with a group of women crowded around their counters. The sandal
maker, the scissors sharpener, the roving vendor hawking fly nets to
put over baby beds, the *darum* merchant selling the soft sticks that
brush a Saudi's teeth as he chews — they were all there. And grouped
in among it all, occupying the same dilapidated quarters, were the gold
merchants.

Of all of the signs of incredible wealth that surrounded me every day, nothing awed me as much as the gold *souqs*. In one shop after another, each no more than a hovel, cracked, tottery showcases held stacks of 18 and 21 karat gold bangle bracelets, heavy earrings, and charms designed to dangle from the pin in a baby's diaper. Glittering in the harsh light of unshaded electric bulbs was wedding jewelry attached to the walls by rusting nails. The gold breastplates, wide bracelets with five matching rings (one for each finger) dangling from gold chains, and big medallions set with pearls and rubies hung in the open with no protection other than the lone shopkeeper. There were items for the Westerner, too. Modest gold chains, strung in groups of twenty and thirty on clumsy metal rings, were thrown in a corner on the back counter. There were some small Western-style earrings and less cumbersome bangle bracelets that appealed to Western tastes and pocketbooks. The gold merchants had little patience with their Western customers, who browsed in the gold *souqs* often just to pass the time. There were serious shoppers among the Westerners, however, and on occasion women as well as men bought a ring or a necklace on impulse the way they would buy a blouse or shirt at home.

Workmanship in a piece of jewelry had no bearing on its price, and the price varied every day depending on the international price of gold. A buyer interested in an item pointed it out to the merchant, who threw it on his scale, figured the weight and the price per gram on his Japanese calculator, and announced the total. The haggling then began, with weight rechecked and figures punched in the calculator again and again until either a deal was struck or the customer left, usually followed by a torrent of abusive language.

Next to gold, Westerners delighted most in T-shirts. Some enterprising Saudi entrepreneur learned about this Western passion very early. The first shirts carried captions like "I'm no tourist, I work here," "Saudi Arabia — Thrill a Minute," or "Smile, You're in Saudi Arabia." Colin once had a mustard-colored shirt adorned with a sober group of Peanuts characters clothed in *gutras* that proclaimed, "Happiness is being one of the gang in Saudi Arabia."

Westerners found themselves spending an inordinate amount of time in the *souqs* largely because there was little else to do. According to the *Guide to Riyadh* published by the Ministry of Information, "Entertainment for expatriates is not commercially organized . . . ." In the Wahhabi world of Saudi Arabia, any form of public entertainment fell into the category of sin. There were no movies, theaters, or clubs.

There were no sporting events except the royal horse races. There was no television. Until after 1980, the Intercontinental Hotel was one of the few places where couples could go out to dinner. The foreigner was, and remains, on his own to make his entertainment. People working on isolated construction sites or living in single villas not attached to a large company truly suffered. Outside of ARAMCO, the major embassies, and the U.S. Army Corps of Engineers, the King Faisal hospital probably had the best recreation facilities available in the kingdom. Much of this was due to the desire of the royal family to staff their hospital with not only Western doctors but Western auxiliary personnel, especially nurses and technicians. With many single women in its employ, the hospital made a serious effort to provide some forms of entertainment. We had swimming pools and tennis courts, and a recreation center where hamburgers were available two hours a day. There was bingo on Monday night, and we had our own in-house television system which showed videotaped movies from the United States several hours a day. I must have seen the 1950s "B" movie *Krakatoa East of Java* at least ten times.

There were softball teams, tennis tournaments, exercise classes, swim meets, water polo teams — all of which the Saudis looked on with wry amusement, wondering why Westerners enjoyed physical exertion. Children played with whoever was available regardless of age, sex, or what language he spoke. They devised imaginative games that occupied them for hours and they seldom complained of being bored.

The adults read or played chess, bridge, or Monopoly. My friend Sarah Day and I made up a board game about the hassles of life in Saudi Arabia called *Bukarah, in-shaalah* ("Tomorrow, God Willing"). Mostly we wandered from house to house, eating and exchanging the latest stories on the trials, tribulations, and joys of life in Saudi Arabia.

There were some less mundane entertainments as well. A few sand sailers — metal tripods equipped with wheels and a sail — made their way into the country. The lucky few who had these skirted across the empty desert in a stiff wind until they were upturned by one of the big rocks that jut out of the desert floor. For those living in Jeddah, the Red Sea offered some of the best snorkeling and scuba diving in the world. Groups equipped with tents and gear drove or flew from Riyadh and camped along the beaches from Jeddah to Yanbu. There were daybreak expeditions to the desert to search for a high-quality quartz called *quasuma* diamonds. Scattered on the desert, they were best spotted at sunrise, when the slanted rays of the sun reflect off the surface. Although some people had theirs cut into stones in Bangkok, it was the thrill of the search rather than the reward that hauled people starved for recreation out of their beds while it was still dark.

Sadly, there were many Westerners who, except for the hours spent on their jobs, stayed entombed in their apartments and compounds. It was their loss. The streets teemed with marvelous scenes of human activity that can never be recaptured. Those who shut themselves up in the Western community missed it all. Even more they missed the beauty of the desert. I never believed that first day in Saudi Arabia that I would come to love the desert with a passion. Within the towns and cities, the natural beauty of earth packed to the strength of concrete, the sharding of low limestone hills, and the gift of a single flower enduring without water or shade are all corrupted by the litter of man. But within an hour of Riyadh, into the valleys of Wadi Hanifa or east to the plateaus beyond Khurays, the desert remained in its virgin state. On weekends we loaded our four-wheel-drive vehicles with everything required for survival and headed for the desert in a convoy. As I left behind the walls I spent so much of my time behind and the restraints of an Islamic state, the desert came to represent freedom, a restoration of the soul. Setting up camp, we piled up wood scrounged from Riyadh's construction sites. Charcoal pits were scooped out of the sand to cook supper. Cots and tents went up. The big mats we bought in the Yemeni *souqs* were unrolled and placed end to end to create the center of the camp community. People scattered out from the campsite to look for fossils or just to walk. Camels swayed across the landscape at sunset or wandered into the middle of the camp, where they stood placidly staring. As the sun went down, the sky came alive with stars we never saw from the city because of the lights and pollutants of modernization. As the evening wore on, different members of the group would break off to go to their tents, until finally the camp was engulfed in an exquisite peace.

But we were always aware that the desert could also be deadly. One summer two Americans, experts in desert survival, left their disabled car in search of help. Their bodies, charred black by the sun, were found four days later within sight of the highway. And another summer, Gerhardt Reiner, a towering Austrian with the body of a conditioned athlete, died of dehydration one Friday afternoon while climbing on a rock formation.

The Westerners' major form of diversion was travel. Like middle-

class jet setters, we traveled everywhere on the fat salaries and generous vacation time provided by our Saudi masters. It was this leave time
that maintained a Westerner's equilibrium. No matter how stressful
conditions might become, there was always the next vacation to look
forward to. I will never forget an all-night flight to Athens on which
two men in front of me were drinking one beer after another and talking and talking and talking. As I was about to scream "Go to sleep!"
I heard them exchanging stories about the three-month stint they had
just completed on an offshore drilling rig in the Arabian Gulf. I smiled
and went to sleep myself.

After a few years in the kingdom, it was the rare Westerner who had
not been on safari in Africa, shopping in Hong Kong, scuba diving in
the Seychelles, trekking in Nepal, or relaxing on a houseboat in Kash-
mir. Many of us routinely went around the world once a year on the
annual leave tickets issued by our Saudi employers. But we gladly
passed up those special bargains Saudia Airlines offered, such as the
nine-day excursion ticket to London by way of Hong Kong.

They were good times. Saudi Arabia was riding the crest of the
wave. The Saudis perceived themselves as masters of the petroleum
universe. Nations bowed down before them, flattered and proposi-
tioned them. The Westerners, although bitterly resented, were seen as
posing no real threat. Perhaps we were an annoyance to their traditional values, but for the most part we did our work and stayed out of
the Saudis' lives. Throughout the political upheavals in Afghanistan,
Iran, and Lebanon, Saudi Arabia appeared to be remarkably stable.
The House of Saud prided itself on the tranquility of its kingdom, a
stability the Saudis took for granted. And the Westerners, lulled by the
same sense of security, stayed on to work, feeling protected from the
tumult that surrounded the kingdom. Abruptly, in one day, it all changed.

Although the political stability in the kingdom and Saudi Arabia's
peaceful relations with its neighbors was much touted by the House of
Saud, 1979 had been a year of uncertainty. To the east, the year began
with the shah's flight from Iran. While the shah was no special friend
of Saudi Arabia, his departure was nevertheless viewed with consternation by the House of Saud on several grounds. The fall of any monarchy in the Arabian Gulf threatened to bring into question the sound-
ness of the House of Saud. But a monarch forced to flee passions
inflamed by a religious leader pierced the House of Saud's Achilles'
heel — its fear of its own religious fundamentalists. Moreover, the
House of Saud interpreted the hesitancy of the United States to prop

up the regime of the shah as treason against its allies. The United States, although kept at arm's length by Saudi Arabia's rulers, is the House of Saud's defense of last resort. If the United States were willing to desert the shah of Iran, with whom it enjoyed a far cozier relationship than with Saudi Arabia's leaders, what were the Americans likely to do if the House of Saud were threatened? These were profound questions for the defenseless oil producer.

Throughout the year, the Westerners in Saudi Arabia were exposed to tales of harrowing escapes from the Islamic revolution by the procession of evacuees arriving in the kingdom to work. In early November, we watched as the blindfolded hostages from the American embassy in Teheran were paraded before the world to demonstrate the impotence of the United States in the face of Islamic vengeance. Although there was no apparent instability in Saudi Arabia, our experience of living in an Islamic state nudged our mild anxieties about the possibility of a fundamentalist uprising.

Farther to the east, the government of Afghanistan had signed a treaty of friendship with the Soviet Union in December 1978. The Saudi press resounded with warnings of danger from the alliance and pleaded for the Carter administration to lead a Western response to the Soviet threat. The Saudis were shaken. More alarmed than the West, the Saudis envisioned the Russians pushing to the Arabian Gulf, planting a Marxist, atheistic, anti-monarchical superpower at Saudi Arabia's door.

To the south, the ongoing squabbles between the People's Republic of Yemen (a Soviet puppet state) and the Arab Republic of Yemen (vassal to Saudi Arabia's foreign aid) were flaring once again. In February, border clashes put the Saudi armed forces on alert, while rumors flew through Riyadh that twenty-five hundred United States paratroopers in full battle dress had landed at the Riyadh airport and crates of ammunition were being moved out of the buildings behind Abdul Aziz's decaying palace in al-Kharj to be shipped south.

Saudi anxieties were ignored by Western governments and presses alike. As I turned out one story after another about the threats Saudi Arabia perceived from Afghanistan, Iran, and Yemen, they were largely passed over by editors more interested in articles about Saudi Arabia's money, not its problems. Even for those of us in the kingdom, those problems were external. Except for a vague disquiet, life rolled on in the flush of the oil boom.

It was Tuesday, November 20, 1979. We had just sat down to dinner when Mary Johnston, my neighbor across the sidewalk in Rainbow Villas, burst through the front door. Pale, clutching her chronically nervous stomach, she gasped, "There has been a coup at Mecca!" Jumping up from the table, Dan and I fired one question after another at her. All she knew was that as her husband, Brent, left the hospital, he passed Dr. Nizar Fetieh, the king's personal cardiologist, racing toward a waiting car. Fetieh told Brent that Mecca was in the hands of rebels. Word shot through our compound, and within minutes neighbors began to collect at my house, carrying a variety of short-wave radios. Fanning out through the house, everyone tried without success to tune in the BBC or Voice of America. Dan, surprised to find the telephone still working, called the U.S. Embassy Liaison Office in Riyadh. Amazed at being able to get through, he asked if there was any word of disorders in Mecca. A flat, dispassionate female voice answered, "I will read a statement from Ambassador John West." The crux of the message was that there had been a disturbance in Mecca but there was no indication that Americans or other Westerners were involved. Americans were advised to stay within their homes or places of employment. "Thank you for calling." Then Dan said, "O.K., that's the official word, now what is really going on?" Without pausing, the efficient voice dissolved into gossipy intimacy. "We have no idea. All we know for sure is that something big is happening at Mecca and all of our international communications lines have been cut." What was happening at Mecca was the most serious challenge to the House of Saud since 1929, when the Ikhwan, proclaiming holy war, rose up against Abdul Aziz.

At 4:30 A.M. on the first day of the Hijrah year 1400, Juhaiman ibn Mohammed ibn Saif al-Utaibi grabbed a microphone in the cavernous courtyard of the Grand Mosque at Mecca and beseeched the approximately fifty thousand assembled worshipers to recognize his brother-in-law, Mohammed ibn Abdullah al-Qahtani, as the promised *mahdi*.* But as events unfolded, it became apparent that Juhaiman ibn Mohammed's proclamation of the *mahdi* was more a political tool with which to attack the House of Saud than theology.

Juhaiman, a wild-eyed man with a heavy, matted beard like the old Ikhwan, shouted to the crowd. Picking up on charges being hurled by

*For the Moslems who adhere to the concept, the *mahdi* is like a redeemer, the *imam* who returns as the spiritual guide of the community.

Iran's Ayatollah Ruhollah Khomeini, Juhaiman railed that monarchies are alien to Islam and denounced the al-Sauds' legitimacy to rule. With the fire of evangelism, he attacked financial corruption among members of the royal family, their foreign travels, and their practice of drinking alcoholic beverages. Over the prayer microphones that carried his words to Mecca's nearby neighborhoods, he demanded that the kingdom be cleansed of the corruption of foreign ways thrust on Saudi Arabia by the House of Saud's modernization policies.

Juhaiman had with him a band of followers numbering between two hundred and three hundred men. They were purportedly armed with an odd assortment of weapons, including AK-47s and various bastardized weapons that commonly circulate among the tribesmen of Yemen. The rebels' stock of ammunition and their food supply of dates and water, the mainstay of the Ikhwan soldier, were reported to have been smuggled in through the service entrances of the mosque the day before. Yet two months after the Mecca uprising, Sheikh Abdul Aziz al-Tweijry, assistant deputy commander of the National Guard, told me that Juhaiman's weapons came directly from the stores of the National Guard and were driven into the mosque in convoys of National Guard trucks.

The leader and the core of his group holding the mosque were cut from the same cloth and motivated by the same ideals as some of their ancestors who fought Abdul Aziz in the Ikhwan revolt. Juhaiman and his followers wore the old Ikhwan *thobe* cut above the ankles and grew shaggy beards and long hair. Juhaiman himself was a member of the politically powerful Utaibah tribe and had served in the Utaibah section of the National Guard when he was a teenager. About the time of the oil embargo, Juhaiman is believed to have rediscovered religion and been drawn into the religious community at the Prophet's Mosque in Medina, where he fell under the influence of the infamous Sheikh Abdul Aziz ibn Baz. Living in one of the free hostels that the Saudi government provides for worshipers and students, Juhaiman increasingly was drawn to those disgruntled about Western influences on the Islamic world. The Westernization of Saudi Arabia under the leadership of the House of Saud would become Juhaiman's own crusade. During 1979 the group acquired another source of inspiration — the escalating power of the Ayatollah Khomeini and the Islamic revival that his revolution in Iran had fired.

Soon after Juhaiman seized the mosque, the impracticality of holding fifty thousand hostages became obvious. He singled out perhaps thirty of the frightened worshipers and let the rest go to stream out of the mosque and sound the alarm. Throughout the morning, no one other than the residents of Mecca and the inner circle of the royal family and the military knew that God's house was being held hostage. At noon all communications with the outside world were cut and civilian aircraft ordered to stand silent on the runways of the airports. Meanwhile, pandemonium reigned among the decision-makers. King Khalid's brothers Sultan and Naif, ministers of Defense and Interior, rushed to Mecca. Crown Prince Fahd was in Tunis at a meeting of Arab leaders, cut off by the communications blackout. Abdullah, commander of the National Guard, was noticeably absent, an indication of the level of concern about the involvement of the military force he commanded. By nightfall, about the time I heard of the uprising, enough organization had emerged to put the Saudi Arabian army and air force on an "A" alert and mobilize the National Guard.

Through much of the night, people continued to wander in and out of my house. Radios crackled and squawked as we searched the dials for news, any news. We gathered up passports, weighted ourselves down with jewelry, and collected all of the cash that we had on hand. Some desperately tried to cram their collections of Oriental rugs into hand luggage in case we had to evacuate. Periodically scouts were sent out on the streets, who reported back that everything seemed quiet. Finally we all went to bed.

The next morning armed guards were on top of the hospital and every car that went through the gate was thoroughly searched. Hospital beds were cleared of noncritical patients to make way for anticipated casualties. At this point, the crucial question facing the king was how to get the rebels out of Islam's most sacred mosque, the mosque for which the House of Saud claimed responsibility. In the pictures of the king that had begun to appear in the papers, Khalid looked anguished, like a father perplexed and disappointed by the behavior of his children. With the rebels using the mosque as a fortress, there was no alternative but to storm it with the Saudi military. The *ulema*, which had been summoned on the morning of the uprising, struggled with the theological problem of bloodshed and violence in God's holiest house. By noon on Wednesday, international communications had been reestablished, and the Ministry of Information began to mobilize the Islamic world in support of a move against the Grand Mosque. At last the *ulema*, citing an "ignoble crime and an act of atheism in the House of God,'' issued a *fatwa* declaring holy war, and the long siege on the mosque began.

The trouble at Mecca had erupted on Tuesday. On Wednesday, Pakistani mobs burned the American embassy in Islamabad, claiming the United States was responsible for the events at Mecca. With Mecca under siege, Americans held hostage in Iran, and now another American embassy in flames, the Western staff at the hospital was called together and told to stay in our compounds for our own safety. The next day, Thursday, happened to coincide with the American observance of Thanksgiving. For several weeks, we had planned to go to al-Khobar for Thanksgiving dinner with friends from home. Never ones to be deterred by undefined peril, Dan and I decided to go in spite of the warning. When we drove to the airport at about 9:00 A.M., the streets were all but deserted and an anxious pall hung over the city. The airport was similarly deserted. Saudia Airlines had one desk open. For once we were able to check in quickly and move on to the security check. This is where the trouble developed. I learned one lesson from the Mecca uprising: never go through airport security in a country in the throes of revolution, carrying a pumpkin pie! The guards, already highly nervous, took one look at me and my pie and went berserk. Every item we were carrying was thrown on the conveyor belt to be scrutinized by x-ray before it was hand searched and examined with a metal detector. As I said over and over, *"Akel, akel, akel,"* which is the Arabic equivalent of "eat," the pie was eyed, poked, and shaken. Apparently not knowing what else to do, the guards finally allowed me and my now disheveled pastry to pass.

It was a week before the mosque was retaken. Saudi soldiers fought pillar to pillar through the great mosque, dislodging the renegades one by one. The rebels, some with their women and children, were holed up in the vast maze of rooms beneath the mosque. On the fourth day of the siege, the self-proclaimed *mahdi* was shot and his body dragged before photographers to prove he was not God's chosen. But Juhaiman and a core of followers still held out, despite tear gas, burning tires, and a desperate plan to electrocute the rebels by flooding the catacombs with water and sending live electrical cables into them. At last, in the glare of Saudi television cameras, Juhaiman was dragged out, still defiant. In all the government claimed that 127 of its men were killed and 461 injured. One hundred and seventeen of the rebels died, as well as a dozen or more of their hostages. The figures for both sides were probably much higher. From the reports I garnered during the week, the hospitals in Mecca and Jeddah were full, forcing the overflow to Riyadh.

On January 9, 1980, sixty-three men were executed in eight cities and towns across Saudi Arabia for their part in the uprising. The sentences and the locations in which they were carried out sent a clear message to those who would challenge the House of Saud. If the magnitude of the beheadings was a surprise to the Saudi population not accustomed to public punishment of political dissidents, so much the better. The locations of the executions, extending across the kingdom, were carefully chosen not only to give maximum exposure but, one suspects, to reach other potential nests of discontent. Mecca and Medina, aside from their religious significance, are both near Jeddah, the heart of the western coastal area. Ten were beheaded in Riyadh, where they could be observed by the large number of Yemenis and other laborers from underdeveloped countries working in the city to warn them of the danger to foreign nationals who involve themselves in the political affairs of Saudi Arabia. Tabuk, another execution site, is near the Jordanian border and is the location of the country's largest air force base. There had been continuing rumors since spring of plots within the air force against the crown, and in the official shuffles that took place in the aftermath of Mecca, the command of the air force was the hardest hit. Buraydah, in the north central part of the country, is a hotbed of fundamentalism even in the most normal of circumstances. Finally, Dammam, the capital of the Eastern Province, is not far from Qatif, the center of Saudi Arabia's Shiite minority of two hundred thousand.*

In choosing the Grand Mosque as the point of attack, the rebels seized the symbol of the theocracy presided over by the House of Saud. But by failing in the attack, the rebels sealed their own fate and gave the al-Sauds carte blanche to carry out public executions for religious transgressions that were in reality crimes of politics. Political dissent is not permitted by the House of Saud. The ban on political parties and protest is defended on the religious grounds that politics is a violation of the Koranic injunction against divisive sects. Throughout its history, the House of Saud has used Islam to justify its policies and legit-

---

*There is another concentration of Shiites in the Assir, but they are ethnically Yemeni and followers of Yemen's own form of Shiism.

imize its rule. But as a result of the uprising at Mecca, Islam was turned against those who claim to be its most aggressive defenders. After carefully cultivating a traditional posture on social and religious matters to protect the ruling elite from being identified too closely with the West, the royal family suddenly found its whole right to rule brought into question by those whom it had tried to placate. Religious doctrine turned on the House of Saud and sought to deny it its right of position and power.

There are several unanswered questions about Mecca. The first is whether the royal family was caught as totally unawares by the uprising as it claimed. As defender of the faith, the king or other high-ranking official from the royal family annually led the prayers at Mecca on the first day of the new year. With November 20 marking the beginning of the year 1400, a new century, the king certainly would be expected to be present. Although King Khalid was suffering from a mild illness, Abdullah, Sultan, or Fawwaz, the governor of Mecca, would have represented him unless they had prior warning. The original plan may well have been predicated on trapping Khalid in the mosque. With the king in custody, the revolt, in the eyes of the perpetrators, might have had some chance for success. As it turned out, their mistake was their failure to anticipate the revulsion the Saudis felt about the armed seizure of Islam's most holy site.

Throughout the ordeal of Mecca, the House of Saud tenaciously clung to its story that the uprising was the work of a cadre of religious fanatics. It was the explanation with which the rulers felt the most comfortable. The House of Saud had a certain confidence in its ability to control the religious issue. But the uprising at Mecca represented a mixed religious, sociological, and political protest. It was first a religious protest against the impious behavior and Westernization of the royal family. But it also represented the long-standing regional tensions that exist between the Nejd and the Hijaz. Moreover, Mecca raised the frightening specter of Saudi Arabia's being dragged into the Middle East's boiling political caldron. The number of foreigners who were executed along with the Saudis proved what the government was never previously willing to admit, that outside agitators were involved.

Of the sixty-three men executed, there were forty-four Saudis, seven Egyptians, six from the People's Republic of Yemen, three from Kuwait, one Sudanese, one Iraqi, and one from the Arab Republic of Yemen. From the beginning the involvement of foreigners had to be suspected because of the proficiency with which the whole revolt was organized. Members of the National Guard may have been drawn into the plot by opposition to Westernization, but it is difficult to imagine that they could have organized the revolt. It would not have been in character for Bedouin soldiers, most of them illiterate and poorly ed- ucated, to draw up an elaborate plan, commandeer arms, and smuggle them into the mosque. Bedouins do not plan and organize, they react.

Yet the great unanswered question about the Mecca uprising con- cerns the whole concept of the *mahdi*, the religious figure in whose name the rebellion was staged, and its relationship to religious funda- mentalism in Saudi Arabia. The idea of a *mahdi* or messiah is alien to Wahhabism and is, at best, fuzzy within the mainstream of Islam. The *mahdi* is never mentioned in the Koran, nor does it have any real place in the traditions of the Sunni sect. Rather the idea surfaced during the leadership disputes over Mohammed's successor and was never seri- ously embodied into Islamic theology based on the *hadith*. The belief in the *mahdi* has its origins in Christian and Persian thought, and within Islam relates, culturally and theologically, to Shiism — a point that never seemed to work its way through all of the speculation that char- acterized the post-Mecca quarterbacking.

Juhaiman, who was so fanatical in his beliefs that he would not sit next to a foreigner and considered eating with anything other than his hands as sinful, was probably nothing more than a Wahhabi zealot. However, the Iranian revolution paradigm, so much admired among religious students in Mecca in 1979, doubtless had a vague and general effect on him.

There is no evidence to confirm that Saudi Shiites played any sig- nificant role in the Mecca uprising although there has been speculation to that effect. Saudi Arabia's Shiites are despised and treated as sec- ond-class citizens in a Wahhabi kingdom. Drawing much of its labor from the Shiites of the Eastern Province, ARAMCO pumped Saudi Arabia's wealth out of the ground and the House of Saud spent it on their grand schemes for Riyadh and the Western Province. The Shiites stayed locked in their ghettos on the east coast, realizing little from the elaborate welfare and development schemes enjoyed by the rest of the country.

If not engineered by Shiites, the Mecca uprising fired their long- held grievances. From across the Arabian Gulf, the Ayatollah Kho- meini spoke to his co-religionists, and the House of Saud answered. In

December, while observing Ashura, the Shiite day of mourning that commemorates the death of the Imam Hussein, the residents of Qatif took to the streets as martyrs, lashing themselves with whips until the blood ran from their backs and limbs. Violence erupted when nervous National Guardsmen apparently interfered with the procession. In February 1980, riots again broke out in Qatif. Breaking windows and burning tires, Shiite demonstrators poured out their wrath against the Wahhabi majority and the economic dominance of the Nejd. The National Guard once again set upon the demonstrators, killing at least fifteen. Qatif was ringed with tanks and sealed off from the rest of the country. Rumors abounded within the kingdom that the Guard's tanks opened fire, leveling sections of the town. Arrests and interrogations followed. Only those directly involved knew exactly what happened, for Qatif remained closed for months afterward. Roadblocks north of al-Khobar manned by the military sealed off the area, its fate hidden by the House of Saud's effective system of censorship.

As soon as the revolt at Mecca was quelled and the Shiites locked in Qatif, the government began a rigorous campaign of public relations and fence mending. Choosing to ignore the foreigners who were beheaded, the House of Saud chose to regard the uprising as a revolt limited to Saudi fanatics on the fringes of Wahhabism.

Mecca was painful for rulers accustomed to being protectors of the faith, the foremost defenders of religious purity. An attack from the fundamentalists, the bedrock of their support, caught them off guard. But members of the upper echelon of the House of Saud are first and foremost politicians and only secondarily monarchists. Like a shrewd political machine, the House of Saud not only heard the voices of discontent but attacked the sources of that discontent. Although shake-ups occurred in the military and governorships that smacked of a purge, the family depended more on its network of personal favors than on retribution to put its political affairs in order. As in the past, the conservatives were played off against the liberals to keep the House of Saud secure.

Several new governorships to be presided over by high-ranking members of the royal family were created. Their purpose was to increase the royal presence in the hinterlands. The religious element was placated by a vigorous crackdown on the enforcement of religious laws. Merchants in Jeddah and Dhahran, formerly immune to the rigid religious restrictions imposed on the interior areas, were forced to follow such conservative religious practices as closing shops during prayer call. There was also an energetic campaign to scout out and close down illegal liquor stills as well as a wide publicity campaign extolling the virtues of veils for women. For a while, I found it prudent to don an *abaaya*.

The most momentous decision to come in the aftermath of Mecca was the announcement that popular participation in the government would be expanded through a nebulous entity called a "consultative council." This council, whose members would be appointed by the king, would be complementary to the Council of Ministers. Like the first modifications of Saudi Arabia's government formulated by Faisal ibn Abdul Aziz in 1958, the new system would "introduce a modern system of government without lessening the prerogatives of the King."*

Crown Prince Fahd undertook an active publicity campaign to extoll the plan. The interior minister, Prince Naif, was appointed to head the committee to draw up the plan, a committee left free of time constraints. There was widespread belief that the House of Saud was, at last, going to formalize the sharing of power rather than depending on their network of personal relationships.** Most saw the council as a concession to the religious fundamentalists who precipitated the crisis at Mecca. Instead, its purpose was to promise some form of participatory government to the new middle class. Lurking behind the whole scenario was a deliberate attempt to bring the progressive urban elements into government to dilute the overwhelming power of the religious leaders.

Mecca shocked the House of Saud, but the incident did little to sway the government from its course. The policies of modernization continued, supported by a majority of the population, who believed rapid progress was what they wanted. Saudis went West to school. Westerners continued to structure the new order. Women pushed on into the limited areas open to them. Video machines kept unreeling tapes of Egyptian belly dancers and Western movies. And traditionalists publicly railed and progressives, more than they were willing to admit,

---

*Arab News, March 24, 1980.
**Few noted that in 1924 Abdul Aziz promised to create a consultative council made up of the *ulema*, village and tribal leaders, and city merchants to act as an intermediary between the king and the people. He also promised Saudi Arabia a constitution. The consultative council never came into being as an organized body and the constitution was never written.

chafed against the erosion of their values by the onslaught of foreign ways.

The House of Saud survived the Mecca uprising, shaken but not bent. Attacked by some of its own fundamentalists, unnerved by the apparent complicity of members of the National Guard, buffeted by riots among its Shiite population, and haunted by evidence of foreign elements rocking its political stability, the kingdom of the al-Sauds saw with Mecca the end of the era when Saudi Arabia had few problems except how to spend its money.

II

The Twilight

1980 AND BEYOND

12

The Press:
Pride and Denial

IN JUNE 1980 I climbed into our dusty cloth-top Nissan Patrol for the last time. Dan's contract was finished as was my job at the Stanford Research Institute. It was time to go home and pick up our lives once again.

Sitting on the scorching seat, I waited for Derek Younge to wind a length of wire around the handle on the back door that frequently flew open when the car struck an unmarked construction hole. While the luggage was shifted one more time so the pesky door would close, I absently looked around Rainbow Villas. The flat-top metal prefabs were baking in the afternoon sun. On the sidewalk that divided the two rows of squat houses, Shelia Kingston was lugging another load of clothes to the wash house, fervently hoping that one of the washers might be working. Squealing children were weaving in and out of the fences that surrounded each of the units, stirring up the dirt with their rubber sandals. Joanne Ratcliffe was irrigating the hard earth around a struggling bougainvillea, the only bit of green that I could see.

Painfully, an acute sense of loss washed over me. I had spent two of the happiest years of my life among these people. We had wandered in and out of each other's houses as if they were our own. We had divided what little was available in the way of material goods. We had entertained each other with stories and games, shared our meals, our books, our sewing machines. Together we had survived in a primitive outpost wracked by the pains of change. And now I was going home, acutely aware of what I was losing and somehow knowing it could never be recaptured.

I felt another sense of loss. I had spent the height of the oil boom at the epicenter of events. I had occupied a front-row seat for one of the true dramas of the twentieth century. And now it was over.

When I arrived home, I found adjusting to normal life painfully difficult. Other than a press tour of Israel undertaken at the invitation of the Israeli government, I floated around, doing some political writing for a Georgia gubernatorial candidate, producing a political analysis of the Virgin Islands for a real estate firm whose client happened to be a Saudi *sheikh*, writing a number of background pieces on Saudi Arabia, and publishing an academic paper on the House of Saud. Meanwhile, I tried to follow events in Saudi Arabia from the sketchy reports filed by journalists on the typical seven-day tour of the kingdom escorted by officials of the Ministry of Information.

Life in Atlanta moved along. I eventually passed through a kind of reverse culture shock but still longed for the Middle East. After having spent two years treating an exotic array of diseases among a population barely touched by modern medicine, Dan was restless in a suburban medical practice. Although the hospital in Riyadh periodically asked Dan to come back, we had resisted, believing it was time to settle down. Then one Sunday morning in the spring of 1982, the telephone rang. It was the King Faisal Specialist Hospital, asking Dan once again to return. Maybe it was the time of year, but wanderlust irresistibly grabbed us. Throwing caution to the winds, Dan closed down his practice. I found a house sitter who would feed the dog, informed the school that Colin would not be back, and excitedly packed our trunks to return to Saudi Arabia.

During my two-year absence, the oil boom had rolled along. In 1981, every second of every hour of every day, Saudi Arabia became $3,500 richer from its sale of crude oil. This amounted to $304 million a day, more than $100 billion a year. The price of oil, which was $28.82 a barrel when I left Saudi Arabia, reached $34 a barrel in October 1981. And the giant Arabian American Oil Company (ARAMCO) had become entirely Saudi owned, an estimated $2 billion exercise in nationalism.

But despite the general euphoria, small clouds were gathering on Saudi Arabia's horizon. While the House of Saud was still assessing the threat from the Ayatollah Khomeini's Islamic revolution, the war between Iraq and Iran broke out on Saudi Arabia's doorstep in September 1981. To protect Western economies, where so much of its money was invested, Saudi Arabia pledged to up its production to cover Iraqi and Iranian oil lost to the war. In return, the United States sent four advanced-warning aircraft (AWACS) to patrol the kingdom's borders,* while the erratic Muammar Qaddafi joined the ayatollah in claiming that monarchy is incompatible with Islam and accused the House of Saud of being a puppet of American interests in the Middle East.

On the oil front, the world's shortage of petroleum was disappearing. Throughout 1980 the demand for hydrocarbons was generally flat. Even as prices peaked in October 1981, Saudi production dropped from 9.6 million barrels per day (mbd) to 8.5 mbd, partly to protect the oil fields from overproduction but also to defend OPEC's benchmark price. By 1982 Saudi Arabia was absorbing much of the continued slump in demand for OPEC oil. Output was averaging less than 6 mbd, which, if it continued to fall, could threaten to cut Saudi Arabia's export revenues by as much as half. Still the House of Saud pumped money into the domestic economy, cushioning its subjects from the shock of the waning boom.

King Khalid died unexpectedly of a heart attack at his summer palace in Taif on June 14, 1982. Without conflict, Fahd became king, and Abdullah, despite the long-standing rumors that the "Sudairi Seven" would seek to deny him his place in the line of succession, became crown prince. As political instability in the Arabian Gulf escalated, the senior princes apparently were in no mood for infighting in the royal family.

The king's body was flown to Riyadh. Wrapped in a plain brown cloth, Khalid was placed on a simple litter and carried through the streets by his brothers, followed by government ministers and the common people. By Moslem law, he was buried before sunset, in an unmarked grave in an unkempt cemetery on the Mecca road not far from Abdul Aziz's old palace. Following three days of mourning, Fahd received the *baya,* the formal pledges of support from his family, the *ulema,* the tribes, the military, and thousands of Saudi citizens.

With Khalid's death, Saudi Arabia was seen as making the final transition from a desert sheikhdom to a modern state. Khalid personified the old ways. Born in Riyadh in 1913, educated in the Koran by a

---

*Saudi Arabia's request to purchase five AWACS as well as sixty F-15s was approved by the U.S. Congress on October 28, 1981.

palace tutor, Khalid was rooted in Saudi Arabia's traditional values. Like his father, he received his subjects almost every day, hearing the same petition:"*Ya*, Khalid, I have no money." Initially a reluctant ruler, he became interested in improving education, health care, and housing, direct needs of his people. His religious piety was never questioned, in spite of the charges made by the rebels at Mecca. And to reaffirm his roots, he drank camel's milk and hunted the kingdom's deserts with the tribesmen for weeks at a time.

Fahd, on the other hand, brought to the monarchy his reputation as a worldly-wise progressive tied to the West. Although he made his appearances at the religious sites and undertook brief visits to the Bedouins in the desert, Fahd's reputation for enjoying worldly pleasures, his knowledge of English, his American-educated sons, his interest in pushing Saudi Arabia into the arena of international diplomacy, and his image as a technocrat committed to moving Saudi Arabia along the road of modernization overshadowed his attempts to fulfill the role of tribal *sheikh*. Fahd became king with neither the breadth of support enjoyed by Faisal nor the emotional ties between ruler and ruled nurtured by Khalid.

Nevertheless, Fahd began his reign in the tradition of his predecessors. He ordered the payment of one month's additional salary to all civil servants, military personnel, and people receiving annual grants or social security pensions. A gift of $4.4 million was made in his name to philanthropic societies all over the kingdom, and an additional $17.6 million was mandated for the construction and renovation of mosques.

The tall gates of Khalid's palace closed on his widow and the seat of power moved across the Diriyah road to the palace of Fahd. From the first days of his reign, Fahd let it be known that unlike his predecessors he would spend little time in the capital. Government moved between Taif and Jeddah, and except for Khalid's burial, Fahd did not make his first official visit to Riyadh until the end of November, three months after I arrived back in Riyadh.

When I walked into the Riyadh airport in July 1982, its order had a haunting quality about it. The throng of runty Yemenis garbed in turbans and skirts that had pushed and shoved as they swarmed over suitcases and tips was gone. The terminal was no longer an obstacle course of sleeping humanity spread across the floor waiting for flights to everywhere from Abha to Bangkok. The jam of battered and dusty taxicabs where drivers leaned on their horns and haggled over fares had vanished, replaced by sleek limousines with fixed rates. When I left the terminal, uniformed policemen sped traffic out onto Airport Road, which was now lined with stately palms and even more stately government buildings. This was only the beginning of the utter transformation Saudi Arabia and its capital had undergone in the two years since I had left.

In a remarkably short time, Saudi Arabia had achieved some of the substance as well as the veneer of development. Traffic, although still death defying, had gained some semblance of order. No longer were 97 percent of the beds in Shamaizy Hospital, Riyadh's largest general hospital, occupied by the victims of traffic accidents. Saudia, the national airline, was successfully forcing passengers to board planes *wahad y wahad* ("one by one"), replacing the stampede of earlier days. The Arabian Cleaning Enterprise had removed 4.6 billion kilos of refuse and rubble, 16,000 abandoned cars, and 23,000 stray dogs from the streets. The first A&P supermarket had opened in the al-Azizia section, with an even newer Safeway down the street. And the public scribes who operate out of the alleyway across the street from the office of the governor of Riyadh now had typewriters.

Saudis no longer held menial jobs such as serving tea or driving trucks. They were now merchants, administrators, and bureaucrats. Even the soft drink vendor who used to work out of a packing-crate hut had a new grocery store with a wide plate-glass window. The change had been so fast that it was the norm and not the exception to see a young urbanized Bedouin whose father had herded goats ten years ago now carrying a briefcase.

The building boom continued unchecked. The tall steel cranes that dotted the landscape in every direction were still the national bird of Saudi Arabia. But the architectural style and quality of Riyadh's new buildings attested to a maturing of tastes and an appreciation of the aesthetic that was abysmally absent during the heady first days of the oil boom.

Shortages were gone and the city was now a vast international bazaar. Dior, Cartier, Sony, Panasonic, General Motors, Rolls-Royce, Nike, and Adidas were all there, hawking their wares to Saudis and expatriates alike. The clock tower and the main mosque were no longer the center of life in Riyadh, as affluent Saudis flocked instead into the temples of merchandise that had been built in the new suburbs. The

Euromarché, the French equivalent of K-Mart, and the expensive shops along Siteen Street had all pulled business away from Tamari and Wassir Streets, while the jungle of shops under the corrugated tin roof of my beloved Dirrah *souq* had burned to the ground.

Riyadh had lost much of the evasive charm that had made it such an interesting place to live. Chicken Street in Malaaz, location of dozens of vendors roasting chickens over open fires along the sidewalks, now had parking meters. But in the strongest statement of the new generation, the open pen behind the Toyota dealer was gone. No longer were Saudis trading in camels for pickups.

Unlike the makeshift housing I had lived in previously, the building we were now assigned to was the luxurious "low rise." It had been under construction when I left, eight of the ten stories of structural steel already up. Then a prince protested that the building would look over the wall of his house, so the ten-story high-rise was reduced to three stories sitting atop a massive base. General living conditions, in fact, had improved so much that the long-time residents lamented the passing of an era of survival without fresh milk, electric appliances, corn-fed beef, sneakers, and Pop Tarts.

The number of foreign workers had risen by a geometric progression. With so many different nationalities working in Saudi Arabia, a perverted English had become the sort of *lingua franca*. Even the Saudis had incorporated English into their own vocabulary. People hung up the telephone with *"Halas, yellah,* bye-bye ("I'm through talking, I'm leaving, good-by). "It's finished" universally meant "out of stock." But it was in the new road signs, somehow regarded as the symbol of a developed country, that the bilingual system was most evident. There was, "Don't fesitate [hesitate] to help an injured person. You may save a life," and "The Prophet Mohammed said to pick up offense is charity." Other signs urged safe driving: "It is dangerous to think or talk while driving"; "Traffic signal is a language to be learned"; and "It is not allowed to carry more weight than prohibited." My particular favorite was, "Do not park here. If you do the air will be let out of your tires."

One of the major changes that had occurred in the everyday life of the expatriate was the government's inauguration of English-language television on the "Second Channel." It was a natural progression, for the history of radio and television in Saudi Arabia reflects the history of the kingdom's struggle with modernization.

In deference to the standards of the powerful religious faction, radio in Abdul Aziz's time was little more than a broadcast of readings from the Koran. When Faisal became king, he undertook to expand the broadcast media for significant political reasons. In 1962, concerned about the divisiveness of tribalism, Faisal authorized the building of radio transmitters strong enough to reach all parts of the kingdom. Radio would become the instrument through which the House of Saud would foster greater domestic unity and a sense of nationalism.

Faisal then approached the issue of television. In the sometimes convoluted reasoning of religious politics in which the House of Saud engages, Faisal saw television as a way of preserving Saudi values. Refusing to recognize cinema as an innocent means of recreation, Faisal introduced television in 1965. Unlike movies, television was acceptable because its programming could be controlled by a government sensitive to religious values. Under Faisal's rule, the role of television was to reinforce the strict Wahhabi social norms. All locally produced shows were about Saudi culture and any imported films were carefully previewed and edited to ensure that they conformed to Saudi social standards. No religion other than Islam could be mentioned, and alcoholic beverages and open displays of affection between men and women were banned. "Both the images and words in the Saudi media reflected the ideas and attitudes of the majority of the society which the media served. . . ."* In all, the Saudi media during Faisal's era were carefully designed to be a force of conservatism, not change. With its strong emphasis on Saudi culture at the expense of foreign ideas, television had the same goal as radio: the building of national unity to overcome the obstacles of tribe and region.

In the end, Faisal died for his carefully controlled, conservatively cast television. When the first television station opened, Faisal's nephew, the religiously fanatical Khalid ibn Musaaid ibn Abdul Aziz, stormed the building with a group of protesters. Coaxed out of the station by the king's call for a meeting, Khalid ibn Musaaid was shot by a nervous Riyadh policeman as he stood shouting outside Faisal's palace. Ten years later, Khalid ibn Musaaid's brother would, in turn, kill Faisal to avenge his death.

The decision to launch an English-language channel was momen-

---

*Willard A. Beling, ed., *King Faisal and the Modernization of Saudi Arabia* (London: Croom Helm, 1980), p. 136.

tous, its reasons multifaceted. In part, it was an acknowledgment that the numbers of foreigners, both Western and non-Western, now working in the country needed some form of diversion. The regime was also alarmed by the number of Saudis using high antennas to pick up television from Egypt, Syria, the United Arab Emirates, and Bahrain as well as ARAMCO's English channel. Evidently the government chose to create its own devil rather than abdicate its viewers to foreign governments. Another reason was that the push to teach young Saudis English so they could join the work force demanded that they be exposed to as much English as possible. And overall, the Second Channel in its concept fit the progressive tone that Fahd's reign was committed to pursuing. The programs, which would be viewed by the more progressive elements in the society, would further educate the Saudis and modify their social attitudes. But like everything else, English-language television was defended on the grounds that it was a tool to promote Islam among the heretics working in Saudi Arabia.

To assuage religious leaders' objections to the revolutionary nature of the Second Channel, the House of Saud used its typical method: give with one hand and take away with the other. Before the Second Channel went on the air in August 1983, there was a period of especially strict enforcement of Islamic laws regarding Westerners and segregation of the sexes. Western women could find themselves hassled if they were not in *abaayas* and the *matawain* increasingly stopped cars with unmarried couples riding together to give them morality lectures.

After the initial phase of the Second Channel, the *matawain* were kept pacified by programming that conformed to the standards of family entertainment. A sample evening's schedule included readings from the Koran, cartoons, *Little House on the Prairie*, *That's Incredible*, the news, and a religious program called *Islamic Horizons*.

Lack of experience and personnel made locally produced programs amateurish. Nowhere was this amateurism more apparent than in news broadcasts. Stories were pulled directly off the satellite and broadcast in the language of the country where the event happened. On the same broadcast, there would be a report of floods in China delivered in Mandarin followed by a segment in French about a one-man glider made in Belgium.

But the main function of the local news is to showcase the royal family. Night after night, the first ten minutes of the broadcast concerns the activities of the king. "King Fahd ibn Abdul Aziz departed

Jeddah today for Riyadh.'' This announcement is followed by a recitation of the list of dignitaries who saw him off at the airport. To the
strains of a Viennese waltz on the sound track, the footage of men
kissing the king unreels and unreels and unreels. The next story is
always: "On his arrival in Riyadh, King Fahd ibn Abdul Aziz was met
by . . ." followed by the same music and hundreds of feet of film of
people greeting the king. On one broadcast, Fahd was shown in six
greeting ceremonies, accompanied by the same waltz and consuming
seventeen minutes of air time.

The other news often consists of such illuminating items as "The
Council of Ministers met today and discussed several issues and took
appropriate action,"* followed by the sports news, which on this particular night was a British soccer match between Ipswich and Arsenal.
Beheadings are announced as the last item on the Friday broadcasts.

The Second Channel has become an important tool for basic public
education. In May 1984, for example, there was a driver safety week.
Films on television taught what road signs mean, explained why a
motorist should not park in the middle of the street while he goes
shopping, and demonstrated what might happen if a driver enters a
one-way street going the wrong way (a dummy graphically flew through
the windshield in a head-on crash).

The foreign influence on the Second Channel is heavy because its
shows are all foreign-produced. And in a sad commentary on Saudi
attitudes about development, the Second Channel never gives Arabic
lessons for foreigners and airs few programs about Arab culture.
Somehow Saudi Arabia does not see its contact with the outside world
as a two-way street of enlightenment for both the Saudis and their
foreign employees.

Television, both Arabic and English, has succeeded by chance and
design to advance change in Saudi Arabia. Neil Armstrong's walk on
the moon in 1969 captivated the Saudi public to such an extent that an
entrepreneur opened a restaurant named "Apollo 14." International
communications have forced Saudi Arabia to adapt to Greenwich Mean
Time in place of the traditional Saudi system tied to the rising and
setting of the sun. But the most calculated moves are in the area of
social change, especially concerning attitudes toward women. In the
infant days of Saudi television, women were forbidden to be seen or

---

*Newscast of November 15, 1983.

heard.* Later, non-Saudi actresses were seen primarily in melodramatic soap operas imported from Egypt. In 1967 a children's program narrated by a Saudi female aired and a girls high school was allowed to perform a short play. And then the conservatives complained so much that by 1968 all Saudi women had once again disappeared. But from the earliest broadcasts of the Second Channel, a woman announced the station breaks. She was never shown on screen, but the presence of a female voice was revolutionary. By 1984 Saudi families were appearing on local shows where they played parlor games such as musical chairs. I found it astounding to see an unveiled Saudi woman, her reputation protected by having her family clustered around her, dive for an empty chair and laugh uproariously if she won.

If the government chooses to push social change, it can use state-controlled radio and television as a powerful and persuasive means of communication. Prosperity plus the easy availability of inexpensive Japanese electronics has put a radio in every tent and a television in the home of everyone who has electricity. In the broadcast media, there is the potential to expand human resource development by integrating social change with education. But the media can help to create an atmosphere for innovation only by proceeding slowly while upholding the culture it intends to serve. As in all aspects of Saudi life, change is accepted only if it comes gradually and does not appear to challenge either the teachings of Islam or the culture's traditional values. No matter how innovative the broadcast media might want to be, they are caught, like the rest of society, between the pincers of modernization and tradition.

Regardless of the advent of English-language television and the other great changes branded with the symbols of the West that had occurred during my absence, many things about Saudi Arabia were still the same. My old boss, Tom Krogh, was back in Riyadh. This time he was untangling the problems of the eye hospital. In another construction fiasco, the air-conditioning equipment had been installed directly underneath the operating rooms and there was so much vibration that delicate eye surgery was impossible. Tom told me the interim solution was to chill the building down to about forty degrees, shut off the

---

*During the mid-1970s, a British woman who was in Saudi Arabia as a dependent read the English news. Her presence reflected the labor shortage, for she was replaced as soon as a man could be recruited.

hospital's air-conditioning system, roll as many patients as possible into the operating rooms, and pray that the temperature inside did not rise above ninety-five degrees before the operations were complete.

And Saudi drivers were still so bad that when King Fahd's motorcade raced through the city, it was followed by a wrecker.

Although the Saudis obsessively shopped and purchased the products of the West, the great consumer society had yet to breach the walls of tradition. In one scene after another that greeted my return, I saw that the painful process of synthesizing the new with the old was still unsure. The ice cream truck with its brightly colored logos and tinkling bells that parked outside the posh new al-Karia mall maintained separate windows for men and women. The brightly lighted supermarkets with their wide aisles and imported foods sporadically posted signs in five languages warning female customers to keep "all limbs covered" while on the premises. In addition to combing the hot, dusty alleyways, the *matawain* with their camel whips now plied the air-conditioned shopping malls, forcing ohio shops to close during prayer call. The Safeway store imported electric curling irons and then drew in a more modest neckline on the girl decorating the boxes. Foreign books were on the newsstands but the front of an Agatha Christie mystery was censored by blacking out a drawing of a woman's leg in fishnet stockings. And Jane Fonda, smiling from the front of her exercise book, had been put in sleeves and long pants by the stroke of an ink brush.

In spite of the large numbers of Westerners and the expanding length of time that they had been part of the scene in the kingdom, the Saudis had yet to accommodate to them. Rather, new attitudes toward Westerners had developed that made life more difficult. Increasing numbers of Saudis had taken up administrative jobs in previously all-Western companies as a result of the government's policy of Saudization. As these Saudis moved into the housing compounds of the large Western-managed companies, Saudi Arabia's problem of balancing its need for Western expertise and its need to defend the norms of its own society proved as difficult as it had always been. Westerners were no longer always totally segregated from the Saudis, allowing them to pursue their own lifestyles. There was a pervasive change in the attitude of many Saudis, particularly the educated. During the 1970s, no matter how strenuously the Westerners were confined to their compounds or how harshly the religious laws were enforced, the Saudis on a one-to-one basis cheerfully welcomed them. Now, following nearly a decade of a significant Western presence, the Westerners had ceased to be an interesting intrusion into the kingdom, who brought with them glittering promises of tomorrow. Instead, the Saudis harbored a nagging uncertainty about what Saudi Arabia had sacrificed in terms of its hallowed traditions to pursue economic development. To the Saudis, modernization had disrupted family life, corrupted the devout, and subjected the society to the disdain of its large Western work force. As a result, the Saudis developed a hostility toward Westerners that had not existed before. No longer were they willing to bend their own way of life to placate the Westerners. Instead, there was a growing attitude that the Westerners should be brought to heel.

In an attempt to accommodate both the Westerners and Middle Easterners living in the same compounds, swimming pools were segregated and in-house video systems purged of "nonfamily" tapes or shut down altogether. I walked into the employee cafeteria at the hospital one day to find it segregated by a solid wall into male and female sections. At the National Guard Hospital, the entire staff (doctors, nurses, technicians, support personnel, and their families) were confined to hospital property for several days after a Saudi guard saw a Western nurse caress her date. After the ban was lifted, men and women were not only forbidden to ride on the same hospital bus unless they were married but the single men and women were taken to different stores in town so there would be no danger of fraternizing while shopping.

In this atmosphere, it was not surprising that the Christian church once again came under intense scrutiny. It had been assumed that Fahd, as king, would lift the restrictions that had been clamped on the Christians after the Mecca uprising. But in January 1983, members of the governing board of the Riyadh Christian Fellowship were suddenly picked up and taken to the Ministry of Interior for lengthy interrogation and then released. In May, the Protestant minister Francis Gregory, John Farr, a founder of the Christian fellowship who had worked in Saudi Arabia since 1977, and all members of the board were rounded up, interrogated, and ordered out of the country within twenty-four hours. When they protested to Prince Naif, minister of Interior and the government's liaison with the Christians, about their expulsions in light of the fact that all of his instructions had been carefully followed, he simply replied, "The rules have changed."

The tense atmosphere between the Saudis and the Westerners that existed in Saudi Arabia when I returned made the job of reporting even more difficult. Most of the problems for any journalist working in Saudi Arabia arise from the character of censorship in the kingdom. It is different from the prototype censorship in the police states of tinhorn dictators or the institutionalized censorship of the Soviet Union. This censorship is nervous, expressing not so much repression as a great fear that somehow the Saudis will be embarrassed. There is a real sense that those in power control the media as much for the defense of Islam and the protection of Saudi honor as for their own political purposes. The Saudis have an acute sensitivity to how they as a people are perceived and how Islam is viewed by non-Moslems. When Saudi Arabia's Information Council proclaims, as it has consistently through the Iraq-Iran war (a war between two Islamic states), its need to keep a vigil on the mass media in view of the challenges the Moslem world is facing, its proclamation is accepted without question by the population. It is also understood, if not necessarily accepted, by Westerners sensitive to the central role Islam plays in the Saudis' self-perception.

But Westerners have difficulty comprehending the depth of Saudi apprehensions when events seen as acts of fate in the West are regarded by the Saudis as blotches on their honor. In my experience, the most clear-cut case of this phenomenon occurred in July 1979. For several weeks, there had been essentially no mail coming into Riyadh. The problem was not just mail coming from a particular country, which happened often as letters fell victim to one postal service or another; no one was receiving anything. Finally the news began to spread that the post office and two hundred thousand pieces of mail had gone up in flames, victims of a careless employee and a nearly nonexistent fire department. The disaster was never publicly acknowledged, since it was regarded somehow as an intolerable loss of face.

For perhaps the same reason, the scorching weather was seldom mentioned until the English-language *Saudi Gazette* finally began to publish the high and low temperatures for the kingdom in 1984. Even then, floods, wind storms, and record temperatures have continued to pass without comment.

Censorship in the kingdom falls in four areas: perceived attacks on Islam, violations of the Wahhabis' moral standards, direct or implied criticism of Saudi Arabia, and political commentary on the House of Saud.

Censorship of domestic publications is managed through government policy. Censorship of foreign material is managed by manual labor. Saudi Arabia employs hundreds of manual laborers from the Third World and arms them with brushes and ink pots to black out ads for alcohol or pictures of scantily clad women in imported magazines. When the international news publications such as *The Economist, Time,* or *Newsweek* are late reaching the stands, it is a clear signal that they contain something that offends the Saudis or those in power. To stop the dissemination of objectionable stories, armies of laborers are mobilized to slash and tear publications, page by page. Consequently, many times I would be reading an article and turn to the next page to find myself in the middle of an entirely different subject. It then became a game to find out what was missing. Westerners leaving the country on vacation carry lists of magazines, dates, and page numbers of censored articles in order to report their contents back to their compatriots. Sometimes when the information arrives back, it is disappointing. I found out, for example, that some missing pages of *Time* contained only an article on the treatment of breast cancer. What had been objectionable to the Saudis was an anatomical drawing of a breast.

The suppression of news in Saudi Arabia is remarkably easy since there is no perceptible public pressure on the government for disclosure. This absence of the demand for the right to know reflects the culture as much as it does the repressive nature of censorship. In a society where the self-esteem of the individual and the privacy of the family are paramount, censorship is almost self-imposed. The Saudi press, for instance, would never print anything about the personal life of any member of the royal family, nor would the public expect it. Officials, from the king to clerks, are not expected to face public scrutiny. It would be an intolerable loss of face, a condition no Saudi imposes on another. Furthermore, unlike in Western culture, where communication is a virtue, in the Arab world, communication is a danger, a threat arising from prying outsiders. It is secrecy, not disclosure, that is the virtue. Security for the individual, group, and nation is thought to reside in unity behind stated values and ideals, not in the divisiveness created by a free press.

In addition to the cultural acceptance of censorship, the House of Saud has its own powerful political motives for keeping a lid on the press. In Saudi culture, only the strongest are accepted as rulers by their subjects. Leaders cannot be called into question and expect to continue to govern. In a population intolerant of human error, political survival depends not just on the suppression of opposition but on the concealment of the mistakes, minor sins, and foibles of various members of the royal family.

It was in this atmosphere that I reported on Saudi Arabia. A journalist in Saudi Arabia functions like no other. Western journalists accustomed to being haunted by every third man on the street seeking a platform for his views find in Saudi Arabia that information and opinion are shut up as if the kingdom were an oyster. Traditionally, reporting the news means reprinting government press handouts with no commentary. Confronted by a culture in which secrecy reigns in all matters and where Western journalists are not permitted entry, the only way a journalist can get a story is to be patient, assiduously filing away isolated facts and then patching those facts together until they begin to mean something. Since the Saudis' dedication to obscuring information is shared by all Arabs, the meetings of the Organization of Petroleum Exporting Countries (OPEC) are a good example of what journalists are up against. There is a hierarchy of reporters who have followed the Saudi and other Arab oil ministers for years. At every meeting, after exhausting their contacts with the Sphinx-like delegates, reporters from competing newspapers cluster together, thumb through their notebooks, and trade pieces of information, hoping to piece together coherent concepts from stray facts. What they come up with is similar to the *New York Times* interview with Sheikh Otaiba of Oman about a 1983 emergency session of the cartel. The *sheikh* slept through the first appointment, skipped the second, and finally sent a vague poem he had written about the meeting, which ended, "In verse I find a bountiful largess / A great refuge at times of much distress."*

In Saudi Arabia, I found that a reporter's most valuable tools are a prodigious memory, keen intuition, and diligence. Whether I was at work, prowling the *souqs*, having dinner in a Saudi home, or talking to Westerners attached to ministries, embassies, or businesses, I absorbed every nuance and then I rushed home to write it all down. I broke this material down into subjects and filed it away with newspaper clippings, government documents, and other tidbits of information for future reference. These files allowed me to work but they also would be my downfall if they were ever found by the secret police.

---

*Quoted in Stuart Diamond, "Reporter's Notebook: OPEC and Its Vagaries," *New York Times*, November 3, 1984.

Anyone who risks being an underground journalist in Saudi Arabia lives with constant anxiety about being discovered. It was particularly important for me to recognize the repercussions if I were caught. I was the only reporter writing in-depth political articles on a regular basis and I was well aware that they had raised the hackles of those in power. Putting the writer of those articles out of action would be sweet revenge. A long prison term would not only punish me for my transgressions but would serve as an example to other writers who were in the kingdom ostensibly in other roles. Even if I were only deported, there was always the specter of spending several months to a year in jail waiting for the Saudis to make that decision. Therefore, a certain level of tension underlay my work. Periodically I got word from a contact in the Western diplomatic corps that the Ministry of the Interior was searching for "Michael Collins," my nom de plume. Hurriedly I would move all my files out of the compound and store them with close friends outside of Riyadh. Even in the best of times, nothing that could tie me to anything that had been published was kept or casually thrown away. My rough drafts and carbon paper stayed buried under the kitchen garbage until I took them to the desert to burn. I hid my stories until they could be sent out of the country by the "Pony Express."* Envelopes were either addressed to my agent, who sent them on, or, in the case of editors with whom I had a working relationship, they were simply addressed to a name and a street address. The only thing that distinguished these letters from the hundreds of others going out was that there was no return address on the envelope. In this net of deception, my most serious bouts of anxiety developed when an article I had written for an American publication surfaced, as they often did, in the expatriate community in Riyadh.

My particular problems were both helped and made enormously more complicated by the fact that I was a woman. The greatest drawback of being female was not being allowed to drive, and the second was that I stirred up an inordinate amount of attention every time I walked into a male enclave. On the other hand, I often could get more information than a man. Saudi men seldom think a woman is intelligent enough to be interested in business or politics and so are not on guard. Sometimes

---

*There was a mail network among Westerners at the hospital. Anyone leaving on the direct Dhahran–New York flight took all the mail for North America. I left the kingdom on more than one occasion carrying an extra bag filled with nothing but letters.

they would talk to me just to get rid of the threatening presence of a woman. And in the world of women, to which my sex gave me access, educated Saudi women would more readily discuss politics with me than men would with my male counterparts.

Still, the role of journalist was difficult for anyone. Just collecting basic facts, which are at one's fingertips in the West, was a major undertaking. There were no public libraries. The library at the University of Riyadh was of little use since women were barred from the premises. (Female students requested books in writing, which were delivered to their own section of the school.) The libraries at the Western consulates were totally inadequate. Although the Ministry of Information made some effort at maintaining a selection of reference books, there were no newspaper files, guides to government documents, or even a partially complete collection of books published in and about Saudi Arabia.

Editors in the West, except the rare one who had some experience with the kingdom, had no appreciation of what it took to dig out the facts for a story. I gradually developed a small network that I worked with consistently, but in the beginning I found it wildly frustrating to try to bridge the chasm of ignorance. I remember when the participants in the Mecca uprising were beheaded I wrote an article about the political implications in the government's public recognition that foreigners were involved in the revolt and the significance of the various execution sites that had been chosen. It was rejected by an editor who wanted a photograph of a victim's grave.

I was once working on a story about the General Organization of Social Insurance (GOSI), Saudi Arabia's social security system. The totally tax-free status of some expatriates ended when employers were directed to deduct 2 1/2 percent from the wages of all employees. As the economic crunch began to become apparent, there were strong suspicions among the expatriates that despite the regulations foreigners would never recover their contributions, either through withdrawal after they left employment in Saudi Arabia or as the pension promised to all expatriates after ten years' service in the kingdom. To even begin to tackle the subject, I needed the labor laws and the social insurance regulations that I assumed would be at the Ministry of Labor and the GOSI office. To get there, I first had to convince someone to drive me. Since I had been tutoring him in a correspondence course in freshman English, Ed Lane, one of the paramedics at the hospital, was more or less coerced into taking me. I donned my regulation long dress, and Ed and I started out at 8:30 A.M. on an incredibly hot summer day. Although Riyadh was always in a state of flux, at this particular time ministries, bureaus, and departments were moving all over town as many of the new government buildings under construction were completed. Our first stop was the Ministry of Information, to get an updated map of Riyadh. I had been in Saudi Arabia long enough to know they were not going to have one, but I could always hope that this time it might be different. Of course, they didn't have one, but fortunately there was a young man behind the desk who had a vague idea of where the Ministry of Labor might be. In the Malaaz district there was a hideous pink-domed building that housed the Institute of Technical Training. According to his directions, the Ministry of Labor was "somewhere nearby."

The usual route to Malaaz was closed because of construction so we wandered around trying to spot that pink dome until the gas tank was almost empty. We then spent the next fifteen minutes looking for a gas station. (For a major oil producer, Saudi Arabia has an absurdly small number of gas pumps.) While Ed was filling the tank, I glanced beyond the mound of rubble across the street and, to my delight, spotted the Ministry of Labor. It was now 9:35. Perspiration was pouring off me as I panted into the ministry and asked for a copy of the labor regulations. Why should I have believed the labor regulations would be at the Ministry of Labor? I was informed they were at the Ministry of Finance.

Armed with a new set of directions, we set off once again. When we arrived, the building that had been the Ministry of Finance was now the Real Estate Development Fund. By 10:30 I had finally located a relatively recent map of Riyadh. Driving toward what I believed to be the Ministry of Finance, we miraculously passed the GOSI building. I screamed for Ed to stop. Thinking things were finally going smoothly, I walked into the building and requested a copy of the GOSI regulations. The young Saudi sitting at the reception desk stiffened and nervously waved me upstairs, saying I would have to talk to the director. My antenna went up. The Saudis were obviously becoming suspicious of anyone asking questions about social insurance. I was right. The director was no fool and immediately exhibited intense interest in who I was and why I was asking questions. As Ed sat on a sofa and squirmed, the director quizzed me at length while I deftly avoided revealing my name. Sinking into my helpless female act, always my repugnant defense of last resort, I spun a tale about my husband being in Riyadh looking at business prospects and since he was so busy he had thought it would be permissible for me to come for the information he needed on the kingdom's social insurance system and its application to foreign workers. Becoming apologetic, I said that being new to the kingdom perhaps I had overstepped the bounds of propriety. My story did not fly. Feeling increasingly trapped, I signaled to Ed and we beat a hasty retreat. By now it was 11:00. There was just enough time to get to the Ministry of Finance before the noon prayer call. More streets were torn up by construction, making the map all but useless. At last we were back on course, retraced our steps, and found the block where the map indicated the ministry was. Excitedly I saw building #1 as indicated on the map, next door was building #2, and building #3 should be the Ministry of Finance. Only there was no building #3, just an empty lot being leveled by a bulldozer. As I screamed with exasperation, I heard the *allahu akbar* of the prayer call waft over the landscape. Ed turned the car around and we went home.

In 1983 I was offered a job by *Saudi Business,* a weekly publication of the Saudi Research and Marketing group. Under the terms of the offer, I was to provide the magazine one article a week. For the magazine's part, I would be provided no transportation or transportation allowance, no leads, no introductions, and no press credentials, and if I found myself in trouble with irate government officials or the Ministry of Information, I was on my own. As far as the magazine was concerned, I did not exist.

In August 1983 my contact in a Western embassy passed word to me that the government was furious about an article I had written for the *Christian Science Monitor* about the deportation of Christians. He had information that the Ministry of Interior had launched an intensive search for Michael Collins. He implored me to get rid of my research material and to stop writing altogether. Shaken, I moved every note, clipping, and document out of my house and burrowed further underground for a while. But after a few weeks, I went back to writing. Michael Collins died rather suddenly, only to be resurrected as "Justin Coe."

Like television, newspapers and magazines in Saudi Arabia are undergoing their own, if less dramatic, set of changes. The print media are relatively new to the kingdom since there had been little need for newspapers in Saudi Arabia until the production of oil made its impact. Besides a low rate of literacy and little interest in the outside world, the small population was too widely dispersed to be reached even by the new technology known as radio. Following his unification of Saudi Arabia, Abdul Aziz recognized the need for a vehicle to promote national unity among his scattered population. Therefore, *Umm al-Qura,* the first newspaper, was started under his auspices in 1924. It remained the only publication in the entire country between 1925 and 1932. During World War II, the publication of *Umm al-Qura* and its few struggling competitors was suspended, and it was not until 1953 that the first daily, *Bilad al-Saudiya,* appeared.

There are now ten daily newspapers and nine weekly or monthly magazines published in Saudi Arabia, all privately owned and subsidized in varying degrees by the government. They represent a wide diversity of attitudes. The spectrum ranges from the English-language *Saudi Gazette,* which caters almost exclusively to Westerners, to the arch-conservative *Al-Madinah,* housed in a building in Jeddah that looks like a mosque. But all follow similar reporting policies. The main difference between the two English-language papers and the Arabic papers is the space devoted to religious topics and the tone of the coverage of Israel. The Arabic papers carry more stories speculating on the dastardliness of Israeli acts and motives and casts blame for all Middle East instability on the Jewish state. The other difference is price. The eight-to twelve-page Arabic-language papers cost SR 1 (32 cents); those in English SR 2 (64 cents).

The Saudi press is dominated by the philosophy of the late King Faisal. Faisal was more concerned with the government being on good terms with a press that he felt was loyal to Saudi principles and ideals than he was with controlling the press directly. Rather than making the press an organ for promoting the political goals of the regime, the Faisal government was more comfortable with a bland, politically passive press, "which would avoid controversial issues if necessary so as not to stir up society unnecessarily."* In 1962 Faisal created the Ministry of Information to encourage development of Saudi-style journalism and to deal with potential problems that might arise between the government and the press.

Today the press is not totally controlled by the government in the sense that every item printed must be approved by official censors.

---

*Beling, ed., *King Faisal and the Modernization of Saudi Arabia,* p. 133.

Rather, the government licenses all book shops, video clubs, printing presses, and public relations agencies and supervises all advertising and publications "to insure that standards of taste and ethical practices are maintained."* With control of their existence, the government maintains a pact between the Ministry of Information and the publishers that sets guidelines. Editors patrol themselves, deferring to government judgment in questionable cases. From the viewpoint of the House of Saud, the system has worked well. Sometimes important news stories are downplayed or totally ignored by the media because editors know the government is not pleased by the events. For instance, both the coup that brought Muammar Qaddafi to power in Libya in 1969 and the Jordanian civil war in 1970 were hardly mentioned in the Saudi press. More currently, the rage of Shiism in the Moslem world is largely ignored.

Saudi newspapers are more noteworthy for what they do not say than what they do say. Lebanese journalist Salem Lozi once said, "The politician remains master of the statement he has not made and slave to the one he has made."** This could be the motto of the House of Saud, carried out by the Saudi press. Newspapers are more like bulletin boards of local and international events and reports on the comings and goings of the royal family than they are actual sources of information. An entire story can read, "The High Executive Committee on the Transfer Project of the Foreign Ministry and Embassies to Riyadh met here Sunday under Riyadh Governor Prince Salman, the chairman of the committee. It adopted a number of decisions."† Or "The Minister of Information Ali Shaer has issued a number of decrees in Riyadh calling for punishment of video shop owners who violate instructions laid down by the ministry."‡ And no opportunity to flatter the king is ignored. The *Arab News*, in editorial comments on King Fahd's speech at the King Abdul Aziz University, said, "What impressed the audience even more than his frankness, his eloquence, his knowledgeable comments and his spontaneity and his wit was his humbleness despite his exalted position."¶

---

*Kingdom of Saudi Arabia, Ministry of Planning, *Third Development Plan: 1400–1405 A.H., 1980–1985 A.D.* (Riyadh, 1980), p. 380.
**Quoted in David Holden and Richard Johns, *The House of Saud* (London: Holt, Rinehart and Winston, 1981), p. 482.
†*Arab News*, October 25, 1983.
‡*Arab News*, August 3, 1983.
¶*Arab News*, October 26, 1984.

Regardless of the controls, interesting things are happening in the Saudi press. After Fahd came to the throne, the newspapers became, if not a vehicle for social change, at least a platform for discussion. Sensitive issues such as the treatment of women, child brides, the plight of workers from underdeveloped countries, and even the competency of Saudi drivers regularly appeared in increasingly blunt and honest letters to the editor. Cartoons depicting people appeared, which in itself was revolutionary in a country governed by a religion that discourages representations of the human body. Furthermore, these cartoons were often used to make statements of social concern about the Saudi work ethic, the treatment of wives, the attitudes of taxi drivers, or the inefficiency of public service employees.

The other factor growing in the press was its attacks on the West. The size of the oil glut could almost be gauged by the level and variety of criticism of the West. The most common subject of editorials was Saudi Arabia's Herculean efforts in the defense of Islam, and the second was condemnation of the policies and practices of Western countries. The media has become an extension of the government's love-hate relationship with the West, particularly the United States. Ignoring a directive from King Fahd to downplay Western subjects in the press, the newspapers continue to run a wide range of stories about Western culture which they juxtapose against bitter anti-Western editorials. Much of this anti-Westernism is born of frustration with American policy toward Israel and Europe's inability to win something concrete for the Palestinians, but it says something more. It expresses the Saudis' confusion about how they want to deal with the West. While absorbing more and more Western products, ideas, and practices into their society, they have become more strident in their claims about the superiority of their own culture, a culture they assert the West does not understand. Without doubt, the West's view of Saudi Arabia is distorted. Yet much of this distortion is due to the absence of foreign journalists in the kingdom. The House of Saud has long had a deliberate policy of excluding foreigners, or at least keeping them at an acceptable distance, as a way to preserve traditional values and regulate the pace at which change proceeds. The same philosophy applies to foreign correspondents. While succeeding internally, the policy has left the world closed out, ignorant of the Saudis and their culture.

But the Saudis' view of the West is also distorted. Much of this is due to the media's unceasing drive to present the West in the worst possible light in order to defend Saudi Arabia's traditional values. Claiming that Westerners have warped ideas about Islam generally and Saudi Arabia particularly, the Saudis use their own press as a showcase for the worst in Western civilization. In the mainline newspapers, I read on a daily basis front page stories such as:

VIENNA — Pigeon-crazy man starves wife to feed birds.

LOS ANGELES, CALIFORNIA — Former choirgirl sues seven priests for drawing her into sexual intercourse with the clerics.

KALAMAZOO, MICHIGAN — An heir to the Upjohn pharmaceutical fortune was sentenced Monday to a year in jail for sexually abusing his 14 year old stepdaughter and was ordered to take a drug made by his family's company that reduces sex drive.

ANN ARBOR, MICHIGAN — U.S. slavery trial ends in conviction.

BRISSAC, FRANCE — A French chef whose baby daughter Valerie cried so much that it disturbed his television viewing killed her, cut her up, and fed her remains to his Alsatian dog.

My return to Saudi Arabia coincided with the beginning of the oil glut. In the economic downturn, the Saudis' fearfulness of the West and Western journalists became even more pronounced. With the oil boom waning, it became increasingly evident that the Saudis had yet to resolve their psychological conflict with the West. Saudi Arabia had made remarkable progress since I had first entered the kingdom in 1978. The basic infrastructure was in place. The educational system was drawing in a large percentage of both boys and girls. Health care was reaching out into rural areas that had never before had access to a doctor. Housing, running water, and electricity were available to most of the population. Saudis now read daily newspapers, supplementing the Koran as their only reading material. Sophisticated communications satellites connected the kingdom with the world and brought the world into Saudi homes via television. In less than a decade, the Saudis had moved out of isolation and ignorance to take a tenuous place in the twentieth century. So impressive were the changes that Saudi Arabia's advancement had to be measured in terms of generations.

But the pace of change could no longer be managed, for it had assumed its own speed. Like a promise released from Pandora's box, the material advances the people had experienced were inexorably undercutting the puritan nature of Saudi society. When the House of Saud, as it had always done, tried to balance the demands of the conservatives with the demands of modernization, it increasingly found that the past and the present could no longer coexist. Unlike in 1963, when movie theaters that operated out of private homes were closed by the *matawain*, those committed to the defense of Wahhabism were now thwarted by the technology of video recorders. The elders of Saudi Arabia will soon face a generation of young Saudis raised on American movies smuggled into the country on videotapes. Furthermore, powerful transmitters and high antennas, which frustrate Saudi censorship, are bringing in broadcasts from less conservative Arab countries. Yet censorship will not die, for it plays a vital role. Censorship allows the whole society to disguise the profound and fundamental changes that are happening in its culture. Control of the media allows not just the government but all Saudis to applaud the physical advancements the country has made and at the same time ignore the great undercurrents altering traditional lifestyles. Unsettled by the kingdom's steadily declining income, the Saudis are reassured by their radio, television, and newspapers that prosperity will continue, Islam will be defended, and the West will be prevented from either humiliating the Saudis or corrupting their values.

13

Jail: A Clear and Present Danger

PEOPLE BEGAN GATHERING early in Justice Square, a broad triangular area in central Riyadh defined by the Governor's Office, the main mosque, and the old clock tower at the head of Tamari Street. Known as Chop-Chop Square to the Westerners, it serves as a parking lot for the main mosque during the week. But on the occasional Friday, it is roped off to accommodate the crowd that gathers for the public dispensation of Saudi justice. It was such a Friday.

Among the first to arrive to witness the beheading of a man convicted of murder were busloads of workers from the many Korean construction companies building the modern Riyadh. The coaches, parked around the perimeter of the square, looked like tour buses waiting for their customers to visit the local sites. The crowd continued to grow, becoming largely Saudi. Policemen clad in drab olive uniforms and cocky berets touched with red patrolled its edges, methodically striking their truncheons against their open palms.

As the noon prayers at the mosque drew to a close, an unheralded procession of vehicles slowly pulled off King Abdul Aziz Street into Justice Square and stopped in front of the ornate building housing the governor's office. In the lead was a distinctive black and white police car, followed by an ominous-looking black van and two buses. As soon as they stopped, the buses quickly disgorged their cargoes of policemen. Armed with submachine guns, the men immediately formed a barrier between the assembled crowd and the execution site. With the area secured, an officer emerged from the lead vehicle. Standing on the running board and supporting himself with his right arm crooked against the roof of the car, he drew a small microphone close to his mouth and began to read the order of death. As he read, the doors of the black van quietly swung open and the convicted man, a white blindfold wrapped around his bare head, his hands tied behind his back, stumbled out, held between two men. It was here that he met his executioner, an enormous black man clothed in a finely woven and intricately embroidered ebony cloak, which hung from his massive shoulders. An ornate broadsword sheathed in a heavy gold scabbard lay tightly strapped against his barrel chest. The docile prisoner, seemingly resigned to his fate, knelt on the black asphalt. When one of the guards lightly touched his neck, the condemned man dropped his head forward. Silence descended on the excited crowd. The executioner dramatically unsheathed his sword and fleetingly held it above his head for the crowd to see. He then took one step forward. With the grace of a dancer, he raised the sword to its apex and swung it down in a perfect arch until metal met flesh. The crowd shouted its approval as the head dropped from the body, sending fountains of blood spurting from the severed arteries. I stood halfway between the mosque and the execution site. I had chosen my position carefully. Stationed behind a stout Chevrolet, one of the few cars parked in the square, I felt protected from the crowd, which becomes highly agitated at the moment of the beheading. Surging forward, the Saudis often mock Westerners and force them to the front, in full view of the dismembered body. As soon as the condemned man's body was tossed into the van for removal, the police, who had been placidly patrolling the square, waded into the crowd, swinging their truncheons. People scattered in all directions while the police shouted the order to disperse. Glancing around me, I realized that I was trapped between the car and the fleeing crowd. Although the impatient policeman approaching me was striking people with his raised club as he waded through the throng, I could not move. I felt no panic, somehow believing that he would not strike a foreign woman, especially since I was swathed completely in black, my hair tightly bound in a heavy scarf. At that instant, a racking pain shot through me as the truncheon landed across my back just below the shoulder. I turned, desperately trying to escape, when a second blow struck me across the ribs. All at once an escape route opened up and I fled, clutching my arms around my battered body. Within minutes the square was as empty as it would have been on a normal Friday afternoon.

Westerners are often shocked by what they consider the brutality of Islamic law as practiced in Saudi Arabia. Unmodified by the philosophies and practices of modern legal systems, the undergirdings of the Wahhabis' law remains as it was in the seventh century — a combination of Hammurabi's code, tribal justice, and Mohammed's teachings. The logic and writings of the great Arab intellectuals were added during the Islamic empire. What emerged was the Islamic body of law known as the *sharia*. There are four formal sources of this law: the Koran; the Sunna, the sayings of Mohammed written down by his followers; *ijma*, the consensus of learned scholars writing on particular issues not clearly defined by either the Koran or the Sunna but which have been validated by tradition; and *qiyas*, decisions deduced by analogies.* Together they form the *sharia*, which serves as the constitution of Saudi Arabia as well as the authority on which every rule and regulation is based.

The Koran was born in a primitive time to a primitive people who were controlled more by tribal traditions than by any code of law. Yet through the centuries of the Islamic empire, the *sharia* underwent great speculation and innovation in Alexandria, Baghdad, and the other centers of Arab learning. The intellectuals of the time regarded the *sharia* as a type of common law from which to develop an ever-expanding legal system. Combining the teachings of Mohammed with the thinking of the Greeks, the Islamic scholars of the ninth century worked through the same logical order that Maimonides undertook for Judaism in the twelfth century and Thomas Aquinas set out for the Christians in the thirteenth century. But the creative thought of the Arabs stopped on the eve of the Renaissance in Europe.

As a result of the desolation wrought by the Mongol invasion (1219–1258), or perhaps because of the repressive domination of the Ottomans, the legal systems of the Middle East ceased to be creative. With the fall of the Ottoman Empire and the imposition of European rule throughout much of the Arab world, Islamic law began to imitate rather than instruct the West. In Saudi Arabia, cut off from contact with either the West or the Arab world, the *sharia* did not develop at all. It

---

*There are several schools of thought in Islamic law, which explains some of the deviations in legal practice from one Islamic country to another. Saudi Arabia's *ulema* chiefly follows the Hanbali school, but decisions may incorporate jurists from other schools where no precedents exist.

has stood unmodified since before the fall of the Islamic empire.

Unlike Western law that ensures the public order but also guarantees the rights of the individual, protects commerce, and defines the functions of government, the sole mission of the *sharia* is to protect the social order. Since the goal in the treatment of any person who violates the rules is never rehabilitation but the defense of Islamic society, the idea of justice is inseparable from the idea of punishment. Therefore, punishment becomes organically related to the social order, pacifying a deep fear among Moslems that the rejection of punishment will eventually involve the rejection of order.

Under a simple and ancient code of law based on the philosophy of vengeance, only a few deeds — theft, rape, adultery, and murder — are defined as crimes. But for these the punishments are drastic and public. In Riyadh, when a thief's right hand is cut off in public by the executioner's sword, a string is tied to the middle finger and it is hung from a high hook on a streetlight in Justice Square for all to see. This public display, appalling to Westerners, is an integral part of the philosophy of punishment. It announces the thief's transgression to the community and casts shame on his family. It enforces discipline in a basically undisciplined society. And it is emotionally satisfying to the needs of the faithful.

Saudi Arabia's criminal justice system, perhaps more than any other, encompasses the true philosophy of "an eye for an eye and a tooth for a tooth." In the customs of Arabia, a person convicted of harming his neighbor was punished by the same act suffered by the victim. In the late twentieth century, in a country committed to rapid modernization, traditions codified by the *sharia* and the opinions of its scholars still reign. In March 1984 a *sharia* court hearing a case from Jaizan ordered a man's left hand and the fingers of his right hand amputated after he inflicted similar wounds on his wife. The verdict was endorsed by the Supreme Judicial Council and approved by the king.

Under the law of the *sharia,* murder is a capital crime. Yet the choice of punishment for a man convicted of murder can be determined by a bargain that satisfies the victim's family rather than by society's fixed price for violating the rules. A murderer can escape the sentence of death by paying the victim's family blood money if that is the family's choice. But only the victim's family can decide, and justice will wait for its decision. In 1983, in two unrelated cases, the murderers in crimes committed in 1966 and 1968 were beheaded. In both instances, the implementation of the death sentence was delayed until the dead men's sons reached maturity to make their choices. In choosing death, the victim's family also has the right to administer it. A family who inflicts the punishment itself does so in order to satisfy its need for revenge in defense of family honor or to end a cycle of violence between feuding families. The most gruesome beheadings are those carried out by the victim's relatives where, lacking the professionalism of the public executioner, the condemned is repeatedly hacked and chopped until he dies.

The sexual transgressions of rape and adultery are also punishable by death. A man guilty of rape is considered to have committed the most vile crime that can be committed against society by robbing a woman of her sexual chastity. Adultery also is a crime against the whole society because of the threat it poses to the family and therefore to the social order. Of the sexual crimes, the punishment for adultery, death by stoning for a woman and beheading for a man, is the most fascinating and the least understood in the West.

Charges of adultery are never made lightly. Since the penalty is so severe, women are protected from unfounded accusations of sexual misconduct. According to the Koran, "Those who defame honorable women and cannot produce four witnesses shall be given eighty lashes."* Unlike the tribal rights of a father to put to death a daughter who has violated her chastity, death sentences under Koranic law are extremely rare. In Saudi Arabia, only one woman is acknowledged to have been stoned to death for adultery in the last twenty years. It is no wonder, since proof of adultery is on the accuser. This proof requires that either a woman confess to the adulterous act three times in front of a *sharia* court, or either four males or eight females who witnessed the actual penetration testify before the court. Just how difficult it is to convict someone for adultery was summed up by a Saudi delegate to a human rights dialogue with European jurists some years ago, who defined the circumstances in which stoning applies. According to the Koran, this is "only when the culprit, prior to his delict, had contracted a legal marriage and if four witnesses known for their righteousness and their integrity were present at the accomplishment of the sexual act in a manner which would exclude the possibility of doubt:

*Sura 24:4.

it would not have been sufficient, namely, that they had seen the accused completely naked and stuck together."*

Whether it is due to severe punishment or public humiliation, Saudi Arabia unquestionably enjoys a remarkably low rate of crime. With no fear, I walked the streets and alleyways wearing several gold chains around my neck and carrying generous quantities of cash in my shopping basket. It was this freedom from the fear of street crime that expatriates almost universally point to as one of the pleasures of life in the kingdom. Yet although no one is mugged, there is crime in Saudi Arabia. In 1982 the Ministry of the Interior reported that in a population of over seven million (Saudis and foreigners), 14,469 crimes were reported during the year. But this number is deceptively large when viewed in the light of what is now reported as criminal.** Among the 1982 offenses, theft accounted for 30 percent of the total; possession or sale of alcohol, 22 percent; murder, 6 percent; attempted murder, 1.2 percent; manslaughter, 1 percent; threats to kill, 7 percent; assaults, 3.7 percent; suicides and attempted suicides, 0.2 percent; bribery, 3 percent; abductions, 4 percent; and moral assaults, 10 percent. This last category included "breaking into homes for immoral purposes, adultery or attempts to commit adultery, sodomy or attempts to sodomize, raping or malesting [molesting] women, running brothels, etc."†

Although the legal system is designed to protect society, not the rights of individuals, it is a system in which every man is equal. But as in the rest of society, women do not share total equality with men. Even so, Mohammed, in a revolutionary act in the tribal society of the Arabian Peninsula, commanded a measure of legal rights for women. Saudi Arabia continues to hew exactly to those commands, and the principle that two women more or less equal one man still holds true in most of the kingdom's legal proceedings. A woman may witness a legal document if another woman agrees to witness it with her. In a trial, it takes the testimony of two women to match that of one man. But in civil matters involving her property, a woman alone has access to the courts. Most of a woman's other legal rights involve her marital rights and the custody of her children.

---

*The Economist, February 13, 1982, p. S-7.
**Although many of these actions exceed the crimes cited by the Koran, all threaten the social order and therefore fall under varying interpretations of the sharia.
†Saudi Gazette, October 31, 1983.

Beyond the general legal categories of criminal, sexual and marital, and what might be termed civil law, most of the *sharia* is concerned with religious practices. Since Islam is so legalistic, perhaps even more so than most orthodox sects of Judaism, there are minute legal rulings on almost every act a human performs. Yet few of these rulings are applicable to the needs of a nation-state functioning in the twentieth century. As the oil boom progressed, more and more claims for action pressed in on a government lacking few points of reference by which to create the rules and regulations necessary for conditions undreamed of in Mohammed's time. But the idea of the *sharia* as the only law of the land is something that no one, including the king, questions, at least not in public. In a speech before the student body of the King Abdul Aziz University in Jeddah in 1983, King Fahd asserted once again that the Islamic *sharia* is the greatest asset of the country and that Saudi Arabia will maintain its strict adherence to it for all time. So ingrained is the concept of religious law and governmental functions being the same that something as far removed from the religious sphere (in Western thought) as a water-use plan emerged from the Third Development Plan as the "Islamic Water Law."

As a result of the total unification of law and religion, civil law particularly has become corsetted in the attitudes and rulings of a 1300-year-old legal system believed to be universally and eternally valid. There is no clearly defined method by which a secular authority can firmly draw the line between what is God's and what is Caesar's. Under Islam, God alone is the lawgiver. Theoretically, the king has no right to legislate except under the authority the *sharia* grants the *emir* of the community to issue regulations to "enforce the commandments of the divine law [and] to implement whatever is deemed necessary for [the] good and well-being of his subjects."*

That Saudi Arabia has been able to function at all with its antiquated and ossified legal system is due to the wiliness of Abdul Aziz and the surprisingly flexible attitude of the *ulema*. When he merged his kingdom, Abdul Aziz inherited a legal system that was composed not only of the *sharia* but also of the Ottoman rules that had governed the Hijaz, the tradition of mediation by the *emir* that characterized the Nejd, and the tribal law of the Bedouins. Claiming to recognize only the *sharia*, Abdul Aziz very carefully and over an extended period of time reor-

---

*Quoted in Willard A. Beling, ed., *King Faisal and the Modernization of Saudi Arabia* (London: Croom Helm, 1980), p. 113.

ganized the judiciary and vastly expanded his right to legislate by decree. Issues that fell outside the specifics of the *sharia* were left to the discretion of the king as long as the principles of religious law were upheld. The *ulema* tolerated these innovations largely because it recognized Abdul Aziz's sincere respect for the *sharia* and benefited from his willingness to incorporate the religious authorities into the political process.

The system worked because Saudi Arabia's long seclusion behind the barricades of its deserts had protected it from "picking isolated fragments of opinions from the early centuries of Islamic law, arranging them into a kind of arbitrary mosaic and concealing behind this screen an essentially different structure of ideas borrowed from the West. . . ." *

Because Saudi Arabia was never colonized, the *ulema* escaped the imposition of foreign law. It was spared the uncomfortable dilemma of either demanding the repeal of alien laws or producing an instant Islamic alternative. The institutions and basic laws of Saudi Arabia have remained indigenous, voluntarily adopted, while at the same time, the system of decree legislation for government administration has allowed the role of government to expand to meet the needs and promises of the oil boom while paying due respect to the *sharia*.

To carry out its governmental decisions, the House of Saud has literally bureaucratized the *ulema* and incorporated it into the mechanisms of the state. Consequently, administrative matters often take on the force of religious law. For example, in October 1979 the Permanent Committee of the Board of Religious Guidance, the kingdom's highest religious body, was asked to issue a religious ruling that would forbid farmers to use white flour as animal feed. Because of government subsidies, the Grain Silos and Flour Mills Organization sold for $3.23 to $3.82 per bag flour that actually cost $23.50 to produce. Lazy livestock owners, taking advantage of the low price, raided supermarket shelves, loaded their pickups, and hauled away the precious flour to feed their animals. The committee for religious guidance decreed the obvious. The purpose of the subsidy was to make good flour available at cheap prices for the benefit of the human population. It was

---

*Joseph Schacht, quoted in Soliman A. Solaim, "Legal Review: Saudi Arabia's Judicial System," *Middle East Journal* 25 (Summer 1971): 406.

additionally pointed out that plenty of animal fodder was available at subsidized prices. The sole reason a religious ruling was necessary at all was that rural farmers could be brought to heel only by the authority of religion.

As the oil boom gathered momentum, the entire approach of defending an outdated legal code with decrees issued by the king but which lacked the force of law quickly clashed with the complexities of an increasingly sophisticated economy tied to the international economic structure. This structural and philosophical weakness was so basic to all aspects of the modernization of Saudi Arabia that the great conflicts between the law of Mohammed and the realities of the twentieth century became an integral part of the boom era. The duality inherent in the civil law built on the *sharia* combined with decree legislation has created a never-never land of contradictions and ambiguities that bears heavily on foreign contractors. Rules and regulations are born, changed, and die in dizzying sequence. What was valid last week no longer applies this week but may be resurrected without notice next week. Furthermore, it seems that 90 percent of the regulations are not written down. I have seen Western businessmen and their Japanese counterparts reduced to bundles of insecurities trying to find out what the law requires for them to operate in the kingdom. Since so little is written down or codified, Saudi lawyers generally advise their clients on the basis of their own experience and their all-important connections. Saudi lawyer Ahmed Audhali once said that his colleagues are very careful about writing anything down for their clients because other lawyers will claim it is incorrect. "And who knows what is correct."*

In an attempt to streamline the adjudication process, commercial courts, labor courts, and other tribunals with limited jurisdiction have been created to hear cases involving decree legislation. But since all matters relate back to the *sharia,* any case can go to a *sharia* court. Western businessmen are well advised to stay out of the religious courts, where for every precedent there is an equally strong opposing precedent, making decisions totally unpredictable. The courts hearing decree legislation cases are somewhat better but are also unpredictable. In these courts, the king becomes the ultimate judge. "If you want to get to the King, you can dispute everything that went before."** But

---

Middle East Economic Digest (April/May 1983): 14.
**Ibid.

as with so much else in Saudi life, this tactic has its limitations. In one case, a German party in a labor dispute refused to accept a compromise settlement. Instead, he hired a Saudi lawyer who took the dispute to the king. The king heard the arguments and nodded, indicating agreement with the German national. With this, the opposing party went to another Saudi lawyer, who for half of his opponent's fee also took his client's case to the king. The king heard his side of the story and reversed his prior opinion, leaving the original ruling of the court standing.

So confused are all of the regulations in the courts governing decree legislation that it is usually easier to seek forgiveness than permission. Compromise is the essence of the courts because, like everyone else, judges in Saudi Arabia abhor making decisions. Instead, reflecting the tribal philosophy that disputes are best settled by reaching a consensus, the courts push litigants into compromise. And the foreigner is wise to accept the court's mediation. For any foreigner wishing to make money in a country whose government almost totally fuels the economy, a clear ruling in the foreigner's favor renders it exceedingly difficult for him to win any further business. A minister who has been embarrassed by an adverse decision in the court simply cuts off any further contracts to his antagonist.

Much of the confusion that reigns between the legalisms set down by the *sharia* and the decrees and regulations of a government no longer in the seventh century flows over into law enforcement.

There are two police forces, the religious and the civil. The *matawain* patrol the public morals and the police enforce civil law. But since all law is ultimately religious, there is a constant overlapping of jurisdictions. And in any jurisdictional conflict with the *matawain*, the civil police are rendered powerless. No one in the political sphere is willing to back its own police in a confrontation with religious authorities. Therefore, the religious police dominate unless the parties involved have sufficient political power to appeal the matter to a higher authority. This sets in motion the consensus process, which can reach the highest level of government and which, at some point, may or may not settle the matter.

Shortly after I arrived back in Riyadh, the al-Azizia area of Riyadh, the most Westernized section of the city, was being intimidated by a young, articulate *matawah* known as Sheikh Ahmed. Believed by the American embassy to be a dropout from Georgetown University, Sheikh

Ahmed, accompanied by several followers, prowled the supermarkets and restaurants in the vicinity. With no official credentials stating that he had any authority, he swept through the aisles of the Euromarché, A&P, Safeway, and other Western-style stores, harassing Western customers. His targets seemed to be couples whom the *sheikh* suspected of shopping together without the benefit of clergy. For those he caught, he confiscated their *iqamas* ("work permits") and threatened the men with three days in jail and eighty lashes. For those who were married, he harangued the women for failing to cover their hair or for wearing dresses with open necklines or knee-length skirts. After seven people had been rounded up and driven off in a truck from the Safeway store the preceding week, the supermarkets in the area became so anxious that they began to stock *abaayas* at the door for their customers.

Women were not the only targets. Sheikh Ahmed took offense at the actions of men that violated the rules of Wahhabism. He viciously berated a man who was wearing gold jewelry and used his camel whip to switch the legs of a big, burly plumber dressed in shorts.

Then one night an American electrician at the King Faisal Specialist Hospital by the name of Ralph Baldwin refused to surrender his *iqama* when the *sheikh* scolded his wife for appearing in public without a head scarf. Sheikh Ahmed called the Riyadh police and Baldwin summoned help from the hospital security department charged with intervening between KFSH employees and Saudi authorities. When everyone had assembled on the sidewalk in front of the al-Johar supermarket, Sheikh Ahmed turned on Mike Field, the security department representative who had been sent by the hospital to try to rescue Baldwin. Releasing everyone else, the *sheikh* detained Mike, the real innocent in the entire affair. Field, realizing he had fallen into the hands of the *matawain,* begged the Riyadh police to intervene but they shrugged their shoulders and left. Afraid to resist, Field was locked in the back seat of a silver Datsun and driven to the al-Badr mosque, Ahmed's headquarters. There five more *matawain* joined the *sheikh,* who was by now threatening to lash his prisoner. Finally, in the early hours of the morning, the badly shaken but unscathed Field was abruptly released.

Eventually Sheikh Ahmed went too far. Staking out the gate leading to the nurses' housing at the hospital, the *matawah* would pick up women coming out to meet their dates and take the couple to his mosque for one of his discourses on sexual propriety. Late one night, a member of the U.S. Diplomatic Corps brought his fiancée home. Just as he kissed her good night, Sheikh Ahmed stepped out of the shadows and grabbed him. Screaming his right to diplomatic immunity, the envoy was hauled off to the al-Badr mosque. However, before the night was over, the American ambassador reached the center of power, the senior princes, and the man was freed. Through the dark corridors of decision-making, the political leaders and the religious leaders reached an agreement to squelch Sheikh Ahmed. The last that I heard of him, he had been placed in a job at the Intercontinental Hotel — in public relations.

When the oil boom hit and the population of Saudi Arabia surged, a civil police force in the real sense of the word did not exist. The House of Saud, always nervous about creating organizations with any authority, had allowed either the *matawain* or the man on the street to do most of the policing. The principle of citizen's arrest was, and remains, a highly developed art. Every Saudi man claims as an inalienable right the power to have anyone arrested on his word. The police usually comply by taking the "offender" to jail, where he can stay until his sponsor secures his release or the court judges whether or not the arrest was justified.

The whole law enforcement system terrifies Westerners, who constantly live with the possibility of landing in jail. An expatriate faces the threat of jail for anything from driving without a license to the possession of alcohol. Yet things have improved. During the early years of the oil boom, the police would determine fault in car accidents by rounding up everyone at the scene, drivers and witnesses alike, and taking them all to jail, where they would be detained until some resolution could be reached. Alan Miller was once held for four hours when he stopped at a police post to ask directions. And my friend Ian Dylan spent two days in jail in 1971 because *his* car was stolen.

Over the years since the oil boom began, a civil police system gradually has been put in place that, on occasion, can create some semblance of order out of the chaos. Always cognizant of the divisiveness within its kingdom, the House of Saud from the beginning centralized control of the police. Consequently, municipalities neither hire nor command their own police forces. Every policeman who patrols the streets works directly for and is answerable to the Ministry of the Interior Security Forces.

The major problem with the police is that they continue to be a law unto themselves until cases reach the courts. Although there is in every country the problem of keeping the police in bounds, seldom is this problem more serious than in Saudi Arabia. As in all areas of the society, the fierce individualism of the Saudis makes it extremely difficult for them to be molded into an organization with established rules and procedures. When a Saudi is given some authority, his ego demands that it be exercised. Regardless of the statement by the respected mayor of Jeddah, Said al-Farsi, that "municipality officials are expected to deal with citizens 'gently,' "* the Riyadh police on occasion can be seen dragging teenage drivers stopped for speeding out of their cars and caning them in the public eye.

Friends or relatives often use police and security officers to settle personal disagreements, especially with Westerners. I once talked to an American who worked for a Riyadh construction company as the receiving clerk, responsible for signing invoices for supplies received. The invoices then went to the accounting department for payment. Unfortunately, one invoice was lost in transit. Holding the receiving clerk responsible for nonpayment of his bill, the supplier had a friend in the Ministry of Interior arrest the clerk. The American stayed in jail for several days under interrogation about why he refused to pay his bills.

Beyond the issue of disciplining the police, the main problem in Saudi Arabia's law enforcement system is the general lack of organization. In late 1983 the long-term influx of foreigners, increasing crime, and the inexperience of the fledgling police establishment finally led the government to issue a set of detention laws that would apply to Saudis and foreigners alike.** According to the executive order of Interior Minister Prince Naif ibn Abdul Aziz, the new rules "forbid arrest or detention of any one unless there is ample evidence calling for his arrest and stipulates that investigation should be completed within three days of detention." † For the expatriate, the most significant provision is that a foreigner arrested in Saudi Arabia is to have his case reviewed by the governor of the province in which the alleged offense took place before the judicial process proceeds further. This procedure gives the governor authority to dispense quickly with cases of way-

---

Arab News, August 9, 1983.
**There is no right of habeas corpus in civil or criminal proceedings.
†*Saudi Gazette,* November 18, 1983.

ward expatriates, primarily Westerners, thus saving the government the embarrassment of formal protests about unjust detentions from foreign governments. Although they do not always work very well, the statutes are at least an attempt to get those accused out of jail, where they often languish for weeks without charges, and into the courts.

The great frustration for Westerners embroiled in Saudi Arabia's legal system is time. There seems to be no procedure for notifying defendants when a case will be heard, or at least no procedure that has ever been explained to those who are not privy to the process. Instead, the defendant sits in jail or is denied an exit visa for months on end while he waits for his case to be heard.

According to most Westerners working with Saudi Arabia's legal system, it works reasonably well once the case makes it way into the courts. Furthermore, once in the court the accused is not subjected to a complex and convoluted trial. "Court procedures are intentionally made as simple as possible to enable the most ignorant Bedouin to come out of the desert, lay his complaint before the court and get a fair hearing." * There are firm judicial procedures established through a series of decrees issued between 1927 and 1975. A defendant has the right of appeal through a sequence of courts, with the Supreme Judicial Council as the final authority. And most would agree that a *sharia* judge is incorruptible, fervently believing that he will go to hell if he makes an unjust decision. Unlike the influence-peddling so prevalent in the rest of the society, a *sharia* judge will usually make a reasonably fair ruling, one not influenced by who the parties to the dispute happen to be.

There are in the *sharia* distinct philosophical similarities to Western systems of law. A man is innocent until proved guilty. The burden of proof falls on the plaintiff. There is a system of appeals. And there is the concept that all men are equal before the law. However, procedures in the *sharia* courts differ from those in the West. All cases require the testimony of two witnesses who saw the actual act. In the absence of these witnesses, the plaintiff is allowed to take an oath swearing that what he claims is true. The testimony of Christians is admissible under a special oath: "In the name of God, who gave Jesus, son of Mary, the Holy Bible and made him cure the sick, the leper, and the deaf, I swear." Oaths are important in the judicial process, especially for a

---

* Beling, ed., *King Faisal and the Modernization of Saudi Arabia*, p. 116.

Moslem, for whom oath taking is a profound act, a personal trust between himself and Allah. Therefore, the court takes little responsibility in guarding against perjury, assuming that any person not telling the truth will be condemned by God to eternal damnation.

There is no jury in a trial and the judge participates in the case. In the lower Saudi courts, the *qadi,* or judge, sits on an elevated dais in the courtroom. The plaintiff and the defendant, sharing the same bench, face him directly. The role of the judge is not to arbitrate but to seek the truth and dispense justice. Consequently he often becomes a mediator, working out a compromise between feuding people. Since the *sharia* is at best vague on many situations in modern life, judges use the precedents of their own culture and their own reasoning to reach decisions. For the Saudis, these decisions are perfectly logical. For the Westerners, they are more often a total mystery. Back in the late 1960s, one of the few Westerners in Saudi Arabia was a British public health worker. He told me that one quiet Friday afternoon he was sitting in the mud house of a Saudi friend, drinking homemade alcohol. The house was situated alone on the edge of town, at the end of a road that was hardly more than a path. Lulled by the peace of the afternoon and the effects of the alcohol, he and his host drifted in and out of sleep. Suddenly, without any warning, the entire front wall of the house collapsed, hit by a Saudi driving one of the few cars in Riyadh at the time. When the lone policeman eventually arrived, he took everyone to jail. The case was heard the next day. The Englishman was sentenced to twenty days in jail and twenty lashes for drinking alcohol. The owner of the house was sentenced to twenty-five days in jail for locating his house in such a place that the driver could run into it. The only one who escaped without punishment was the driver of the car.

While I was working for Tom Krogh, the maintenance contractor, a Mercedes water truck rammed into one of his pickup trucks, totaling it. The case went to court, where the judge ruled that the driver of the water truck had caused the accident, but since he had six children he was more burdened with responsibilities than the owner of the pickup, who had only one child. Therefore, the driver was relieved of paying damages.

Passengers riding in a taxi involved in a wreck are responsible for the accident. The theory is simple and reflects the fatalism of Islam. If the passenger had not hired the taxi, it would not have been where the accident occurred.

Westerners who are veterans of survival in the kingdom are generally philosophical about the minor scrapes and monumental inconveniences generated by the legal system. Most people involved in negligible incidents realize they will be released from jail within a few hours or a few days. And since being in jail is so common, to be arrested carries no social stigma in the foreign community. This cavalier attitude radically changes when Westerners find themselves in jail on serious charges.

Some Westerners who go to jail have become trapped in disputes with their Saudi partners. The regulation requiring all business enterprises to be Saudi owned locks every foreigner into either an immediate or indirect relationship with a Saudi national or the Saudi government. On entering the country, the foreigner surrenders his passport to his Saudi partner and is dependent on him to obtain his visa to exit the country. The character and ego needs of the Saudi sponsor are crucial to the well-being of the foreigner. There have been hundreds of incidents of foreigners being held in Saudi Arabia by their employers. In any disagreement, the foreigner simply does not get out of Saudi Arabia or he stays locked in jail until the matter is settled to the satisfaction of the Saudi or is resolved months later by the court.* It is often the issue of Saudi honor that causes the Westerners so many problems. A Saudi partner has great need to maintain status among his peers. If his business is not as successful as the Saudi expected or if it falters, the Saudi will not bear the shame of failure. Charges of embezzlement fly and the foreign partner usually lands in jail.**

Although many foreigners find themselves in jail unjustly, there are those who are there because they are guilty of any number of transgressions. Every scam devised by man has probably been pulled on the Saudis. During the golden days of the oil boom, an appalling number of supposedly reputable businessmen and professionals inflated prices, forged invoices, sold low-quality goods at high-quality prices, and committed outright embezzlement, all under the guise of helping the Saudis modernize. At one time so many Westerners were stealing files from the Ministry of Planning to peddle to project bidders abroad that

---

*One of the great legends of the Western experience in Saudi Arabia was the American who, unable to get out by other means, had himself crated as cargo and shipped out of the country.
** All of these disputes can be mediated. To stay out of jail, one contractor hid out in my house for six weeks until his Saudi partner agreed to apply for an exit visa in return for $40,000 he claimed was owed to him.

the ministry was forced to adopt a policy that amounted to holding hostages. None of its employees could leave the country unless another employee signed a paper assuming all of his debts and obligations in the kingdom in perpetuity. And that person could only leave if he were able to transfer his obligations plus those he had assumed from the first person to someone else.

But even with all of the financial chicanery, it is the possession of alcohol that lands most Westerners in jail. In spite of all the import restrictions, Saudi Arabia is far from alcohol free. There is the quota of legal alcohol that the government allows the diplomatic corps to import. Then there are the bootleggers. Before the Mecca uprising, bootleg alcohol was relatively easy to buy, although at $75 to $100 a fifth very costly. Bootleggers, some of them Saudi, operated all over the kingdom and claimed a regular clientele. And then in about 1980, stocks of imported alcohol evaporated and prices shot up to $120 or more a fifth. A number of theories about the sudden drought emerged. Speculation swirled around Prince Turki ibn Abdul Aziz, deputy minister of Defense and Aviation and one of the Sudairi Seven. It was rumored that Turki had provided protection for bootleggers before his involvement became too blatant for the political health of the House of Saud, shaken by the Mecca uprising and the growing Islamic revolution. The story gained credence when the black market in alcohol shrank about the time he left the government "for health reasons." But in the end, it may have been Saudi Arabia's new security concerns that permanently crippled the bootlegging industry. The first winter after the outbreak of the Iraq-Iran War, roadblocks were set up on the highways and back roads leading into the cities, where trucks were stopped to search for arms. At about the same time, the first AWACS, whose mission it was to fly air surveillance for the defense of the kingdom, arrived in Saudi Arabia. On one of the sophisticated aircraft's first flights, it was reported to have spotted convoys of trucks transporting bootlegged whiskey across the desert. Suddenly the whiskey runs had become too dangerous for those supplying anyone but the most rich and powerful.

Westerners outside the privileged circle of diplomacy and unwilling to pay the exorbitant prices of the bootleggers make their own alcohol. Wine, being the easiest to formulate, is the most popular. Westerners line up at supermarket checkout counters with their shopping carts loaded with cases of grape juice. Securing themselves behind the locked doors of their houses and apartments, they mix the juice in five-gallon plastic jerry cans with sugar and yeast, smuggled through customs hidden in everything from guitars to the socks on their kids' feet. The mixture is allowed to ferment for three weeks or so, occasionally stirred with a broom handle. The finished, if grossly immature, product is then drained through rag filters into the empty grape juice bottles and corked.

Among these home vintners are the connoisseurs who rig up elaborate wineries in their bathrooms and regularly engage in fierce wine-tasting competitions. The beer brewers, largely British, stage random "Octoberfests" where everyone brings his home-brewed beer for judging. Those with no fear of "jake leg," the neurological disease that strikes from impure moonshine, distill a usually wretched concoction called *sedeeqi,* or "my friend" in Arabic.*

As a result of all of this illicit activity, Saudi Arabia has produced the world's largest breed of high-tech moonshiners. Stills are rigged with an elaborate array of pirated technology and the freshly distilled liquid is passed from bubbling jugs through a variety of sophisticated valves and filters, where it eventually drips into a boggling array of bottles. (I knew a high spirited, boisterous Canadian who colored his *sedeeqi* blue and poured it into Aqua Velva bottles, which he blithely carried through police roadblocks.)

Westerners brewing their own alcohol are usually left alone by Saudi authorities as long as the product is kept in the Westerners' homes and is neither served nor sold to Saudis. But as relatively open as home distilleries are, anyone caught with alcohol is punished. Most go to jail, although in 1978 a furor erupted when two British nationals were publicly flogged in Riyadh for selling *sedeeqi.*

Escaping a jail term often depends on the political clout of the detainee's Saudi sponsor. The more politically important a Westerner's sponsor is, the easier and faster it is to get him out of trouble, if the sponsor chooses to do so. Some Western companies maintain contracts with important princes who use their influence to have culprits guilty of minor offenses deported rather than imprisoned. But nothing is done for people like the employee at the Military Hospital in Riyadh, where a raid uncovered six thousand bottles of liquor stashed in his small dormitory room.

---

*Westerners insensitive to the mores of the society and the ever-increasing number of Saudis who speak English sport T-shirts that say "Sid-eeqi is my friend."

As the House of Saud has come under increasing internal and external religious pressure, the leniency of Saudi authorities toward home
distilleries has waned. Companies like ARAMCO are integrating their
formerly all-Western housing compounds with Saudis and other Moslems, making it difficult for company officials to choose to remain
ignorant of illicit alcohol. If Moslem residents call in the local police,
who themselves often prefer to be left out of issues involving minor
violations of the alcohol laws by expatriates, employers will usually
not intervene. The new atmosphere is forcing Westerners to pour their
homemade alcohol down the drain when rumors spread of an impending raid by authorities, for there are few remaining protections from
jail.

A Westerner's legal problems seldom arise from the failure to be
warned about the seriousness of breaking Saudi law. Western embassies post notices throughout the country describing the severe penalties
for offenses related to drugs and alcohol and for financial malfeasance.
Large companies hold orientation sessions that stress the differences
between Saudi law and the laws of their own countries. Most listen,
many do not. Americans particularly have difficulty in accepting the
fact that the U.S. government has no jurisdiction in Saudi Arabia.
There is some illusion that the American eagle will spread its protective wings over its citizens foolish enough to flout Saudi law. As one
weary ARAMCO official stated, "We try to prepare them but many
don't take our counsel to heart."*

Conditions in the jails of Saudi Arabia vary. Only the rare facility is
heated in winter or cooled in summer, and all serve as a haven for
Saudi Arabia's enormous fly population. In the urban jails, a brief stay
is usually spent in a massive cell with as many as five hundred men,
who share the one toilet that dominates the center of the room. One
man complained that his cell was so overcrowded that for four days he
was unable to find space to lie down. Those who are held for weeks or
months awaiting trial are most often provided clean, if spartan, accommodations and adequate food but nothing else.** Clothing, toiletries,
and reading material are furnished by the prisoner's family or friends.

---

*Quoted in Judith Miller, "Americans in Saudi Prisons Say They Are Being Abused," *New
York Times*, October 17, 1983.
**Women are housed in separate, less austere quarters. The female jail population is quite small
compared to that of males and is predominantly composed of Africans and Asians. The most
startling aspect of women's jails is that the inmates bring their children with them.

Jails in the smaller communities are primitive and the treatment of prisoners often harsh. But everywhere prisoners are treated as a serious threat to the social order. Westerners being moved anywhere outside of their places of incarceration are handcuffed and clamped into irons. A prisoner at Diriyah who was paralyzed and desperately ill from urinary problems was put in leg irons and chained to his hospital bed.

Curious to find out what it is like to be locked in a Saudi jail, I posed as a visitor to an incarcerated Westerner and went behind the forbidding walls of Riyadh's Malaaz jail.

When I entered the small, cramped visitors' room, it was dark except for the thin shafts of strong sunlight that forced their way in through the narrow ventilation spaces near the roof. The room, enclosed by thick mud walls and a single metal gate, was not much larger than ten feet by ten feet and smelled damp. The prisoners, an assortment of Westerners in khakis and sport shirts, sat huddled together on the dirt floor, which was partially covered with cheap, grimy rugs. After introducing myself to the men, I sat down on the hard-packed dirt, which was strangely wet and cool. Conversation moved around the circle clustered about me, as each man recounted for perhaps the hundredth time the circumstances of his running afoul of Saudi law. They were typical stories. There was the overweight Eugene, who claimed he had been in jail for four months awaiting a decision on whether or not the over-the-counter diet pills he had purchased in the United States and which were discovered in his luggage by customs officials constituted a drug offense. Wayne was there because customs officers had found a marijuana cigarette in his coat pocket, placed there "as a joke by my friends at my farewell party in the States." Neal was only nineteen, a construction worker. On his first trip into Saudi Arabia, he had tried to smuggle in a "commercial quantity" of marijuana and had been caught. Walter, a slight, middle-aged man, fidgeted nervously and whined about his arrest for selling *sedeeqi*. The common denominator among the men was that they were scared. Except for one brief contact with an embassy official, who could do little but acknowledge their plight, they were alone, lost in an alien legal system.

Eugene and Wayne were eventually freed and deported, but Neal and Walter went to trial and were sentenced to terms in prison. Several months later I went to see how they were faring.

The al-Hair prison stands alone on the rocky landscape southwest of Riyadh, its walls rising starkly out of the desolate waste of the desert.

It was Thursday, visiting day for women. I stood with the other female visitors who hugged the prison wall, trying to capture the shrinking shade. Every major population group in Saudi Arabia was represented. Arab women clutched the hands of small children. Westerners carried grocery sacks filled with magazines and paperback books. And Asians stood by passively, delicately holding small baskets of fruit. Eventually two benign-looking Saudi guards appeared at the high narrow desk just outside the gate that served as a check post. After they examined our sacks and purses, we were allowed to pass through the gate into a large bare area that stood between the walls and the barracks where the prisoners were housed. Rounding the first building, I saw the inmates standing in a long, tall covered cage set in a concrete slab, strikingly similar to the cages in a zoo. Unlike in Malaaz, where I sat down with the prisoners, I stood outside the cage in the broiling sun while the men clung to the metal bars.

The prisoners whom I interviewed had surprisingly few complaints except boredom and uncertainty about when they would be released. Most were somewhat philosophical about their plight. Neal, the young drug smuggler I had first met in the Malaaz jail, had adjusted to prison life. Deeply chastened by the experience, he spoke of going home someday and putting his life in order. Walter, the bootlegger, was there too. Badgering me for everything from extra clothes to intervention with the American embassy, he said he was not sure he could last through his year-long sentence. With the exception of Walter, the prisoners generally agreed that they were treated reasonably well. Except for being confined in an alien culture, most said they would rather be in prison in Saudi Arabia than in the United States because of the absence of what they termed "hardened criminals."

Yet the charges of physical and psychological abuse that are lodged against Saudi Arabia's prison system by Western governments are too often true. Torture of prisoners is not permitted or condoned by official government policy. But as in so many other areas of the kingdom's day-to-day functioning, there are few people in positions of authority and those who do have authority are routinely absent from work. A prison guard can cane prisoners on the soles of their bare feet for weeks before the line of command can grind into action to order it stopped or to punish the guard.

On the whole, psychological abuse is greater than physical abuse and comes from many sources. It arises primarily from the culture gap between the Westerners and their Saudi guards. A guard can make life miserable not because he is inherently mean but because he will harass prisoners to kowtow to his authority or fail to understand that prisoners want their mail when it arrives, not two weeks later. Even more stressful are the structural weaknesses of the whole administrative system that begins with a foreigner's arrest. The process of sorting out those who should stand trial and those who are unfortunate victims of circumstances is interminable. Prisoners live with a sense of being totally abandoned and powerless. One of the major complaints of Western embassies about the treatment of prisoners is the lack of access to their nationals. Just trying to find out where a foreigner is being held and getting in to see him is difficult. There is no centralized system that lists a prisoner's name, where he is being held, or what the charges against him are. Overzealous officials in the local jails make arbitrary decisions about who can be seen or who can receive mail or reading materials. Not surprisingly, it is the language barrier, for which the Saudis are not responsible, that can create perhaps the most severe form of psychological stress. A prisoner can spend weeks in a detention facility with dozens of men, none of whom speaks his language. Several years ago, a Korean hanged himself after being incarcerated for over a year in a jail where he was unable to speak to another soul.

Among the lawyers, representatives of foreign governments, and inmates whom I interviewed, there is a nearly unanimous opinion that inmates in the Saudi prison system are victims more of poor administration and bureaucratic red tape than of a deliberate government policy that orders the physical and mental torture of prisoners. But the reasons for poor treatment and long delays in the legal process are of little comfort to those caught in the system. Even so, there are those rare foreigners in Saudi jails and prisons who acknowledge they broke the law and willingly pay the price. The most interesting inmate I met during my rounds of Saudi jails and prisons was Jimmy, a Dutch citizen of Indonesian descent who had been a big-time bootlegger in Dhahran. An infectious smile lighted up his face when he frankly admitted that he and his wife recognized the risks in breaking the law and had made the decision to net all the money they could before they were caught and then to pay the consequences. They were eventually arrested. She was deported and he was sent to prison. When I talked to him, he was within a few weeks of completing a three-year sentence in the al-Hair. As Jimmy awaited release, his wife was preparing for his homecoming to the couple's palatial home in the Hague, which they had purchased with their earnings from their bootlegging empire.

The Saudis have little patience with foreigners who violate their laws. While still comfortably low, Saudi Arabia's crime rate has risen noticeably since the oil boom began and the fault is laid on the foreigners. Officials single out the foreign work force for certain types of crime, foremost among which is "bribery as well as bouncing checks and crookeries."* Like people everywhere, the Saudis are concerned about crime. But in addition, their society, firmly anchored in fundamental Islam, is one of the most rigorous law-and-order societies in the world. Among the antagonisms that have arisen between the Saudis and the Westerners is the conflict between the enforcement of Saudi law and the interests of Western governments in protecting their nationals. The Western press periodically exposes the predicament of Westerners in Saudi jails, prompting their embassies to increase their pressure on the Saudi government. The House of Saud then becomes nervous, fearing the issue will create a negative image of Saudi Arabia in the West, at the least, and affecting arms purchases from the West, at the worst. Therefore, the government periodically releases its Western prisoners. The February 1985 state visit of King Fahd to Washington provided an excuse to release Americans being held in Saudi jails. The move did not go unnoticed in Saudi Arabia. To the Saudis, the granting of amnesty was yet another indication that the House of Saud is willing to sacrifice the principles of its own people to preserve the kingdom's relationship with the West.

Confused and frustrated by the centuries-old legal code, Western business learned to accommodate during the oil boom. The contracts were lucrative enough and the threats to profits small enough to soothe the troubled waters. Then in 1982, when the oil glut coincided with the completion of major construction projects, the inadequacies of *sharia* law, from a Western viewpoint, surfaced. The issue was creditor rights. The Saudis chose not to pay their bills on time and the foreign contractors were left with no legal recourse. Since that time, increased pressures to modernize the legal system have come from the Western legal force working in Saudi Arabia as well as major Western financial institutions. The House of Saud can fend off these attacks from the West; its major problems are within the kingdom itself. Domestic business suffers as much as foreign business from the vagueness of the law. The increasing scope of government requires that regulations concerning

---

* Saudi Gazette, November 1, 1983.

everything from social security to berthing rights in the ports carries the force of law. Both the Saudi leadership and the new Western-educated middle class recognize that the *sharia* is inadequate for the kingdom's present stage of development. What is lacking is the political will to move the legal system off dead center.

The fundamental problem of forcing an overhaul of an ancient code of laws is made even more difficult by the political needs of the House of Saud. Saudi Arabia is locked into a political system that originally drew its authority from its defense of the Wahhabis' rigid teachings. The protection of the *sharia* as it now stands is a means by which the House of Saud continues to defend and justify its existence. Political parties and even petitions are banned on religious grounds. Labor unrest, such as the strikes of ARAMCO oil-field workers in 1953 and 1956, is squelched by citing the divisiveness that Mohammed forbid. With only the *sharia*'s rudimentary laws on land tenure based on tribal grazing rights, land without clear title becomes royal property and is distributed to favored people to sell. To call the *sharia* into question is to call everything else about the al-Sauds' own particular form of theocracy into question. The privileged position of the royal family becomes even more threatened when the new middle class voices its demands for constitutional government guaranteeing the rights of citizens.

It is not that the House of Saud is not cognizant of the resistance to its authority, especially coming from the educated classes. Ever since the 1950s, each time the regime has faced a serious challenge at home or abroad, it has promised to institute some form of constitutional government. It happened in 1958 in the succession struggle between Saud and Faisal; in 1962 during the Yemen war; in 1970 after a military coup d'état failed; in 1975 after Faisal's assassination; in 1979 following the incident at Mecca's Grand Mosque; and in 1982 after King Khalid's death. And each time the promise is ignored as soon as the immediate crisis passes. "The fact that various Saudi leaders have felt it necessary to make those promises shows the extent of their awareness of an unsatisfied demand that needs to be appeased. The fact that those who made the promises have been unwilling or unable to deliver on them betrays an ingrained opposition within the regime's power center that paralyzes its capacity for political adaptation." *

---

*Nadav Safran, *Saudi Arabia: The Ceaseless Quest for Security* (Cambridge, Mass.: Belknap Press of Harvard University Press, 1985), p. 227.

The need both to overhaul the legal system and to adopt clear principles and practices under which to govern the country also represents in microcosm the conflict besetting Saudi Arabia. The House of Saud is caught between two opposing forces, neither of which it is willing to abandon. While sensing that an updating of the *sharia* would be supported by the middle class, the leadership is terrified of the fundamentalists. For the House of Saud to appear to move away from the current rigidity of *sharia* law and to adopt some type of constitution or basic law to appease the progressives would only fuel the opposition of the religious bloc to what they see as the Westernized rule of the royal family. In essence, the struggle over the legal system is another aspect of the dilemma of trying to forge the future while clinging to the past. To bring even a modicum of order to a legal system emasculated by conditions created by the oil boom, a review and updating of the law of the *sharia* must come and a formal voice in the decision-making processes of government extended. Unfortunately, it has now been delayed so long that the mounting pressures for change are coming in a period of deep internal and external uncertainty.

14

Swords and Missiles: The Search for Security

WITHIN THE KINGDOM of Saudi Arabia, a quarter of the world's proven oil reserves lie in 865,000 miles of largely empty land, bordered on two sides by 1300 miles of coastline fronting two seas. All this must be defended by a population of perhaps six million people, three-quarters of whom are women, children, and the elderly. Saudi Arabia's vulnerability to outside attack, on one hand, and internal chaos, on the other, has haunted the kingdom since its inception. Through a combination of internal control and consummate diplomatic skill, kings Abdul Aziz and Faisal wound their way through the foreign and domestic minefields surrounding them. Their successors have done less well. Struggling with far more serious problems, the present leadership is intimidated and confused in its response to the escalating threats to the kingdom. Tied up in the recurring dilemma of balancing its own political interests against the interests of the country, the House of Saud keeps the military fractured into several competing forces. These forces are, in turn, overwhelmed by a grim shortage of manpower and a culture that frustrates the basic requirements of military organization. Now facing serious threats from Islamic fundamentalism spurred by Iran and the hard-line Arab states and profoundly questioning the value of its alliance with the United States, the House of Saud in a desperate attempt to defend the kingdom has laid Saudi Arabia's security on the altar of high technology, sold and serviced by the West.

The fragile military establishment in Saudi Arabia has always played the dual role of defending the country and protecting the royal family from its internal opponents. Historically, the House of Saud has trusted its internal political interests to its Bedouin army. What is now the National Guard, an integral part of the current military structure of Saudi Arabia, was originally a military organization formed from tribes loyal to the king and pledged to defend his personal safety. The National Guard grew out of the 1929 Ikhwan revolt, which nearly destroyed the regime of Abdul Aziz. The Ikhwan were fanatical religious zealots who rose against the king when Abdul Aziz refused to allow his former allies in the unification of the kingdom to stage tribal raids beyond Saudi Arabia's borders. Fearing the raids would result in armed conflict with the British in Iraq, Abdul Aziz gambled his kingdom by turning on the rebellious Bedouins. It took two years before Abdul Aziz crushed his enemies. The decisive battle took place at Sibilla on March 29, 1929, and was "the last great Bedouin battle ever fought, the last in the series which had continued since the time of Abraham."* But the revolt was not to end until Abdul Aziz mechanized his army. Word reached the king that the rebel leader, Faisal al-Duwish, had once again mobilized his forces in the al-Hassa. Commandeering every automobile from Mecca to Jeddah, Abdul Aziz's army raced seven hundred miles across Saudi Arabia with no spare parts and no mechanics. Although they arrived in the al-Hassa in broken-down wrecks riding on their axles and held together with leather thongs, the sight of an army no longer dependent on camels was enough to cripple the spirit of the rebels, and the rebellion ended. Rather than punishing the participants, Abdul Aziz settled the Ikhwan in communities and won their loyalty by creating a select pseudo-military establishment that tied the *sheikhs* and their sons to the power structure. Abdul Aziz's need to provide these Nedji tribesmen with employment and cash in order to keep them in their communities and loyal led him to institutionalize the ties of suzerain and soldier in the form of the National Guard. Through the guard, Abdul Aziz funneled money and favors to the major tribes to keep them passive and his kingdom united.

The National Guard remains the most visible branch of the military. Although the army, air force, and navy were strengthened after the oil boom, the guard still dominates the showcase events in which the king appears. As in ancient pageantry, dozens of men adorned in rich-col-

---

*David Howarth, *The Desert King: A Life of Ibn Saud* (Beirut: Continental Publications, 1964), p. 168.

ored vests proudly sit, stirrup to stirrup, astride flawless white Arabian horses. Above their heads, their green and white Wahhabi standards flap in the wind. As the king approaches, they draw their mounts into a rigid stance and grasp the hilts of the swords strapped at their sides. Releasing from their throats the loud guttural cry of the desert warrior, the guardsmen raise their drawn swords high above their heads in salute to their ruler. So the Bedouin army remains a kind of Praetorian guard for the House of Saud, the royal family's defense of last resort against internal opposition.

The House of Saud assiduously cultivates its historic ties with its tribal force. Once a year the King's Camel Race, held under the auspices of the National Guard, gathers in the last of the Bedouins still wandering the desert. There they pit the best of their camels in a grueling eighteen-kilometer race across the moonscape plains of the Nejd. Days before the actual race, the participants, many of whom have sons serving in the National Guard, begin to collect. Gradually, the empty spaces beyond Riyadh's ultramodern King Khalid International Airport fill up. The camels, hundreds of them, are transported in from their grazing grounds, somehow folded up in the back of their owners' dinky Toyota pickups. In the camp, housing hundreds of people, veiled women hover near their tents behind the smoldering campfires while children play amid the cantankerous beasts on whose existence traditional society depended for centuries.

On the day of the 1984 race I arrived early. Staking out a choice spot on the crusty earthen hill that was the viewing stand for the Westerners, I spread out my small rug. As if to confirm the constant blending of old and new in Saudi Arabia, I was immediately approached by a Pakistani offering me a sample cup of a new soft drink called "Coka." Before I had finished swallowing the overly sweet cola, truckloads of National Guardsmen began to arrive, taking their places near the finish line. They were armed with small paddles, each with a number painted on it. Their assignment was to meet the riders as they crossed the finish line. As I watched, an officer carrying a swagger stick called the Bedouin soldiers to attention. They lined up. Each man turned his head sharply to the left and extended his arm to measure the distance to the next man. They held this perfect formation approximately three minutes before they began to sit down, a few at a time. Realizing what was happening, their commander shouted, ordered them to their feet, and lined them up again, over and over. Meanwhile, other guardsmen strutted and preened before the stands.

Most of the day at a camel race is spent waiting for the racers to appear. In good Saudi tradition, the race has no firm starting time. Instead, the racers accumulate far out on the desert, and when they do start it is two hours or more before they approach the finish line. Sitting in the sun on my rug, I watched the crowd and waited. The first clue that the camels were approaching was the excitement heralding the arrival of King Fahd and his guests. The royal entourage, which had followed the race across the desert, blazed by the viewing stand in one of those big luxury cross-country buses, escorted by six red custom-ized Mercedes convertibles loaded with the king's armed guards. Just after them, I saw a long cloud of dust preceded by a grand parade of camels. They were running at full tilt in their absurd splay-legged gait, their riders clinging precariously to the back of the great humps. The field of approximately seven hundred made two passes in front of the spectator stands, with the royal bus and armed escort streaking by in pursuit of the leaders, before making the final pass toward the finish line.

Many of the camels refused to finish. The spent beasts balked as their riders repeatedly hit them with their whips before climbing down and leading their mounts off the track. One camel, the color of the dust that covered it, collapsed, trapping its head under its enormous body. I gasped, afraid it had died. But several Saudis on the sidelines dashed out to right it. There it sat on its haunches, looking dazed and puzzled but fit to race another day.

By this time I had also regrettably moved to the finish line. When the sweating, foaming camels crossed the line, an overpowering stench washed over the entire area. The fumes hit me, momentarily paralyz-ing my sense of smell, only to be followed by another wave of the numbing odor. The boyish riders, aged from about nine to fourteen, seemed immune to the smell; all that mattered was that they had fin-ished. Each of the top five winners appeared before the king to receive his prize, which ranged from a GM water truck, a thousand bags of barley, and SR 35,000 ($10,294) in cash for first place, to a tent, seven hundred bags of barley, and SR 22,000 ($6,470) for fifth place. (The newspapers somehow felt it necessary to point out that the barley was for the camels.) The last I saw of the champion, he was driving his bright red water truck home, his head barely visible over the dash-board.

The king departed, the expatriates boarded their buses, and the Bed-ouins loaded their complaining camels back into their Toyotas and struck their tents. They would return next year to renew their bond with the House of Saud.

The great camel race is evidence that despite the sophisticated hardware that the oil boom bestowed on the National Guard, it has retained many of the characteristics of its early history. And these were the characteristics that served Abdul Aziz so well.

The Ikhwan, the precursor of the National Guard, provided Abdul Aziz with an army that although untrained could be mobilized and demobilized swiftly. The Bedouins were not needed for prolonged campaigns since Abdul Aziz's chances of becoming involved in a foreign war were small as long as he stayed within his own borders and out of the way of the major powers in the area. Except for the 1934 border dispute with his southern neighbor, isolated internal uprisings were the main threat to Abdul Aziz's rule. Therefore, a loosely organized, poorly defined military establishment was in his best interests. Conversely, a highly structured and visible military was not only unaffordable but dangerous. An armed force with its own structure and staffed by people with a vested interest in the power of their organization did not fit Abdul Aziz's own unique political equation. Nevertheless, the resumption of oil production at the end of the Second World War forced Abdul Aziz and his successors to begin to think about protecting themselves from the events swirling on their borders.

To keep its enemies off guard, the House of Saud traditionally has kept the whole military structure clouded in shadowy obscurity. Outsiders had little knowledge of Saudi Arabia's defense capabilities until after World War II, when in 1950 an American military advisory group arrived in Riyadh to help Abdul Aziz organize his meager armed forces. But the Americans were not the first to attempt to bring some order to the Saudi military. The British, who had arrived six years earlier, had left in disgust when their mission was rendered impossible by the complexities of Saudi politics and culture. The frustrated British military experts found themselves unable to recruit adequate officer material, a situation compounded by the arbitrary granting of commissions to the king's relatives and friends. The already inadequate funds Abdul Aziz allocated for equipment routinely disappeared in the pipeline of corruption. The final blow came when the movements of the British mission within the country and its contacts with Saudi troops were all but forbidden for fear it might discover information Abdul Aziz chose to keep to himself. When the American mission arrived, the number of Saudi troops was still unknown, even though a nine-month survey of the Saudi defense establishment preceded the Americans' arrival. Three years later, they were able to estimate that there were probably somewhere between seventy-five hundred and ten thousand regular army troops. Another ten thousand might be commandeered from the king's personal guard, paramilitary police, and the Bedouins who were on the king's levy. By the time the Americans had formulated their estimates, the knowledge of the numbers and location of troops loyal to the House of Saud had taken on added urgency. The first challenge to the al-Sauds' rather cavalier military strategy came from a combination of the founding of the state of Israel and the rise of Arab nationalism under the sway of Egypt's Gamal Abdul Nasser.

Saud ibn Abdul Aziz became king of Saudi Arabia in the year following Nasser's 1952 seizure of power in Egypt. Nasser's charisma among the Arab masses and his emotional appeal to Arab nationalism would buffet Saudi Arabia both internally and externally throughout Saud's reign and into Faisal's. Representing the Saudis' first confrontation with revolutionary Arab politics aimed at pulling down the Middle East's conservative monarchies, Nasser was the prelude to what has been Saudi Arabia's major foreign threat until Iran's Ayatollah Khomeini entered the scene.

Initially attracted to Nasser as a check against any move Jordan's King Hussein might make to regain the Hashemite kingdom his grandfather lost to Abdul Aziz,* Saud invited the Egyptians to send a military training mission to Dhahran to try its hand at organizing the Saudi military. It was a move the House of Saud soon regretted. While Saudi Arabia was keeping a wary eye on Jordan, Nasser was moving toward rabid revolutionary rhetoric against the monarchies of the Middle East. Nasser's message took root in the kingdom, leading to a 1955 coup attempt by Saudi army officers against the House of Saud. King Saud mobilized his tribal army against the regular army, hastily patched up relations with Jordan, and turned for protection to the United States, a major opponent of Nasser and the developer of Saudi Arabia's petroleum industry. It was in the Nasser era that the strategic relationship between the United States and Saudi Arabia was born. For the next twenty-five years, the American option would serve as the underpinning of all of the Saudis' defense thinking.

---

*Britain failed to support its ally, the Sherif Hussein, against Abdul Aziz during his drive to unify Saudi Arabia. Instead, Hussein's sons Abdullah and Faisal were placed on the thrones of the British mandates of Transjordan and Iraq.

But the American military guarantee could not protect Saudi Arabia from Nasser's ideology. In 1962 Saudi Arabia faced yet another threat from Egypt, this time along the kingdom's southern border in Yemen. A Nasser-inspired military coup in Yemen overthrew the traditional ruler, the Imam Badr. Fleeing to the north of the country, the *imam* gathered an army of friendly tribesmen for his defense. To bolster its stand Egypt poured an expeditionary force into Aden and southern Yemen. Alarmed that Nasser's troups would march north into Saudi Arabia, the House of Saud found itself facing its first serious foreign threat. The crisis had all the elements the House of Saud fears most: the defenselessness of the kingdom, the threat of revolution against its rule from its own military, and dangerous dissension within the royal family. The crisis in Yemen is deserving of some detailed scrutiny because Saudi anxieties and behavior during the war and its associated events have come to characterize the House of Saud's diplomacy and its military responses to all threats against the kingdom ever since.

To begin with, the al-Sauds were confused about how they should respond to the challenge. The House of Saud is always burdened with the possibility that a military defeat of its national army might lead to the renunciation of the king. Like a tribal *sheikh*, a king no longer regarded as able to provide for the security of his people falls victim to his rivals. For the House of Saud to send in an undisciplined, poorly equipped army against the Egyptian army invited defeat, which in turn invited revolution. Consequently, the House of Saud was willing, as it continues to be willing, to go to any lengths to avoid armed conflict. The second problem to emerge from the confrontation with Egypt was the split in the Saudi royal family. Again, this is characteristic of the House of Saud in times of stress over foreign threats. This episode of disunity simply happened to be more public than others. Prince Talal ibn Abdul Aziz and several other princes had been exiled from Saudi Arabia after they publicly called for a constitutional government that would impose restraints on the power of the royal family. Talal and the other royal dissidents who formed the Committee of Free Princes established themselves in Cairo prior to the coup in Yemen, apparently to be in readiness to claim leadership of Saudi Arabia if the Yemen adventure drove Saud and Faisal from power.*

---

*The House of Saud has an interesting way of handling its opponents. Abdul Aziz decided early on to make his enemies allies by returning them like lost sheep to the fold. Prince Talal and the Free Princes were eventually brought home, and Talal himself now holds an honored and visible position in the royal hierarchy.

But Saudi Arabia never went to war. Recognizing his country could not defeat Egypt, Faisal, crown prince and acting head of government at the time, used the kingdom's oil income to hire surrogates from among the tribes of northern Yemen to hold off the Egyptians. Having bought off Saudi Arabia's opponents in Yemen, which also fended off the challenge of the Free Princes, Faisal moved to divide the kingdom's military forces in order to keep the military weak and, therefore, out of politics.

While the disarranged army and cursory air force muddled along, the tribal levies,* numbering somewhere between ten thousand and sixteen thousand men plus an undetermined reserve force, became noticeably better organized. Still, they were equipped only with light arms, were largely untrained, and had little transport. Since they were considered loyal to the king, they were assigned the important jobs of guarding the Tapline (the major oil pipeline) and other strategic points not trusted to the army.

The Royal Guard, the elite of the military, had about twenty-seven hundred men, who were regarded by American intelligence sources as crack troops. The guard clustered around the king and existed solely for the protection of the House of Saud. Its members had received more training than any other branch of the military and possessed enough equipment to overpower the National Guard. The two together could roll over the ragtag army. This completed the military scheme. The National Guard checked the Royal Guard, which checked the army. No opponent could challenge the king without controlling at least two of these three independent forces.

The system worked. During the final episode of the succession struggle between Saud and Faisal, the divided military prevented Saud from staying in power against the wishes of most of the royal family. In 1964 Saud tried to reclaim the throne by calling out the Royal Guard and deploying it around his pink palace. The National Guard declared its support of Faisal while the army stayed neutral. Consequently, neither brother was in control of two of the three components of power. The stand-off ended when the commander of Saud's Royal Guard was surprised and captured by officers of the National Guard who arrived at his home in Riyadh's minuscule fleet of taxicabs.

With Saud finally gone and Faisal firmly in control, the military was reorganized once again. The Royal Guard was dismantled and the main

---

*Variously called the White Army or the National Guard.

body incorporated into the National Guard. The core, which still acts as personal guards of the king, went into the Ministry of the Interior. This new ministry became yet another element in the power configuration. Its power is derived from its control of the Department of Public Security (the police), the Frontier Guards, the Coast Guard, and royal intelligence. Leaving the National Guard, or tribal force, as its own entity, Faisal also created the Ministry of Defense and Aviation (MODA) made up of the army, navy, and air force. To govern over the new military structure, the king appointed his conservative brother Abdullah as commander of the National Guard and his progressive brother Sultan as minister of Defense and Aviation, positions both still hold. Fahd, the future king, became minister of the Interior.

By 1967 the House of Saud had emerged intact from the war in Yemen and the internal crises it had triggered within the kingdom. Nasser had been forced to withdraw his support from Yemen because of his calamitous defeat in the 1967 war with Israel. The question of what to do about Saud's incompetent rule was finally settled. And a military equation that protected the House of Saud from its opponents had been formulated and put in place. The problem with the new structure — a problem that has never been solved — was that in trying to combine the administrative needs of the military with measures designed to secure the power and privileges of the thousands of members of the royal family, Saudi Arabia wound up with a military that could not defend the country. This was of little concern to the House of Saud, for the confirmation of Faisal's wisdom in organizing the military in such a way that a coup d'état against the ruling house was almost impossible was not long in coming.

In May 1969 a Nasser-inspired group colluded with segments of the Saudi military in a scheme to overthrow the House of Saud and replace it with a republic. Before the plan could be executed, the plot was discovered. The National Guard went on alert and the internal security forces in the Ministry of the Interior went after the culprits. As the layers of the Arab Nationalist Movement, the group responsible for the coup attempt, were peeled away, officers of the army and air force were exposed. Among them were sixty air force officers, the director of the Air Force Academy in Dhahran, the director of military operations, commanders of the military garrisons of the al-Hassa and Mecca, and a minor prince from the Sudairi family. The discovery of the plot led to waves of arrests and dismissals of officers of the regular military and senior civil servants. Although the rumor was unconfirmed, many believed the leaders were flown over the Empty Quarter and pushed out. Considering the seriousness with which the House of Saud regards challenges to its power, it was plausible that all might have suffered excessive punishments. But on one of my excursions into a *hareem*, I met a stunning Saudi woman in her mid-fifties who disproved the theory.

I had become engaged in conversation with the woman because I was fascinated to learn that although she had been married for many years she had always had a job, putting her in the vanguard of Saudi career women. Casually, I asked her what type of work her husband did. She lowered her head perceptibly and said he was "in business." Sensing she was going to say something else, I waited. She shifted slightly on the soft sofa and then looked directly at me, her eyes probing mine. "He used to be an important officer in the military until he was arrested during the trouble in 1969." I was so astonished that she would mention the episode at all, much less her husband's involvement in it, that I said nothing in response. Perhaps because of my silence, she again went on. Looking away from me toward a wall across the room, she related her tale in the tone of a philosophical journey through the past. Her husband had been arrested by the internal security forces and spent six years in jail somewhere in the central part of the country. She and her children were allowed to visit him from time to time. Other than being confined, he was treated well. She even spoke kindly of King Khalid, who had released her husband, along with the others involved in the plot, during the amnesty following Faisal's assassination. When she finished her story, she looked at me once more and said, almost passionately, "You know, none of the men wanted to overthrow the king. They just wanted to do things differently."

On the eve of the oil embargo, the al-Sauds had their house once more back in order. But two important truths about Saudi Arabia's military lingered as a result of the events surrounding the war in Yemen, the succession struggle, and the 1969 coup attempt. Both are still valid. The first was that Saudi Arabia discovered it was powerless in a military confrontation with its neighbors. Militarily, its troops and supplies were too limited to be an effective fighting force, and politically, the House of Saud could not chance a fight it would probably lose without risking revolution from its opponents at home. Second, the rivalries within the royal family coupled with threats to its rule from dissident

elements within the kingdom mandated that the military forces be split
so no one organization could dominate. One military force checking
the other was good internal politics but left Saudi Arabia defenseless
against foreign threats. Although bestowing great wealth on the kingdom, the 1973 oil embargo in some ways only increased the kingdom's
security problems. No longer could it stand on the edges of the caldron
of Arab politics. Its oil resources and its wealth forced it to become a
player in the Arab struggle against Israel, and at the same time, whether
the Saudis wanted to acknowledge it or not, Saudi Arabia became more
dependent than ever on the United States for the technical and military
assistance it needed to build any viable defense. The only thing the oil
boom did not change was the kingdom's fundamental defense objectives.

Since 1948 Saudi Arabia has had three consistent security goals.
The first is to keep Yemen disunited and weak so that it can neither
recover the Assir lost to Abdul Aziz or be used by a foreign power as
a base of operation against Saudi Arabia from the south. The second
is to shore up the vulnerability of the oil fields to protect them from
encroachment by a foreign power. The third of Saudi Arabia's security
objectives, and the most difficult to orchestrate, is to maintain a stance
against Israel that insulates the kingdom from the hostility of its Arab
neighbors while at the same time allowing it to nurture its defense
alliance with the United States. Despite all of its sudden wealth after
1973, Saudi Arabia quickly recognized that it was unable to translate
money into military power. Its dearth of manpower, the technical ineptitude of its population, the political considerations of the House of
Saud, and the dictates of the Saudis' own culture conspired to keep
Saudi Arabia impotent. What the oil embargo did accomplish was to
give the Saudis enough credit with its Arab neighbors to move ahead
with its defense plans based on the American guarantee of security.

In 1974 Saudi Arabia adopted a ten-year military preparedness plan
drawn up by its American allies. Under its provisions, the army by
1984 would increase from 45,000 men to 72,000; the air force from
14,000 to 22,000; and the navy from a few hundred men with almost
no ships to 3,900 seagoing sailors. The National Guard was to stay at
35,000 men. Even with its expanded numbers, the armed forces would
remain pitifully small, spread out across the kingdom's great land-
mass. No one envisioned Saudi Arabia fighting a war. The pivot of
defense strategy was to adequately arm the Saudis so they could defend
themselves long enough for their allies to arrive. The American plan

sought to overcome as much as possible the lack of manpower by creating relatively small but highly mechanized land, air, and sea forces heavily endowed with fire power, ground and air mobility, strong air support, and the best infrastructure money could buy. By depending on high-tech weapons systems rather than manpower, Saudi Arabia was to purchase its security from the West. In building the protective shield, Riyadh, al-Kharj, and Dhahran would be molded into one defensive triangle; Jeddah, Taif, and Mecca into another. The four corners of the kingdom, largely empty in 1973, would literally be filled up with new or expanded military facilities. With the Empty Quarter employed as a buffer zone, Khamis Mushayt was designed to repel an attack from the Yemens. Tabuk, the main air base, looked toward conflicts centering around Israel. And at Hafar al-Batin a whole city would be built to create some defense on the empty plain that runs from the border with Iraq directly to Riyadh.

It was with the King Khalid Military City at Hafar al-Batin that the Saudis would test their ability to turn money into security. In 1976 Saudi Arabia began raising a city for a projected seventy thousand inhabitants out of a spot that is so isolated and so inhospitable that an uncarthly aura hangs over it. Sitting in a *wadi* in the middle of a stark, barren desert, it is three hundred and fifty miles from Riyadh and, when construction began, four hundred miles from the nearest port. Its isolation made a staggering problem of logistics for men and materials. Building stocks were blocked in the congested ports or sat on the docks because there were no trucks to transport them to the site. Although the first men on the site worked out of tents, the mass of workers needed for construction of the permanent buildings could not be recruited until support facilities were in place. Unbearable heat and sand storms raged for days. In addition to all of this, the Saudis threw their own stumbling blocks in the way. There was a rule that no aerial photographs intended to locate sources of gravel could be taken for security reasons. The use of short-wave radios was so restricted by the military that communications were next to impossible. There were bureaucratic tie-ups within the bowels of the Ministry of Defense and Aviation. The already severe labor shortages were made even worse by the Saudis' reluctance to use labor from any country suffering political unrest. And there were the ever-present visa problems. In just one instance, experts needed to fire up the generators that were to supply the site's major source of power refused to return to the kingdom. On a previous trip when they were sent by the American electrical equipment supplier to Saudi Arabia for two weeks, they found their stay forcibly extended for two months when the Saudis denied them exit visas to keep them on the job. The mutinous employees complained about their "shabby treatment" and that "slavery went out a hundred years ago," assailing their employer with a torrent of expletives. When I was typing and filing at the Corps of Engineers, I remember seeing an intercorps telex from the United States reporting on the progress in coaxing these experts back to Saudi Arabia. The go-between bluntly stated, "I get the impression these guys don't think much of playing with camels and walking barefooted in the sand."

The King Khalid Military City was in the early stages of construction when I finessed a permit to visit the site in late 1978. Very early in the morning, I arrived at the far end of the runway of the Riyadh airport to board the six-seater plane that ferried contractors, construction supervisors, and officials from the Ministry of Defense and Aviation (MODA) between Riyadh and al-Batin. The flight that morning was full, as it was every time it made the run, since the cadres of people demanded by such a mammoth construction project fought to get aboard. Ducking my head in the cramped cabin space, I took a seat facing a Saudi from MODA, who eyed me curiously but never spoke. The other passengers were contractors and engineers, who also ignored me, sensing, no doubt, that my presence was highly irregular. As soon as we were buckled in our seats, the motors sputtered to life, shaking the plane as the rpms mounted. We had barely cleared the ground before we were out over the desert. As the engines groaned through the dusty air for the next hour, I saw absolutely nothing below me except for the bleached gray of the packed sand of Saudi Arabia's northeastern desert. Not until the twin propellers of the small plane slowed signaling our descent did I spot the naked strip of black asphalt that marked al-Batin. The plane taxied to a stop on the empty runway, and I stepped out into what seemed like endless nothingness. Then I spotted my contact, signaling to me from underneath a ten-gallon hat. We hurried out of the sun and climbed into his four-wheel-drive vehicle, where I met the others responsible for my presence on what the Saudis liked to think of as a highly secretive military site.

Al-Batin was desolate. Except for a Bedouin camp on the edge of the construction site, the only sign of life I saw outside the small cluster of construction trailers was a stray donkey startled by the noise of the jeep. As we jarred over dirt roads that appeared to come from nowhere and connect to nowhere, my escorts pointed out small blue flags, barely visible, that marked the sites of future buildings. Construction, then in its second year, was expected to take five more, at an estimated cost of $1 billion per year. We eventually arrived at a stark obelisk that marked "Centrum," the center point of the future city, which someday would fan out in interlocking octagons of headquarters, housing, shops, mosques, and maintenance and training facilities. Leaving Centrum, I saw six Pakistanis standing next to a wheelbarrow and a hole in the ground that would someday be the maintenance shed for the sophisticated tanks scheduled to be stationed there. Another spot had a small motor perking along, drawing up water. This would someday be the water plant for the whole city. Looking at the advance cadre of construction workers and engineers clawing their way into the hostile desert, I thought it hardly seemed possible that they could build a city in this environment. Yet I knew that with enough money the Saudis could accomplish miraculous things. And so it was. The King Khalid Military City was eventually inaugurated by King Fahd in 1985, two years later than scheduled. After spending in excess of $5.2 billion on construction to house fifty thousand people, the total number of men in the entire Saudi army at the time it opened was no more than twenty-five thousand.

Al-Batin was more a monument to the dream of turning wealth into protection than it was a viable military establishment. But its construction had barely begun when the military and economic planners were already envisioning the expenditure of $100 billion on defense during the upcoming Third Development Plan. Most of this money was designated for infrastructure projects for every branch of the military. And much of the money would not be spent wisely. At al-Batin, away from the dirt and noise, beyond the cramped barracks of the manual laborers and the spartan trailers housing the engineers, the temporary VIP villas stood alone. Built especially to house King Khalid and his immediate entourage for one night when the KKMC site was dedicated, the villas had cost $3,246,352, including the accessories flown in from Tiffany's in New York.

The 1974 defense plan of which al-Batin was a component part was the most comprehensive and ambitious move Saudi Arabia had ever made in its own defense. Yet it had serious weaknesses, weaknesses that were inescapable for a country that had little to defend itself with except money. By adopting high technology as a basic strategy, Saudi Arabia bought a military structure that required absolute organization and technically sophisticated officers, administrators, and soldiers. These were qualities the Saudis lacked and that plagued every area of development Saudi Arabia undertook. But it was in the military perhaps more than any other sector of the new Saudi Arabia where Saudi culture so dramatically conflicted with modernization.

There is no military tradition in Saudi Arabia and little commitment to the concept of the nation-state. As fiercely independent individuals who survived on the desert for centuries with nothing but their own wits and fortitude, the Saudis are not about to submit to the discipline of the army. Family and tribe remain the center of any Saudi's existence, and for this reason it is difficult to keep the military recruits the country does have at their posts. Unit assignments are haphazard, as commanders respond to special requests from relatives or people in positions of power to place a particular man in a particular post. Then his assignment might never make it onto a central registry. If an alert is issued, both soldiers and commanders are left with no idea of where to report. Emergency situations become chaotic because so little importance is placed on routine training. The air force commonly has only 25 percent of its pilots appear at scrambling exercises and being absent without leave is an accepted military tradition in all branches of the armed forces. When the army was mobilized in March 1979 to meet the threat posed to Saudi Arabia by clashes between North and South Yemen, the first order of business was to issue frantic calls for missing soldiers who had simply drifted off. While U.S. military personnel were taking up stations in Riyadh, the only visible sign I saw of the Saudis' all-out military alert was a lone truck pulling the Ramadan cannon down the main road to Mecca.

Since concerns beyond today have little place in the national psyche, maintenance depends more on Allah's will than it does on his suppliants. Lack of routine care turns sophisticated hardware into useless junk. This endless crisis of maintenance is not as much a matter of ability as of commitment. The forceful status system within the culture forbids a Saudi to work with his hands. As a result, Saudis can be trained to be excellent pilots but service and repair of their aircraft depend on the large numbers of foreign workers imported for almost all military support functions. If for no other reason, Saudi Arabia's defense strategy, built around sophisticated weapons requiring exacting upkeep, is fatally flawed by Saudi attitudes toward maintenance.

Overall, the officer class is well trained and motivated. Yet no matter how competent the officer corps, Saudi Arabia's forces lack numbers and depth. While there is no problem in recruiting pilots to fly F-4s and F-15s, there is a chronic shortage of pilots for the forty-eight C-130 transport planes that tie the kingdom's defenses together. The lower in rank, the less competent and committed is the military man. Although there is as little glory in being a foot soldier in Saudi Arabia as there is anywhere else in the world, building morale is enormously complicated by the fact that those soldiers are basically Bedouin in their attitudes and patterns of behavior and not easily welded into cogs in a late-twentieth-century defense force. The contrast between the educated, status-conscious officer corps and the troops is no more graphically depicted than by the street vignette in which I saw an officer impeccably attired in his tailored uniform standing next to a private who was making his last stand for independence by refusing to put shoelaces in his combat boots.

The cultural constraints on military preparedness further aggravate the basic organizational nightmare inherent in the division of the military. The entire military structure is plagued by a shocking lack of coordination, both at the highest levels of command and between the branches. At the same time that it is committed to high technology that has cost billions of dollars, the kingdom's military is paralyzed by the rivalry between the religiously conservative National Guard and the generally progressive armed forces. They compete with each other for everything from elaborate officers clubs and favors from the king to legitimate requests for needed military hardware, thereby draining away both manpower and resources. Nevertheless, in the eyes of the monarchy, the long record of military coups in the volatile Middle East spearheaded by ambitious young officers proves the wisdom of keeping military power equally divided between fiercely competing groups.

The National Guard, now numbering in the neighborhood of twenty thousand men, remains the most politically powerful division of the military. The ruling regime continues to rely on the tribal origins and the financial prerogatives of the guard to keep it loyal to the House of Saud. Coveted positions within the officer corps of the guard are secured through the influence of fathers who have, in turn, proved their loyalty to the crown. Promotions of enlisted men are made by the commander, Prince Abdullah, while promotions of officers are made by the king himself. Although the National Guard originally filled a largely ceremonial role, it is now a heavily equipped, full-blown military machine.

The National Guard was not directly covered by the 1974 defense plan because of the House of Saud's insistence on keeping the affairs of the guard completely separate from the affairs of the regular military. Therefore, in March 1973, a seven-year agreement was concluded between Saudi Arabia and the United States that put the U.S. Department of Defense in charge of three private American contractors hired to modernize the guard. At a cost of $335 million (raised to $1.9 billion in 1976), the guard's twenty battalions would be mechanized into infantry battalions with their own artillery support and air defense capability for its internal security functions and to back up the army in case of a foreign invasion. The Vinnell Corporation of Los Angeles, California, one of the contractors, hired a number of Vietnam veterans, largely logistics experts rather than Rambo-type mercenaries, to train the Saudis to be modern soldiers.*

The efforts are paying off. My first impression of the guard was of disheveled Bedouins who had been taken out of their *thobes* and put in an alien attire of pants, shirts, and combat boots. Looking more confused than competent, they slouched against walls or sprawled in the nearest shade, oblivious to military order or mission. Guard members now look comfortable, even snappy, in their olive drab uniforms topped by the traditional red and white *gutra*, held in place by an *agal* sporting the guard's insignia. When they are on parade, they march in unison and salute on command, at least most of the time. But although it is housed in impressive new headquarters and armed with sophisticated new weaponry, the guard, despite outward appearances, still remains in attitude a Bedouin army.

I had been hearing from my friends at the National Guard Hospital near Riyadh about a malady among guardsmen that the impatient medics had dubbed the "Dead Soldier Syndrome." According to the reports, it occurs when guardsmen are lined up to do calisthenics and presents itself as a type of hysteria where the patient feels faint and becomes stiff as a board. Arriving at the hospital by the busload, the victims are rushed into the emergency room, where they instantly kick

---

*One of the things Saudi Arabia got for its money was a cadre of experts from the United States who trained the Saudis in the art of desert survival.

off their shoes, open their pants flies, and yell "I need air." Believing the doctors and nurses were kidding, I stationed myself in the emergency room of the National Guard Hospital one day. Within an hour, the wide glass doors of the ambulance entrance swung open in a flurry of excitement, and a soldier, escorted by five comrades, shuffled in stiffly, leaning on a wheelchair. Through the shouting and gesturing flowing from the group, I realized that the man clutching the wheelchair was claiming that his limbs had become paralyzed by the day's exercise drill. It was an authentic case of "DSS" precipitated by the man's affront at being required to do physical training. As an orderly motioned him toward an examining room, he straightened his stiffened neck, looked around him, and announced to all within hearing that he was a Bedouin, a man of honor.

The other arm of the modern military is the Ministry of Defense and Aviation, which administers the army, navy, and air force. Though it has a force larger than that of the National Guard, it does not enjoy the same political clout. Because the officer corps provides an appealing career choice for status-seeking young men without connections, its members come largely from the urban middle class, which is outside the network of family and tribal relationships that runs the country. The troops are primarily drawn from lower class non-Nejdis or former slaves. Since its personnel is drawn from groups who have a high potential for social discontent, the army is almost invisible in Saudi Arabia. Stationed in military cities near the border areas, the army is kept outside the strategic areas and therefore, the government hopes, outside the political arena.

The army can probably be managed. It is the air force that the House of Saud truly fears. Flying jets is an appealing career choice for the status-conscious Saudis. The air force attracts the elite of the military recruits. Young, traveled, and often Western-educated, pilots are more outspoken than any branch of the military about the excesses of the royal family. Their hostility to the top echelon is not as great as their resentment of the second and third tiers of royal relatives that continue to increase geometrically and which still demand their share of royal revenues. To maintain its critical viability in the defense of the kingdom while at the same time protecting the royal family against military coups, the air force is staffed as much as possible by bright young men from the House of Saud. The remaining positions are filled by men chosen more for their loyalty than their ability. To further frustrate potential coups emanating from the air force, commandants and wing commanders are constantly rotated, making it difficult for them to build up personal loyalties among the men they command.

Although it is usually assumed that the National Guard is the balance to the army and air force, it actually requires the combined resources of the Ministry of the Interior with those of the National Guard to make the comparison of the relative strength of the tribal army and the regular forces valid. The Ministry of Interior through its command of the border guards and the civilian police has the capacity to put a significant force in the field. But it is through its control of the intelligence apparatus, the secret police, that the ministry's shadowy presence is most strongly felt. Ever since rebels seized the Grand Mosque at Mecca in November 1979, internal security forces have been draining manpower from the military. It is as if every time the military is used in a defensive capacity, it is reorganized in the hope that the new power configuration will create security. One of the government documents I saw while working on the Third Development Plan revealed that the Ministry of Interior in 1979 had more than 42,000 men engaged in actual fieldwork, supported by another 22,000 civil service employees. The ministry's manpower request for 1985 was a staggering 115,000, more than the army, navy, and air force combined.

The discovery of the duplicity of some elements of the National Guard in the Mecca uprising sent shivers through the royal family. The assumption had always been that the armed forces, not the House of Saud's own militia, would be the source of any insurrection. Although the major contingent of the National Guard stayed loyal, it appeared to spend as much time fighting the army as it did the rebels. And the competition for glory between their commanders paralyzed what operations were launched against the rebels. Commanders screamed conflicting orders to confused troops. The National Guard, the army, and security forces, if they fought at all, fought as individuals not units. It was the minister of Defense and Aviation, Prince Sultan, acting as a field commander, who finally bestowed order on the mass of confusion. The army and the National Guard performed so poorly at Mecca that King Khalid subsequently created a twelve-hundred-man special antiterrorist unit, which was equipped with helicopters and placed under the control of the Ministry of the Interior.

Besides keeping the military broken down into its component parts, loyalties to the royal family in all branches of the military are cultivated as other political loyalties are cultivated, with money and privileges. With the air force leading the way, officers are provided generous salaries and quality housing and treated to a whole range of fringe benefits. The first well-designed and well-constructed building to go up in Riyadh after the oil boom was the Officers' Club on Airport Road. Every time I passed by, its quiet dignity elicited a kind of awe amid the junky buildings that surrounded it. Looking like a country club in Palm Springs, it is heavily staffed with foreign waiters, who set the tables with gold-plated flatware and Limoges china. Now after a decade of heavy investment in the military infrastructure, every branch of the armed forces possesses impressive headquarters, academies, and sports facilities reserved for the exclusive use of the kingdom's guardians. The physical benefits that each branch of the military enjoys reflects to some extent the political power of its commander. For not only are the kingdom's military forces divided to protect the House of Saud against its enemies, they are divided to protect the royal family against itself.

In Saudi Arabia, where religion is politics, the military is part of the constant tension generated by the struggle between the religious conservatives and the progressives. Discord frequently rages within the mammoth royal family, where each camp possesses its own military power.

Prince Abdullah, commander of the National Guard, is King Fahd's half brother and is assumed to be next in line for the throne. Abdullah, regardless of his royal lineage, is pure Bedouin in his attitudes, making him beloved by his troops and the religious fundamentalists. The minister of Defense and Aviation, Prince Sultan, is a full brother of Fahd's and Abdullah's major rival. The Ministry of the Interior is under the control of Prince Naif, also Fahd's full brother but one who also has strong ties with the tribes. While Khalid was king, rumors periodically ran rampant about a new outbreak in the power struggle between Abdullah and Sultan backed by Fahd. When Fahd became king, the major conflict was believed to be between the king and Abdullah. On at least two occasions after Fahd assumed the throne, stories surfaced and were reported by the Western press that Fahd and Abdullah had engaged in an altercation in which one or the other had been shot. Prince Abdullah told Dan that one rumor had started when he was seen at Shamaizy Hospital visiting a friend. There are rows, but neither man is known to have been injured in what are probably verbal battles. Rather, the wild tales and the subsequent disclaimers confirm the existence of intense rivalries among members of the upper echelon of the House of Saud, supported by various factions within the family. Insiders believe that the progressives were poised for a showdown with the conservatives when it was all interrupted by the 1979 takeover of the Grand Mosque in Mecca, forcing the family to pull together for survival.

Compelled to mend their fences with the National Guard after the uprising, the traditionalists in the House of Saud were once more on the ascendancy, causing Abdullah to rise noticeably in the public arena. Suddenly Abdullah's picture was everywhere. Rather successfully ignored during the height of the oil boom as an embarrassment to the family, Abdullah was now obviously a public relations ploy for the House of Saud. His visits to the King Faisal hospital took on a certain fanfare, and the hospital's medical research center launched a study of diseases among the Saker falcons with which Abdullah hunts. After Khalid died, Abdullah, rather than being passed over by the Sudairi Seven, became crown prince apparently unopposed. Perhaps more interesting was that he retained his command of the National Guard. There had been intense speculation that Abdullah would be forced to relinquish command of the guard on becoming crown prince. Instead, he gathered in both the political title as second to the king and the military position as commander of a major force in the military equation, one primarily responsible for protecting the royal family.

Before the oil boom and into the latter years of the 1970s, the royal family regarded its fragmented military establishment and its lack of military preparedness as a desirable thing. Internally, it preserved the political system. Externally, Saudi Arabia made no pretense of being a military power and obviously posed no real threat to its neighbors. But conditions had changed and Saudi Arabia was no longer an isolated desert kingdom. On the heels of its sudden wealth, forces beyond its borders began to draw Saudi Arabia into the whirlpool of international power politics. Avoiding any move that would make the kingdom a target of Israel, the Saudis still had to be concerned about leftist elements in the Arab world and clients of the Soviet Union. Saudi Arabia's rulers found themselves facing a dilemma: a weak military was good politics, but was it good self-defense? Whether the House of Saud wanted to or not, the external situation demanded that manpower and weaponry be increased so that Saudi Arabia could forge some semblance of a defense force. But in the end, no matter what the Saudis did to arm themselves, the defense of the kingdom depended on the intervention of a foreign power. As the decade of the 1970s drew to a close, the manpower projections of the 1974 defense plan were obviously falling short. Although every time an external crisis arose there was talk of a military draft, everyone knew it was politically unacceptable to institute and impossible to administer. The use of foreign mercenaries was explored, but the House of Saud's paranoia and xenophobia made this unacceptable except in the most limited situations. Still depending on the strategy of the 1974 defense plan, the Saudis if attacked expected to employ delaying tactics until the Iranians, the backbone of United States strategy in the Arabian Gulf, arrived, followed ultimately by the Americans. By 1980, in the aftermath of the Iranian revolution, the political scene had changed so drastically that the underlying assumptions of the 1974 plan were dead.

Saudi Arabia's confidence in the reliability of the American defense commitment began to collapse when the Soviets made their moves on the horn of Africa. Despite dire warnings from the Saudis, the Carter administration essentially ignored the introduction of troops and supplies from the Soviet bloc into Ethiopia in 1977. By the following year, the Marxists were in control of vital real estate directly across the Red Sea from the Arabian Peninsula. While north, across the Arabian Gulf, alarm bells were ringing in Afghanistan, which were heard in Saudi Arabia long before the message reached Washington. The blatancy of the Soviet attack on fighters of the Afghan *mujahideen* finally captured the attention of the Carter administration as to the realities of Soviet power politics around the gulf. Regardless of the success in arousing the American giant, Afghanistan remained a frightening reminder of the vulnerability of militarily weak states.

These were symptoms of instability in the gulf. The real threat to Saudi Arabia came when the kingdom's relationship to Iran and the United States was fundamentally and abruptly changed by two events: the American-sponsored peace agreement between Egypt and Israel (1978) and the Iranian revolution (1979). The specter of Egypt making peace with the Arabs' sworn enemy fractured the Arab bloc. The confrontation states led by Syria rallied against the agreement and demanded that the moderate Arab states fall into line. Because of the kingdom's special relationship with the United States, the American-promoted peace agreement between Egypt and Israel made Saudi Arabia a special target of Arab venom. At the same time, the United States was exerting firm pressure on the Saudis to join the peace process. Disagreement about the Saudi response to both the Americans and the Arab bloc raged among the senior princes and sent the pro-American Crown Prince Fahd into self-imposed exile for several weeks. Caution, as always, won out, and Saudi Arabia joined with the other Arabs in rejecting the peace accord. The American commitment to the defense of Saudi Arabia emerged from the debate unbroken but perhaps bent more than either side recognized at the time.

Of even more immediate concern to the security of Saudi Arabia and the future of the House of Saud was the fall of the shah of Iran. The Islamic revolution had turned Iran from a shield for Saudi Arabia into a major threat. While the Western press often fueled the perception that the House of Saud feared the territorial ambitions and military strength of the shah, the reality was more complex.

> Saudi Arabia's problem in the Arabian Gulf was two tiered: at one level there was the threat of radical, hostile Iraq to the regimes of Saudi Arabia and the Gulf emirates, and the related threat to oil facilities and transit; at another level there loomed the threat of Iranian hegemony and its potential implications. The Saudis could not do much by themselves to counter either danger. They essentially counted on Iran to check Iraq, and on the United States to check Iran.*

Although the Saudis were wary, they saw Iran as an important part of their security shield and also as a test of American honor of its commitments. Day after day of the final crisis of the shah, I read articles in the government-controlled Saudi press that superficially extolled the Islamic experiment in Iran but at the same time sent out subtle but passionate pleas for the United States to intervene in defense of the embattled ruler. Instead, the shah was allowed to fall, a ruler more strongly tied to the United States than the House of Saud ever was. Among the overlooked results of the Iranian debacle for the United States was the Saudi royal family's reaction to the shah's plight as a homeless exile. Regardless of a number of sound motives, there was no comprehension among the Saudi hierarchy about the refusal to grant the shah immediate asylum in the United States. The al-Sauds as a

---

*Nadav Safran, *Saudi Arabia: The Ceaseless Quest for Security* (Cambridge, Mass.: Belknap Press of Harvard University Press, 1985), p. 214.

result came to believe that by tying themselves too closely to the United States they were guaranteeing neither the throne nor their personal protection in case of political turmoil. Furthermore, the United States not only had failed to move to protect the shah but had allowed a regime to come to power that was determined to destroy American presence in the gulf and to pull down the House of Saud.

At the beginning of the 1980s, American policy toward Saudi Arabia and Saudi attitudes toward the United States were ambivalent. Since the oil embargo, relations between the two countries had been floundering over oil policy, the Soviet threat, Saudi nationalism, and the United States' reluctance to push Israel on a solution for the Palestinians. In many ways, the alliance was in danger of becoming a commercial agreement in which the United States sold hardware and expertise to the affluent Saudis and Saudi military and foreign policy stayed clear of the United States. This state of affairs was strengthened by Saudi Arabia's rejection of pleas to station American troops on Saudi soil. Although the presence of the United States military within the kingdom would prove the American commitment to Saudi Arabia's defense and make that defense infinitely easier in case the American option became a reality, the House of Saud would not assume the political risk. Fearing the reaction of the radical Arab states, Saudi Arabia chose instead to buttress its defenses by purchasing even more sophisticated hardware from the United States, which it would use to erect its own protective umbrella over the Arabian Peninsula. For the United States, the commitment to defend Saudi Arabia was still a vital part of its military policy in the Arabian Gulf. But for Saudi Arabia, the United States as the ultimate security guarantor in a grand strategic design was a concept that had failed.

15

The World Creeps Closer

THE OIL BOOM provided enough money for the House of Saud to explore new avenues in its search for security. An extraordinary number of heads of state paraded through Riyadh seeking contracts, trade, and aid at the trough of Saudi plenitude. No sooner were the flags of one nation pulled off the streetlight poles on Intercontinental Road than those of another nation went up. Since the King Faisal Specialist Hospital was a major stop on the official sightseeing tour of Riyadh, I could sit on my doorstep and literally watch the world go by. France's Valéry Giscard d'Estaing came, Prince Philip of Britain, and Libyan leader Muammar Qaddafi, as well as a parade of lesser notables, including the head of some obscure African state who was encased in a leopard skin and carried a fly flicker. All of this activity was a procession of homage before the superrich Saudis. The cavalcade reached its height in February 1979 with the state visit of Elizabeth II of Britain. The queen faced a substantial challenge as the first female head of state to call on the Wahhabi kingdom. After so many famous figures had passed tranquilly through Riyadh, the quiver of excitement and the explosion of publicity in the capital prior to the queen's arrival was astounding. The dour figures in the House of Saud were swept up in the excitement, impressed by the longevity and glamour of the British monarchy. In retrospect, I think they may also have been fascinated by a visit from a lady.

Before the queen arrived, I was not exactly sure how it would go. After all, this was male-dominated Saudi Arabia. But the queen came and Saudi Arabia's men sailed through the ceremonies with aplomb. Although the Western press reported that the king surmounted the problem of being seen in public with a woman by declaring Elizabeth an honorary man, the story is doubtful. There was no reason that female political figures from the West should not take on the same status as female professionals working in the kingdom. The Saudis simply deal with them on a different psychological plane than other women, which allows them to shuck all of the sexual taboos surrounding female chastity. Still, Queen Elizabeth's dress designers were put to a real test to create a wardrobe that respected local tradition without clamping the queen into a veil and *abaaya*. Her Majesty was swathed in turbans and tulle in her public appearances with King Khalid. And at the horse and camel race that the king held in her honor, I saw the queen step from her car attired in a simple red and white two-piece dress with a long skirt. On her head sat a matching bowler hat with a whispy veil that subtly fell to her chin.

When Queen Margrethe II of Denmark arrived in Riyadh four years later, the demands on female dignitaries had decreased remarkably. Her majesty stood in a receiving line in a knee-length dress with her head uncovered, firmly shaking hands with smiling Saudi men. But when her picture appeared in the newspaper, Margrethe had been discreetly hidden behind a giant pot of tulips.

This grand caravan of foreign visitors was indicative of Saudi wealth, not Saudi power. The ceremonies the House of Saud attached to political hospitality marked the reality that Saudi Arabia was militarily impotent and politically under siege.

King Faisal was the architect of the kingdom's grand scheme of promoting its security by buying off Saudi Arabia's enemies and cultivating the American option. After Faisal's death, Khalid continued his predecessor's policies of staying in the Arab mainstream while preserving a close, if strained, relationship with the United States. But by 1980 Saudi Arabia was facing a whole new set of strategic problems. As the decade of the seventies was characterized by the challenge of leftist ideologies from within the Arab world, the eighties would be characterized by the challenge of Islamic fundamentalism. Instead of adopting a whole new strategy to meet the added challenges, the Saudis have made military and diplomatic decisions since 1980 on an ad hoc basis. Like a covey of quail startled into flight, the Saudis go scurrying in all directions as every new crisis startles them to action. Yet every action taken by the House of Saud seeks to achieve the same goal of protecting Saudi Arabia's resources and political system. As a result of this crisis diplomacy, the House of Saud has become tangled in a morass of conflicts. These have been created by the essential dichotomies of its present situation: its support of the mystique of the Arab nation and its fear of revolutionary Arabs; its image as the defender of the Islamic nation and the burden of accusations that monarchy is incompatible with Islam; its practice of buying off the kingdom's enemies and its financial insecurity arising from the oil glut; and, finally, the reality of war in the Arabian Gulf and the threat of rejection by its major arms supplier, the United States. External political forces on the left and right have menacingly joined against the kingdom, which is desperately in search of policies and weapons to shield its vulnerability. From riding the crest of power in the 1973 oil embargo, Saudi Arabia has been reduced, more by circumstances than ineptitude, to a country forced to panhandle for its own protection.

Basic to Saudi Arabia's problems is the issue of Israel, the festering sore on the Arab body politic. To maintain what the House of Saud regards as the kingdom's all-important place in the Arab world, Saudi Arabia maintains a belligerent stance against the state of Israel. This, in turn, enormously complicates the kingdom's relationship with the United States, the guarantor of Saudi security and the cornucopia from which Israel draws so much of its military and economic resources. The struggle to balance the demands of its Arab brothers against the demands of its Western ally consumes prodigious amounts of the Saudis' diplomatic energy, a feat little understood by the United States.

One must understand how Saudi Arabia views the world to appreciate the importance the Saudis attach to their standing among other Arabs. The Saudis see the world as a series of concentric circles, with Saudi Arabia in the center, surrounded by the Arab world, surrounded by the Islamic world. In this scheme, the world is largely bipolar — Moslem and non-Moslem. Central to this concept of bipolarization is an acute consciousness of being a member of the second ring, the Arab nation, a consciousness shared by all Arabs. Yet there exists an enormous gap between the ideal of Arab brotherhood and the national interests and ambitions of individual countries. Consequently, all relations between Arab countries are conducted on the basis of unity and discord. Although profoundly confusing to Westerners, this is not contradictory to Arabs, who view the Arab nation much like a family. Furthermore, the rules worked out for the survival of the Arab family are applied to the Arab nation: I against my brothers; I and my brothers against my cousins; I and my cousins against the world. Within this psychological context, all conflicts are viewed as temporary and any unity as permanent.

From the standpoint of its American ally, a great deal of the confusion about where Saudi loyalties lie (with the United States or with the Arabs) is in the nature of Arab diplomacy. Arabs, to a large degree, deal with their disagreements by mediation and meeting in conference. These traditional patterns of conflict resolution, which for centuries maintained a certain equilibrium, are now applied to new situations that have arisen from the absorption of elements of Western culture, not the least of which is diplomacy conducted in the glare of publicity. A typical summit conference dealing with the Palestinian issue, for instance, opens a day or two late. The participants are usually unable to convene or end the sessions at the appointed time. Arab disunity is expressed by frequent boycotts of one or several countries, walkouts of delegations during the conference, or open displays of animosity. There is fiery and flowery oratory disproportionate to the concrete issues being discussed. And the conference often closes days behind schedule. But these conferences should not be viewed by the West as either comic or pathetic. Being Arabs, the parties cannot resist the pull of coming together again and again in the hope that agreement, as happened in the tribal council tent, will come out of what seems to be irreconcilable differences. Therefore, the most fundamental and painful conflicts between Arab nations are regarded as little more than temporary disagreements that will in time give way to unity. While they last they in no way encroach on the principle of Arab brotherhood or the mystique of Arab unity.

Although there is a historical identity among Arabs, the actual concept of the Arab nation did not emerge until the twentieth century. Following four hundred years under the yoke of the Ottoman Empire, Arab nationalism was awakened by the promises of independence made by the Allied powers in World War I. Nonetheless, after the war the imperialistic demands of Britain and France dashed the hopes of the Arabs, forcing them once again under the rule of foreign powers. Only after another war destroyed Europe's empires did the Arab states of Iraq, Jordan, Syria, and Lebanon become independent states. But at the same time, another form of Western imperialism was taking root in the Middle East. Regardless of how anyone else viewed the issue, the Arabs saw Jewish immigration to Arab-occupied and British-ruled

Palestine between 1920 and 1948 as nothing less than European colonialism, this time packaged as Zionism. The 1948 declaration of the state of Israel by the Jews of Palestine and the displacement of seven hundred thousand Arabs from their land served to stoke the passions of Arab nationalism. Since then, through four wars, multiple domestic economic crises, and persistent territorial expansion, the United States has provided enormous sums of military and economic aid to Israel. In the process, America has become to the Arabs the arch-imperialist of the Middle East. Four decades after the state of Israel was born, whether the issues involve the leftist government of Syria or the conservative monarchy of Saudi Arabia, Arab intercourse with the United States takes place within the framework of the Arab-Israeli imbroglio.

From the time Franklin Roosevelt brought Abdul Aziz to Cairo in a failed attempt to charm him into supporting the Jewish state, Saudi Arabia has stood, however reluctantly, with its Arab brothers in opposition to Israel. Yet unlike the front-line states of Egypt, Syria, and Jordan, Saudi Arabia's fight against Israel has been verbal and financial, not military. Abhoring instability above all else, Saudi Arabia sees the threat from Israel in terms of the unrest the confrontation with its Arab neighbors churns up on the kingdom's borders. Consequently, in the frequent flare-ups between Israel and the Arabs, the kingdom seeks whatever course promises it the most security. Saudi Arabia supports the Arab cause enough to protect the kingdom against repercussions from radical Arab regimes while being cautious enough not to ignite an Israeli military strike against Saudi territory or an open break with its American ally. Except for the token presence of a few soldiers, the kingdom stayed out of the 1948 war that created Israel. The Saudis also avoided the 1956 Suez war. But with the 1967 war, the six days that so upset the territorial and psychological balance of the Arab world, it became more difficult for the Saudis to distance themselves from the central struggle between Arab and Jew. While the Arabs were humiliated by the scope of their defeat, Saudi Arabia was profoundly affected in another way. Jerusalem, the third holiest site in Islam, passed into the hands of the Israelis. As the self-proclaimed guardian of Islam's holy places, the House of Saud starkly faced the need to confront Israel in the name of Islam. Yet King Faisal's concern about the new Israeli territorial conquests was more political than religious. Faisal saw the Arab-Israeli struggle as one that strengthened the influence of the Soviet Union among the Arab states and fueled Arab radicalism in the Middle East.

During the 1950s and 1960s, the Saudis had learned an important lesson about the disfavor of radical regimes.* In 1966 Egypt, using Yemeni expatriates, executed a series of sabotage bombings targeted against various installations of the Saudi government and its American ally. The radicals delivered their message to a defenseless kingdom. The incidents fueled anew the House of Saud's anxieties about internal violence. The fear of what is now called terrorism haunted Saudi Arabia in the period between the 1967 and 1973 wars.

With the vacuum of political leadership in the Arab world created by the 1967 war, fear of Egypt was replaced by fear of the Palestinians. Charging forth from their refugee camps, the Palestinians declared vengeance on Arab regimes tepid in support of their cause. The Saudis ranked as a special target because of their strong connection to the United States. And the kingdom held the promise of a terrorist's delight because of the logistical impossibility of protecting a highly exposed oil delivery system and thousands of members of the royal family. As if to justify these fears, the Popular Front for the Liberation of Palestine was suspected of blowing up on May 30, 1969, a section of the Tapline that carried twenty-three million tons of oil a year to Mediterranean ports.

As the Saudis watched with alarm, the Palestine Liberation Organization captured international attention in the swirl of publicity surrounding airline hijackings and the massacre of Olympic athletes. All the while, Nasser continued to rail against "reactionary forces" within the Arab fold while he imported more and more Soviet arms and advisers. But then Gamal Abdul Nasser died, opening the way for Faisal to pursue his goal of banishing Soviet influence from the Middle East and reining in the radical Arabs. The 1973 alliance of Egyptian manpower and Saudi oil forged by Nasser's successor, Anwar Sadat, and Faisal ibn Abdul Aziz was an alliance to restore Arab honor and open the way for some accommodation with Israel. Although Egypt wanted the return of the Sinai, Sadat's major goal was to be freed of the enormous military costs associated with the Arabs' wars against Israel. What Saudi Arabia wanted in any agreement with Israel was the liberation of Jerusalem from the hands of the Zionists and some agreement between Israel and her Arab neighbors that would protect Saudi Arabia by defusing the radical Arabs.

---

*In Saudi terminology, a radical Arab state is defined by its political and/or economic system and its level of hostility toward Israel.

The Yom Kippur War in Jewish terminology and the Ramadan War in Arab terminology was a war in which everyone miscalculated. Sadat's army could not sustain its early advances. The Israelis, surprised by the attack, were pushed back from the Suez Canal and lost many of their weapons. The United States, failing to appreciate the political nature of the war, resupplied the Israelis even in the face of the oil embargo. And Saudi Arabia, suddenly finding itself incredibly wealthy, sacrificed the luxury of staying somewhat aloof from the deadly quarrel between the Arabs and Israel. The oil embargo and subsequent escalation of oil prices threw Saudi Arabia onto the main stage of Arab politics, a role that presented the kingdom with as many dangers as it did opportunities. It quickly became clear that in its new position in the Arab world, the kingdom was expected not only to use its oil as leverage but to bankroll the Arabs' military effort against Israel and perhaps even contribute its meager armed forces. For an action that Faisal anticipated would help stabilize the Middle East, the oil embargo created even more perils for defenseless Saudi Arabia.

From the outset, Saudi Arabia was extremely uncomfortable in its new position of leadership in Arab politics. The conservative King Faisal found himself forced to bend to the hardline Arab forces in the Arab-Israeli dispute, which conflicted with the monarchy's need to maintain its relationship with the United States.

The House of Saud's first defensive move was to keep the radicals out of Saudi Arabia. One of the prime reasons for Saudi Arabia's tight visa policy was to control the immigration of the Middle East's political instability into the kingdom. The House of Saud was determined to prevent the kingdom from becoming a haven for Palestinians, dragging Saudi Arabia into the execution of the Palestinians' political agenda. The Palestinian issue had emotional appeal for the Saudis only as long as Israel held Jerusalem and as long as the Saudis were not pulled into direct confrontation with the Jewish state.

Saudi Arabia's insatiable appetite for labor during the oil boom and the Palestinians' high level of skills made some Palestinian immigration inevitable. But the Saudis' apprehensions about the Palestinians they did allow in the kingdom were so acute that few of the Palestinians I knew would readily admit their origins. Not until I became well acquainted with them would they confess that their lineage extended beyond the Hashemite kingdom of Jordan. And most Palestinian professionals or managers holding jobs in ARAMCO or the government buried their nationality behind an apolitical façade.

In 1973, in the wake of the Ramadan War, Faisal had reluctantly allowed the largest faction of the Palestine Liberation Organization, al-Fatah, to open an office in Riyadh. The move illustrates Saudi Arabia's policy of extending the symbol but not the substance of commitment to the dreaded Palestinians.

By the time I arrived in Saudi Arabia, two hundred thousand Palestinians were working in the kingdom and the PLO was discreetly housed in a two-story white stucco building on a side street at the top end of Wassir. The only outward indication of the PLO's presence in the nondescript structure was the modest quadricolored flag of black, white, green, and red that flew from a short staff on the roof. One hot day in late spring, I dropped in on the PLO to find out how it functioned among its hostile hosts.

I approached the headquarters with a certain amount of trepidation arising more from the uncertainty of what the Saudi government might do to a Westerner making contact with the Palestinians than from any fear of the PLO itself. Just as I passed into the shade of the portico that extended from the building out over the sidewalk, a man in fatigues with a small Palestinian flag pinned to his shirt snapped to attention. Behind him, lolling in the shade on a rather dilapidated folding chair, was a Saudi in a *thobe*. I assumed the Ministry of Interior had posted him on the site to observe who came and went. Since he made no move to stop me, I walked in the front door, turned left, and popped my head into the nearest doorway. Except for the absence of women and the way in which the men were dressed, the room looked surprisingly like a campaign headquarters in the West. There were two desks, a large beat-up table, a well-worn sofa, and a collection of mismatched chairs scattered across the room. In the far corner, a young man stood cranking out handbills on an antiquated duplicating machine. Other men sat at the table folding flyers, while others stood in front of a clattering window air conditioner to take advantage of the pitiful output of refrigerated air. One by one, as they saw me, the men stopped whatever they were doing and fell silent. Standing there with everyone's eyes riveted on me, I felt somehow like an apparition of Western imperialism that had suddenly materialized. In time one of the young men sitting at the table recovered enough to rise and greet me. I introduced myself and explained that I was there because I was interested in learning something about the organization and activities of the Palestinians in Saudi Arabia. Still suspicious but conforming to the strong dictates of Arab hospitality, the man summoned the tea boy and I was asked to sit down. A few of the others came within hearing distance, but responsibility for conversing stayed with the young man who had greeted me. In answer to my prodding questions, he told me that most of the men in the room were students at the University of Riyadh, some were Palestinian, some were other Arabs, including a few Saudis. Pressing him further, I asked him what activities the PLO sponsored at the headquarters and what restrictions the Saudi government placed on those activities. He explained that the membership met every other Monday night for commando training. Since the Saudi government forbid them to possess weapons, they trained with wooden guns. Then he nervously added that any type of instruction in explosives was strictly banned.

At this point, a middle-aged, aggressively hostile PLO field organizer blustered into the room and immediately took over. Challenging me in a voice that was just below a scream, he demanded to know who I was and what was I doing there. Assuming I was a spy for the CIA, he launched into a tirade about American policy in the Middle East. Patiently I waited while he ticked off the Palestinian grievances against the United States. Finally, he paused. Before he could collect his thoughts for another verbal assault, I asked him what the PLO hoped to accomplish in Saudi Arabia beyond providing a contact point for Palestinians working in the country. He looked at me, stunned. Becoming totally flustered, he dropped his aggressive demeanor and went on the defensive. Jumping to his feet, he firmly declared that he was not allowed to respond to that, the answer would have to come from higher authority. After repeating this for the third time, he rose and whirled out of the room.

The students took over again. Ushering me to another room, which served as a library, they presented me with a head scarf in the design of the black and white *kufiyyah* that Yassir Arafat wears, with the PLO flag set in two corners. Remembering Saudi sensitivities, I stuffed it deep in my pocket and bid them good-by. As I passed back through the foyer, the Saudi lookout was on the phone, shouting to someone on the other end that a Western woman was in the PLO headquarters.

In 1978 the Saudis' ability to tiptoe through the minefield of Middle Eastern politics while retaining the American option faltered in the face of the Camp David accords, signed by Israel and Egypt and mediated by the Saudis' ally, the United States. American strategy was to use Camp David as the core of a Middle East peace settlement, drawing in one Arab country at a time until a comprehensive settlement between the Jews and the Arabs was reached. The key to this strategy was Saudi Arabia, which in the first phase of the plan the Americans had assigned the role of bringing the moderate Arabs to the conference table. But because the agreement contained no firm guarantees for the Palestinians or on the future of Jerusalem, Saudi Arabia feared its compliance would open the kingdom to charges from the radical Arabs of being a lackey of American interests. If the Saudis refused, they would incur the anger of the United States.

In the aftermath of Camp David, opponents of the peace agreement banished Egypt from the Arab countries' political organization, the Arab League. With Syria and Libya in the lead, Arab attention shifted to Saudi Arabia. Did the kingdom intend to stand with its Arab brothers or with its Western ally? As the House of Saud wavered, it was possible to feel the tension of indecision hanging in the air. Finally, the regime, as always, opted for caution and stayed in the Arab fold. In March 1979, shortly after the decision was announced, the news that Crown Prince Fahd had gone into self-imposed exile because of his brothers' refusal to support the United States flashed through Riyadh like an electric current. Fahd had in fact left, and he did not return until mid-May. But exactly what Fahd was doing during this time still remains somewhat a mystery. He was without doubt making a statement in support of the American alliance. At the same time, he was grossly overweight and had been ordered by his doctors to use his home in Spain as a royal fat farm. There was also a rumor circulating in the *hareems* that Fahd left Saudi Arabia in order to take a Moroccan woman as a third wife. In a period of growing nationalism, it was politically wise for the crown prince, if he chose a foreign wife, to keep her hidden on the Costa del Sol. The story still lives but the wife has never been identified in Spain or Saudi Arabia.

Regardless of the auxiliary reasons for Fahd's absence, the Saudi decision to opt out of the Camp David process has plagued U.S.-Saudi relations ever since 1979. The United States harbors resentment against Saudi Arabia for refusing to seize the chance to break the Arab-Israeli impasse and for expecting American military support while simultaneously sabotaging American peace efforts. The Saudis accuse the Americans of failing to understand their fragile position within the Arab world and of not appreciating Saudi Arabia's efforts during the period of severe shortages to maintain high rates of oil production in order to hold down prices and keep the West supplied with petroleum. As the United States drew even closer to Israel after the Saudi rebuff over Camp David, the Saudis once again intensified their search for an alternative to the American alliance.

In the late 1970s and early 1980s, Saudi Arabia's rulers, driven by the absence of any military strength or political leverage beyond money, hit on the strategy of forging Islamic fervor into a tool to promote Saudi Arabia's own national interests. Not since the days of the evangelical union of the missionaries and the imperialists of nineteenth-century Europe was religion to play such a commanding role in the foreign policy of any country.

The architect of this linkage of foreign policy to religion was Saudi Arabia's foreign minister, Prince Saud al-Faisal. The tall, brooding son of the late King Faisal sought to mobilize Saudi Arabia's resources of oil, cash, and diplomatic influence, and above all the spiritual legacy of custodianship of Mecca, to establish Saudi Arabia's position as a major force in the Moslem world and to assure the kingdom's dominance over the entire Arabian Peninsula.

By promoting universal Islamic solidarity, the House of Saud was striving to escape the specter of pan-Arabism that had haunted it since the 1950s. Through the stormy years with Gamal Abdul Nasser and into the period of the revolutionary ascension of Syria's Hafiz Assad and Iraq's Saddam Hussein and on into the heyday of the PLO, the Saudis had never been comfortable with the concept of Arab unity hawked by the pan-Arabists. The secularism and socialism preached by the pan-Arab movement had little appeal to all but a tiny minority of Saudis. There was either no firm understanding of the philosophy or it was seen as diluting the position of religion. Even more important, though, was the threat the Saudis perceived from the pan-Arab appeals of the Arab socialists. Any political theory that implied that the wealth from the oil-rich Arab states should be distributed among its poorer Arab brothers was appalling to a people who had endured centuries of poverty more severe than most of its neighbors now knew. All the Saudis wanted, royalty and commoner alike, was regional stability that would give Saudi Arabia the opportunity to control its pace of modernization and to enjoy the advantages of its wealth in peace.

The meteoric rise in oil prices following the oil embargo and the political dividend of seeing the Western world crawl on its knees to the oil producers was not lost on the image-conscious Saudis. From this pinnacle of Saudi Arabia's influence and power, the concept of "petro-Islam" was born.* Under this policy, the prestige and money derived from the energy shortage would be used to forge a new alliance among not just Arabs but all Islamic peoples. This would allow the House of Saud to move out from the prison of pan-Arabism with its threats of violence and socialist unity into the broader, safer world of Islam. For as long as the oil boom lasted, Saudi Arabia was determined to shift the balance of power in the Middle East from the forces of *thawra* ("revolution") to the forces of *tharawa* ("fortune").

Saudi Arabia's image as leader of the Moslem world was promoted by the sheer circumstance of being the cradle of Islam. The House of Saud believed that by coupling its image as the champion of Islam with its vast financial resources, petro-Islam could mobilize the approximately six hundred million Moslem faithful worldwide to defend Saudi Arabia against the real and perceived threats to its security and its rulers. Consequently, a whole panoply of devices was adopted to tie Islamic peoples to the fortunes of Saudi Arabia.

The House of Saud has embraced the *hajj*, or pilgrimage to Mecca, as a major symbol of the kingdom's commitment to the Islamic world. Every year the Saudis host over two million foreign visitors making the *hajj*. These "guests of God" are the beneficiaries of the enormous sums of money and effort that Saudi Arabia expends on polishing its image among the faithful. The Ministry of Pilgrimage and Endowments at the time that Saudi Arabia had more money than it could spend brought in heavy earth-moving equipment to level millions of square meters of hill peaks to accommodate pilgrims' tents, which were then equipped with electricity. One year the ministry had copious amounts of costly ice carted from Mecca to wherever the white-robed *hajjis* were performing their religious rites.

During the petro-Islam offensive, the goodwill generated by the *hajj* was followed up. Through its generosity, Saudi Arabia established departments of Islamic studies at universities throughout the world, which were regularly visited by members of the Saudi royal family on the road as roving ambassadors. Lavish funding for elaborate mosques in places as divergent as Islamabad and Regency Park in London's fashionable West End was provided by Saudi Arabia. In fact, one never knew when one might stumble on another symbol of Saudi philan-

---

*"Petro-Islam" is a term coined by Middle Eastern scholar Fouad Ajami.

thropy. I was once standing in the shade of an ornate mosque under construction on the Israeli-occupied West Bank, halfway between the Jewish settlement of Qiriyat Araba and the Arab town of Hebron. As I was glancing up toward the surrounding hills, a handsome brass plaque embedded in the wall of the mosque caught my eye. Simply inscribed on its polished face was "Gift of Saudi Arabia."

In addition, a steady stream of Islamic political figures both famous and obscure passed through Saudi Arabia's elaborate hospitality routine. Ghazi Algosaibi, minister of Industry and Electricity at the time, tells the story of a visit to Saudi Arabia by the infamous Idi Amin Oumee Dada, President for Life of Uganda. With the endless procession of personalities coming through Saudi Arabia, cabinet ministers hosted the visiting heads of state on a rotating basis. When Amin arrived, it was Algosaibi's turn. The welcoming delegation, made up of the crown prince, the chief of protocol, various ministers, and the military band, was standing on the tarmac when Amin's plane rolled to a stop. As soon as the engines shut down, the cabin door opened and a steward stepped forward. He reached for a hook just above the opening and pulled down what looked like a giant window shade on which was painted a life-size portrait of the Ugandan leader. Not knowing what to expect next, the Saudi chief of protocol ordered the band to strike up its music. As if on cue, the portrait rolled up and out stepped Idi Amin. In an attempt to impress his hosts, the tall, rotund Amin was clad in what he thought were Saudi clothes. On his ample body was a tight nightshirt split around the bottom every six inches, creating long strips that extended above his pudgy knees. And on his head lay a big white handkerchief with a knot tied at each corner. Fahd, the crown prince, went into paroxysms of laughter. Pulling the end of his *gutra* to hide his face from the television cameras, he turned to Algosaibi and said, "Take this man and find him some real Saudi clothes!"

Heads of state like Idi Amin stay in King Saud's old palace, which has been turned into a guest house. Decidedly theatrical, it looks like a Hollywood version of an Arabian villa. Down the street, the government built a multimillion dollar center for international conferences of Moslem leaders and organizations. In a style that can best be described as "Arabesque modern," the impressive complex contains a multistory hotel, with an interior atrium paneled with rich, dark wood, an imposing mosque, and a vast round conference hall, wired with all the most advanced audiovisual technology and dominated by a heavy crystal chandelier that cost more than a million dollars. But the opulence of the hall pales in comparison to the dining facilities in the hotel. There are banquet halls and tearooms everywhere, all furnished with sleek chrome tables and Arabized Louis XIV chairs embellished with overwrought damask and heavy fringe. In room after room, elongated dining tables seating dozens are lined up and dressed in silky cloths, fine china, pristine crystal, and the gold-toned flatwear that the Saudi taste so much admires. The only credential required for leaders from Bangladesh to Senegal to share in the grandeur is that the visitor be Moslem.

During the petro-Islam blitz, Saudi Arabia mobilized its oil revenues to sponsor a multitude of political and financial organizations aimed at proving that Islam is a cohesive force that transcends nationality and culture to unite all believers in brotherhood. Bypassing the Arab League, Islamic diplomacy was carried on through the thirty-seven-member Organization of Islamic Conferences (OIC) and the Moslem League, created and nurtured by Saudi Arabia. Through these groups, the Sau dis channeled financial aid to the poorer Islamic states, making Saudi Arabia the major financier of the Moslem world. Unilateral government-to-government funds were dispersed through the Saudi Development Fund, which granted loans totaling approximately $557 million during the 1979 fiscal year alone. In addition, Saudi Arabia was a highly visible, generous contributor to the Islamic Development Bank, which between 1975 and 1980 financed projects totaling $930 million in thirty countries, to the Islamic Center for Trade, to the Islamic Chamber of Commerce, to the Islamic Industry and Commodity Exchange, and on through an entire collection of Moslem associations.

All the while, members of the Saudi royal family constantly moved through the Islamic countries, pouring oil and its golden residue on troubled waters. Through petro-Islam, Saudi whims and desires could, for a time, make or break the designs of many leaders. The Saudis used their leverage openly with every country from monarchist Dubai to leftist Syria. But the Saudis were never able to control the Arab League.

The Arab League, composed of twenty-one member nations plus the Palestine Liberation Organization, not only exerts the most pressure within Arab affairs but also dominates the Organization of Islamic Conferences. The challenge to Saudi Arabia's preeminence within the League and its whole Islamic foreign policy came from the infamous, mercurial, and violently antimonarchial Colonel Muammar Qaddafi. Riding his own wave of oil wealth, the diminutive Qaddafi, bemedaled and bedecked in a multitude of uniforms, whirled out of North Africa. Everything that Qaddafi would stand for was anathema to the House of Saud. Brandishing an irresistible charisma among the lower classes throughout the Arab world, Qaddafi proclaimed himself the new Moslem messiah. In his rhetoric, he summoned forth a new pan-Arab movement that would merge the Arab states, rich and poor, under some form of Islamic socialism with himself at the helm. To the horror of the House of Saud, Qaddafi succeeded in promoting his own foreign policy by combining the emotion of Islam with the economics of socialism. In essence, he not only challenged the Saudis with the very threat they were trying to escape, pan-Arabism, but he had done so by capturing the al-Sauds' own platform — Islamic unity.

Even though relations between Libya and Saudi Arabia were strained, Qaddafi was a frequent visitor to the Guest Palace. In July 1979 he prayed at Riyadh's al-Maadhar mosque, prominently stationed between King Khalid and Crown Prince Fahd. It was a grand act in the House of Saud's constant struggle to hold Arab animosities toward the kingdom in check. But Qaddafi would not be checked. When the early-warning surveillance planes provided to Saudi Arabia by the United States arrived in October 1980, Qaddafi launched a vituperative verbal assault on the House of Saud. He claimed that the idea of American-owned planes manned by American crews flying over Mecca was intolerable to the Moslem nation and urged the Saudi people to rise up against the House of Saud to restore their honor. In response, Saudi Arabia broke diplomatic relations with Tripoli.

Each using its own combination of oil money and religion, the House of Saud sought to stabilize the Middle East and Qaddafi sought to foment conflict. Through the rhetoric of Muammar Qaddafi, Saudi Arabia trembled at the possibility that Libya would disrupt the Middle East, which was tantamount to destroying the political stability that was the whole goal of petro-Islam.

Since some accommodation to Israel was central to any kind of stability, Crown Prince Fahd launched a new peace initiative among the Arabs in 1981. The Fahd plan would replace the Camp David accords as the basis for negotiation between the Arabs and Israel. Requiring Israel to withdraw from the occupied territories and to accept a Palestinian state with Jerusalem as its capital (terms considered impossible by the Israelis), the plan nevertheless implied more clearly the recognition of the state of Israel than any previous Arab position. Saud al-Faisal as well as Jafar Allaghany, Saudi Arabia's representative to the United Nations, both stated that Saudi Arabia was willing to recognize Israel under the terms of the Fahd plan. As the plan originally escaped the condemnation of Syria and appeared to be acceptable to the PLO, the possibility emerged that Saudi Arabia might deliver the PLO and the United States might deliver Israel to the conference table. Then everything began to fall apart. Syria and Iraq, recipients of massive amounts of Saudi economic aid, went on the offensive against the plan. The acquiescence of Yassir Arafat fell victim to his own radical wing. And the United States, after originally endorsing the plan, began to back off in order to mend relations with Israel. Frightened, the Saudis failed to press ahead, allowing the plan to be sabotaged by the radicals. It was finally laid to rest after the Israeli invasion of Lebanon in 1982.

Saudi Arabia's main problem in its excursion through Islamic politics was that its push for regional stability left an ideological vacuum that petro-Islam was not capable of filling. Islam standing alone, unsupported by either a charismatic figure or a message of rage against the corrupting influence of the West, could not mobilize the Islamic world or bypass pan-Arabism. Petro-Islam was not so much a viable policy as an entrenchment of a conservative moral and political ideology backed up by little but oil money. And because petro-Islam depended as much on money as religion, the oil glut effectively ended Saudi Arabia's attempt to weld the Islamic world together in its own defense. Over the ashes of petro-Islam, a new Islamic crusade began to push into the Middle East from Iran.

When the Iraq-Iran war began in 1980, the Arab world was divided into the familiar pattern of the moderate camp versus the radicals. Egypt, shepherded by Saudi Arabia, had tenuously returned to the Arab fold to join Jordan, Kuwait, and the sheikhdoms of the Arabian Gulf to form the moderate bloc. Allying themselves with leftist Iraq as common enemies of Khomeini's ideology, the oil states would bankroll the Iraqi war effort. Syria, leading the opposing camp, supported Iran because of Hafiz Assad's long-standing rivalry with Iraq's political regime. Libya's Qaddafi, touting Islamic revolution, joined Syria. Saudi Arabia as the richest of the oil states directed policy toward its own ends. Iraq would be supported with enough money to stop an Iranian victory. At the same time, the House of Saud would continue to pur-

THE SAUDIS

chase a measure of security by its time-honored mechanism of funneling monetary grants to the leader of the opposition, Syria, and to Yassir Arafat's Fatah, the most moderate of the politically viable factions of the PLO and one under heavy attack from Syria.

The Saudis had no hesitation in pulling out all the stops to support Iraq, its former adversary. The threat from Iran under Khomeini is proving far greater than the somewhat limited territorial ambitions of the former shah. Khomeini and his Shiite followers are pushing a religious and political revolution that recognizes no national boundaries. It aims to wash away established governments, especially Iraq and the gulf monarchies, and to replace them with Islamic republics or "societies of the just" and to drive Western influence out of the world of Islam. Saudi Arabia is a particularly vulnerable target of Khomeini's fanaticism because it is a monarchy tied in an alliance with the United States. Major plots by Khomeini disciples to destabilize Bahrain and Saudi Arabia were uncovered in 1981. By 1983 the Saudis were compelled to sell anywhere from 200,000 barrels of oil per day (by Saudi government estimates) to 800,000 barrels a day (by the estimate of an American intelligence agent) in support of the Iraqi war effort. Even the *hajj*, the linchpin of Saudi Arabia's Islamic strategy, came under attack by Iran. On the eve of the 1983 *hajj*, Prince Naif, the minister of Interior, charged that since 1980 Iranian pilgrims to Mecca had engaged in "political and demagogic activities," distributed pro-Khomeini pamphlets, called for revolution against the monarchy of Saudi Arabia, and even attempted to carry concealed weapons into the Holy Haram, the sacred area around the mosque. Saudi Arabia was facing the grim truth that militant Iran intended to pursue its revolutionary goals in the Arabian Gulf by means the Saudis had always dreaded: the combination of external pressure and internal subversion.

Saudi Arabia, baffled about how to combat an assault from the right, organized the 1983 military maneuvers, the first ever held with its partners in the Gulf Cooperative Council (GCC). The military exercises fulfilled more a symbolic than a military function by serving notice on the West that the Saudis and their gulf neighbors were prepared to stake out their own position, free of the menacing American connection. The Gulf Cooperative Council, an alliance of the sheikhdoms of Kuwait, Bahrain, Oman, Qatar, and the United Arab Emirates in concert with larger, richer Saudi Arabia, is the culmination of the Saudis' latest plan to defend themselves. The organization was originally constituted in 1976 in an effort to pool information on criminals and political dissidents in the gulf region. As strategic considerations in the area changed, it would become the framework for a defensive alliance that was outside the Arab League and its radical politics and outside the sphere of either superpower, East or West. In 1981 the GCC was formalized and expanded. Although the council has moved forward to free up the movement of capital and manpower between its members, to create its own trade zone, to connect its members with roads and bridges, and even to talk of unifying its currencies, its prime objective is to provide a security shield in the gulf. Members of the GCC coordinate their armies through training, strategic exercises, integrated weapons systems, and their own light arms industry. But can they actually protect themselves?

In December 1983 a Lebanese Shiite group loyal to Iran set off a series of bombs in neighboring Kuwait, just to the north of Saudi oil fields.* Consternation reigned in Saudi Arabia as Saudis clustered around television screens unreeling films of the destruction. Government pronouncements about Saudi Arabia's ability and determination to defend itself filled the newspapers. The night following the incident, I was changing planes at the airport in Dhahran, Saudi Arabia's major air facility on the gulf. With the level of alarm the attack had set off in Riyadh, I expected to find security forces of the military on full alert and conspicuously placed. Instead, as I walked through the terminal I saw nothing beyond the usual number of unarmed airport guards watching the normal movement of passenger traffic. It was 2:00 A.M. when I emerged from the unattended door of the terminal. The area outside was largely deserted. The only clue that anything out of the ordinary was happening was that the incandescent lights that usually flood the parking lot had been dimmed. Otherwise, there was stillness. And then out of the dark, humid night, a jeep quietly approached. One soldier, with the *gutra* under his military helmet drawn across his mouth and nose, sat behind the wheel. Another man faced the rear, his arm slung across an M-60 mounted on a tripod. They slowed then crept on, leaving me once again in the hushed stillness.

The terrorist attack on Kuwait was only one episode in a steady progression of events that have shaken the Arabian Gulf since 1980. Early in the war, Iran threatened to close the vital Strait of Hormuz,

---

*This is the group suspected of holding the American hostages in Lebanon.

the narrow passage in the gulf through which all oil tankers must pass. And Iraq and Iran both bomb and strafe gulf shipping with impunity. To protect its markets from these potential bottlenecks in the gulf, Saudi Arabia has stored oil at various times in critical locations in western Europe and the Caribbean. Forty million barrels of oil are believed to have been in floating storage in 1985. By 1986 Saudi Arabia's trans-peninsula pipeline was carrying Iraqi as well as Saudi crude from the Arabian Gulf to Red Sea ports, bypassing the dangers of the gulf. Through these measures, Saudi Arabia has ensured that a level of oil shipments will continue as long as the vulnerable fields and the delivery system do not fall victim to Iranian encroachment.

Iranian testing of the oil fields defense system began in the spring of 1984. In May a Liberian tanker was attacked by an Iranian fighter in or very near Saudi Arabia's territorial waters. Although the Saudi defense ministry was loath to admit the incursion, before the week was over a U.S. Air Force unit was in residence at the Riyadh Marriott Hotel and the United States had shipped the Saudis four hundred Stinger missiles.* In June, one, possibly two, Iranian planes skirted the coastline near the Ras Tanura oil-loading facilities. Picked up on the sophisticated radar of the AWACS, one plane was downed over the gulf by an F-15 of the Royal Saudi Air Force. This time the government had to admit that its territory had been violated. That night I stood on my small balcony, watching as planes, in a continuous circle, took off and landed from the direction of Dhahran. After years of successfully staying out of armed conflicts, it seemed that Saudi Arabia might now be threatened with war at its frontiers. A tension that I had not felt since the uprising at Mecca permeated the atmosphere. Westerners once more wondered how much longer they might be able to stay.

The crisis passed. The shipping lanes were still being assaulted, but the Strait of Hormuz stayed open. The land war bogged down once again in the marshes of the Shatt al-Arab. Iraq, as long as Saudi money held out, appeared to be holding the Iranians at bay. Then in the spring of 1986, two years later, Iranian troops broke out, crossing the Shatt al-Arab to occupy the Faw Peninsula. Iran was sitting on the doorstep of Kuwait. Across the city-state is the open plain to Riyadh.

Short of intervention by the United States, the only defense the gulf

---

*The Stinger is an ideal weapon for Saudi Arabia. It can be carried and fired by one man, maximizing Saudi manpower, and it is particularly effective in use against low-flying aircraft.

states have is the arsenal of weapons the members of the GCC buy in prodigious amounts from the West. In 1985 Saudi Arabia alone spent $17.7 billion on defense, nearly a third of all government spending. The kingdom and its GCC partners have bought sophisticated aircraft, missiles, tanks, armored personnel carriers, air defense systems, and surveillance planes. Yet so short is manpower that together they have been able to assemble only one five-thousand-man force, which is stationed at the King Khalid Military City near the border with Kuwait. There they wait in case the Iranians come. Although the GCC, led by Saudi Arabia's American-made fighter planes, probably has better equipment than Iran, the unknown is how well the Saudis and their partners would perform under fire. Except for the 1984 air skirmish over the Arabian Gulf, the GCC forces have no combat experience, have a cultural tradition that shuns military discipline, and lack the revolutionary fervor that has sustained the Iranians through six years of grueling war. Now they have another grave problem: access to the hardware that would give them any chance of fending off attack.

The United States, the Saudis' supplier of first choice, appears by the actions of Congress to be shutting down arms sales. The 1981 sale of the AWACS surveillance planes to Saudi Arabia was a political donnybrook. The Saudis' request to buy additional F-15s in 1985 was turned down. The arms package the Saudis sought in the spring of 1986 was originally voted down by Congress. Later when the arms sale proposal was stripped of the Stinger missiles, President Reagan's veto of the Congressional rejection was sustained with just enough votes.

Congress and the president sidestepped the issue of whether or not the AWACS Saudi Arabia was given permission to buy in 1981 could be delivered. It is not only weapon supplies that are at issue. The Saudis' public humiliation at being forced to grovel before the American Congress strikes at the heart of Saudi honor. Begging for the arms to protect itself from Iran, an enemy that Saudi Arabia shares with the United States, offends the sensitive Saudis as nothing else in the long, difficult relationship between the two countries. Nevertheless, a combination of diminished dependence on Saudi oil, the domestic political reality of Israel's allies in the American electorate, and the misconception in the American mind of all Arabs as terrorists is straining the American alliance as it has never been strained before.

Much of the current difficulty between the Americans and the Saudis lies in how each perceives the power of the other. The United States throughout the history of the alliance has expected the Saudis to deliver something concrete in the way of Arab willingness to accept the existence of Israel. Misled by the kingdom's ability to influence oil markets with its vast petroleum reserves, the United States deludes itself that the Saudis can effectively moderate Arab opposition to Israel. Ever since the Camp David accords were signed, the Carter and Reagan administrations have shared one miscalculation. Both have overestimated what the House of Saud can actually deliver. Defenseless, threatened by opposing political philosophies, custodians of a society still emerging from the feudal era, Saudi Arabia does not lead, it muddles through. It is folly to count on the Saudis for what they cannot be — a powerful force within the Arab political constellation.

But the misconceptions in the alliance are by no means one-sided. The Saudis have as little appreciation of what the United States can extract from Israel as the United States has of what the Saudis can extract from the Arabs. Barry Rubin of the Georgetown Center for Strategic Studies has said,

> . . . the local actors in the Middle East expect the United States to provide a solution [for the area's problems], and they invariably overstate American power. They expect the United States to do all the work, make the concessions, and take the blame. In this game, questioning American credibility is simply a bargaining chip.*

Thus the alliance stands, each partner trapped in its own myths.

The value of the American alliance has already split the House of Saud. The family has been long divided between the pro-American faction led by King Fahd and Prince Sultan, the defense minister, and the nationalists who rally around Crown Prince Abdullah and Saud al-Faisal, the foreign minister. The pro-American faction believes that no matter how much the kingdom seeks other defense strategies, in the end America is its only option. The nationalists, whom many would claim are simply anti-Western, fervently believe that Saudi Arabia always has been in a one-way alliance with the United States. While the Saudis produced enough oil to sustain Western economies during the

---

*Barry Rubin, "Two Years Later, Lebanon's Lessons," *New York Times*, August 29, 1984.

years of the oil drought and risked their own political well-being by serving as the counterweight to radical Arabs, the United States did nothing to wring concessions from Israel. Furthermore, the United States, instead of moderating its policy toward Israel, has become increasingly supportive of it during the years of the Reagan administration. The Israeli invasion of Lebanon, the bombing of the PLO headquarters in Tunis, American acquiescence to Jewish colonization of the West Bank, the bombing of Libya, and the denial of arms to Saudi Arabia on the grounds that the Saudis support terrorists have all combined to convince the nationalists that the interests of the House of Saud lie in opposing the United States. To bolster the argument of the nationalists, Saud al-Faisal frequently discusses the Saudis' option of seeking Soviet support. But although the Saudis periodically vent their frustrations with the United States by threatening to improve relations with the Soviet Union, the Russians are even more unpalatable to them. The Soviets are socialists politically and atheists religiously, neither of which is compatible with a conservative monarchy that functions like a pseudotheocracy. Riyadh and Moscow may exchange ambassadors in the near future, but as long as the House of Saud rules, relations are likely to stay at arm's length.

Instead, to balance the factions in the royal family and to return to the tried-and-true practice of buying off their enemies, Saudi Arabia is scurrying to mend its fences with the radical Arabs. The primary beneficiary of the Saudis' latest diplomatic stance is Syria, ally of Libya, supporter of Iran, and major destabilizer of the Middle East. In a period of severe economic strain, Saudi Arabia is providing Syria with perhaps as much as half a billion dollars a year in aid. Stopping short of subjugating themselves to Hafiz Assad's leadership, the Saudis are gambling that they can moderate Assad's actions toward Israel and his sponsorship of the anti-Arafat faction of the PLO. Most important, the House of Saud seeks to win Assad's intervention with Iran to convince the ayatollahs to stay clear of Saudi territory.

Unless the House of Saud falls to a radical political regime, the United States remains the ultimate guarantor of the kingdom's security in spite of the Saudis' alternative defense pacts. Despite the opposition of the nationalists, the House of Saud also largely accepts this truth. As a result, the Saudis have built military facilities and purchased equipment with an eye toward the use of friendly forces in an emergency. Military bases have been built large enough to accommodate

Pakistani mercenaries as well as a Jordanian rapid deployment force to fill the role that Iran was to fill under the shah, to hold off a hostile attack until the United States arrives. Airfields have redundant runways to handle the aircraft of the U.S. Air Force. Military hardware, including radar and communications equipment, has been bought for its compatibility with the equipment of an American intervention force.

The United States in its current relations with Saudi Arabia is also forced to face the hard truth that the kingdom falls within its vital interests. Commanding oil reserves of 160 billion barrels, Saudi Arabia has as much oil as the total proven reserves of the United States, the Soviet Union, Mexico, and Venezuela combined. Those reserves will loom even larger when the next cycle of want and plenty in the petroleum market hits the Western industrial nations in the 1990s. Current American policy is simply making the task of safeguarding Saudi Arabia more difficult. Because of the political pressures within the United States, Saudi Arabia is being forced to turn to the British and French for military supplies. And the Europeans are happily filling the void. While the Saudis secure their weapons and Congressmen and presidents gauge the domestic political scene, Saudi Arabia and its gulf allies are acquiring a hodgepodge of incompatible equipment that cannot be easily supplemented by the Americans in case the United States does have to intervene.

Ironically, the crisis in American-Saudi relations is coming at a time when the two countries share a remarkable compatibility of interests in their defense against the insidious hatred fanned by Iran's Islamic revolution. The oil monarchies of Bahrain and Kuwait have both been victims of a war of subversion from Iran. Nor in all probability has Saudi Arabia escaped. In the spring of 1985, Riyadh, the physical, historic, and visceral center of the kingdom of the al-Sauds, was hit by two terrorist bombs. Little damage resulted, but the symbolism was profound. The House of Saùd had been struck at its heart, its inland capital. And the targets were manifestations of the Western presence: a compound housing American advisers for the Saudi Arabian National Guard, and a nearby pizza parlor, one of the more odious icons of Westernization. The perpetrators escaped and responsibility was never assigned. No one seriously believed it was the work of either Saudi liberals or religious fundamentalists. This left the whole range of Saudi Arabia's foreign opponents to consider: radical Palestinians, terrorist groups under the sponsorship of Muammàr Qaddafi, or Shiites under the sway of Iran's Ayatollah Khomeini. The most likely source was any one of a number of opposition groups answering to the ideology of the Islamic revolution. Appealing to the significant numbers of Shiites and other disaffected Moslems scattered through the gulf region, Khomeini and his followers cry out for revolution against the evil, Western-tainted monarchies. These calls to battle in the name of Islam carry with them an acrid condemnation of the West, especially the United States, the "great Satan."

Western passions in the Arabian Gulf have waned in proportion to the rise in oil supplies. But the peninsula remains one of the most strategic regions in the world for Western interests. Any interruption in the flow of gulf oil would generate a major Western economic crisis that would carry over into the military, affecting the viability of NATO. The present threat to Western oil supplies lies with the fomenting revolution against Westernization that is stoked by the rhetoric coming out of Iran. "It is in the Gulf that the Iranian revolution will either be contained or will receive the fuel it needs to spread." * Consequently, the West is facing a new battle of ideologies. The major East-West conflict in the Middle East has ceased to be the struggle over Marxist ideology between the surrogates of the superpowers. The new East-West conflict is between the traditions of Islam and the cultural imperialism of the West. As a result, the Western nations, especially the United States, can no longer conduct their relations with Saudi Arabia solely in terms of the Arab-Israeli dispute.

---

*Mazher Hameed, *Arabia Imperiled: The Security Imperatives of the Arab Gulf States* (Washington, D.C.: Middle East Assessments Group, 1986), quoted in the *Christian Science Monitor*, July 10, 1986, p. 21.

16

The New Realities

BY 1982 the oil glut was an ugly reality. Saudi Arabia's oil revenues had dropped $32 billion or 31 percent in twelve months, with the outlook for recovery dismal. But if the average Saudi was disturbed by the turn in the kingdom's fortunes, it was not evident in the marketplace. Sea route imports were up once again, making Saudi Arabia the largest importer of foreign goods next to North America, Western Europe, and Japan. There were still 350 gold shops in Riyadh, whose proprietors continued to toss their 21 karat gold merchandise on the scales and ring up their sales, while the well-dressed young Saudi shopping in the *souqs* might chose to wear a black velvet jacket with wide sequined lapels over his traditional *thobe*.

The home furnishings craze had escalated as a result of the proliferation of luxury villas. Furniture and accessories were pinker, gaudier, and more expensive than ever. A shop in Jeddah was selling two silver-incrusted chairs with a matching hookah for $46,000. Shop windows in Riyadh featured expensive Victorian-style serving carts with crystal branches and fussy curlicues sprayed with gold, displayed in a setting of art deco furniture.

If the elite ventured into the desert, it was in a mobile home the size of a semitrailer called the "Desert Palace," pulled by a diesel truck. The interior was decorated in chintz and damask and outfitted with a stereo sound system, several VCRs, and a microwave. There were still tents, but the Bedouins no longer wove the black hair of their goats into the timeless architecture of the desert. Instead, they bought canvas tents of garish print from the Yemenis and attached a television antenna to the top.

The car market was as outrageous as ever. Young Saudis were buying inexpensive Japanese Isuzu Troopers and equipping them with color television sets and video machines. Bavaria Car Styling of West Germany sent in a pearlized Mercedes embedded with sparkling specks of silver and trimmed in gold-toned aluminum. There was also a Mercedes jeep customized for falcon hunting. The body had been extended, the top cut off, and four bucket seats installed, each upholstered in black and white mink paw.

The colorful old *souqs* continued to crumble, to be replaced by air-conditioned malls with slick advertising campaigns. "London has Harrods, New York has Saks, Jeddah has the Galleria. A prestigious complex in a setting of Italian marble, water fountains, balconies and hanging greenery creating a relaxing atmosphere where the most discerning clientele can wander and browse."*

All of this was possible because salaries stayed high. Western-educated Saudi bureaucrats made about $2,000 a month plus perhaps another 50 percent from the copious fringe benefits provided by the government. Western companies paid more, about $5,000 a month, and technicians at the Jubail industrial complex could earn as much as $6,500 a month.

Furthermore, the welfare state under the House of Saud was still in full motion. In spite of the economic slowdown, the rulers continued to go to extraordinary lengths to provide for the well-being of the citizenry. "Residents and tourists visiting Fifa mountainous area will no longer be worried about lightning . . . as giant devices will be installed to protect them from . . . hazards."** The Saudis' expectations as recipients of the government's largess had risen to new heights. King Fahd, in his speech dedicating the King Khalid International Airport in Riyadh, said the graceful buildings and elegant furnishings did not belong to the government but to the Saudi people. His listeners took him at his word. Potting soil was ground into the new carpets as Saudis picked Terminal 3 clean of the tiers of lush plants that surrounded the central fountain. Men atop other men's shoulders pried signs from the wall as souvenirs. And one farmer was seen loading into his pickup a six-foot-tall palm tree that he had just dug out of the ground. At the cafeteria of the King Fahd Hospital at Nassim, young Saudi employees arrogantly walked past the cashier, always a for-

Arab News, June 16, 1984.
**Al-Madinah*, July 15, 1983.

eigner, without paying for their food. And the push to not only "Saudize" but create a culturally acceptable job for every Saudi national expanded an already bloated bureaucracy, while jobs more critical to the functioning of the country's infrastructure continued to be filled by foreign labor. This seemingly limitless prosperity was not illusory, but how long it could be sustained by government spending became an overriding concern by the beginning of 1983. The combination of a sluggish world economy, the aggressive conservation policies of the industrial countries, and new sources of oil developed after 1973 perpetuated the glut on the world oil market. From a production high of close to 10 million barrels a day, Saudi Arabia in the early months of 1983 was producing only 4 million barrels a day. By March, the Organization of Petroleum Exporting Countries had been forced to make the painful decision to drop prices from $34 a barrel to $29 and, in an attempt to stabilize prices, set production quotas for its members. In this climate, Mana Said al-Otaiba, the United Arab Emirates' representative to the OPEC Market Monitoring Committee, issued another of his pungent poems:

> It's a buyer's market, a flexible fluidity,
> And the buyers are now quite changed,
> Sometimes showing coyness,
> At others cupidity,
> No longer fearing boycotts,
> Or shortages in supply,
> They now dictate conditions,
> And harsh rules apply.
>
> The market, alas, is stagnant,
> To the whims of buyers' over-pliant.
> For sellers, that is a heavy care,
> A great predicament.*

Saudi Arabia was central to OPEC's scheme to stabilize prices. The kingdom, with its enormous capacity, would become the swing producer of the organization. If in the face of production restraints a market surplus still existed, Saudi Arabia would cut its production to bring

---

* *Saudi Gazette*, July 19, 1983.

supply and demand into line and to defend the price of oil established by the cartel. If the price rose, the Saudis would increase production.

The oil glut brought into question once again the whole philosophy behind Saudi Arabia's oil policy during the boom, a policy that never enjoyed unanimous support. Since 1973 Saudi Arabia has sought to use its oil wealth to achieve four general objectives: to maintain the kingdom's security and stability; to increase Saudi Arabia's stature in the world arena; to diversify the economy away from its nearly total dependence on crude-oil exports; and to price oil at a level that would slow down the rate of oil substitution by the consuming nations. Saudi Arabia was able to pursue these objectives in an orderly fashion as long as the kingdom remained the dominant voice in OPEC's oil pricing decisions.

Between 1974 and 1979, OPEC, despite the cries of the oil consumers, was not a true cartel and had little to do with setting oil prices. That was done by Saudi Arabia. Zaki Yamani, the oil minister, entered OPEC meetings with instructions on a price band from the senior princes. After consultations with its partners, the Saudis set the marker price of oil within that band. Since Arabian light gravity crude* was the marker crude in international markets, the other oil producers secured what they could for their oil in relation to the premium price. If an OPEC member tried to overprice its crude, the international oil companies operating the fields refused to lift its oil. Or if an oil company were on a long-term contract, it had the contractual right to reduce the amount it lifted. Short of crude in either of these scenarios, the companies turned to Saudi Arabia and lifted their shortfall from the kingdom's excess capacity. The whole system functioned on the basis of Saudi Arabia's setting the price of the marker crude and the oil companies, acting as policemen, keeping the other producers in line by using the Saudis' surplus capacity.

In 1979 Saudi Arabia lost control of the pricing mechanism. Amid the confusion and exhilaration of the revolution, Iran's Islamic government reduced petroleum output by some 3 to 4 million barrels a day. In order to make up the deficit, Saudi Arabia upped its own production to 9.5 mbd, close to the limit of its capacity. But production at this level could not be sustained. It soon became apparent that oil pumped

---

*Light gravity crude oil is the easiest and therefore least expensive crude oil to refine. Saudi light became the benchmark crude because it was the first discovered in large quantities.

at such a high rate was doing irreparable damage to pressure in the fields and had to be cut back. When Saudi Arabia lost its surplus capacity it lost control of prices, which subsequently went berserk.

To a segment of Saudi planners, this forced cutback on production was a welcomed development. Throughout the oil boom, Saudi policymakers were divided on the wisdom of producing the maximum amount of oil in order to moderate prices and protect the Western economies where Saudi Arabia's surplus revenues were invested. Basically, the debate was over the value of oil in the ground versus the value of oil produced. The strategy of those who might be termed the "slow growthers" stressed the conservation of oil resources, slower economic growth, and a more moderate rate of social change. These advocates of oil in the ground argued that a barrel of oil sold created revenues that the domestic economy could not absorb. Therefore, they had to be invested abroad, subjecting Saudi monetary assets to foreign exchange fluctuations and the risk of sequestration and/or freezing. Their most persuasive argument was that high production benefited the West more than Saudi Arabia. And arming themselves with the figures, the conservationists early in the boom pointed out that "in terms of 1974 dollar prices [the currency in which oil is traded], the $129.5 billion gross foreign assets of OPEC that are denominated in dollars would be worth only $75.1 billion in early 1979 simply because of dollar devaluation." *

But by the time Saudi Arabia lost control of OPEC, it was already too late to moderate policy. The progressives among the senior princes, spearheaded by Fahd, already had the kingdom firmly set on the path of rapid economic development, financed by huge oil revenues deposited in the West. An intricate part of the progressives' plan was to maintain oil production at a high enough level to insulate the Western industrial countries against the worst excesses of the price hawks in OPEC, who were led by Iran. The rationale behind the high production philosophy of oil minister Yamani and Crown Prince Fahd was that a relationship exists between oil prices and rates of consumption. Low production and high prices drive consumers out of the market in search of alternative energy sources. From the standpoint of Saudi interests, this would leave Saudi Arabia with enormous oil reserves and fewer

---

*Ragaei El Mallakh and Dorothea H. El Mallakh, eds., *Saudi Arabia: Energy, Developmental Planning, and Industrialization* (Lexington, Ma.: Lexington Books, 1982), p. 31.

markets. By 1981 high prices had indeed driven the rates of oil consumption down. At year's end, Yamani, like an oracle predicting doom, said, "As we approach the year 1982 and enter it . . . we will most likely encounter a big glut in the oil market at a time when we are not ready for it. . . . Then the chances of a price collapse will be great."* Events proved Yamani right.

Nineteen eighty-three was the year that Saudi Arabia was compelled to seriously confront the new reality of too much oil and too few customers. Exports fell another 56 percent in the first six months of the year, with production dropping to 3.5 mbd, or about half the 1982 level. By the beginning of the second half of the year, production had plunged to a new low of 2.3 mbd as Saudi Arabia, OPEC's swing producer, continued to drop its output to hold the line on prices. Although by August the Saudis were producing 5.5 mbd, three-quarters of a million barrels of that was needed for domestic consumption, and it is estimated that close to 800,000 barrels a day went to fund Iraq's war with Iran.

Beyond the number of barrels of oil produced and the dollars collected, the House of Saud began to clearly sense the threat to its own political fortunes inherent in the economic downturn. Theoretically, Saudi Arabia's economy was so underdeveloped at the beginning of the oil boom that the level of income depended on the level of oil production. When oil production was increased or reduced, government revenues and, therefore, national income either rose or declined. But as a result of rapid development, the government of Saudi Arabia found itself in the difficult position of always having to trade off three factors: oil production, development expenditures, and financial surpluses. A high level of oil production combined with conservative development expenditures produced large financial surpluses. A low rate of oil production combined with a large expenditure on development produced low financial surpluses or deficits. In each case, the government's ownership of oil resources, its control of development expenditures, and its command of financial surpluses made the public sector solely responsible for balancing these forces.

Since oil is Saudi Arabia's only real source of income, government ownership of oil reserves means that the government alone determines the specifics of diversification through the major investment projects it

---

*Quoted in Joseph Kraft, "Letter from Saudi Arabia," *The New Yorker*, July 4, 1983, p. 52.

chooses. There is no feedback on the wisdom of these decisions from
market mechanisms built up through a gradual process of economic
development by the private sector. After a decade and a half of frantic
developmental efforts that have included extensive efforts to direct private investment into productive ventures, the oil sector has yet to be
integrated into the rest of the economy through various backward and
forward linkages. Therefore, the overall performance of the Saudi
economy can only be measured by the growth of the government budget, the vehicle through which oil revenues reach every segment of the
economy. As a result, the burden of finding a solution to the economic
crisis caused by the oil glut falls squarely on the shoulders of the government. And the government, as perceived by Saudi Arabia's population, is the House of Saud.

The al-Sauds' predicament in dealing with economic recession is
made even more difficult by the patriarchal nature of their rule. The
average Saudi largely escaped demands of citizenship before the oil
boom and after the boom became the beneficiary of an elaborate welfare state. The sudden drop in wealth and government spending has
proved a jolting experience to a well-cushioned society that had become all too accustomed to easy money, huge profits, and little work.
With the House of Saud accepting the political reward of plenty during
the golden years, it realizes it is also likely to suffer the blame for the
drought years.

The al-Sauds' first line of defense in the oil glut was denial. Government ministries cranked out reassuring statements in which Mohammed Aba al-Kahail, minister of Finance and National Economy,
claimed the kingdom was unaffected by recession, and Abdul Rahman
Zamil, minister of Industry and Electricity, said, "We are going through
a new era of our society. It is an era that will be extremely positive to
the Saudis."*

Yet the signs of slowdown in the government's largess were clear.
"Riyadh — The Ministry of Finance has issued a circular . . . ban-
ning the publication of advertisements about deaths and condolences
at government expense."** Saudi ships no longer benefited from cut-
rate bunker fuel. The handsome coffee table books about the kingdom
that the Ministry of Information passed out to expatriates disappeared,
to be replaced by packets of postcards. One of the large money-chang-

*Arizona Republic, June 5, 1983.
**Al-Jazirah, January 31, 1983.

ing firms collapsed and there were rumors of impending bankruptcies among some members of the great merchant families. On Saudia Airlines flights I saw the signs of decline graphically. My family was still flying first class on tickets provided by the hospital. However, the expensive printed menus that were the size of newspapers, the handsome gifts passed out to passengers, and the Christian Dior perfumes and colognes in the toilets had all disappeared.

The 1983–84 budget, still totaling $76.4 billion, showed cuts of between 14 and 40 percent in almost every area of government spending. As an example of the magnitude of some of the reductions, the pediatrics department of the King Faisal hospital was allotted discretionary funds for July to October 1983 of SR 100, or $29.41. Most cuts, though, came in the form of stretching out the completion dates of construction projects. This chiefly hit foreign firms, leaving the holdings of the royal family and most other Saudis largely unscathed.

As oil production continued to slump and prices rocked, the question became whether or not Saudi Arabia would be forced to dip into its foreign reserves to meet the projected budget deficit of $22 billion for fiscal 1983–84. The answer was never announced; it simply evolved. As early as 1982, the government reduced the amount of money it paid to construction companies to cover startup costs from 20 percent to 10 percent of the price of the contract. No longer would contractors like "Red" Blount of Blount, Inc., collect $200 million up front. Later, the government, rather than drawing on reserves, simply stopped paying its bills to its foreign contractors. There were long delays in contractual in-process construction payments. These delays were described by the government as a "technical problem" rather than as fiscal policy. Whatever it was called, contractors could not collect their money. While average delays at first were between 90 and 120 days, soon they began to drag on for as long as six months. As the economic situation worsened, contractors were waiting eighteen months for their money. To meet their payrolls and buy materials, most companies operated on borrowed money. Shutting down operations ceased to be an option when the government announced that if a contractor stopped construction because he was not paid on time, he did not get paid at all. For Western construction companies, which had made so many millions of dollars during the years of plenty, the boom was over.*

---

*Western companies are still carrying millions upon millions of dollars of the Saudis' unpaid bills on their balance sheets.

In 1984 revenues dropped another $15 billion to $42 billion. Stung by the reports some of us were filing in the Western press about contractors' cash flow problems, the minister of Finance and National Economy was still claiming that the delays on the payment of government bills was not because of a budget deficit but because of the time necessary for his ministry to examine the technical terms of contracts. But at the same time, the Saudi Arabian Monetary Agency was repatriating close to $20 billion in foreign reserves. A businessman friend of mine who had relatively small amounts of money due him routinely bribed employees in the Ministry of Finance to move his invoices from the bottom of the pile of the government's unpaid bills to the top. By now, Saudi businessmen were also feeling the pinch. The financially frail among the legions of trading establishments that imported and sold everything from construction equipment to consumer goods quietly folded. Of those left, many realized that although profits were poor this year there might not be any profits next year. The percentage of private money flowing out of Saudi Arabia into Swiss bank accounts and American real estate escalated accordingly. The only positive factor in the economic downturn was its effect on inflation. Prices stayed stable and in the case of real estate dropped precipitously. While housing costs were still high, the astronomical rents of the 1970s had crashed.

At the time I left Saudi Arabia in the summer of 1984, the kingdom stood in suspended animation. Many Westerners had either made the decision to leave or were considering it. Those who had no jobs waiting at home or who could not abandon their investments in Saudi Arabia anxiously waited the next round of bad economic news.

I went to a party one night at the home of an American construction contractor who had been in Saudi Arabia since the earliest days of the oil boom. Throughout the evening I had the vague feeling that I was living the movie *Casablanca*. In a corner of the room, someone languidly picked out a tune on an old upright piano. The room was dominated by an elaborate and well-stocked bar, a certain sign that the host had high-placed political connections. Critically stationed at the bar, pouring drinks, was the CIA's unacknowledged Riyadh station chief. As he mixed, he tipped his ear toward whoever was standing before him to catch the bits of information they passed along. Except for the host, it seemed everyone at the party was waiting for an exit visa to leave the kingdom for good. A young British farm equipment salesman, who although dressed in a pink Polo shirt looked like an Oxford don, was going home after eight years. A former U.S. army officer who had been in Riyadh for three years, training the National Guard, would be leaving in two weeks. A distraught French architect would depart the next day, giving up on collecting his fee for designing a building finished two years before. Behind me, I heard a lawyer say he and his wife were returning to the United States the following week. I instantly recognized the voice. Sidling up to him, I casually asked, "Are you Bryan Lynch?" He looked puzzled and said yes. I whispered, "I am Michael Collins." A broad smile came over his face and he said, "I'm glad to meet you after all this time." While Bryan was practicing law in Saudi Arabia, he was also part owner of a Middle East business magazine published in Washington, D.C. Since 1980 I had been writing for that publication. Bryan and I had spoken many times over the telephone about stories, but we had never dared meet. His wife, who edited several of my articles, joined us and we reminisced about our time in Saudi Arabia and what lay ahead.

I left the party melancholy. Perhaps I was still thinking of Ingrid Bergman and Humphrey Bogart playing out the last days before World War II. Saudi Arabia was in no danger of going to war, but it was in danger of losing much of the wealth that had fueled development and the great consumer society.

The 1984–85 budget held level at $76.4 billion, the same as the previous year. To boost government revenues, the price of a gallon of gasoline was hiked from 21 cents, as was the price of other low-cost petroleum products consumed domestically. Even with the threat from Iran, military spending was cut 20 percent. The number of Saudis being sent abroad to study was severely cut back. Salaries and benefits for both Saudis and expatriates were cut from 30 to 50 percent. Layoffs were sending as many as fifty thousand expatriates a month home. Still, the budget deficit was estimated at $30 billion. The *riyal* was adjusted downward against the dollar to raise import prices and discourage the purchase of so many foreign goods. The gold shops were no longer so crowded that people were forced to stand on the street waiting for a place at the counters. The pace of trade from the shopping malls to the *souqs* was somber. Businesses saw their profit margins strangled, and empty stores began to scar Riyadh, Jeddah, and al-Khobar like pockmarks. The average Saudi, at last, had begun to feel the pain of recession.

Nineteen eighty-four was also the year that the goals for the Fourth

Economic and Social Development Plan (1985–1990) were unfolded. While the Third Plan was unveiled in 1979 at the height of the boom, the Fourth Plan was born in uncertainty. With most of the major infrastructure projects completed, the new plan's goals would be infinitely more difficult to accomplish than those of the building years. The plan has four objectives, which are more themes than goals. The first is to draw on the infrastructure built during the Third Plan to diversify the economy through manufacturing, agriculture, and finance. The second is to encourage the private sector to play an expanded role in the economy. To reduce the government's near total dominance of the economic system, local businessmen are to be provided with a range of incentives to establish enterprises aimed at increasing the gross domestic product rather than businesses geared to the importation and sale of foreign goods. Third, taking a page from every government budget in the West, Saudi Arabia has pledged to increase government efficiency to cut costs.* And finally, the gist of the plan is to reduce the kingdom's dependence on foreign labor. "Saudization," a term introduced in the Third Plan, not only would put Saudis into jobs held by foreigners but would raise the quality of that manpower through education and training. The delicate issue of women's role in the labor force was addressed with promises that fields other than medicine and teaching would be open to women. And then, as if to cover his bases with the religious fundamentalists, Minister of Planning Hisham Nazer said the new plan would exert all effort in "the preservation of Islamic values and the propagation of the divine faith."**

Significantly, the Fourth Plan stressed two subjects barely touched on in the Third Plan: the necessity of adapting to revenue constraints, and the need to bolster the kingdom's defenses and internal security. The figure for projected expenditures over five years (1985–1990) — $278 billion — may be an illusion. In all public discussion of the plan, officials stress that, rather than committing a designated amount of money to development, the Fourth Plan establishes a set of desirable objectives on which money will be spent in line with the country's income.

On the threshold of the Fourth Plan, the promises of the Third Development Plan appeared as impermanent as oil shortages. Among the

---

*As an example of this efficiency, 326,000 new government jobs were added in fiscal 1984–85.
**Arab News, December 3, 1983.

more serious repercussions of the oil glut was the future of Saudi Arabia's fledgling petrochemical industry. The commitment of the Third Development Plan to diversify the kingdom's economy by building on Saudi Arabia's abundance of oil raised not only economic but political questions as the Saudis struggled to maintain an acceptable level of oil production and to find markets for their petrochemicals.

As they had questioned the high production oil policy, many questioned the government's original decision to invest billions of dollars in heavy industry. There were strong arguments against industrialization in a country that had colossal capital costs, high operating costs, and essentially no indigenous labor. In addition, there were projections of marketing problems intrinsic to the cyclical slumps of the petrochemical industry and the great distance of Saudi Arabia from the major markets of Europe and North America. So dismal were the projections on profit margins that at the time Jubail and Yanbu were under construction, some experts predicted that the six major petrochemical projects would yield less revenue than the sale of 250,000 barrels of oil a day. But the proponents of industrialization believed the kingdom had no other course if it were to maximize the downstream potential of its oil resources. So the money was committed and the bulldozers went to work. The most obvious goal was to capture the gas, a by-product of oil production, that burned in towering flares across the oil fields. A mammoth gas gathering and processing system was constructed, which could collect and process 3.3 billion cubic feet of gas a day to power industry, electric generating plants, and seawater desalination facilities while providing ethane as feedstock for the petrochemical industry. The original cost of the gathering system was to be $4.5 billion, but before it was finished it had absorbed $12 billion of the Saudis' oil revenues. Nevertheless, unlike the glamorous steel and aluminum plant projects, the gas-based industries made economic and developmental sense at the time. Saudi Arabia could produce the feedstock for its petrochemicals at a cost of $.50 per million British thermal units of energy, or what amounted to $3 per barrel of oil, thus making the Saudis competitive in international markets. But as oil prices declined, whatever advantage Saudi Arabia had gained from cheap gas began to be lost to other factors. It cost twice as much to build a plant in Saudi Arabia as it did to build the same plant in the United States or Europe. The highly specialized technicians who were available only in Europe or North America charged about twice as much for their services

in Saudi Arabia as they did domestically. Technology, dominated by
American firms, was obtained largely through expensive leasing arrangements. Even more basic was the ever-present cost of water. The
only way Saudi Arabia could meet industry's enormous demands for
water was by desalination, at a cost of probably $2.50 per cubic meter.
And then, to complicate the prospects of Saudi industry further, political events in the Arabian Gulf that were unforeseen at the time the
decision to industrialize was made threatened to impede, if not immo-
bilize, shipments out of Jubail.

Confirming the warnings of the doomsayers, the performance of the
early Arabian industries was disastrous. There were labor shortages,
management problems, and a succession of technical breakdowns. Over
the first seven years of its operation, the fertilizer plant was never able
to run at more than 55 percent capacity for any sustained length of
time. Gradually these problems were brought under control, only to be
replaced with an even greater problem: the threat to markets indirectly
caused by the oil glut.

After seven years of construction and billions of dollars, Saudi Arabia's infant petrochemical industry was just coming on line about the
time the surplus in the petroleum markets became endemic. The atmosphere in the country when industrialization was the buzz word among
Saudi economic planners was much different from the atmosphere when
the plants actually went into operation. When ground was broken for
the Jubail and Yanbu projects, Saudi Arabia loudly boasted that the
success of the ventures was assured. Industrial nations would be coerced
into buying a quota of Saudi petrochemicals to qualify for a share of
Saudi crude oil. But when the industrial cities went into production,
Saudi Arabia was faced with doing business in the real world. No
longer master of limited oil supplies, the kingdom was reduced to marketing its petrochemicals through the give and take of international
trade governed by competition and trade barriers. By 1983 the Saudis,
frustrated in their attempts to break into European markets, were
threatening a trade war with the European Economic Community (EEC).
The government insisted with little success that the EEC lower its import taxes of 13 to 19 percent on Saudi Arabia's chemicals as a recip-
rocal measure to compensate the kingdom for the largely duty-free
status of European products imported into the country. The issue was
pointed and it was public because the government was concerned not
only to recover its vast investment in petrochemicals; it was growing
increasingly concerned about the kingdom's income needs.

Hoping eventually to capture 5 percent of the world's petrochemical market, Saudi industry with its advantages and handicaps is chiseling away at the competition in Europe, the United States, and the Far East, as well as India and Africa. As long as the oil surplus wears on, Saudi Arabia has a more immediate problem than its market share in petrochemicals. Although the government desperately wants to recoup its costs and increase income, the immediate concern is to produce enough oil to maintain the pressure in the gas lines needed to fuel its petrochemical plants. In some respects, industrialization, rather than freeing Saudi Arabia from its total dependence on oil, has made oil production hostage to industry.

Agricultural policy, another cornerstone of the Third Development Plan, has also fallen victim to dearth and plenty in the oil markets. Reacting to veiled threats by other countries to embargo food exports to Saudi Arabia in retaliation against another oil embargo, the Saudi government in 1977 hit on the idea of making the kingdom self-sufficient in the staples of the Saudi diet, particularly wheat. If industrialization was a questionable policy, growing wheat on the desert was ludicrous. Nevertheless, Saudis were offered free land, interest-free loans for machinery, fertilizer, and seed, and a government guarantee to buy their total production for just over $28 a bushel. (The average price per bushel of wheat in the United States in 1977 was $2.28.) With almost unlimited capital and foreign management, Saudi entrepreneurs turned into gentlemen farmers.

Al-Madani Farms, owned by Sheikh Fahd Ghandourah, is near the oasis town of al-Kharj. My guide on this tour of a Saudi wheat farm was the *sheikh*'s Egyptian manager, Abdul. It was early April and the wheat harvest had begun. I had grown up in wheat growing country in the western United States, but this farm was unlike any I had ever seen. With Abdul at the wheel, we drove over miles of dry, crusty desert interspersed with dots of green. The wheat, planted in circles, or pivots, was being fed water at 1250 gallons a minute. Thousand-foot sprinklers, anchored in the center, moved over the field on heavy tires, spraying a combination of water and liquid fertilizer to make fruitful soil devoid of animal or vegetable matter. Near the pivots it became almost steamy, as water, heated by the sun as it came through the pipes, sprayed out at 85 degrees. As I stood in the sun looking over the willowy wheat, it seemed only slightly less than miraculous. But an inch beyond the reach of the water and fertilizer, the ground remained what it truly was — desert.

The crop around al-Kharj was good. On the highway I had passed a line of trucks ten kilometers long, waiting to unload at the grain elevators. Although Al-Madani would also have a bumper crop, Sheikh Ghandourah was having problems. His specially built, $32,000, sixty-metric-ton trailers, which had just been delivered from the United States, were banned from Saudi roads for excessive weight. He had been talked out of his cherished plan to buy from an Italian con artist $1 million worth of earthworms to irrigate the soil. And the government was slowing down on its payments for wheat. Originally paying farmers on delivery to the silos, in 1983 the government began to stretch out payments in three installments. By 1984 no payments were made until ten months after the harvest.

In 1986 Saudi Arabia would produce two million bushels of wheat, one million more than it could consume. Not only has the surplus required more silos for storage, but the whole agricultural program has become exceedingly expensive. To stem the bounty, no new land is being provided for additional wheat acreage. Loans for increased production are difficult to obtain. Delays in payments to farmers have gotten even longer. And the price the government will pay for wheat has been cut to $14 a bushel, still five times the world price. But as with other projects of the oil boom, once the agricultural program was set in place, it acquired its own momentum. When the government in 1986 tried to reduce production by backing out of its commitment to buy all the wheat grown in the kingdom, such a commotion erupted that the plan was hastily withdrawn. Politically the House of Saud is locked into high costs for overproduction of wheat largely by city dwellers turned farmers who are now financially tied to guaranteed government payments. As serious as the economic drain is, other costs are even higher. To keep the farms going requires foreign labor and the resource Saudi Arabia can least afford to waste — water. Agriculture now consumes 84 percent of the kingdom's water, 70 percent of which comes from the nonreplenishable underground aquifers. With the water table in some areas dropping two meters a year and desalination costs so high, the search for water, somewhat ignored during the growth years, is on once more. The iceberg idea has resurfaced, as well as cloud seeding. And Wales has offered to buy Saudi oil and send the tankers back filled with spring water. None of this is enough if the current level of water consumption continues. In the end, the misguided agricultural policies of the boom era may turn Saudi Arabia into more of a desert than it was before.

The Saudis' reaction to the ups and downs of their economic fortunes has followed a clear pattern. The initial shock over their sudden
wealth was followed by a period of supreme confidence that lasted into
the 1980s. The second phase, 1983 to early 1986, was marked by
doubt and indecision as the crisis in the oil markets began to press
down on the kingdom. OPEC, usually meeting in the cool and tranquility of Geneva, saw one emergency session after another flounder
over the issue of production controls to support a unified price on oil.
Unlike the period from 1973 to 1979, when oil minister Yamani would
enter OPEC meetings with a predetermined price band and the others
would fall in line, the production hawks now refused to bend. The plan
by which Saudi Arabia would either shrink or expand its own production in response to market conditions was the only deal Yamani was
able to strike to support prices. And that proved to be counterproduc-
tive to the interests of Saudi Arabia. As the Saudis' OPEC partners
routinely exceeded their production quotas, the kingdom's own production became smaller and smaller to keep OPEC within its production guidelines. With oil production at one time as low as 1.9 mbd,
the House of Saud needed the revenues from at least 5 million barrels
of oil a day to shelter both the benefits of its welfare state and its own
political well-being against the storms of the oil glut. As production
dropped, the high level of government spending was maintained by
allowing foreign reserves to fall over three years from an estimated
high of $150 billion in 1983 to less than $90 billion in 1986. To shore
up its own economy, Saudi Arabia had to increase its share of petroleum markets.

With essentially no hope of bringing OPEC in line, Saudi Arabia in
February 1986 unilaterally abandoned its position as the swing producer in OPEC. In a bold move for the cautious Saudis, the kingdom
declared it intended to use its dominion over a quarter of the world's
proven oil reserves and its low production costs to recapture its oil
markets. Throwing off the constraints of OPEC's failed production
quotas, Saudi Arabia went into the marketplace to crush the high cost
non-OPEC producers, such as Britain and Norway, and to force its
OPEC partners to suffer the consequences of falling prices. OPEC's
united front crumbled. As persuasive as the economic arguments were
for Saudi Arabia's move to humble the dreaded OPEC of the boom
years, the House of Saud's decision was made as much for psychological as economic reasons.

The oil glut had been a cruel blow to Saudi honor. In addition to the plenteous material rewards, the other real dividend of the oil boom for Saudi Arabia was what it did for the Saudis' perception of themselves. Before the oil era, it was their devotion to Wahhabism, the most puritanical and demanding sect of Islam, that the Saudis believed set them above all others. And the House of Saud defended the Saudis' pride in their piety by being the most vigorous protectors of the faith. However, despite their piety the Saudis still were derided for generations by their Middle Eastern neighbors, who regarded them as little more than illiterate Bedouins. Then with the House of Saud at the helm, the kingdom burst forth from the backwater to bask in the glory of unimaginable wealth. The world groveled at the Saudis' feet to win contracts and jobs. And everyone was made to pay court. Through a multitude of personal humiliations imposed on non-Saudi Arabs working in the country and through the systematic use of Saudi aid to other Arab governments, the Saudis extracted their pound of flesh for the years they suffered as objects of scorn. As for the West, the Saudis perceived the economic price that the oil shortage extracted from the industrial countries as revenge for Western acts against Arab honor dating back to the Crusades. In a sense, the oil boom was seen by the Saudis as restoring their pride, soiled by their years of poverty and isolation.

In a culture where a man's greatest fear is an affront to his honor, this was heady stuff. Under the House of Saud, oil had vindicated Saudi honor, satisfied its pride. It is this sense of power, the ability of Saudi Arabia to force others to do its bidding, that the oil glut destroyed. The downward spiral of oil production and prices has shaken the Saudis more severely psychologically than economically. No longer able to command the awe of the outside world, the Saudis are plagued with self-doubts. And as with a tribal *sheikh* who has failed his people, these doubts transfer directly to the House of Saud. In the scramble to recoup, the al-Sauds wisely saw that their best interests lay in restoring the Saudis' self-image. The decision to flood the world's petroleum markets with oil had had an economic rationale; but at its soul was the kingdom's desire to cause the world to tremble or rejoice at Saudi Arabia's will.

17

Castles of Sand

OIL PRICES TUMBLED as Saudi Arabia upped production and sold at terms highly favorable to buyers. Income inched upward even as the price of oil per barrel plunged. Unlike most of its competitors, Saudi Arabia could continue to make money at almost any price because of its low production costs. I often heard Western oil company executives joke that the oil of the al-Ghawar field is so near the surface that all it takes is turning on a spigot to fill the tankers that pull into berths at Ras Tanura. The truth is that Saudi Arabia can produce oil for between $.50 and $2 a barrel, depending on the variable cost factors. North Sea oil becomes unprofitable at less than $20 a barrel, and the economics of the high-priced Texas wells drilled since 1981 knocks out their production every time the price of petroleum drops. Furthermore, Saudi Arabia has no foreign debt requiring large profits from oil simply to service oil boom loans. Nevertheless, even if the price war that Saudi Arabia undertook in 1986 had forced a rise in oil prices, this would not have solved the kingdom's unique set of problems. Nor would it in the future. All that was created during the years of plenty must now be maintained or it will be reclaimed by the relentless punishment of the desert. From basic maintenance to the level of oil that the Saudis must produce to keep their industries operating, infrastructure costs are an albatross around the kingdom's neck. The gap between the glamour of building and the toil of operation touches on every facet of Saudi culture — resistance to organized and defined tasks and revulsion to manual labor in a paltry and proud population — that hindered development in the first place.

In every corner of the kingdom, generators for electricity are in place.

Water is being delivered to homes and industries. Municipal buildings and hospitals stand ready to receive Saudi citizens. The rural areas have roads and the cities have cloverleaf highways, skyscrapers, and high-rise housing. Yet the life expectancy of a car in the kingdom is less than five years because of the lack of maintenance on the part of car owners and the shortage of service facilities and repairmen. The King Saud University in Riyadh is a beautiful monument of learning but the kingdom has almost no public libraries. Saudi Arabia now has a water supply of 500 million gallons a day but the water table is dropping so fast that the gracious old date palms in the *wadi* at Diriyah are dying. The government creates public parks and the Bedouins graze their goats on the grass. SAPTCO, the Saudi Arabian Public Transport Company, buys sleek buses of blue, white, and orange and then puts one route number on the front, another on the side, and a third in the rear.

Compounding the challenges of making everything work are Saudi attitudes fostered by the government's paternalistic policies during the oil boom. Motivated to keep the cost of living down, the government subsidized food, charged consumers only a fraction of what it cost to produce electricity, and kept fuel prices ridiculously cheap. Education was free. Basic needs such as housing and health care flowed from the government. Although some benefits have been reduced, there is still an extraordinarily high level of expectation among the citizenry. As early as 1979, a confidential memo within the Ministry of Planning summed up the Western economic planners' concern about public attitudes toward the maintenance of the infrastructure Saudi Arabia was building. In this case, it was water and sewage systems.

The way in which municipal projects have been funded has caused the cities' populations to expect that progress in the future will continue as in the past. More importantly, the general population believes that they are only to be beneficiaries of these expenditures and do not need to contribute directly to raising the capital required to attain or maintain these projects and services. Not only do such services then become expected, but also more sophisticated, higher quality and, therefore, more costly services become considered necessities. This crisis of expectations will haunt further investments . . . as citizens continually force municipalities to forgo the less visible and glamorous operation and maintenance expenses for the new, highly visible projects. If the cycle of creating the desire for more, without the burden of paying for more, is not stopped, this will constrain municipal investments from serving the vast majority of the Kingdom's urban and village populations with either essential water and sewage, or maintaining the investments in-place.

During the oil boom, the solution to the problem of basic maintenance and every other problem was to throw more money at it. No longer master of endless wealth, Saudi society will now be tested to see how it measures up in maintaining what it has created.

Members of the Western-educated elite are making the transition from observers in the development process to managers, with a reasonable degree of success. Lower-echelon bureaucrats are doing less well but have become part of the systems structured during the boom. Shopkeepers and peasants are largely following their traditional occupations. It is the low-level jobs in the new economic order against which the Saudis are the most defiant. A Saudi may be put behind the wheel of a scheduled intercity bus but he is still a son of the desert, master of his own destiny. The following letter to the editor appeared in the *Arab News* on February 11, 1984.

On February 2, I went from Medina to Jeddah by bus. While going, after all the passengers boarded, the bus was taken to the garage for [a] checkup, which should have been done before the scheduled time of departure. While coming from Medina [after the service stop], the bus was being driven at a speed of over 140 kph causing panic among the passengers. Those in the upper decks were frightened and started crying with fear when other passengers forced the driver to stop the bus. Instead of tendering an apology, the driver declared that he would better not drive, if he had to reduce the speed. This led to a controversy which was intercepted by the police passing by who then arranged to get another bus from Medina to take us to Jeddah.

The director general of SAPTCO, put to shame by the conduct of his employee, chose to deny everything in a subsequent letter. He claimed that the SAPTCO buses would only go 120 kph; drivers were forbidden to drive over 100 kph; the shaking of the bus was due to a sudden malfunction in the bus's support system, not excessive speed; and the driver, a Saudi, was considered one of the best as far as his character was concerned. And then he gave it all away. The company was considering placing an iron bar under the accelerator to make it impossible to exceed the mandated speed.

The Saudis might be better able to run the country if development had not come so fast and had been more balanced. As it is, too much of everything was built on too grand a scale. Hisham Nazer, former planning minister, summed up the oil boom when he said, "We built four lane highways when two would do. We overbuilt housing. We created an excess of electric generating power."* There was also a strong tendency to duplicate facilities, most of which had low standards. In 1983 Jaizan, a town of thirty-two thousand, had seven hospitals with three more under construction. The hospital in Diriyah was small and grossly inadequate yet it was on a major bus route, only fifteen minutes from major hospitals in Riyadh. With so much, it is impossible for the Saudis, still inexperienced in technology, untrained in mechanics, and fatally handicapped by a scanty population, to take over and manage their vast infrastructure successfully. The King Khalid International Airport, just one of three major airports, requires the labor of ten thousand people for its daily operation and contains mountains of computer banks that have to be serviced. Every facility constructed during the oil boom now requires plumbers, air-conditioner repairmen, electricians, a manager, and someone to sweep the floor. Saudi Arabia is learning that although the desert can be made beautiful, for every tree and blade of grass that is planted, it takes technology to pump the water and manpower to tend the soil to make them grow. As a result, the xenophobic Saudis have come out of the oil boom inextricably bound up with their foreign work force.

One of the jokes making the rounds of the expatriate community during the boom was about an interviewer who asked an American, a German, and a Saudi if sex were work or fun. The American said, "Fun, of course." The German said, "I work in my office all day, I come home, and I have more ahead of me to do. Sex is work." When a Saudi was asked, he paused, thought for a while, and then said, "It is fun. If it were work I would have a Pakistani do it."

The human components of the oil boom were the Saudis, as masters, the Westerners, as highly paid servants, and the great mass of manual laborers from the Third World, as beasts of burden. The TCN, or third country national, was a name coined by the U.S. Army Corps of Engineers early in the oil boom to define a worker who was neither an American nor a Saudi. The name soon came to define any non-West-

---

*Quoted in Joseph Kraft, "Letter from Saudi Arabia," *The New Yorker*, July 4, 1984, p. 50.

erner working for the Saudis, an identification that has endured. TCN is not a derogatory term but rather a harsh statement of fact that divides the clerks, maintenance men, drivers, and construction workers from the class of privileged Westerners. These "petromigrants" are a new slave class. They dig the ditches, build the buildings, sweep the streets, farm the land, drive the trucks, stock the supermarket shelves, clean the houses, and care for the children of the Saudis. Yet they cannot apply for citizenship, own property, or claim Saudi law for their children born on Saudi soil. They can be deported at will and are looked on by their Saudi masters with disdain. Despite the wealth of the Saudis and the technical expertise of the Westerners, much of what was achieved during the oil boom was done by the sweat of the TCNs.

There has always been a foreign worker class in Saudi Arabia, largely clustered along the coasts. There were the *hajjis* who stayed on to work to earn their passage home. There were Africans who migrated across the Red Sea. Omanis who were escaping political unrest in Oman during the 1950s were followed by Yemenis in the sixties. But it was with the oil boom that Saudi Arabia actively sought and willingly paid for a large foreign worker class, which permeated every region of Saudi Arabia including the Nejd. As the boom wore on, these workers became ingrained in the economy, an indispensable commodity. In 1975 the expatriate work force (Western and non-Western) was 41 percent of total employment. In 1980 it was 46 percent, and by 1985, even in the face of recession, it had grown to 48 percent of the total work force.

Not far into the boom, the Saudis shifted from predominantly Arab labor to Asian labor. The Arabs, primarily the Yemenis and rural Egyptians, often lacked the skills needed for modernization, and those who were skilled, the Palestinians and the Lebanese, had about them the aura of political unrest. The Asians, on the other hand, provided an enormous pool of skilled, semiskilled, and unskilled labor that was both inexpensive and politically safe. By 1980 the Asians had become the Saudis' major source of manpower. At one time, there were so many Koreans living in barracks and lining up to march to work that some Westerners speculated that they were in reality a mercenary army masquerading as construction workers. But the Saudis were not content with just Koreans or Thais or Filipinos. The composition of the work force was constantly adjusted so the kingdom would not become overly dependent on the labor of any one country. Checkout lines at the supermarkets were illustrative of government policy in the private sector: every three cash registers were run by a Filipino, a Pakistani, and a Sri Lankan. This fluidity of nationalities was also due to the government's policy of shifting to the cheapest labor of the moment. Migrants from Bangladesh were among the last to arrive, willing to work for less than even the Pakistanis. But the symbol of the lowliest foreign laborer always remained the same: the rubber bucket made from an old tire that was used to move dirt, shovelful by shovelful, from one place to another.

In the Saudi embassies in Cairo, New Delhi, and Bangkok, I pushed through corridors crowded with men squatting, anxiously waiting for a precious Saudi visa. And every time I went through immigration in Saudi Arabia, I saw a new shipment of workers, clad in jeans and rubber sandals and wearing bright-colored company shirts with matching billed caps, lined up waiting to enter the kingdom. Their dark, sad eyes spoke of their acceptance of the inevitability of their fate, yet they undoubtedly were thankful for a two-year job in the dust and heat of Saudi Arabia.

Recruiting Third World labor was big business during the oil boom. There existed a whole international trade in indentured servants. In 1978 a contractor's advertisement in the *Far East Report* read, "Ample skilled, semiskilled, and unskilled workers available for immediate processing and transfer to Saudi Arabia." Pakistanis were recruited for wages of $200 a month through ads in Karachi's newspapers. Other companies promised Saudi employers quality manpower from Bangladesh, India, the Philippines, Sri Lanka, and Thailand.

The TCNs were exploited by everyone — recruiting agencies, their employers in Saudi Arabia, and their own governments — as unscrupulous operators on both sides took advantage of men desperate for work. At the height of the boom, a number of Third World countries became remittance economies dependent on the money their nationals working in Saudi Arabia sent home. In 1982 Pakistani workers delivered $2.16 billion in foreign exchange to Pakistan's economy, 93 percent of the country's merchandise export earnings. Not only were workers in Saudi Arabia filling the coffers of their home countries with foreign exchange, but what they eventually realized from their earnings often fell victim to the currency manipulations of their own governments. Saudi Arabia paid Korean workers in dollars through the government of Korea. The workers' families were then paid in local currency so the government could maximize on the foreign exchange. And the Marcos government of the Philippines forced its citizens to remit a percentage of their earnings through Filipino banks paying the official exchange rate instead of sending money to their families in dollars that could then be exchanged on the black market.*

The economic downturn in Saudi Arabia has been devastating to the remittance economies of the Third World. With the end of the giant construction projects of the Third Development Plan, the number of TCNs would have declined regardless of economic conditions. But it was the recession in Saudi Arabia that forced the government to cut back on every activity possible. The ripple effect then wiped out the jobs of stone masons and hod carriers, clerks and drivers, as one small business after another went under. There are still thousands of Third World nationals working in Saudi Arabia, and with their governments heavily dependent on their earnings, no embassy presses for its workers' rights. Unlike the Western employees, whose embassies push for the release of their jailed nationals, the TCNs are forgotten men. One government official of the Philippines told me quite frankly that some Filipino workers he was charged with protecting would "fall through the cracks."

The conditions in which a TCN lives and works in Saudi Arabia depend on his employer. Although the government sets minimum standards in housing and food, maintains strict labor laws on working conditions, mandates compensation for workers or their families in case of injury and death, and provides a labor court known for its fairness to foreign workers, the system fails in protecting foreign workers. There is neither the commitment nor the numbers among the Saudis to enforce the rules. Employers are not responsible to anyone on a routine basis for the welfare of their employees. The only enforcement of the law comes after a worker appeals to the labor court. Handicapped by ignorance and language, most workers either are unaware of their rights or have no knowledge of how to press their claims. And the court is slow. It takes months for a case to be heard. A worker who has filed a claim often receives no salary from his embittered employer and is forbidden to work for anyone else without risking his work permit while the case waits to go before the court.

---

*In the end Marcos lost. The army ran the black market in currency. When Marcos cut out its profits, sectors of the army began to turn against him.

One of the functions the Saudi press served in the later years of the boom was to air workers' written grievances against their employers. Obviously a privilege reserved for the educated, these letters painted a true picture of the plight of many from the Third World. Chauffeurs, paid no more than $500 a month, were worked fourteen to sixteen hours a day with no overtime pay. An Indian doctor working in a private clinic was denied his annual leave. An engineer employed by a construction company had not been paid for six months. A group of Filipinos and Pakistanis had not received their salaries, bonuses, or vacation pay for periods of eight to sixteen months. The 5 percent social security tax was being deducted from the wages of another group but their employer had never enrolled them with the General Organization of Social Insurance.

During the construction explosion, most foreign workers were employed by large construction companies and lived in camps. Accommodations were spartan by anyone's standards. They lived two to a room hardly larger than a stall and ate in a common mess. The work day was ten to twelve hours. The work week was six days. Left with no recreation except a basketball hoop and perhaps a big metal tank in which to sit to cool off, the one day off a week was spent wandering the *souqs* or cutting each other's hair. The camps, though smaller, still exist. As depressing as they appear, there is a camaraderie in which men share the burden of separation from home. Nevertheless, a desperate depression arising from loneliness, grueling work, an alien culture, and no social outlets stalks even the most cheerful of personalities. Suicide is an occupational hazard, especially in the summer. What keeps most TCNs going is the knowledge that at the end of a two-year contract they can go home with more money than they ever believed possible. Passengers on flights going east out of Saudi Arabia are burdened with mammoth multispeaker tape players, television sets, bits of gold jewelry, boxes filled with presents for relatives, toys for their children, and even clusters of grapes carefully packed in woven plastic shopping bags. Men who came to Saudi Arabia in sandals go home in shoes, and their pockets are filled with enough money to handsomely support the family for the year. Some accumulate enough to buy land, moving them from the peasantry to the landed gentry.

The female domestics who arrived in numbers in the 1980s provided a whole new dimension to the foreign labor scene. The first thing that caught my eye when I walked into the airport on my return to the kingdom in 1982 was a group of Sri Lankan women in bright colored saris asleep on the floor in front of the immigration counters. During my first two years of residency in Saudi Arabia, they would not have been there. Previously barred from Saudi Arabia on the grounds that they were a social disruption, women are now briskly recruited by employment agencies to serve the well-to-do among the Saudis. Foreign women are now as much a part of Saudi Arabia as the foreign men. But in some ways, their lives are even harder than those of the men. Farmed out as domestics to individual homes, they are denied the companionship of the work camps. Even if the working conditions are reasonable, a woman can suffer by living in a state of total isolation. Usually speaking no Arabic and no English, she toils away in solitude for her master. At the end of each year, she goes home for her one month's annual leave and then returns to begin another year separated from anyone with whom she can even talk. Other women not only experience the loneliness but endure difficult working conditions. Some are put on strict food rations or live in closets. At the beck and call of their employers, they often labor twenty-four hours a day, seven days a week. Not knowingly behaving as unconscionable or cruel taskmasters, the Saudis, as a whole, have yet to learn the difference between service and slavery. In Saudi culture, hiring is commonly confused with possessing. Periodically, domestics are driven to desperate acts. A Sri Lankan woman, working for $117 a month for a middleclass Saudi family in Riyadh, jumped off the balcony of the apartment house where she lived because her employer never allowed her to leave the premises. But for others life can be quite different. The diminutive, usually young Oriental women serving as nannies for the wealthy can enjoy an extravagant lifestyle. Educated and hired because they can speak English, the nannies share in the life of the *hareem*. They attend the weddings, are clothed by their employer, receive lavish gifts, and sometimes travel abroad with the family.

Yet the threat that hangs over the head of the female servant of the wealthy as well as the servant of the middle class is that her duties can also include serving as a concubine to the men of the house. Even though Mohammed formulated exacting instructions for servants and slave girls, the new slavery in Saudi Arabia does not fall under the rules. Since they are outside of Arab culture and beyond the protection of a man, foreign servants are fair game for the sexual advances of men. The typical victim of sexual slavery is a non-Moslem woman of south Asia who suffers from a combination of a wife who makes her life miserable, a master who believes he has hired a mistress, and adult sons who think of the baby sitter as an adult plaything. Evoking a reaction somewhat like the stimulus of foreign travel, the foreign nanny can trigger the same chasm between Islam's exacting rules and the Moslem's internal system of ethics. Their excesses restrained by their presence on Saudi soil, some Saudi men nevertheless see the maid as a test of their sexual prowess. A domestic who becomes pregnant by her employer can be incorporated into the household as a wife or as an *umm walad,* or mother of a child. But most return home in disgrace, sometimes with a generous settlement and sometimes at their own expense.

The plight of foreign domestics is viewed as a serious social problem by Saudi Arabia's religious and political leaders. Yet the root of their concern is not so much the well-being of foreign domestics but rather the disruption in the social fiber caused by the introduction of foreigners into the family domain. Unlike the manual laborer who is confined to his work camp, the female domestic enters the sanctity of the home. Among the issues that arise out of this phenomenon is the ambivalent hostility of Saudi women toward their own domestics. While prizing the maid's services, the wife fears her servant may be taken into her husband's bed or, even worse, brought into the family as another wife. Ultimately, the issue of female domestics is another facet of the Saudis' paramount concern about their foreign work force. While dependent on their labor, the Saudis are tormented by the shadowy threat of social and political disorder they see arising from the presence of foreigners.

The government's official attitude toward the hordes of TCNs is control. *Amils,* or workers, are regulated through visas, work permits, permits to travel within the country, and jail. Periodically, the police and immigration officials stage roundups of workers illegally in the country. The Overstayers Bureau, charged with responsibility for the illegals, loads them on trucks and transports them to the nearest airport for deportation to their countries of origin. As many as four thousand can be held in jail at one time, awaiting deportation.

Any kind of labor unrest takes on the specter of political unrest. Periodic explosions of violence from frustrated men is a common theme in work camps, disorder that sends tremors of fear through the House of Saud. When Turkish workers rose up at Tabuk in 1977, the government immediately dispatched a C-130 Hercules from the Royal Saudi Air Force to fly them directly back to Turkey. As a security measure, Iraqi workers were removed from the King Khalid Military City when

King Khalid visited the site in 1978. I once lost a part-time house boy to a brawl between Pakistani and Thai waiters at the Atallah House hotel when all were deported in less than twenty-four hours. But brute force against the *amils* is a rarity for the House of Saud's own political reasons.

Saudi Arabia's ruling family is tied up in the dilemma of its fear of foreigners and its self-proclaimed obligation as the major defender of Islam. The government openly follows a policy of discrimination against immigrants in every walk of life. The "separate development" of the native and immigrant communities is a politically acceptable way, from the standpoint of domestic politics, to discourage foreigners from seeking permanent residence in Saudi Arabia. Typically the immigrants are looked down on by the Saudis, who generally mistrust and suspect other Arabs, are contemptuous of south Asians and regard Far Easterners as "infidels." This attitude of superiority, based upon the Saudis' view of themselves as Islam's chosen people, makes the Saudi national insensitive to the tide of feeling among non-nationals. Furthermore, the Saudi population continues to cling to the myth that the kingdom can be rid of its foreign workers whenever its chooses.

While escaping criticism of its treatment of non-Moslems, the House of Saud is increasingly suffering a stain on its piety in its treatment of non-Saudi Moslems. Palestinians want a home and a passport. A group of Burmese who fled to Saudi Arabia to escape religious persecution after the Second World War are demanding citizenship. Pakistanis, Syrians, Indonesians, Sudanese, and Eritreans want to be treated with a respect they believe is due all Moslems. It is this exclusiveness of the Saudis that opens the House of Saud to the charges of being "un-Islamic" by Muammar Qaddafi, the Ayatollah Khomeini, and other opponents of the regime.

. . . The very notion of using Muslims and Arabs as "foreign workers" who are denied the rights enjoyed by Saudi citizens, introduces a discrimination based on nationality that runs counter to basic Islamic and Arab principles proclaimed by the regime as the foundation of its legitimacy. This contradiction leaves the regime vulnerable to devastating criticism by potential domestic opposition and hostile outside powers, and the workers themselves receptive to agitation on those grounds.*

---

*Nadav Safran, *Saudi Arabia: The Ceaseless Quest for Security* (Cambridge, Mass.: Belknap Press of Harvard University Press, 1985), p. 224.

Although recognizing that its tough immigration policies are destructive to its image, the royal family values the reality of internal security over the illusion of its image in the Moslem world. And like the presence of Westerners, the large work force from the Third World is forcing profound changes in the society. In 1983 a joint meeting of the interior ministers of the GCC countries stated in an official paper that the economic development of the region had made substantial changes in the social life of the gulf peoples. "Some of these changes were positive but the rest were negative because of the presence of alien manpower which . . . carried a lot of customs and traditions which did not suit us."*

Some Saudis speak ominously of *waqt-al-takhreeb*, the period of destruction of the entire indigenous social system, which they claim came with the influx of petrodollars. Saudi society no doubt has been corrupted by the expatriates. When I came to Riyadh, it was possible to drive around the city with a box of cash on the back seat of the car and never worry about theft. By the time I left, some stores were checking parcels to prevent shoplifting. Cars and houses could no longer be left unlocked. Pickpockets prowled the aisles of supermarkets and the baggage claim areas of the airports. Somali women had staked out a section of Riyadh and turned it into a red light district. Customs officials became more concerned about searching for drugs than for alcohol. And the Ministry of the Interior was giving cash rewards for information on criminal acts. Most of the petty theft and drug trafficking is blamed on members of the Third World work force. (Westerners are more sophisticated and are guilty primarily of white collar crime.)

Throughout the oil boom, the Saudis talked endlessly about effectively reducing the number of expatriates in the kingdom but they were able to do little about it.

The hiring of expatriates on an increasing scale for government office duties . . . is the concern of the Civil Service Agency. A committee therefore has been set up . . . to consider the issue from all sides. There was a previous committee for the same purpose. . . . The present committee is an extension of the former, and is seeking comprehensive solutions to the problem.**

Arab News, December 1, 1983.
**Saudi Gazette*, November 3, 1979.

The economic recession has succeeded in reducing the number of TCNs in Saudi Arabia but their presence is still large and inescapable. The Westerners continue to manage. The Egyptians and Indians are civil servants. The Filipinos run the grocery stores, repair the cars, operate the telex machines. The Pakistanis, Sri Lankans, and Bangladeshis dig the ditches and sweep the floors. Oriental nannies, who cannot speak Arabic and are alien to the culture, raise the children. And a host of nationalities from the Arab world educate the next generation of Saudis.

As a result of the presence of so many foreigners, the urban areas of Saudi Arabia have become huge caldrons of Third World humanity and American fast-food chains. The number of foreigners increased so dramatically over the ten years of the oil boom that Riyadh, Jeddah, and al-Khobar became nondescript cities, stripped of their Saudi character by the economic planners and masses of foreigners. The Saudis themselves became lost in the crush. The Baatha *souqs*, usurped by the aggressive and cunning Yemenis, assumed the milieu of a totally different country. As I prowled the covered alleyways of the bazaar, the dwarfish Yemenis would badger, wheedle, and connive to make a sale. There was seldom a Saudi merchant in sight. It was as if the Saudis had abdicated their traditional bazaar skills to the foreigners in order to retreat behind the walls of their new houses to ponder the crumbling values of their society.

I remember being in Baatha one Friday afternoon, pushing through the crowds of Pakistanis, Afghanis, Bangladeshis, Koreans, and Sri Lankans and suddenly wondering what would happen if even a portion of these poor and tired men had guns. It was far from an original thought. The Saudis do feel threatened by the TCNs. Groups of various nationalities are present in the kingdom in such large numbers that in rare unguarded moments Saudis of influence voice fears that they are a potentially hostile army. Yet the more realistic threat of the influx of Third World nationals to Saudi society is that they will never go home. For many, life in Saudi Arabia, no matter how strained, offers more than the ravaged economies of their overpopulated countries.

Saudi Arabia is not a melting pot. Even after ten years of economic boom times that brought in hordes of foreigners, the Saudis remain a rigidly insular people, shutting out everyone except their own kinship group. If by the second generation of their residency in Saudi Arabia these foreigners, especially the Moslems, are not integrated into the social and political structure, they may become a source of serious political opposition. This is a threat not only to the House of Saud but to any Saudi government that discriminates against non-Saudis. To believe that the present distinction between Saudis and non-Saudis will not survive past the current regime is to fail to understand the nature of the Saudis themselves.

As contemptuous and distrustful as the Saudis are of the third country nationals, it is still the Westerners whom the Saudis most resent and fear. Western xenophobia has always existed in Saudi Arabia, although during much of the boom it was masked by a strong tradition of politeness and hospitality. But as the economic downturn accelerated, the hostilities began to emerge. Invitations to Saudi homes, which poured in when I first went to Saudi Arabia, all but disappeared except from very Westernized Saudis. Isolated incidents of vandalism against Westerners occurred. At the Oleya Villas, a Western compound occupied by King Faisal hospital employees, vandals smashed the hoods and trunks of cars parked on the street and then scaled the wall to damage the rest of the cars parked inside. When the Saudi soccer team defeated Korea and qualified for the 1984 Olympic Games, the victory parade contained ugly incidents of attacks on Westerners watching the festivities. As the economic outlook worsened, the more strained the atmosphere became. The Saudis' natural reserve took on subtle tones of hostility. Behind their masks of civility, Saudi suspicions about the Westerners' motives and resentment of their lifestyle rose. The Saudis' ability to disguise their feelings of inferiority in the presence of Western skills was wiped away by doubts about their financial future. Even though the salaries of the Westerners were sliding along with those of the Saudis, silent resentment of the Western presence was as strong as it had been when Saudi Arabia was first awash in money. In saying my good-bys to Saudi Arabia, I went to Jeddah's Old Town, the kingdom's historic window on the West. I walked through the dim, twisting streets too narrow for a car, enjoying the traditional architecture distinguished by closed wooden balconies suspended above the street, where the women could gather to watch the scenes below. Shortly I became aware that my presence was not welcome. A motor bike brushed by me as if deliberately trying to hit me. Boys threw orange peels before dashing into an even darker alleyway. Turning onto another street, I was confronted by a collection of several young men who shouted at me in perfect English, "Go back where you came from."

It was as if the words of Abdul Aziz uttered on the horizon of the oil rush were ringing back through the decades. "My kingdom will survive only insofar as it remains a country difficult of access, where the foreigner will have no other aim, with his task fulfilled, but to get out." *

---

*Quoted in David Holden and Richard Johns, *The House of Saud* (London: Holt, Rinehart and Winston, 1981), p. 406.

18

Stalled Between Seasons

IT WAS THE SUMMER of 1984 and it was time to go home. In a fitting conclusion to my journalistic career in Saudi Arabia, I spent my last two weeks in the kingdom ducking the authorities. For months Saudi Arabia had been in the throes of a major political upheaval involving the minister of Health and the director of the King Faisal Specialist Hospital. With the secret police prowling the premises, Dan was approached one day and asked about the rumor that his wife was writing a book on Saudi Arabia. Quickly reeling off my cover story about a textbook, Dan seemed to satisfy the inquirer. Unable to call me on the hospital's tapped telephones, he dashed home to sound the alarm.

Since Christmas I had been sending my most incriminating notes out of the kingdom with special friends who mailed them on from New York. What was left was composed largely of newspaper clippings, government publications, and the all-important computer disks containing my research. While I packed my worn flight bags to go into hiding one more time, Dan returned to the hospital to apply for an exit visa for Colin. Afraid of arousing suspicions by abruptly leaving Saudi Arabia earlier than scheduled, I turned my fifteen-year-old son into an international courier. The night he left for home, I bundled my remaining material into school notebooks and put them in Colin's cavernous backpack. At the very bottom, I laid two tough plastic cases containing the computer disks on which two years of research were recorded. As it was the end of the school year, many expatriate children were leaving Saudi Arabia, often traveling alone. The chances of Colin's being stopped were minimal. Still, my stomach was in knots as I stood on a balcony at the airport and watched him go through immigration and security. When his flight was called, he ran his arms through the straps on the backpack, turned, and with a big grin on his face waved good-by. The next morning, knowing he was safely in London, I had nothing to do but wait until my departure date.

I spent much of that time walking, as I had done when I first arrived in Saudi Arabia. In 1978 the excitement of the oil boom and my fascination with the duality of twentieth-century technology in a feudal society had drawn me into twisting, narrow streets. In 1984 I walked on wide sidewalks that ran along multilane roads. As I walked, I took in the changes wrought by the oil boom. The hospital was no longer on the edge of the desert. Large walled-in villas stretched out from it in every direction except into King Faisal's garden which still retained its tranquility. Most of his former date grove was occupied by the new Palm Villas where I now lived. A new wing was being added to the hospital and a grand new entrance opened onto a six-lane divided thoroughfare. The quiet that used to fall with the night was gone as cars and trucks raced by under the amber glow of the arching incandescent lights lining the streets. The only thing that still stood undisturbed was the ruins of the villa on the corner, a quiet reminder of Faisal's assassination and the fate of those who strike against the House of Saud.

On Oleya Road, the City Supermarket, the queen of the markets in 1978, struggled to compete with the Greenhouse, Panda, Safeway, and A&P. The fruit and vegetable stands with their flats of broken eggs were still in business, but the traffic was so fast and heavy that it was no longer safe to cross the street to browse among their produce. The office buildings that had gone up in the early eighties were now mostly empty, as contracting firms, those business creatures so unique to the boom times in Saudi Arabia, quietly died. In the new concrete-block Dirrah *souqs,* the fabric shops were deserted. Except for those in Baatha, the gold shops now had more Western customers than Saudi. Even the vegetable *souqs* beyond the main mosque had lost their climate of frenzied activity. The area next to the Bedouin women's *souq* had been turned into a secondhand market where lower-class Saudis swapped used clothing and dented household goods.

I found leaving Saudi Arabia for what I felt would be the last time less difficult than it had been in 1980. I shared the general realization that for most of the Westerners the Saudi experience was over. More and more Saudis were moving into jobs formerly held by Westerners. The business opportunities were largely gone and companies were pulling their people out of the kingdom. But even more, there was somehow the sense that it was the proper time to end the large-scale Western involvement in Saudi Arabia. The Westerners had done what they could best do for the Saudis — build a physical infrastructure and frame the organizational models for a modern country. It was time for the Saudis to take control.

The Westerners had done miraculous things for Saudi Arabia. We had also done great harm. We too often expected the Saudis to live up to our expectations rather than their own. We expected them to change too fast. We imposed our own culture, largely in the material sense, on a culture of great pride steeped in long tradition. We were not always sensitive enough to the forces tearing at Saudi Arabia, as a people isolated for centuries was bombarded with such a variety of alien ideas. Too many among us cheated them for no other reason than naked greed. And too few among us ever extended the Saudis the proper respect for what they were — a fervently religious people, protective of their own culture, and deeply frightened of foreigners.

Dan and I ate our last meal in Saudi Arabia with our dear friend Phil Weaver. In an apartment identical to the one in which we had stepped that first night over six years ago, we reminisced about how we had arrived in the kingdom within months of each other and about the years in between. Together we had struggled with Arabic, shopped the *souqs*, and spent wonderful hours in the desert. Phil, like so many of our other long-time friends, was also planning to leave within a few months. Dinner ended. It was time to leave for the airport. I looked out one more time on Phil's riotous bougainvillea, which had mysteriously survived over all those years without ever being watered. Then I turned and walked toward the front door, past the hanging rug we had found in the *hajj* camp. With the luggage loaded, I climbed into Phil's GM Jimmy for my last ride through the gate of Medical City Village.

The drive to the airport was poignant. Partly this was because I knew that once this book was published I would never be allowed to return to Saudi Arabia. And partly it was because I was reflecting over an era. I remembered that first drive into Riyadh from the airport — the torn up road, the incessant activity of building, the feeling of confidence and promise. That night, at the end of the boom, we glided along on a four-lane highway interspersed with overpasses, along clusters of new houses, past strip shopping centers with flashing signs beckoning customers to buy the products of the West. The mud walls of the combination shops and houses that stood when I first arrived were gone, swept away by the hurricane of change. Gone also was that feeling of confidence in the future. As we passed by a residential neighborhood, there was the same quiet that I so acutely felt the night I arrived in Riyadh. But in 1978, the Saudis slept blissfully as their foreign workers built the new Saudi Arabia; after this night, they would awake to an uncertain world.

By outward appearances Saudi Arabia had achieved an authentic miracle in the desert in ten years. But would the miracle last? There was too much to manage and too little money, at least in the short run, and I wondered how much of the new Saudi Arabia would be reclaimed by the ruthless desert. No one who spent the boom decade in Saudi Arabia can escape feeling that somehow he was a small part of a revolution that carried the kingdom from the past to the present. Having taken part in that revolution, I cared what was to come.

I was jerked out of my reverie when the car slowed under the graceful arches of the airport terminal. I was to leave Saudi Arabia by way of the pomp and grandeur of the new King Khalid International Airport. Cars lined up at the curb in an orderly fashion, while Filipino porters in iridescent orange coveralls loaded bags onto bright chrome luggage carts. Somehow this all seemed an anticlimax to my whole experience in Saudi Arabia. That feeling changed when I entered the terminal. It was bedlam. Expecting that night to see the new moon signaling the end of Ramadan and the beginning of the Eid al-Fitr holidays, Saudis, Egyptians, Sudanese, Pakistanis, Lebanese, and a few Asians and Westerners were all fighting their way to the crowded ticket counters dragging huge suitcases. There was mayhem among the ticket agents, who screamed at passengers screaming at them. After being shoved around in the swarm around the ticket counter for forty-five minutes, we succeeded in checking our bags and securing a boarding pass. As the immigration officer canceled that last exit visa in my passport, I glanced up and smiled. At the entrance to the departure gates a black-veiled Bedouin squatted next to her husband stretched out asleep on the floor. It seemed in some ways that all that had changed since I first entered the kingdom was that I was walking out of Saudi Arabia, holding my head high, in a knee-length skirt.

After ten years of breakneck development, Saudi Arabia is hovering in an uncertain twilight. Confronting a multitude of threats — declining oil revenues, sagging confidence, a bureaucracy and infrastructure both beset by decay — the exaggerated promises of the oil boom are rapidly fading away. Behind the walls of the palatial homes of the nonroyal rich and in the apartments of the new middle class, a disquiet lurks that is alien to the political experience of the House of Saud. Facing the rising politicization of the middle class and dissatisfaction among much of the rest of the population, the House of Saud is mired in its own internal struggles and burdened with a political system incapable of addressing the postboom era. Complex questions loom over the future of Abdul Aziz's dynasty, now that it is no longer master of a bottomless pot of gold. The first is how to equably divide the kingdom's finite economic resources among a people whose expectations were fueled by ten years of unbelievable wealth. The second and more profound question is how a society turned upside-down by wealth and the invasion of foreigners is to be governed as it struggles to define itself. How well the al-Sauds accommodate to the new political and economic environment in which they find themselves will determine in what form the House of Saud will survive or if it will survive at all.

In its short history, the House of Saud has endured the early threats of intervention by European powers, two revolts of fanatical Moslems, drought, poverty, and the radical economic transformation of the kingdom in the decade following the 1973 oil embargo. The royal family has succeeded in ruling a fractious, contentious people divided by family and tribe largely by personally identifying the monarchy with the religious and egalitarian values of the culture.

The House of Saud successfully contained liberal political dissent during the 1960s, and the golden days of the 1970s were to a great extent free of overt political opposition. With the exception of the dramatic Mecca uprising, the pockets of dissent that did exist were either weak and unorganized or were placated by government policy and revenues. Opposition groups tended to be specific and controlled. There were the Shiites, with their deep-seated hostility to their status as second-class citizens. The grumbling Hijazis still harbored animosities about the imposition of Wahhabi rule over the more freewheeling Western coastal areas. And the non-Shiites of the Eastern province were resentful at being shortchanged on developmental money and political appointments. Otherwise, the Saudis as a whole were so caught up in the consumer society that political conflict was virtually absent except for the ever-present religious question, kept under control largely by religious leaders beholden to the House of Saud.

During the oil boom, the monarchy benefited from rulers who were respected as individuals and, therefore, as leaders of the Wahhabi state. Exemplifying the image of the righteous *sheikh,* both Faisal and Khalid provided generously for their people. In much the same style in which Abdul Aziz fed anyone who came to his tent, the kings showered their subjects with money, and political participation stayed in the context of the petitioner appearing before the king at his *majlis.* While personifying traditional values that played to the conservative Saudi temperament, Faisal and Khalid at the same time were casting Saudi Arabia's whole economic and bureaucratic system in the mold of the West. Operating like an eastern Tammany Hall, the al-Sauds kept the religious leaders happy by enforcing religious law and providing financial support to the religious establishment. The small farmers and the Bedouins were subsidized and left alone. Middle-class merchants and upper-class families made hefty sums of money in a wide range of commercial activities. Young Saudis, many with no economic or political ties to the existing power structure, were pulled out of the cities and villages and sent West to study. In an era of galloping change, the quiescence of the Saudis' political behavior was the subject of endless speculation. Was it fear of reprisal? Were the Saudis by their nature apolitical? Or did the policies of the al-Sauds have to be considered highly successful? In retrospect, it appears all of these were factors. But the missing element in the continued success of the House of Saud's political formula was the realization of how much the policies of development were changing the society and, therefore, the balance of forces by which Saudi Arabia was ruled.

When King Khalid died in the summer of 1982, Fahd ascended the throne among predictions that Saudi Arabia's march toward modernization would advance at an even more rapid pace. Because Fahd in essence ran the government for the ailing Khalid and was known to be the foremost proponent of modernization, his reign was seen as marking Saudi Arabia's move to its postdevelopment phase. After Khalid's benign tenure, it was assumed Fahd would be a strong king. Instead, Fahd's reign is crippled both by the mountain of problems that have descended on him and by his own personal image.

Like every king in the lineage of the House of Saud, Fahd's personality and style influence the strength of the family and, therefore, its ability to rule. Because the king is the embodiment of the old tribal *sheikh,* who was chosen by his people for his piety, generosity, leadership, and courage, the image of the ruler is paramount to how well he can rule. Fahd, who is all but fatally tarnished by his early reputation as a high-rolling playboy, meets few of the criteria of a successful *sheikh*. An aura of corruption hangs around the king and his sons. He is identified not with the tribes and religious leaders but with the technocrats who are outside of the al-Sauds' traditional power base. His aloof personal style is vastly different from that of his predecessors. But most of all, Fahd is seen by his subjects as a high-living captive of the West. Although Fahd's public decorum in Riyadh is conservative, the people are contemptuous of him. They deride him as a hypocrite, a rogue masquerading as a pious Moslem. And because he is frequently absent from the kingdom, the population is quick to believe that the king is a heavy drinker and fond of foreign women.

While practicing a certain level of discretion, Fahd is nevertheless more public about the lavishness of his lifestyle than any king since the discredited Saud. While Fahd publicly claims that the royal family is a family of simple tastes and boasts of the pride he takes in being a "servant of God," he builds one elaborate palace after another. His palace on Spain's Costa del Sol has made Marbella an international playground. He has another palace in Geneva. He plays country squire on an elaborate farm outside Riyadh and has yet other palaces in Jeddah and Taif. Several years ago he built a house in Riyadh that is a near replica of the White House in Washington, D.C.* And now an official palace has been constructed between Riyadh and Diriyah, the original capital of the al-Sauds. In a disturbing throwback to the time when King Saud lived behind the walls of his own royal city within Riyadh, the new structure is actually a small city enclosed by high, thick, and fortified walls that run for several miles.

Unlike all the previous kings, who identified Riyadh as the heart of the kingdom, Fahd is restive in the capital. To escape the prying eyes of the religious authorities who place strict demands on his decorum, the king maintains a yacht the size of a luxury liner off the coast of Jeddah. Floating in the steamy waters just beyond the harbor, the yacht allows Fahd to stay in the country and, at the same time, live as he wishes. When the king escapes the kingdom, he flies in his private 747-SP, outfitted with two posh sitting rooms and a master bedroom

---

*Fahd never moved into this palace, which was begun when he was crown prince. The political repercussions of the Saudi king imitating the American president were too politically risky.

decorated in pink and staffed with a cabin crew of eight comely women, mostly Western.

Fahd's elaborate lifestyle elicits more comment from Saudis than any other facet of his rule. Much of the criticism is directed not just at the king but at his sons, who are notorious for the number of government contracts they win and the margin of profit involved. There has always been some corruption in the royal family, which is related to the mores of the patriarchal rule established by Abdul Aziz. Before Faisal's reign, the state was seen as the property of the ruler and little differentiation was made between public funds and the king's private purse.

> But the prince, in turn, was perceived as the father of his people, and his benevolence was based on the fairness with which he distributed material and abstract goods among his subjects. The *sheikh* of the tribe was not much richer than his men and his life-style was not that different from theirs. Avaricious rulers were held in contempt and often lost their legitimacy and their rule.*

Fahd seems to invite reproach through his family's extensive business interests and his various forms of self-indulgence. Unlike the revered Faisal and to some extent the kindly Khalid, Fahd and his sons appear shabby.

Yet the worst of Fahd's image problems may be his inability to project himself as a man with the soul of a Bedouin. In contrast to Khalid, who was happiest among the Bedouins, Fahd prefers the city. When he does venture into the desert to meet his subjects, he moves in a procession of Mercedes eighteen-wheel trucks, which includes his private operating room and clinic. After three years as king, Fahd in the spring of 1985 uncharacteristically spent weeks in the desert with the Bedouins. It was as if he had suddenly recognized that he had lost touch with the core of the al-Sauds' support and was trying to reestablish the House of Saud's traditional roots. As the mastermind behind Saudi Arabia's massive modernization effort, Fahd may have moved too far from the average Saudi's perception of his king to restore the aura binding ruler and ruled. For Fahd has been as much corrupted by

---

*A. Reza S. Islami and Rostam Mehraban Kavoussi, *The Political Economy of Saudi Arabia* (Seattle: University of Washington Press, 1984), p. 78.

the oil boom as many of his subjects. While Abdul Aziz rode with his Bedouin army on a saddle made of rough wood covered with the skins of Nejdi sheep, Fahd rides forth to meet his people on a saddle of fine leather custom crafted by Louis Vuitton.

One of the major facet's of Fahd's lack of political authority is that the political constituency with which he is identified is not part of the power configuration with which the House of Saud rules. Fahd's reputation was built through the middle class, a creation of the oil boom. Faisal drew on his image of piety. King Khalid identified closely with the Bedouins. Abdullah, the current crown prince, is allied with the National Guard and the traditionalists in the country. Fahd's only identity has been with the technocrats, a nebulous group in terms of the power configuration, and the expanding middle class. Yet Fahd's partnership with the middle class has neither been lengthy nor intimate. While Fahd was championing the middle class during his tenure as crown prince, he was operating in a climate of almost unlimited wealth, in which the king's generosity to all segments of the society involved few choices. Fahd simply devised the mechanics for spreading enormous amounts of money among a small population. As long as the interests of the middle class did not clash with the prerogatives of the royal family, Fahd was free to push for the expanded political input of nonroyal family members, such as Hisham Nazer and Ghazi Algosaibi. But by the time Fahd became king, the economic slowdown was beginning to cause a clash between the interests of the royal family and those of the middle class. Caught between Saudi Arabia's foreign and economic problems and the quarreling between the various factions of the royal family and the population, Fahd, rather than ruling as a strong king, is immobilized.

Few expect Fahd to enjoy a long reign. His health is imperiled by obesity and the al-Saud family history of heart disease. Always a tall man of wide girth, Fahd is now so fat that he moves in a wheelchair if he is required to walk much farther than a few steps. Just as Fahd succeeded Khalid after only seven years, it is probable the House of Saud will once again need to choose a new king following a relatively short reign. And once again the royal family and the religious leaders will undertake the precarious and imprecise process of selecting a man to head the House of Saud.

The uprising at Mecca, the Islamic resurgence triggered by the Iranian revolution, and the blighted hopes of rapid economic development have all combined to strengthen the power of the traditionalists, led by Crown Prince Abdullah. No longer do the progressives among the senior princes rule almost alone. And the old political theory of Fahd and the Sudairi Seven rolling over Abdullah and the conservatives has collapsed.

Abdullah, tall and thin, with a small beard extending from his chin, looks like a king. Except for his speech impediment, he commands the presence of the tribal *sheikh*. Though Fahd is more competent to deal with the outside world, Abdullah has brimmed with self-confidence ever since the Mecca uprising resurrected the fortunes of the traditionalists in the House of Saud. Abdullah's picture is now spread across newspapers and public buildings, unlike during the boom years, when he was largely ignored. As if orchestrating them himself, conditions have seemed to conspire to ensure that Abdullah's visibility remains high. His long-time opposition to rapid modernization has been vindicated by the forced reduction in development projects dictated by the economic recession. The rise of Islamic political groups on Saudi Arabia's borders has strengthened Abdullah's fundamentalist constituency to the detriment of the progressives. But it is in foreign policy that Abdullah's rising stature has been the most noticeable. Often condemned by Westerners as being anti-West, Abdullah is an ultranationalist who believes the kingdom should shun alignment with either of the superpowers. Even at the pinnacle of the Saudi-American alliance, it was Abdullah who was outspoken in his opposition to the kingdom's dependence on the West for its defense. As the American alliance has come increasingly into question and the anti-West campaign of Iran more strident, Abdullah has been sent in search of new allies for the vulnerable Saudis.

Part of the reason for Abdullah's diplomatic activity is the nature of his tribal connections. Abdullah's mother belonged to an important family of the Shammar tribe, whose tribal lands and relationships extend into both Syria and Iraq. Therefore, Fahd has wisely used Abdullah as a major emissary to Syria ever since he became king. With ties to Syrian president Hafiz Assad, Abdullah is regularly sent to Damascus to buy Syria's intervention with Iran as well as the Saudis' various leftist enemies. Nevertheless, the old animosities and political rivalries between the progressive Fahd and the traditional Abdullah still live. Abdullah, confident in his own power base, refuses to pay court to Fahd. He voices clear opposition to those policies of the king that dilute the power of the family or the traditionalists. And to Fahd's displeasure, he continues to command the National Guard, a post Fahd believes Abdullah should have resigned when he became crown prince. Yet neither the Sudairis nor Abdullah can unseat the other without destroying the all-important balance of power in the royal family and within the military.

Abdullah in all probability will become king in his turn, upsetting the predictions during Khalid's reign that the Sudairis would never tolerate him on the throne. But Abdullah, approaching his mid-sixties and having suffered a heart attack, also might not rule long. Fahd and Abdullah as individuals are much less important than the power bloc each represents. The House of Saud without either of the two men will still be racked by the philosophical division between the progressives and the traditionalists and the power rivalries between the competing factions within the family. And since each group has a vested interest in control of its own military power, it will be with Abdullah's death that the real struggle for power within the royal family will ensue. For at that point, perilous decisions will have to be made about control of the National Guard and the Ministry of Defense and Aviation (MODA).

Unless the progressive branch of the family can force him to strike a bargain at the time of his ascension, it is assumed that Abdullah as king will retain control of the National Guard, either himself or through a commander he appoints. With Sultan due to succeed Abdullah as king, authority over both the Ministry of Defense and Aviation and the National Guard comes up for grabs at Abdullah's death. The natural order of promotion could move Prince Naif, now minister of the Interior, to the National Guard, opening up the Ministry of the Interior to his deputy, Ahmed ibn Abdul Aziz, a Sudairi. The Ministry of Defense and Aviation, never in the traditionalists' power constellation, would go to a progressive. That would put the Sudairis or their allies in all of the power points: the National Guard, the Ministry of the Interior, and MODA, a situation intolerable to the Abdullah faction. On the other hand, if control of the guard went to Abdullah's son at the time Abdullah became king, the long-delayed power shift to the second generation of Abdul Aziz's descendants would be set in motion, challenging the orderly succession of Sultan.

For the House of Saud to avoid a period of destructive infighting, some decision about the distribution of military power must be made at the time Abdullah becomes king. In this compromise, the succession of Sultan will also have to be determined, for Sultan will have problems laying claim to the kingship. First, Sultan as defense minister is a bitter foe of the Abdullah faction. And second, Sultan is the most pro-Western of all the senior princes. His sons are Western educated. One of his sons, Bandar, is ambassador to the United States. Sultan himself is the most active and vocal member of the family in support of the American alliance. And like Fahd, he has essentially no roots in Saudi Arabia's political system outside of the nontraditionalist military.

If Sultan cannot put together a strong enough coalition in the family to become king, the House of Saud will likely be reduced to intrafamily squabbling while it searches for a leader acceptable to all. Yet the family has an instinct for survival and an enormous pool of personalities from which to draw for a ruler. The al-Sauds range from traditionalists in the mold of Abdullah to liberals like Talal, one of the "free princes" who challenged Faisal. Or there is the family mediator, Prince Salman, governor of Riyadh, who might emerge as a compromise candidate. Or an alignment of the grandsons of Abdul Aziz, known as the "party of the nephews," could compete for the throne. The most likely candidate among the nephews is Saud al-Faisal, son of King Faisal and long-time foreign minister. The tall, distinguished Saud al-Faisal, who was educated at Princeton and would be assumed to be pro-Western, is nevertheless more closely associated with Abdullah's policies than those of the Sudairis. A nationalist who eloquently argues the case for a nonaligned foreign policy, he is also perhaps the most condescending of any of the leading members of the royal family about the Sudairis' opulent lifestyle. Unlike so many of their relatives, Saud al-Faisal and his brothers live sedately in sensible houses near their father's palace, where no hint of scandal has yet touched them. The al-Faisals, who all look remarkably like their father, hold a series of posts in the provinces and the central government. Riding on their father's reputation among the Saudis who staff the military, the secret police, and even the National Guard, the al-Faisals could be a formidable power bloc if they so chose. But in any of these scenarios, a deviation from the precarious balance of forces within the royal family threatens to bring the House of Saud tumbling down.

The royal family realizes it is in trouble. Even during Khalid's reign, the longevity and the legitimacy of the House of Saud was strengthened by its publicly restoring to the dynasty the deposed Saud ibn

Abdul Aziz, purged from the history of Saudi Arabia by King Faisal. Government publications listing the kings of the House of Saud had omitted King Saud as if he had never existed. Then Khalid resurrected him. First Saud's picture began to appear in public buildings, placed in proper order between the pictures of Abdul Aziz and Faisal. Various government buildings and institutions began to carry Saud's name, the grandest being the King Saud University outside Riyadh. But it is not just Saud who is being promoted. When Fahd appears around the kingdom, people in the villages are turned out for the television cameras, waving palm fronds along his route. Considering the depth of opposition, these are ridiculous attempts to treat cosmetically the political problems that engulf the House of Saud at every level of the population.

The ten years of the oil boom (1974–84) were a period in which educational levels soared, when a principally agricultural and nomadic population became rapidly urbanized, when tribal and regional divisions were muted by a sense of nationalism, and when traditional values running the gamut from religion to the work ethic came under attack. At the same time, a people who had always prided themselves on their independence and freedom from authority became tied to an economic system dependent on the distribution of oil revenues by the central government.

The state, the private monopoly of the House of Saud, clove unto itself all economic and political power and ruled by buying off interest groups that were holdovers from a fragmented tribal society. The House of Saud, so successful in tying the people to the person of the ruler, allowed no political philosophies or abstractions to develop, no impersonal rules and procedures. Its efforts to create new structures to deal with the new Saudi Arabia were aimed at neutralizing potential threats to its authority rather than mobilizing support for a modernizing nation. Consequently, responsibility for the economic downturn and its resulting impact on personal purchasing power is not, in the Saudi mind, attributable to history, circumstances, or simple luck. Having failed to develop any institutional supports, the House of Saud is held directly responsible for the state of the economy and the inequities in the distribution of wealth and power. To it falls the blame for policies that created artificial and unjust differences in a society that believes itself to be basically egalitarian. "Given the royal family has depended on a diffuse sense of legitimacy rather than a concentrated base of support, such as a party or a bureaucracy, its loss of legitimacy is even more destabilizing than it would be in other regimes that have solid organized support.'' * At the end of the boom era, the economic and political policies of the House of Saud are bankrupt. The population is dissatisfied and restive. And in Arabian society, when there is misery, rebellion is imminent.

Unlike the political unrest during the oil boom, which was isolated and contained, there is now either outright or measured opposition to the royal family in almost every segment of society. Some merchant princes who have suffered economically in the recession have become part of the political opposition. The middle-class entrepreneurs who feasted on the crumbs of the economically powerful have been left with trading establishments bereft of trade and in search of new economic allies. The technocrats and the urbanized element of the military are demanding political power. The tribal army and the traditionalists chafe under the Western-tainted policies of the House of Saud. There are certain lingering regional groups and isolated leftist groups who have always opposed the al-Sauds. And there are the Shiites. Each configuration has its own dissatisfactions with the government.

Outside the traditionalists, the most explosive group is the middle class, supported by elements of the regular armed forces. The largest element in the new middle class, and its backbone, is the educated technocrats. Although some questioned oil policy and the accelerated rate of development during the oil boom, all technocrats accepted the basic philosophy of modernization. Typically holding Ph.D.s from UCLA, they were men who went West early in the oil boom and returned to take up positions in the upper levels of the bureaucracy. For the most part, they were sons of urban merchants or other families who were outside the tribal power structure. Created by the oil boom, the technocrats had nothing to gain from the traditional order. In the political equation, they came to occupy an intermediate position between the wealthy entrepreneurs and the religious fundamentalists. As the oil boom rolled on, the technocrats who were no longer satisfied with being impotent cogs in the bureaucracy came to demand some political power as the price for their expertise in managing the bureaucracy. Believing they would be pulled into the process of decision-making by their mentor, the crown prince, they waited for Fahd to become king.

---

*Islami and Kavoussi, *The Political Economy of Saudi Arabia*, p. 78.

Yet when Fahd did become king, the political equation remained the same and the position of the technocrats even declined. In contrast to the 1970s, students returning home from foreign schools in the 1980s found that they did not rocket into high-level government jobs as their older brothers had. With government expansion limited to jobs with no other purpose than creating employment; the most recent wave of the educated elite has been wedged into mid-level positions with little hope of advancement. Stagnating economically and politically, the middle class's lingering illusions that the House of Saud was willing to share power were shattered in 1984 when Ghazi Algosaibi, minister of Health and leader of the technocrats, fell from power.

The political upheaval at the King Faisal hospital at the time I left Saudi Arabia was, on the surface, a struggle for control of the hospital. But in all its dimensions it represented a wide-ranging power struggle between the royal family and the new middle class. The antagonists were Nizar Fetieh, director of the hospital and guardian of the medical privileges and secrets of the royal family. On the other side was the popular Ghazi Algosaibi, minister of Health.

Through the 1970s and into the eighties, Algosaibi was a model and a mentor for the generation of young bureaucrats that emerged as a result of Saudi Arabia's development policies. The Western-educated Algosaibi was regarded as the most effective of the technocrat ministers. A leading intellectual and social commentator, he is considered among the best Arab poets writing today. Through his writing in both Arabic and English, he has publicly challenged such hallowed topics as the Saudi prohibition of women drivers and Henry Kissinger's basic understanding of the Middle East. But it is in his poems that he most effectively pricks the sacred cows.

Nurtured by Fahd, Algosaibi rose through the ranks of the Saudi bureaucracy to become minister of Industry and Electricity in 1975. He won the admiration of Saudis and Westerners alike by untangling the hodgepodge of electrical systems and launching Saudi Arabia's vast industrial projects. He sat on the Council of Ministers, where insiders say he was the most outspoken of the nonroyal members. A superb administrator, Algosaibi also had the reputation of being among the most incorruptible men in Saudi Arabia. Perhaps for this reason, he was moved to the Ministry of Health in 1982. In the postboom era, the Ministry of Health was potentially one of the most expensive government agencies, with a 1983–84 budget of $6 billion, and by common agreement one of the most poorly managed.

Algosaibi's attempt to build a comprehensive health care system depended on bringing both the military and National Guard hospitals, controlled by Crown Prince Abdullah and Defense and Aviation Minister Prince Sultan, as well as the King Faisal Specialist Hospital, under the Ministry of Health.

Seeking to gain control over the military hospitals, Algosaibi claimed that he could operate the hospitals of MODA and the National Guard hospitals for much less than their current budgets. The implication was that the extra costs were going into the pockets of Sultan and Abdullah. He bluntly challenged Sultan on the propriety of a Spanish defense contract that the Ministry of Defense and Aviation had awarded without a public bid. And for extra measure, he insulted Abdullah's close friend the deputy commander of the National Guard on the quality of his poetry. All of this was behind the scenes. Public was the row with Fetieh, director of the King Faisal Specialist Hospital.

Fetieh, a cardiologist of mixed Saudi and Syrian ancestry, had built an empire by taking care of the politically troubling drug and alcohol cases in the royal family and by catering to the whims of the daughters, wives, and derelict sons of the mighty. In November 1983 Fetieh became the subject of a scandal involving allegations of administrative malfeasance and a string of Western mistresses. Algosaibi seized the moment to force Fetieh out and win control of the hospital. In response, Fetieh mobilized his royal patrons against the health minister.

King Fahd's personal intervention in the dispute was drawn in early by Algosaibi. The relationship between Algosaibi and the king approached that of a father and son. It was Fahd who had shepherded the brilliant Algosaibi from the directorate of the railways into the Council of Ministers, where he reigned as the czar of the Third Development Plan's industrialization projects. By pitting the director of a hospital and his royal allies against the minister of Health and the middle class, the King Faisal hospital controversy brought into focus the whole question of whether or not Saudi Arabia would be able to move beyond its status as the personal fiefdom of the House of Saud or whether the kingdom would continue to be controlled by the whims of the royal family and its cronies. Algosaibi became the test of the House of Saud's commitment to the expansion of some political power to the middle class.

Regardless of the king's affection for Algosaibi, irresistible pressures from the royal family were building for his dismissal. The senior princes wanted him out because he had trod on their turf; Fetieh's supporters blamed him for their doctor's problems. In March 1984, five months into the battle for power, Algosaibi published in the newspaper *Al-Jazirah* what will probably go down as his most famous poem. It was written in the style of a famous epistle to an Egyptian ruler by al-Mutanabbi, the tenth-century laureate of Iraq, in which al-Mutanabbi laments his disappointment in the ruler Ikhshidid Kafur. His poem was a plea to be released from his duties before he was further victimized by slander and backbiting from those around the king. Algosaibi's poem was written in the same vein and caused a storm of political discussion. Although Algosaibi never stated that it was addressed to Fahd, its content left little doubt.

> Why should I go on singing while there are a
> thousand slanderers and backbiters going
> between you and me?
> My voice is lost and you do not feel its echo
> and I am used to seeing you enchanted when I
> sing.
> Now, I barely see you between the crowds and I
> do not see that smile which used to grace your
> features.
> Your eyes gaze at me and then turn away quickly
> just like a stranger who is frightened and
> cautious.
> There are thousands of slanderers between you
> and me.
> They lie, you hear them and believe their
> falsehoods.
> They deluded you and you liked their
> deceitfulness, but you used to abhor the
> artificial perfume.
> . . . .
> Tell the slanderers that I am coming with white
> banner held high so that they may walk and run
> in my earth.*

Within days, Algosaibi was fired. The dismissal, which was announced on the front pages of the newspapers, caused consternation among segments of the middle class. Evidently the king was concerned

---

Al-Jazirah, March 5, 1984.

enough about the outcry that he subsequently appointed Algosaibi to the politically safe but trivial job as ambassador to the sheikhdom of Bahrain.

Algosaibi's dismissal ranked as the major domestic political event in Saudi Arabia since the Mecca uprising. It marked the watershed in the House of Saud's laudable ability to deftly balance political forces to hold its kingdom together. During the oil boom it was postulated that the senior members of the royal family were too astute politically to ignore the middle class's rumblings of discontent. Yet the Algosaibi episode demonstrated that probably no king has the ability to control the royal family to the extent needed to force any limitations on its power. Although the major decisions involving the kingdom and the family are made by the king and the senior princes, these decisions can be implemented only with the broad support of the total family. When two of the senior princes joined by a panoply of underlings in the royal family can combine to force a major political upheaval, the prospects of evolution to any type of representative government are dismal.

As if to underscore this truth, the best known of the technocrats, Ahmed Zaki Yamani, Saudi Arabia's oil minister of twenty-four years, fell from power in October 1986. While speculation in the West focused on the effect on the kingdom's oil policy, Yamani's dismissal said a great deal more about the political climate in Saudi Arabia than it did about the Saudis' future moves in the oil markets.

Zaki Yamani became Saudi Arabia's oil minister in 1962 at the age of thirty-two. One of a handful of Saudis who on the eve of the oil embargo possessed a Western education and a knowledge of the outside world, Yamani became the protégé of King Faisal. In spite of the stature his position afforded him, Yamani, over all the years that he served as oil minister, was never granted the privilege of decision-making. While he advocated sacrificing high prices to protect Saudi Arabia's share of international oil markets, oil policy was set by the senior princes. Yamani frequently left OPEC meetings to call Riyadh for instructions or to fly back to the kingdom for consultation. Nonetheless, he became an international superstar. A superb negotiator, he was a poised and graceful spokesman not only for Saudi Arabia's oil interests but for issues affecting the entire Arab world. It was the respect and recognition afforded Yamani that so irritated King Fahd and his brothers. As egotistical as he was competent, Yamani cast a long shadow over Fahd's troubled and lackluster regime.

Animosities between Fahd and his oil minister brewed over several years and his dismissal should have come as no surprise. Even the abruptness of the departure followed the model set by Algosaibi's dismissal. Purported to have heard of his ouster over the radio, Yamani was forced out more by the weakness of the royal family than by its strength. As the economic downturn stretches out, the royal family more and more adopts a siege mentality. Anxious of the future, usurpers of the respect and affection that the royal family regards as its own private reserve cannot be tolerated. So Yamani like Algosaibi was fired.

Ironically, the new oil minister, Hisham Nazer, is the third star in the triumvirate of commoners who reigned during the oil boom. Longtime minister of Planning, Nazer directed all four of Saudi Arabia's five-year development plans. A Western-educated progressive, he draws support from the same constituencies as Yamani and Algosaibi. He was chosen partly because in a glutted oil market the royal family saw it as advantageous to create the illusion that oil policy is in the hands of someone other than an al-Saud. But more important, there were few men from whom to choose to fill the post. The bureaucratic structure of Saudi Arabia is such that men have positions, not responsibilities. Responsibilities remain with the senior princes. Consequently, the only men who can assume a post such as oil minister are the same ones on whom the House of Saud called when Saudi Arabia burst out of its medieval mold in the 1970s. These are also the same men, now joined by thousands of others who have been educated in the West, whose services are vital to Saudi Arabia but who still have no political power. It is as if the House of Saud can live neither with nor without the technocrats. Furthermore, by putting them into positions of power and then driving them out, the House of Saud is creating its own political opposition with the brightest and the best of Saudi Arabia at its core.

Although the middle class as a whole lacks the cohesiveness to act as a revolutionary class, its growing alienation contributes to the atmosphere for insurrection from other groups sharing similar interests. The urbanized elements of the regular armed forces have certain of the same goals as the middle class. There are also the long-held grievances of the populations of the Hijaz and the al-Hassa, which fit into the same mode as those of the middle class.

But it is not only the progressives and the non-Nejdi Saudis who are at odds with the House of Saud. Insurrection from the other part of the military, the National Guard, could come on behalf of a religious rebellion against the societal decay of the oil boom. The kingdom's traditionalists are indignant about how much the development policies of the boom weakened the Saudis' religious values. Fewer Saudis are praying in the mosques. Western words such as "sandwich," "bus," and "radio" have crept into Arabic, corrupting the purity of the language of the Koran. Artistic expression that was conveyed through religious calligraphy has been superseded by such outrages as the sixteen-foot-tall Carrara marble sculpture of a prince's thumb that dominates a thoroughfare in Jeddah. Traditional Saudi society, rather than being defined by its fierce defense of the standards of Wahhabism, has become marked by apathy, alienation, and political opposition to the policies and behavior of the House of Saud.

The state encompassed by the House of Saud is no longer seen as the defender of the faith but as the creator of artificial and unjust differences. Religious leaders including Sheikh Abdul Aziz ibn Baz have fallen to charges that by putting their knowledge of theology and jurisprudence at the service of the House of Saud, they have become as corrupt as the rulers. This has wide-ranging implications for political stability. For in the absence of a religious hierarchy, the authority of the *ulema* has depended on its ability to cultivate a relationship with the masses. Historically, the ties between the learned scholars who comprise the *ulema* and the people have served as a conduit of support from the people to the House of Saud. But during the oil boom, the *ulema*'s close association with the House of Saud severely damaged its credibility with the traditional Saudi. If a revolt of the traditionalists comes, it will not be instigated by the *ulema* but will originate, as it did in the Mecca uprising, with marginal elements of the religious community claiming to represent the purity and certainty of religion.

The nature of the fundamentalists' opposition is drawing in others, for religious unrest is not limited to the fanatics of the ilk of the Ikhwan or the rebels at Mecca. Although the average Saudi does not frequent the mosque as often as his father did, the urbanization of the Saudi population has increased the pull of religion among all those who migrated to the cities during the oil boom. The passive symbols of religion have taken on new meaning and importance as "the detribalized city dweller looks to religion as a cultural map to guide him through the unfamiliar and expanding city." * In an alien environment, religion

---

* Islami and Kavoussi, *The Political Economy of Saudi Arabia*, p. 88.

has been revived and strengthened to suit the emotional needs of the believer. Even among the educated classes there is a worry that increasing Westernization will soon relegate religion to the subordinate position Christianity occupies in the secular nations of the West. In essence, there hovers within every Saudi the fear that the price he paid for the gifts of the West was his soul.

That leaves the position of the Shiites, the most readily identifiable of the opposition groups, to be pondered. By the Shiites' numbers, geography, and the disdain with which they are regarded by the rest of the Saudis, the House of Saud can move its military against them with impunity. There are perhaps 150,000 Shiites, conveniently congregated in settlements around Dammam, Qatif, Dhahran, and Ras Tanura. With the tacit support of the Saudi Wahhabis and Sunnis, the House of Saud has used force against the Shiites in the past, specifically during the labor unrest of 1956 and during the rioting in 1979. But since 1979, it has become obvious that although a town such as Qatif cannot defend itself against tanks, the Shiites command their own sources of power. Through their willingness to do manual labor and their ambition for education, the Shiites have become heavily concentrated in both the oil fields and the management of ARAMCO. If the Shiites chose to rise up in support of Iran's Ayatollah Khomeini or simply because they hate the other Saudis, they could close down oil operations. This possibility terrified the House of Saud particularly between 1979 and 1984. But when Iranian planes threatened Saudi Arabia, the Shiites, as a whole, seemed to have cast their lot perhaps not with the House of Saud but with Saudi Arabia. Although isolated acts of sabotage do occur, the real threat of the Shiites against the House of Saud is not so much physical violence as it is the spiritual appeal of the Islamic revolution.

It is tempting to write off the House of Saud as another victim of the greed and avarice for power that too often seems to characterize Middle Eastern political regimes. Saudi Arabia's ruling family has always been regarded as something of an anomaly. The Arabist D. G. Howarth, writing in 1925, said,

I see nothing in the circumstances or constituents of the present Wahhabite expansion to promise it a longer life than has been enjoyed by early Nedjean ebullitions. These, to take only one test, have prevailed in Mecca for ten years on the average. . . . I prophecize therefore, that Arabia is not in for more than a decade, at the most, of Wahhabite domination outside the Nejd.*

The House of Saud has endured and it will not easily be dislodged. The royal family is a massive corporation, fanning out across the kingdom. It holds the governorships of the provinces. It is integrated into all elements of the armed forces. Its righteous pray with the religious leaders and fund their work. Its members command the major positions in the bureaucracy. Its secret police are in place in every organization and institution. The carefully built system of checks and balances between the military forces and the National Guard, each representing not only a different political bloc but a different style of life, frustrates the military from uniting against the political system. That leaves the opposition, although far-ranging, fragmented and leaderless and all but fatally handicapped by a culture that shuns planning and organization and seems incapable of sustaining any emotion-charged activity beyond a short span of time. Without an external invasion or a military defeat that could ignite the fuse of revolution, nothing short of sudden, total rebellion is likely to dislodge the House of Saud.

That is not to say the regime is secure. To the contrary, the empire of the al-Sauds is tottering. The House of Saud is sitting on top of a political system on the verge of collapse. The political system in its present form in all likelihood cannot endure. The question is how it will change. With the various factions of the family snarling over the skeleton of the al-Saud dynasty, one or the other may eventually produce a king. But the future of the House of Saud in some respects is a question not so much of whether it will survive but whether it can rule.

Unless the House of Saud can produce a strong leader, it may simply crumble. Political opposition in the Arabian Peninsula has long employed its own unique weapon — noncompliance. Traditionally, tribal alliances held as long as one man could command the loyalty of all. A *sheikh* rejected by his people had no choice but to withdraw, for he could not force his authority. The same mechanism is inherent in the new order. Saudi Arabia is built of private empires that respond to a personal relationship between the leader and his followers. These empires might be tribal or bureaucratic or military, but all are dependent

---

*In Ragaei El Mallakh and Dorothea El Mallakh, eds. *Saudi Arabia: Energy, Developmental Planning, and Industrialization* (Lexington, Mass.: Lexington Books, 1982), p. 99.

on personal relationships and economic reward. With a scant population, no large underprivileged class from which to draw manpower,
and a social structure that is not built on class suppressing class, it is
all but impossible for the House of Saud, with its fear of mercenaries,
to rule through armed repression. And economic repression offers the
royal family no better chance of forcing cooperation. Although the
Saudis are now tied into a cash economy fueled by oil and distributed
by the government, an embargo on government payments to the people
is perhaps the most risky move the rulers could make.

Money has been the glue that has cemented the al-Sauds' kingdom
since before the oil boom began. As the economic downturn exacer-
bated the House of Saud's political problems, so could an upturn in oil
prices help mollify some of the opposition. In a glutted market, the
princes of the House of Saud prefer to hold production down to force
oil prices up. But if its partners fail to abide by production quotas and
if non-OPEC producers continue high levels of production, then the
Saudis must either support prices by cutting their own production or
they must once again flood the oil markets to try to force the others
into line. For oil income is directly tied to the political survival of the
House of Saud. With the next cycle of petroleum shortages predicted
to hit in the early 1990s, the House of Saud is faced with feeding the
appetite of its family and placating its subjects until oil shortages perhaps alleviate the money crunch.

In the meantime, left with no tools of coercion and limited sources
of persuasion, the House of Saud must win the Saudis' consent to rule
or it is left reigning over chaos. If it fails to gather in the disparate
political groups that came out of the oil boom, the House of Saud as
now constituted will die. And whatever government replaces it — a
leader rising from the ruins of the House of Saud, an oligarchy of
religious oppression, or a government representing the progressiveness
of the middle class — it must be aggressively anti-Western if it is to
rule. The Saudis have been a people without ideology beyond Islam.
One of the major reasons the House of Saud survived the oil boom
without obvious political opposition was that the Saudis fit none of the
models for political dissent. Before the oil boom, there were no great
class divisions. Everyone was poor except for the royal family and a
few merchant families who were a little less poor than the rest. While
the oil boom did create more distinct class divisions, there was still no
proletariat, no oppressed working class. Rejecting communism as
atheistic and Middle Eastern–style socialism as tainted by pro-Soviet

political regimes, the Saudis proved barren soil for political ideas much removed from those of the House of Saud. There were no political institutions or traditions that could rally sufficient political support to overcome the restrictions on the press or political organizations. With no structured religious hierarchy in Wahhabism, even theology re-sisted being mobilized into a competing political movement. But the Saudis have now found an idea with which to oppose the House of Saud that is not dependent on sharp class distinctions or a competing political philosophy. That ideology is anti-Westernism. Anti-Western-ism rose out of the oil boom, was nurtured in the economic downturn, and was inspired by the revolutionary rhetoric from Iran. Anti-West-ernism is the force that can reach across region and class, traditional-ists and progressives, air force pilot and Bedouin foot soldier, to unite the Saudis against the inequities and alienations fostered by the House of Saud.

Not since the Moslems broke out of the reclusiveness of the Arabian Peninsula in the seventh century have the Saudis faced a challenge to their sense of self comparable in magnitude to the one represented by their encounter with the modern West. As if to justify the anxieties their fathers felt when Major Frank Holmes first crossed the desert in 1922 in search of oil, the Saudis now realize that their culture has been inescapably altered by their embrace of Western technology and know-how. Although the frustrations of Western governments and the hos-tilities of the Western work force toward the insults and humiliations they have suffered at the hands of the Saudis are parallel to the Saudis' resentments against the West, in the long run, the West has always held the psychological advantage over the Saudis.

Much of the Saudis' confusion about Westernization has resulted from their inability to differentiate between the worth of the material benefits of the West and the worth of the traditional values of their own society. In the Saudis' quest for modernization, Western superi-ority in material, economic, technological, and organizational fields endowed the Westerners with superior power. Unable to resist imitat-ing the West, the Saudis judged themselves by Western standards of organization and technical know-how that pointed up their own weak-nesses. It was as if the Saudis imported criteria by which to judge their own impotence.

Furthermore, Western governments unwittingly contributed to Saudi alienation by encouraging the rapid development of Saudi Arabia as the solution to the problem of recycling petrodollars. But as a result, the Saudis are now left with excessive industrial and infrastructure projects that they cannot manage. The massive construction effort of the oil boom has left in its wake an infrastructure that stands as a symbol confirming the Saudis' sense of inferiority.

Having escaped foreign domination throughout its history, Saudi Arabia was finally colonized during the oil boom. It succumbed not to foreign conquest or economic imperialism but to Westernization that was chosen, bought, and paid for in the form of technology and technically skilled people. This colonization, under the name of modernization, disrupted family life, made women restless in their traditional roles, corrupted the devout, and subjected the society to the disdain of a large Western work force. By giving up that which was secure and predictable, the Saudis achieved several years of unbridled prosperity. But the policies of the oil boom failed to deliver easy solutions to the painful process of modernization. Instead they brought with them the breakdown of domestic political institutions and the cultural seduction of Saudi society, a society the Saudis believe is built on the timeless virtues of the desert.

Whether the gain of a modern infrastructure was worth the disruption of their society is not an issue the Saudis consider rationally. Instead there is a visceral reaction to what they see as a debasement of their values and, in a sense, of themselves. Saudi society in many ways has been turned upside-down, leaving a people deeply committed to their traditions awash in a culture they no longer understand. Old and new are locked in a curious collage in which everything has changed and nothing has changed. Veiled women wear *abaayas* over T-shirts and tight-fitting pants. A complete recitation of the Koran in space was an important mission of the first Saudi astronaut. The Saudi Arabian Monetary Agency has installed automatic teller machines at banks but requires that they close during prayer times.

Through the labyrinth of modernization, the Saudis have acquired the characteristics of a marginal people. "The marginal man is marginal, not because he is unable to acquire the intellectual thought processes of the culture to which he wants to assimilate, nor because he is unable to free himself of the thought processes of the culture on which he has turned his back. He is marginal because emotionally he is unable to identify with either of the two cultures." * The Western

---

* See Raphael Patai, *The Arab Mind* (New York: Charles Scribner's Sons, 1976), p. 190.

presence in Saudi Arabia was so pervasive, reaching into every geographic area and touching every social class, that no Saudi escaped the cultural confrontation with the West. And the Westerners, just by the enormity of their presence, lay siege to most facets of Saudi culture. The Westerner, organized in his habits of work and thought, demanded that the Saudi, who found reward in leisure that allowed his mind to drift to the cadence of poetry, conform to the Western work ethic. The Saudis, who pride themselves on the purity of their Arabic, nevertheless had to learn English to survive in the multinational society created by the oil boom. Saudi education ceased to be training in the Koran. Instead, the scientific approach to problem solving, a concept absent in Arab culture, became the method by which Saudis were taught. The further a Saudi went in the educational process, the further he became separated from those Saudis who dealt with the Westerners only in the marketplace. And the more an educated Saudi came to live with Western culture, the more acute his sense of internal division became. The well-to-do spent months each year in London or on the Riviera and then returned to resume life under the dictates of Saudi culture. The middle class went West to earn degrees in technological subjects created by the West and then returned to manage Saudi Arabia's Western-built infrastructure with Western-style management techniques that are inappropriate to Saudi culture. The marginal Saudi was irresistibly attracted to Western culture while at the same time fearing and despising it.

Members of the educated elite have become psychologically debilitated by their encounter with the West, leading them to withdraw from the culture they attempted to assimilate. Regarding the lower classes with disdain during the oil boom, the middle class now has a certain empathy with them, fostered by an economic recession in which all but the royal family are losing. Economic uncertainty has brought into play, more strongly than would have been possible during the boom, the concept of the equality of all men that is the cornerstone of Wahhabism.

Fundamentalism holds tremendous appeal as a vehicle of political opposition embracing all social classes against the House of Saud. The emotional attraction to the eternal qualities of Islam has the effect of chipping away at the modernized Saudi's carefully constructed veneer. Islam restores the claims of his heritage over the false values he believes the West has imposed on his culture. It gives a philosophical basis for attacks on corruption, privilege, and the unimaginable fortunes and the sexual liberties of the royal family. For the lower classes, never separated from the puritanism of Wahhabism, religion provides their reason for railing against the class system that came with development.

But fundamentalism also has an economic base. The wrath of the fundamentalists and the middle class coalesces around the foreign entrepreneurs, with their superior technology and skills, the Saudi middlemen who became rich in partnership with the foreigners, and the royal family, who provided the contracts and government money that made them all rich. The return to all things Saudi is becoming the rallying cry of those whose expectations were not realized by the prosperity of the boom. The appeal of the Saudis' own culture is part of the mechanism by which the Saudis seek to gain control of their own resources.

> If foreigners were getting their way with the help of middlemen, it must be because of the fawning devotion to things alien; as for the success of middlemen, it must be the product not only of access to court but also of the willingness and capacity to move in the foreigner's universe: to discourse in a foreign language, to move easily in the foreigner's hotels and boardrooms, to allow one's unveiled wife to mix with infidels. Politics and culture intersect, and the only way to break the hold of the triangle on vast national wealth is to break it where it counts: challenge the ruling authority, reclaim the political system in order to perform the twin functions of cultural purification and economic autonomy. Those who lead such a revolt are never those anonymous masses ritually spoken of in radical polemics. They are comparatively better off, they have resources, they are articulate.*

In all traditional societies, there is a strong temptation to return to things one knows, things with which one is comfortable. "Yesterday's *grande idée* was the withering away of tradition, the triumph of that great universal solvent, modernization. In yesterday's imagery, societies were to leap, as if by magic, historical stages; they would move instantaneously from traditional society to the rational bureaucratic stage."**

---

*Fouad Ajami, *The Arab Predicament: Arab Political Thought and Practice Since 1967* (Cambridge: Cambridge University Press, 1982), p. 184.
**Ibid., p. 139.

Today's Saudi is reaching not toward modernization but toward the security of Islam, the gateway back to the past.

Since 1979, Shiism has potently established its credentials as a culturally indigenous force that is both revolutionary and anti-Western. This gives the Islamic revolution, spearheaded by Iran, a broad appeal that cuts across the borders of states and even sects. In the immediate aftermath of the Iranian revolution, the fragile states of the Arabian Peninsula felt the powerful appeal of resurgent Islam. While these countries sought to reach some accommodations with militant Islam, Iraq attacked it across its common border with Iran. Throughout the bloody Iraq-Iran war, the puritanism and anti-Westernism of the Iranian revolution has attracted the sympathy of many of Saudi Arabia's Sunnis and Wahhabis. Unlike the leftist revolutions that overthrew the Middle East monarchs in the 1950s, Khomeini and his Shiite followers attract Moslems for the reason that they are both anti-communist and anti-Western. And for segments of Saudi Arabia's population, the revolutionary philosophy of Iran is alluring because it is closer to the ideals espoused by Mohammed than those of their own Wahhabi rulers, who are so enamored of the West.

Iran poses a real threat to Saudi Arabia both militarily and ideologically. Events seem to conspire to keep this dual threat potent. In 1985 Saudi Arabia's fear of Iran's presence on Kuwait's border led the House of Saud to moderate its support of Iraq and to revert to its policy of buying off the kingdom's enemies. Over the next eighteen months, clandestine operations supplied Iran with refined petroleum and undetermined amounts of credit for arms purchases. While pursuing its own policy for its own reasons, Saudi Arabia in late 1986 was caught up in the public brouhaha surrounding the Reagan administration's arms deal with Iran. Every innuendo that linked Saudi Arabia to the affair added fuel to the widespread dissatisfaction within the kingdom, for the revelations coming out of Washington tripped anti-Western emotions and highlighted the shameless riches of Saudi middlemen suckled by the royal family. As a result, the House of Saud became trapped in a scenario in which it appeared to have played lackey to American interests by funding the United States' covert operations in Central America and by perhaps committing the unforgivable sin of allowing itself to become involved with the hated Israel in funneling American arms to Iran. These arms shipments were brokered by Saudi businessman Adnan Khashoggi, a confidant of King Fahd and Prince Sultan.

In the eyes of the Saudis, Khashoggi is the archetype of the middle-man who acquired incredible wealth during the oil boom. Exploiting his ties with the royal family, Khashoggi became the agent for a broad range of Western products and weaponry sold to Saudi Arabia during the oil boom. His fat commissions skimmed the cream off the king-dom's oil revenues. Anyone making money on the scale Khashoggi did would have caused hostilities among the Saudis; but Khashoggi was especially resented because he is an outsider. Of mixed Turkish and Syrian descent, he has always been on the periphery of the tribal relationships that govern the kingdom, and few look on him as a true Saudi. Furthermore, his ardent embrace of Western ways and his flam-boyant lifestyle have largely cut him out of Saudi society. Khashoggi personifies all that the Saudis detest in the House of Saud and its co-horts.

With the House of Saud weakened by its own deficiencies and often discredited in its relations with the West, is Saudi Arabia likely to follow the Iranian recipe for change? In both Iran and Saudi Arabia enormous wealth and rapid economic development were suddenly thrust on a traditional society. Both have had monarchies that rule alone and have attachments to the West. Both have populations easily aroused by religious causes. Yet there are fundamental differences. First, the House of Saud has not isolated itself from the people. While they live lavishly, the al-Sauds still have not surrounded the monarchy with the Oriental pomp and ceremony the shah did. Nor is there the adoration of the person of the king that the egomaniacal shah demanded. And rather than publicly rejecting religion in the name of secularization as the shah did, the House of Saud has assiduously cultivated the tie be-tween Wahhabism and the monarchy.

Second, a highly structured religious organization, which was the vehicle for revolution in Iran, does not exist in Wahhabism. The *ulema* is made up of men learned in the Koran, not members of a religious hierarchy claiming great wealth and the titles of *mullah* and *ayatol-lah*.* And where in Iran the clergy controls great wealth, the collection of offerings is not part of the rituals of the Wahhabi mosque. Almost all the money at the disposal of the religious establishment comes di-rectly out of the government's coffers controlled by the House of Saud. Finally, the Saudis' psychological makeup lacks the sense of martyr-

---

*Similar in status to a priest and a bishop, respectively.

dom that characterizes Shiism. Although prone to short outbursts of highly charged emotional activity, the Wahhabis see no glory in dying in suffering.

What Saudi Arabia and Iran do share is similar anger over the assault on their traditions that came with modernization. And there is the same profound desire for "Western detoxification" that turned the religious message of the Ayatollah Khomeini into revolution. Khomeini's success was due to the fact that there was not one but two revolutions, which occurred simultaneously. One was the liberal revolution of the middle class against the monarchy, and the other was the religious revolution of the lower classes against Westernization. The example of the ideology and militancy of the Iranian revolution could tear at the walls of class, tribe, and region and unite the Saudis against the House of Saud. Militarily, Iran could force the Saudis into defeat on their borders, triggering a general uprising against the al-Sauds. And ideologically, its campaign in the name of Islam against the pro-Western monarchies could cut across all of the checks and balances so carefully constructed by the House of Saud for its own protection.

This is the challenge to the political system in Saudi Arabia. The struggle is not between the philosophies of the United States and the USSR but between Islam and the West. Mutiny against the established order will come. It may not take the form of an armed rebellion to overthrow the House of Saud, but there will ensue a rebellion of contempt against the Westernization of Saudi Arabia. Trapped between the dissatisfactions of its own people and the military presence of a crusading Iran on the kingdom's borders, the House of Saud vacillates between the past and the present. It is a game that it has played well but a game it cannot sustain. Political instability will linger as long as the men in power defend their existence with the symbols of Saudi Arabia's pristine past while serving as handmaidens to the West.

In the end, the oil boom has to be understood in terms of a people who have lost their way, whose heritage proved unequal to the demands of modernization, whose leaders became corrupt, whose ideals floundered. Anti-Westernism will not solve the Saudis' problems, but it does intoxicate those who can no longer endure the enfeebling challenges of an alien world created by the West.

Afterword

During the storm of charges and denials that raged between the Americans and Saudis in the aftermath of September 11, 2001, I found myself emotionally drawn back to the kingdom that I had left in 1984. I wanted to once again roll across the arid desert where the spirit of the Bedouin still reigns, and walk the streets of the cities that now hold many of the aristocrats of the sands, to observe once more the clash of modernization and traditionalism within Saudi society. But I knew I could not return. As I expected when I wrote this book, I was banned from the kingdom. So was the book. Friends still living in Saudi Arabia told me of the stacks of copies confiscated by customs officials and of copies sneaked into the country in all the various ways that Westerners used to get contraband reading material past Saudi censors. Evidently, the Saudis were smuggling it in also. I received a few irate letters from Saudis protesting my treatment of Islam. Yet other Saudis, in letters mailed from outside the kingdom, told me that they agreed with my analysis of the political forces at work in their country. Meanwhile, the House of Saud kept its collective mouth shut, although Prince Bandar ibn Sultan, the Saudi ambassador to the United States, referred to me in private simply as "that woman!" Thus with no access to the country, I have been forced to watch from afar events that have followed the path laid out by the oil boom that spanned the midseventies to the mideighties.

Three decades after the explosion of oil prices catapulted Saudi Arabia into the modern era, the Saudis are continuing their disordered search for the definition of their society. Bringing with them the complexities of tribe, region, and sect, they have come to be grouped within two broad dynamics. The first is driven by the quest for modernization. The second is stoked by a fervor to recover tradition through the zeal of faith. Each viewpoint has produced its own extreme element.

On the outer fringe of the modernizers, there is a rebellion of the young who are coming of age in an era of satellite television, the Internet, and the ubiquitous presence of brand names that the Saudis have come to believe is Western culture. In a society where the patriarchal family dictates tradition and monitors behavior, rowdy groups of young men periodically defy both custom and authority. Denied almost all forms of recreation by religious and governmental dictate, the rebels lure police officers into 120-mile-per-hour chases on the freeways, toss firecrackers into crowds at soccer matches, jump out of cars to engage in wild street dancing, and even disguise themselves as females to infiltrate women-only spaces principally for the thrill of harassment. Refusing to obey their elders, they represent to most Saudis the erosion of the moral fiber with which Saudi society is woven.

The extreme element among the traditionalists is populated by both young and old who hold the West and the House of Saud responsible for the perceived destruction of traditional culture and the inequities in the political system. Representing multiple viewpoints of Islamic theology and defined as a whole as Islamists, they gather around sheikhs with long shaggy beards, yellowed *thobes*, and faded *gutras* who speak from modest mosques or sit on dusty carpets in canvas tents preaching the return to pristine Islam as the salvation of Saudi society.

In important ways, the rambunctiousness of the rebels and the piety of the Islamists reflect the demographic, economic, and social problems that now stalk Saudi Arabia. Since the peak of Saudi prosperity in 1981, one of the world's highest birthrates has increased the population from seven million to nineteen million, oil revenues have shrunk from $227 billion to an estimated $49.6 billion, and per capita income has fallen from $28,600 in current dollars to below $8000. With a shrinking job market and an educational system in which 50 percent of the students pursue religious studies, Saudi Arabia can no longer guarantee every college graduate the once standard government job that provided comfortable salaries for a four-hour workday, interspersed with frequent tea breaks. The kingdom's once fabulous infrastructure, constructed during the boom, is now crumbling, and the country remains utterly dependent on foreign workers, who constitute perhaps 90 percent of the private-sector and 70 percent of the public-sector labor force. And for the first time in this puritanical society, drugs, guns, and crime are being reported among a Saudi population in which 60 percent is under the age of twenty. Sitting on top of it all is the House of Saud.

Just as they have since Abdul Aziz created the state of Saudi Arabia, members of the royal family still dominate all political positions, hold a major stake in every economic sector, and exercise extensive control over the religious institutions. What is new is that the House of Saud is now confronting a level of discontent that has never existed before. The dissatisfaction of the population over the issues of authoritarianism within the political system, management of national wealth, inequity in the economy, and the seemingly permanent presence of U.S. military forces that began with the 1991 Gulf War is broad and deep. This discontent has produced the question of whether or not the House of Saud can survive the paradoxes of its rule that have always been present in the kingdom and the events that have unfolded since this book was originally published.

When I left the kingdom in 1984, the attention of the House of Saud focused more on the internal challenge of balancing tradition and modernization than it did on external threats to the kingdom. Although Iran's Islamic revolution was casting its shadow over Saudi Arabia as it had since 1979, the ruling regime was buying a measure of security by financing Saddam Hussein's war with Iran. That war ended in 1988 when the combatants, exhausted by eight years of bestial fighting that took perhaps a million lives and cost roughly $1190 billion, agreed to a cease-fire sponsored by the United Nations. The Saudis exhaled a collective sigh of relief as a level of stability returned to the Persian Gulf. But in July 1990, the economic stresses the war with Iran had inflicted on Iraq once more plunged the Gulf into crisis. Desperate for money for his war-starved economy, Hussein demanded money from Saudi Arabia, Kuwait, and the sheikdoms of the Arabian Peninsula as payment for Iraq's efforts in holding the Islamic revolution at the door of the Arab world. In a series of maneuvers, Arab leaders of the Arabian Peninsula attempted to ease the tension. Then Kuwait balked, refusing to meet Hussein's financial demands.

Thus in the darkness of August 2, 1990, Iraqi troops, in violation of the near sacred creed that no Arab state invades another, crossed the Kuwaiti border and moved on Kuwait City. Within hours, all of Kuwait belonged to Baghdad. If the million-man Iraqi army moved south again, it would enter the oil fields of Saudi Arabia. Yet for five days the House of Saud remained silent. On August 7, U.S. Secretary of Defense Richard Cheney arrived in Jeddah carrying satellite photographs of Iraqi military deployments along the Kuwait-Saudi border. Throughout the evening, he huddled with King Fahd, Crown Prince Abdullah, and others in the al-Sauds' inner circle. Fahd finally emerged, his face lined with stress and fatigue, to announce that Saudi Arabia was calling in American troops to defend the kingdom. With Hussein knocking at the door, neither Saudi Arabia nor the United States could afford to play any longer the political game that kept the American military over the horizon of the desert kingdom. For Saudi Arabia, and particularly the House of Saud, American muscle meant survival in the face of an overwhelming external threat. For the United States, the fields of Saudi Arabia, producing 17 percent of the oil imported by the industrialized world, translated into a military mandate. This was the reasoning that had always lain at the heart of the American-Saudi alliance. Consequently, the 1974 defense plan, battered and bruised by years of doubt on both sides, came to life. And with it came a new Western incursion into Saudi Arabia.

The empty desert stretching out from King Khalid Military City at Wadi al-Batin quickly filled with the tents, tanks, and troops of the United States and to a much lesser extent its Western allies. In Riyadh, the House of Saud juggled the imperatives of security and politics. Drawing on the experience of the boom years, the regime attempted to impose on the Western military forces the same restrictions it had always placed on foreign civilians working in the country. Benefiting from the fact that the Iraqi-Saudi border stretched across the empty northern plateau, the House of Saud bottled up Western soldiers in the desert much as it had bottled up its Western workforce in housing compounds across the kingdom, and it locked war correspondents out of Saudi Arabia like it had the journalists of peace time. Dependent on Saudi soil to mount the attack against the Iraqi invasion of Kuwait, the U.S. military went along with Riyadh. Americans on the home front were warned not to send anything to soldiers in Saudi Arabia that smacked of pornography. And American brewers geared up to manufacture thousands of gallons of "near beer" for the troops.

As additional troops and equipment arrived, Saudi authorities moved aggressively to bring the new elements that had been introduced into Saudi Arabia into line with the pre-war rules. On orders from the Saudi government, Red Cross emblems atop ambulances were painted over lest they be interpreted as symbols of an alien religion; chaplains took the crosses off their caps when they left their bases; a scheduled USO show staged for the troops by singing, high-stepping Western expatriates was canceled. But it was the female contingent of the American military presence—10 percent of the total—that posed the most serious challenge to Saudi culture and control.

Refusing to bend to Saudi demands on the supersensitive domestic issue of gender equality, the U.S. military sent female mechanics, supply officers, and flight coordinators to work side by side with American men and often in the same hangars and workshops as the Saudi contingent of the military force. Quickly realizing that female soldiers were an inescapable part of the U.S. protection package, Riyadh encapsulated them in their own code of conduct. T-shirts, even in the 115-degree heat, were prohibited. Legs had to be covered when female soldiers left their bases. Outside the strict confines of an encampment, no woman was to appear behind the wheel of a vehicle. Jogging was forbidden. Yet in the time-honored custom of the oil boom, a formerly men-only gym at a Saudi air base was opened to women of the U.S. military—with the proviso that they enter the back door and leave after the two-hour "women-only" time elapsed.

Outside the ruling circle, the arrival of thousands of Western troops into Saudi Arabia in the late summer of 1990 once more fueled all the Saudis' doubts of the oil years. With the Westerners as employees, the Saudis at least had had a chance to control their impact on Saudi culture. But what they now faced was an army fielded by a superpower invited into the kingdom by the House of Saud to defend not only the country but the family itself It came bearing all its technology and all its ability to operate effectively in the world of the late twentieth century. Thus, these Western forces became another symbol of Saudi subjugation to the superior power of the West. And Saudi honor was once more in danger of being humbled at the hands of Western "infidels." One man in particular, among others, raised the voice of protest. His name—Osama bin Laden.

Since the halcyon days of the oil boom, the bin Laden name had marked construction projects, mercantile ventures, and anything else that made money for those with the right connections to the House of Saud. Like the other merchant families, the bin Ladens operated as a unit, not as individuals. But in 1979 the modest, almost shy, youngest son made a name for himself by organizing Moslem zealots to fight against the Soviet Union's invasion of Afghanistan. Claiming victory in driving the Soviets out of Moslem Afghanistan, bin Laden returned to Saudi Arabia infused with the passion of jihad against the encroachment of the West. In August 1990, when King Fahd invited American forces into the kingdom, bin Laden charged that the presence of infidel forces in the shadows of Islam's holy cities of Mecca and Medina stripped the ruling al-Saud family of its legitimacy.

By 1992 bin Laden was calling for the toppling of the House of Saud. Speaking from his austere, fundamentalist view of Islam and expressing the feelings of many Saudis, he denounced the thirty-thousand-strong royal family as corrupted by wealth and Westernization. Words that appealed to many Saudis sounded and alarm in the royal chambers of Riyadh. In the tradition of the tribe with which it governs, the House of Saud sent emissaries from bin Laden's family to tempt the political blasphemer back into the fold. He would not be seduced. Even after he was sent into exile, his name continued to circulate through the religious and political underground of Saudi Arabia. There the bearded zealot took on the aura of a warrior for the poor and the excluded, the ideal Moslem who preserves the faith within a just society. Over the following decade, the seemingly permanent presence of American troops in Saudi Arabia gave additional form and force to the Islamic militancy of Osama bin Laden, which attracted, among others, the Saudi hijackers who collapsed the World Trade Center and damaged the Pentagon in September 2001. Yet political Islam was not new to Saudi Arabia.

At its founding, the House of Saud installed Islam as a political system. Over several decades, religion as politics succeeded largely because most Saudis refused to cut the umbilical cord of tradition. Even in the euphoria of the oil boom, most Saudis were willing to remain in the womb of a theocratic state because outside was a world in which Western institutions and Western culture challenged what was known and what was secure. As long as Saudi Arabia escaped serious entanglement with outsiders, the semi-theocratic state worked reasonably well for ruler and citizen alike. But beneath the surface, things were not as the al-Sauds assumed.

The Islamists, those who see religion as politics, were being churned out of an Islamic educational system that grew during the 1980s through generous government grants. This lavish funding of Islamic studies by the regime was an endeavor to shore up the al-Sauds' legitimacy as the oil boom waned. By the early 1990s, one-fourth of all university students were enrolled in religious institutions. From there, they moved on to become bureaucrats, policemen, military officers, commanders of the National Guard, *matawain*, *sharia judges*, and preachers in some of the twenty-thousand mosques in the country. Thus religion and governance created a circle drawn by action and response. In its first phase, disaffected Saudis of the desert and the cities saw the House of Saud deviating from what they perceived as the true path of Islam. In the second phase, the al-Sauds countered by pouring money, more than attention, into the cause of Islam. In the third and final phase, the products of the religious schools supported with government money enlarged the ranks of the Islamists.

In the 1990s when conflicts in Bosnia, Chechnya, and elsewhere targeted Moslems, a broad range of Saudis reached deep into their pockets to draw out hundreds of millions of dollars to finance schools, refugee camps, and other humanitarian works. Government participated also, for the al-Sauds' social contract with the Saudi population was still written in terms of protecting Islam. Behind the process of alms collecting, some of these charities leaked money to extremist Islamic causes. If those in the ruling elite knew, they ignored it. After all, this was the government's way of doing business—throw money at nasty problems and leave the unpleasant details under the rug. It was not until September 11, 2001, that the House of Saud fully realized that it had been funding its own demise.

Islam has always been a double-edged sword for the House of Saud. One side of that sword has granted to the al-Sauds legitimacy as protectors of the faith. The other side has dictated behavior and policies of government that are compatible with religious law. In what has been a quid pro quo, the *ulema* has given cover to the regime and the regime has preserved the conservative Islamic character of the state. But today this formula of mutual benefit between the regime and the clergy no longer functions as it once did. What was an official clergy that stood in alliance with the House of Saud lost much of its authority in 1999 when Saudi Arabia's principle cleric, the revered Sheik Abdul Aziz ibn Baz, died.

Yet almost a decade before, at the time preceding the Gulf War, the official clergy appointed by the king was already being supplemented by a popular clergy that was both articulate and vocal. By the end of the Gulf War, the clerical ranks in Saudi Arabia were split between Islamic authorities who lived in big houses, drove big cars, and presumably collected big government salaries as a reward for hewing to the line of the al-Sauds and what was a popular Islamic clergy who denounced the House of Saud for authoritarianism, corruption, and cultural defilement. In the theological arena, the official clergy wrote *fatwas* that justified the presence of U.S. troops on Saudi soil while the popular clergy, using the same Islamic vocabulary, offered counter-*fatwas*. It amounted to politics according to Islam.

In the spring of 1991, 453 religious scholars, judges, and university professors out of the popular clergy issued a strongly worded petition that called for a restoration of Islamic values and twelve political reforms, including a consultative assembly, a fair judiciary, the redistribution of wealth, an end to corruption, and the primacy of religious law. People who were always thought to be the pillar of support for the House of Saud not only endorsed sweeping changes but also did so in a public way by circulating the petition through the mosques and religious schools before presenting it to the king.

In July 1992, a "memorandum of advice" to King Fahd, signed by 107 religious scholars, was even more defiant than the petition drafted the previous year. Deploring what they considered "total chaos in the economy and society . . . widespread bribery, favoritism, and the extreme feebleness of the courts," it criticized virtually every aspect of the al-Sauds' domestic and foreign policy.* Furthermore, the communication was made public, breaking the long-standing norm of keeping disputes between ruler and subject private. In some mosques, Friday sermons became blatant political messages. That led to the arrest and imprisonment of several prominent sheikhs among the popular clergy.

Pressures for reform were not limited to the Wahhabis. Other Sunnis as well as the Shia joined in. All constructed their own alternative history of Saudi Arabia using language and cultural symbols to link people across divisions of class, region, gender, and status. These groups often revisited the agreements made between Abdul Aziz ibn Saud, the Hijazi notables, representatives of major families, and the clergy that shaped an implicit understanding of the acceptable relationship between the House of Saud, religion, and society. Speaking from multiple platforms, the Islamists charged that in material terms the House of Saud had abrogated the political pact that defines the relationship between state and society in Saudi Arabia. What the Islamists were demanding was a renegotiation of the social contract in order to change what the al-Sauds considered their private realm into a public state, to establish governance by the rule of law, and to abolish the official state clergy. Some of these Islamists were willing to achieve reform by nonviolent methods. Others sought jihad.

Even under the constraints of an authoritarian political system, the Islamic movement in all its forms was able to forge effective underground networks throughout the country that propelled the political discourse. It was largely the pressure of Islamists that moved Fahd in 1992 to deliver the consultative council promised since 1975 and to create provincial councils. But neither satisfied the opposition, for both proved to be cosmetic rather than real reform.

By 1993, actual organizations were disseminating the Islamists' message. Demonstrations—a rarity in the al-Sauds' authoritarian regime—demanded the release of the sheikhs imprisoned for criticizing the gov-

---

*Quoted in Gwenn Okruhlik, "Networks of Dissent: Islamism and Reform in Saudi Arabia, "Current History 101, no. 651 (January 2002), pp. 22–29. Quote accessed from web site www.ssrc.org/sept11/essays/okruhlik.htm, March 28, 2002.

ernment. The most significant of these by far occurred in Buraydah in September 1994. In the very heartland of the ruling family's support since the days of Abdul Aziz, the voice of the disempowered echoed across the desert. It sounded harsh criticism of Fahd's personal behavior, his methods of governance, his domestic and foreign policies, and his decision to allow the stationing of American troops in the shadow of Mecca and Medina. As it had been in 1929 and 1979, the legitimacy of the al-Saud family was being challenged from the Nejd, the core of al-Saud support.

The ability of the Islamists to organize and protest could be traced in part to a succession struggle that divided the leadership within the House of Saud for three years. The contest for the throne between Abdullah and the Sudari Seven that was predicted at the death of Fahd came instead in 1995 when the king suffered a stroke that rendered him incapable of ruling. In 1998, Abdullah, perhaps benefiting from the support of the Islamists, rose through all the internal rivalries of the family to become the de facto king. Regarded by most Saudis as a pious, incorruptible leader, responsive to the people, and the strongest nationalist voice in Saudi Arabia, he began to shore up the House of Saud's battered legitimacy. In a series of moves, he released the jailed sheikhs, allowed a bit more freedom of the press, tolerated some criticism by the popular clergy, reined in the more ostentatious behavior of the princes, and reportedly limited the extent to which the royal family dips into the state's revenues.

In his role as de facto king, Abdullah has proved to be a gifted politician who is highly respected by most elements of Saudi society. He understands the need for educational reforms to prepare Saudis as carpenters, electricians, and plumbers capable of rebuilding the aging infrastructure built during the oil boom. He is committed to economic reforms aimed at building an economy capable of creating the jobs needed by an overwhelmingly young population. He also has the courage to attack the defense budget that so many Saudis believe wastes national resources and to confront the United States in the name of the Arabs. Authoritarian but not autocratic, the Crown Prince has proved to be the best hope for political stability in Saudi Arabia by working quickly and effectively to repair the cord of legitimacy that ties the House of Saud to the Saudi people. But Abdullah is seventy-eight years old. If his health holds, he will become king on Fahd's death. It is on his own death, after what will probably be a short reign, that the real test for the House of Saud will come.

As at the time of the oil boom, the House of Saud still has not formulated the means to choose a king who is both capable of a long reign and acceptable to a broad spectrum of the Saudi population. Instead, most members of the family are locked in the old model that seems destined to pass the succession through the Sudairi Seven. Prince Sultan, the stained defense minister, Prince Naif, the longtime minister of the Interior, Prince Salman, the governor of Riyadh, and perhaps Prince Turki, the brother who is currently and mysteriously out of favor, are waiting in the wings for their turn to take up the title of "Custodian of the Two Holy Places." Who comes next, no one knows. Even the grandsons of Abdul Aziz are aging.

As of now, the House of Saud is suffering from the steady denigration of its support rather than the immediate threat of revolt. What makes this decline of legitimacy so serious is that the dissent against the existing system bridges the cleavages of region, class, gender, ethnicity, ideology, and school of Islam. As a result, private entrepreneurs and public bureaucrats, industrialists and small shopkeepers, Sunni and Shia, men and women are united in demanding what amounts to social justice. Because of this convergence of so many within Saudi society, the House of Saud can no longer resort to its time-honored strategy of playing one group against another. Thus, change is coming to Saudi Arabia. The question is when and in what form.

Providing the vocabulary, the symbols, and the historic reference points, the Islamists have captured the discourse in Saudi Arabia, made conversation about reform permissible, and begun the process of renegotiating the social contract. Exceeding the force of tribe, regional identity, commercial interests, or nationalism, they are, by far, the most coherent, powerful, and organized social force in Saudi Arabia. But the Islamists, demanding a return to the path of the Prophet, are only one side of the equation. The other side is the modernizers. To them, the central problem of Saudi Arabia is not the government's commitment to Islamic tradition. It is the challenge of the future. According to a Western-educated, middle-class Saudi, "The problem here is not Islam. The problem is too many young men with no job and no university and nowhere to go except to the mosque, where some [radical preachers] fill their heads with anger for America. Every home now has two or three not working. This is the real problem."*

The modernizers came out of the frenzied years of the oil boom. They were part of the rising middle class that was sent in waves to study at colleges in the United States, Britain, and elsewhere in the West. There they not only got an education but also lived in an atmosphere of loosened social restraints and observed the political process in a nonauthoritarian secular state. Since then, they have matured and their attitudes have moved

---

*Quoted in Thomas L. Friedman, "The Saudi Challenge," *New York Times*, February 20, 2002, p. A22.

far beyond the days when the government could win allegiance by giving the Bedouin the means to ride in from the desert to trade a camel for a Toyota. Today many of these Saudis are looking for less paternalism and more inclusion. They want freedom of expression and freedom of assembly. They want to participate in the development of their country. They want better education, health, and employment opportunities, and an improved and expanded infrastructure for a booming population. What they do not want is to continue to waste precious national resources on arms purchases from the United States. These basic desires as citizens are not too different from those of the Islamists.

Even though the Saudis are divided into two broad categories, the portrayal of internal politics in Saudi Arabia as a contest between Westernized "moderates" and puritanical "Wahhabis" is grossly oversimplified. Saudi Arabia is a heterogeneous country regionally, ethnically, religiously, and ideologically. The complexity of the society that was intensified by the oil boom precludes either of two stark choices: an absolute monarchy aligned with the West or a revolutionary Islamic state bent on driving the West out of the Middle East. In truth, the modernizers and the traditionalists occupy parts of each other's realm. No matter how Westernized they regard themselves, the modernizers neither are able to nor want to escape their own culture, for Islam weaves its way into every aspect of Saudi culture, mandating that every Saudi is to some degree an Islamist. By the same token, Islamists have not escaped or totally rejected the forces of modernization. As an example, the most militant and influential Islamists now post their sermons calling for a return to the past on the Internet. Looking at Saudi Arabia today, anyone who was there during the oil boom realizes that nothing has changed and everything has changed.

Occasionally real truth can be found in advertising. On November 6, 2001, the Saudi Ministry of Information ran a full-page ad in the *International Herald Tribune*. In overblown copy lavishly praising King Fahd was this paragraph:

> Achieving security and stability has not always been entirely straightforward. The demands of modernization have inevitably created tensions from time to time in a conservative society. Striking the balance between those who wish to modernize as quickly as possible and those who are concerned that modernization could threaten the unique character of the Kingdom has demanded a high degree of skill. . . . There have always been channels for every party to express their views. That has not necessarily helped King Fahd to find solu-

tions but it has made him and his Government aware of any problems and sensitive to the balance of opinion on any issue.

Finding that balance and accepting the limitations of its own power are the challenges facing the House of Saud and American interests in the Persian Gulf.

Selected Bibliography

Alford, Jane [Sandra Mackey]. "Saudi Banks Experiment with Branches for Women." *Atlanta Constitution*, November 6, 1983.

Ajami, Fouad. "Stress in the Arab Triangle." *Foreign Policy* 29 (Winter 1977/78).

———. "The End of Pan-Arabism." *Foreign Affairs* 57 (Winter 1978/79).

———. *The Arab Predicament: Arab Political Thought and Practice Since 1967.* Cambridge: Cambridge University Press, 1981.

Algosaibi, Ghazi A. *Arabian Essays*. London: Kegan Paul, 1982.

Alireza, Marianne. *At the Drop of a Veil*. Boston: Houghton Mifflin, 1971.

Anthony, John Duke. *The Middle East: Oil, Politics, and Development.* Washington, D.C.: American Enterprise Institute, 1975.

Arabian Government and Public Services Directory, 1982. Northampton, England: Parrish-Rogers International, 1982.

Arnold, José. *Golden Swords and Pots and Pans*. London: Gollancz, 1962.

Atkins, James E. "The Oil Crisis: This Time the Wolf Is Here." *Foreign Affairs* 51 (April 1973).

Beling, Willard A., ed. *King Faisal and the Modernization of Saudi Arabia.* London: Croom Helm, 1980.

Bhatty, M. Akram, M.D., Hishm al-Sibai, and Surindar M. Marwah, M.D. "A Survey of Mother and Child Care in the Saudi Community in Rabaiyah, Tarut Island." *Saudi Medical Journal* 4 (January 1983).

Bill, James A., and Carl Leiden. *Politics in the Middle East*. Boston: Little, Brown, 1979.

Binzagr, Safeya. *Saudi Arabia: An Artist's View of the Past*. Lausanne, Switzerland: Editions des Trois Continents, 1970.

Callen, M. A. "The Changing Role of Banks in a Booming Environment." *Middle East Executive Reports* 4, no. 8 (August 1981).

Carter, Jimmy. *The Blood of Abraham*. Boston: Houghton Mifflin, 1985.

Carter, J. R. L. *Leading Merchant Families of Saudi Arabia*. London: Scorpion Publications (The D. R. Llewellyn Group), 1981.

Chamieh, Jebran, ed. *Saudi Arabia Yearbook*. Beirut: Research and Publishing House, 1981.

Chubin, Shahram. "Soviet Policy Toward Iran and the Gulf." Adelphi Papers no. 157. London: International Institute for Strategic Studies, 1979.

———. *Security in the Persian Gulf I: Domestic Political Factors*. London: International Institute for Strategic Studies, 1981.

Collins, Michael [Sandra Mackey]. "Maintenance, Training, and Management

Opportunities Arise from Labor Dilemma." *Middle East Executive Reports* 4, no. 5 (May 1981).

———. "Riyadh: The Saud Balance." *Washington Quarterly* 4, no. 1 (Winter 1981).

Conant, Melvin. *The Oil Factor in U.S. Foreign Policy, 1980–1990.* Lexington, Mass.: Lexington Books, 1982.

Crane, Robert. *Planning the Future of Saudi Arabia: A Model for Achieving National Priorities.* New York: Praeger, 1978.

Dawisha, Adeed I. "Internal Values and External Threats: The Making of Saudi Foreign Policy." *Orbis* 23, no. 2 (Spring 1979).

———. "Saudi Arabia's Search for Security." Adelphi Papers no. 158. London: International Institute for Strategic Studies, 1979–80.

———. "Iraq and the Arab World: The Gulf War and After." *The World Today* 37, no. 3 (March 1981).

Dawisha, Karen. "Moscow's Moves in the Direction of the Gulf—So Near and Yet So Far." *Journal of International Affairs* 34 (Fall/Winter 1980/81).

Deese, David A., and Joseph S. Nye, eds. *Energy and Security.* Cambridge, Mass.: Ballinger, 1981.

De Gaury, Gerald. *Faisal: King of Saudi Arabia.* London: Arthur Barker, 1966.

Demaree, Allan T. "Arab Wealth, As Seen Through Arab Eyes." *Fortune* (April 1974).

Diamond, Stewart. "Reporter's Notebook: OPEC and Its Vagaries." *New York Times*, November 3, 1984.

Dickson, H. R. P. *The Arab Desert.* London: George Allen and Unwin, 1970.

"Equable Solution for Off Shore Boundaries. The Saudi Arabia–Iran Agreement." *American Journal of International Law* 64 (January 1970).

Eveland, Wilbur Crane. *Ropes of Sand: America's Failure in the Middle East.* New York: W. W. Norton, 1980.

al-Farsy, Fouad. *Saudi Arabia: A Case Study in Development.* London: Kegan Paul, 1982.

Fisher, Sydney Nettleton. *The Middle East: A History.* New York: Alfred A. Knopf, 1969.

Friedman, Thomas L. "The Saudi Challenge." *New York Times*, February 20, 2002.

Ghorban, Marsi. "The Changing Role of Petromin." *Arab Gulf Journal* I (October 1981).

Goldberg, Jacob. "How Stable Is Saudi Arabia?" *Washington Quarterly* 5, no.2 (Spring 1982).

Hameed, Mazher. *Arabia Imperiled: The Security of the Arab Gulf States.* Washington, D.C.: Middle East Assessments Group, 1986.

Hartley, David R.W. "One Thousand Obstetric Deliveries in the Asir Province, Kindgom of Saudi Arabia: A Review." *Saudi Medical Journal* I (April 1980).

Hawley, Donald. *The Trucial States.* London: George Allen and Unwin, 1970.

Helms, Christine Moss. *The Cohesion of Saudi Arabia: Evolution of Political Identity.* London: Croom Helm, 1981.

Holden, David, and Richard Johns. *The House of Saud*. London: Holt, Rinehart and Winston, 1981.

Howarth, David. *The Desert King: A Life of Ibn Saud*. Beirut: Continental Publications, 1964.

Ignatius, David. "Royal Payoffs." *Wall Street Journal*, May 1, 1981.

Islami, A. Reza S., and Rostam Mehraban Kavoussi. *The Political Economy of Saudi Arabia*. Seattle: University of Washington Press, 1984.

Katukara, Motoko. *Bedouin Village: A Study of Saudi Arabian People in Transition*. Tokyo: University of Tokyo, 1977.

Kerr, Malcolm. "Rich and Poor in the New Arab Order." *Journal of Arab Affairs* I (October 1981).

Kingdom of Saudi Arabia, Ministry of Education, Department of Antiquities and Museums. *Saudi Arabian Antiquities*, Riyadh, 1985.

Kingdom of Saudi Arabia, Ministry of Information. *Saudi Arabia and Its Place in the World*. Riyadh, 1979.

Kingdom of Saudi Arabia, Ministry of Planning. *Third Development Plan: 1400–1405 A.H., 1980–85 A.D.* Riyadh, 1980.

Kingdom of Saudi Arabia, Ministry of Planning. *Fourth Development Plan: 1405–1410 A.H., 1985–1991 A.D.* Riyadh, 1985.

Kissinger, Henry. *The White House Years*. Boston: Little, Brown, 1979.

———. *Years of Upheaval*. Boston: Little, Brown, 1982.

Kraft, Joseph. "Letters from Saudi Arabia." *The New Yorker*, October 20, 1975.

———. "Letter from Riyadh." *The New Yorker*, June 26, 1978.

———. "Letter from Saudi Arabia." *The New Yorker*, July 4, 1983.

Kuniholm, Bruce. "What the Saudis Really Want: A Primer for the Reagan Administration." *Orbis* 25 (Spring 1981).

Lacey, Robert. *The Kingdom: Arabia and the House of Saud*. New York: Harcourt Brace Jovanovich, 1981.

Lees, Brian. *A Handbook of the Al Sa'ud Ruling Family of Saudi Arabia*. London: Royal Genealogies, 1981.

Lippman, Thomas W. *Understanding Islam. An Introduction to the Moslem World*. New York: New American Library, 1982.

Lipsky, George. *Saudi Arabia: Its People, Its Society, Its Culture*. New Haven: Hraf Press, 1959.

Looney, Robert E. *Saudi Arabia's Development Potential*. Lexington, Mass.: Lexington Books, 1982.

MacDonald, Charles G. *Iran, Saudi Arabia, and the Law of the Sea: Political Interaction and Legal Development in the Persian Gulf*. Westport, Conn.: Greenwood Press, 1980.

El Mallakh, Ragaei. *Saudi Arabia: Rush to Development*. Baltimore: Johns Hopkins University Press, 1982.

El Mallakh, Ragaei, and Dorothea H. El Mallakh, eds. *Saudi Arabia: Energy, Developmental Planning, and Industrialization*. Lexington, Mass.: Lexington Books, 1982.

Malone, Joseph. "America and the Arabian Peninsula: The First Two Hundred Years." *Middle East Journal* 30 (Spring/Summer 1976).

Melikian, Levon, and Juhaina Al-Easa. "Oil and Social Change in the Gulf." *Journal of Arab Affairs* I (October 1981).

Miller, Judith. "Americans in Saudi Prisons Say They Are Being Abused." *New York Times*, October 17, 1983.

Moliver, Donald M., and Paul J. Abbudante. *The Economy of Saudi Arabia.* New York: Praeger, 1980.

Mosley, Leonard. *Power Play: Oil in the Middle East.* New York: Random House, 1973.

Naipaul, V. S. *Among the Believers: An Islamic Journey.* New York: Alfred A. Knopf, 1981.

Niblock, Tim, ed. *Social and Economic Development in the Arab Gulf.* New York: St. Martin's Press, 1980.

———. *State, Society, and Economy in Saudi Arabia.* New York: St. Martin's Press, 1982.

Ohlsson, Arne. "Range of Diseases at a Public Pediatric Clinic of Saudi Arabia: Two Year Study of Pediatric Patients in Riyadh." *Lakartidningen* 78 (1981).

Okruhlik, Gwenn. "Networks of Dissent: Islamism and Reform in Saudi Arabia." *Current History* 101, no. 651 (January 2002).

Patai, Raphael. *The Arab Mind.* New York: Charles Scribner's Sons, 1976, rev. ed. 1983.

Pelly, Lewis. *Report on a Journey to Riyadh.* Cambridge: Oleander-Falcon, 1979.

Peterson, J. E. "Tribes and Politics in Eastern Arabia." *Middle East Journal* 31 (Summer 1977).

Philby, H. St. John. *Arabia of the Wahhabis.* London: Constable, 1928.

———. *Sa'udi Arabia.* London: Ernest Benn, 1955.

Quandt, William B. "Riyadh Between the Superpowers." *Foreign Policy* 44 (Fall 1981).

———. *Saudi Arabia in the 1980's. Foreign Policy, Security, and Oil.* Washington, D.C.: Brookings Institution, 1981.

———. *Saudi Arabia's Oil Policy.* Washington, D.C.: Brookings Institution, 1982.

Raban, Jonathan. *Arabia Through the Looking Glass.* London: Collins, 1979.

Rabinovich, Itamar. *The War for Lebanon: 1970–1985.* Ithaca, N.Y.: Cornell University Press, 1985.

Ramazani, Rouhollah K. "Security in the Persian Gulf." *Foreign Affairs* 57 (Spring 1979).

———. *Revolutionary Iran: Challenge and Response in the Middle East.* Baltimore: Johns Hopkins University Press, 1986.

Reinhold, Robert. "Uncovering Arabia's Past." *New York Times Magazine*, August 23, 1981.

Ross, Heather Colyer. *The Art of Arabian Costume: A Saudi Arabian Profile.* Fribourg, Switzerland: Arabesque Commercial, 1981.

———. *The Art of Bedouin Jewellery: A Saudi Arabian Profile.* Fribourg,

Switzerland: Arabesque Commercial, 1981.

Rubin, Barry. *The Arab States and the Palestinian Conflict.* Syracuse, N.Y.: Syracuse University Press, 1981.

————. "Two Years Later, Lebanon's Lessons." *New York Times*, August 29, 1984.

Rustow, Dankwart A. "U.S.–Saudi Relations and the Oil Crisis of the 1980's." *Foreign Affairs* 55 (April 1977).

Safran, Nadav. "Arab Politics, Peace, and War." *Orbis* 18 (Summer 1974).

————. *Saudi Arabia: The Ceaseless Quest for Security.* Cambridge, Mass.: Belknap Press of Harvard University Press, 1985.

Sampson, Anthony. *The Seven Sisters.* New York: Viking, 1975.

Saudi Arabia: An Inside View of an Economic Power in the Making. New York: Business International, 1981.

Schmidt, Dana Adams. *Armageddon in the Middle East.* New York: John Day, 1974.

Sciolino, Elaine, and Neil MacFarquhar. "Naming of Hijackers as Saudis May Further Erode Ties to U.S." *New York Times*, October 25, 2001.

Shaheen, Jack G. *The TV Arab.* Bowling Green, Ohio: Bowling Green State University Popular Press, 1985.

Sheean, Vincent. *Faisal: The King and His Kingdom.* Tavistock, England: University Press of Arabia, 1975.

Singer, Fred. "Limits to Arab Oil Power." *Foreign Policy* 30 (Spring 1978).

Solaim, Soliman A. "Legal Review: Saudi Arabia's Judicial System." *Middle East Journal* 25 (Summer 1971).

Sullivan, Robert R. "Saudi Arabia in International Politics." *Review of Politics* 32 (October 1970).

"Survey of Saudi Arabia." *The Economist*, February 12, 1982.

Thesiger, Wilfred. *Arabian Sands.* New York: E. P. Dutton, 1959.

Tucker, Robert. "The Persian Gulf and American Power." *Commentary* (November 1980).

Turner, Louis, and James Bedore. "Saudi Arabia: The Power of the Purse Strings." *International Affairs* 54 (July 1978).

Van Hollen, Christopher. "North Yemen: A Dangerous Pentagonal Game." *Washington Quarterly* 5, no. 3 (Summer 1982).

Wells, Donald. *Saudi Arabia Development Strategy.* Washington, D.C.: American Enterprise Institute, 1976.

Who's Who in Saudi Arabia, 1983–84. Third Edition. Jeddah: Tihama, 1983.

Winstone, H.V. F. *Gertrude Bell.* London: Jonathan Cape, 1979.

Wright, Robin. *Sacred Rage: The Crusade of Modern Islam.* New York: Linden Press, Simon and Schuster, 1985.

Zakzouk, Siraj M. "Deaf Children in Saudi Arabia." *Saudi Medical Journal* 3 (July 1982).

Index

Hyatt Regency Hotel (Jeddah), 83

Iffat (wife of King Faisal), 163
Ignatius, David, 213*n*
Ikhwan ("Brotherhood") communities,
   196, 231, 296, 391; rebellion of,
   197, 218, 230, 231, 293
Illiteracy, *see* Education (Saudi)
Image, obsession with, *see* Value
Imam (as title), 206–7
Imperialism, 326; Israel as pawn of,
   91; British mandates, 297*n*,
   319–20; French, 319; U.S., 320
Imprisonment, *see* Crime
Income: national, 5–6, 43–49 *passim*,
   54, 59, 65, 76, 175, 218, (separated
   from king's) 200; new wealth, 5–7,
   12, 29–30, 121, 174, 302, (distribution of) 49, 59, 114, 217–18, 222,
   (vs. tradition) 72, (women and)
   134, 145. *See also* Consumer
   goods (conspicuous consumption
   of); Labor (salaries); Monetary and
   banking systems; Oil revenues
India, 64, 197; labor from, 362, 364, 369
Indian Army (British), 43, 115
Indonesians, 80, 82, 367
Industrialization, *see* Petrochemical
   industry; Technology
Industry and Electricity, Ministry of,
   25, 328, 346, 386
Inflation, *see* Monetary and banking
   systems
Information, Ministry of, 5, 232, 244,
   259, 260, 346; and the press, 4,
   261, 262–63; quoted, 184, 225;
   Council of, 255
Institute of Technical Training, 260
Intelligence services, 300
Intercontinental Hotel (Riyadh), 134,
   192, 226, 278
Interest rates, *see* Monetary and bank-
   ing systems
Interimco Projects Engineering, 57

Interior, Ministry of the, 232, 272,
   279, 332; and secret police/
   Security forces, 4, 51, 278, 323;
   and entry visas, deportations, 31,
   32, 254, 258, 261; and Christians,
   95, 254; in power structure, 194*n*,
   202*n*, 209, 214, 300, 310, 311; and
   crime, 368
International Herald Tribune, 413–14
International Monetary Fund (IMF),
   174
Internet, 404, 413
Iran, 11*n*, 80, 81, 337; 1979 revolution
   in, 43*n*, 95, 236, (impact of), 52,
   244, (and Islamic revival) 95, 99,
   231, 380, 392, 399–401, 405, (and
   U.S./anti-Westernism) 228–29, 233,
   313–14, 338, 395; Islam established in, 65, 66; shah of, 95, 99,
   203, 228–29, 314–15, 338, 400;
   and Persian thought, 236; as threat,
   292, 297, 333–35, 338, 381, 392,
   399, 401; oil policies of, 343, 344;
   U.S. arms deal with, 399. *See also*
   Iran-Iraq war
Iran-Iraq war, 244–45, 255, 283, 314,
   331–32, 333–34, 399, 405
Iraq, xv, 39, 80, 235, 293, 303, 326,
   388; Saudi tribes in, 114, 381;
   statehood of, 297n, 319; vs. Israel,
   331; workers from, 366. *See also*
   Iran-Iraq war
Irish expatriates, 58
Irrigation, *see* Water supply
Ishmael/Isaac story, 65, 79, 90–91
Islam: women as viewed by, *see*
   Women; rigidity of, 5; Jerusalem as
   holy site, 7 (*see also* Jerusalem);
   Saudi Arabia as birthplace of, 13,
   64, 327; and prayer, 20, 51–52,
   72–75, 77, 89, 105, 151, 238, 396,
   (enforcement of call) 70, 205, 253;
   as barrier between Moslems and
   non-Moslems, 34, 64, 68, 83–84,

United States (*cont.*)
230, 233, (Gulf War in) 405–8;
Saudi ambassador to, 194, 383; and
Israel, 264, 313–26 *passim*, 331,
335, 336, 337, 399; Arab world
view of, 320, 339, 399; arms deal
with Iran, 399. *See also* ARAMCO
(Arabian-American Oil Company);
Engineers, U.S. Army Corps of;
Foreigners; West, the
Universities: of Riyadh, 88, 98, 140,
259, 324; King Abdul Aziz, 132,
136, 263, 273; King Khalid, 164;
King Saud, 205, 358, 384. *See also*
Education (Saudi)
Urbanization, *see* Population (native)
Utaibah tribe, 112n, 204, 231
Uthman (Mohammed's third succes-
sor), 66

Values, 103–7, 109–12, 115–21, 384;
obsession with image, 4, 30,
117–21, 133, 167, 255, 282, 326,
356, 368, (as progressive government) 139, 140, 142; honor
("face"), 25, 64, 84, 117–32 *passim*, 139–41, 152, 183, 255, 256,
309, 356; pride, 30, 103, 104,
119–21, 356; traditional, of Arab
world, 64, 65, 228, 246, 265, 377,
384, 403 (*see also* Modernization);
hospitality; 64, 107, 110, 116–17,
196, 202–3, 207, 323; chivalry
system, 104n, 133; Bedouin influence on, 105, 115 (*see also*
Bedouins); loyalty, 109, 111–12,
114, 186, 207, 208, 318–19; fighting and revenge, 112, 115, 139,
200, 356; concept of time, 179,
181–82, 251, 319; aversion to
labor, 183 (*see also* Labor
[native]); Western, 187, 397,
(rejection of) 188. *See also*
Decision making; Equality;

Family, the; Islam; Islamists;
Language; Marriage; Tribe(s);
women
Veil, the, *see* Women
Venereal disease, 156. *See also* Sexual
behavior
Venezuela oil reserves, 338
Vinnell Corporation, 308
Visa process, *see* Foreigners

Wahhabism, xv, 14, 35, 175, 196, 199,
294, 356, 410; rigidity/restrictions
of, 13, 83, 86–88, 96–97, 129n,
225, 249, 269, 290, (and women)
37, (*matawain* and) 69, 70, 71, (vs.
non-Moslem religions) 82, 83,
(violation of) 223, 255, 277; xenophobia of, 30, 33, 67, 83–84, 98,
236, 399; -Shiite conflict, 66, 67,
195, 236–37, 392; equality as concept within, 74–75, 397; and politics, 85, 99, 195, 376–77, 395,
400–401; in rural areas, 205;
defense of, 266, 391; and social
class, 398; oversimplified conflict
of moderates and, 413–14. *See also*
Islam; Islamic/government restrictions; Islamists; Law
Wadi Hanifa (region), 104, 195, 227
Wales, 354
Wall Street Journal, xv, 211, 213n
Washington Quarterly, 3
Water supply, 7, 19, 47, 67, 358;
desalination plants, 48, 53, 57–58,
352; underground (aquifers), 56,
57, 354; irrigation, 57, 353; plans
for, 58, 204, 273, 305, 354. *See
also* Climate and topography
Wealth, *see* Income; Monetary and
banking systems; Oil revenues;
Saud, House of
Welfare state, 183, 217, 236, 341, 346,
355; Faisal and, 45, 202, 222. *See
also* Monetary and banking sys-